Wild Rivers
of
North America

ALSO BY MICHAEL JENKINSON

Ghost Towns of New Mexico (WITH KARL KERNBERGER)

Tijerina: *Land Grant Struggles in the Southwest*

Wild Rivers
of
North America

BY

MICHAEL JENKINSON

Illustrated with Photographs by
Karl Kernberger, and Maps

A SUNRISE BOOK

E. P. DUTTON & COMPANY, INC. | NEW YORK | 1973

Library of Congress Cataloging in Publication Data

Jenkinson, Michael.
    Wild rivers of North America.

    Bibliography: p.
    1. Canoes and canoeing—North America.   2. White-water canoeing.   3.
Rivers—North America.   4. United States—Description and travel—1960–   —
Guide-books.   I. Title.
GV783.J38   917   73–158604
ISBN 0–87690–099–6

Photos copyright © 1973 by Karl Kernberger, unless otherwise specified.

Maps by Richard Mogas, except those on pages 52
and 302–303, which are by John Hill

Published simultaneously in Canada by
Clarke, Irwin & Company Limited, Toronto and Vancouver

Dutton-Sunrise, a subsidiary of E. P. Dutton & Co., Inc.

For Constance, who knows how it feels
to be thrown into a rapids,
and Sean, Kristen and Jennifer,
whose rivers are mostly yet to be run

Contents

8 Contents

"If there is magic on this planet, it is contained in water."
Loren Eiseley, *The Immense Journey*

"Something hidden. Go and find it. Go and look behind the ranges—
Something lost behind the ranges. Lost and waiting for you. Go."
Rudyard Kipling, "The Explorer"

Maps

Wild Rivers
of
North America

Introduction

My first river float was years ago, when a beautiful young woman and I drifted down a gentle section of the Rio Grande in a rubber raft. It was her birthday and we ate fresh strawberries, drank lemonade and a little rum. We watched the shadows of drifting clouds on the changing shores. The wildlife took little notice of us; instead of crashing into their domain afoot, we were silently drifting through it. We might have been invisible.

Later, I floated other rivers. Each had a character of its own. Some pounded thunderously through rapids; others slipped drowsily beneath canopies of leaning trees. I remember fireflies, parrots, and northern lights; the sensation of being catapulted out of a boat into the boil of a rapids; being three days' float from anywhere and down to a solitary cup of oatmeal when a companion killed a moose; blue-green waters rushing beneath house-high boulders upon which an Indian sat, playing a simple, haunting melody on a bamboo flute; a campfire in Grand Canyon next to which a New Jersey jeweler gazed up at the stark, towering walls and murmured, "This is a long way from West Orange."

In places, there were people living on the rivers—Indians, homesteaders, miners, and hermits. They are part of a river's character, as much as the flow, the rocks, the flora, and the fauna. And so is the past—the violent, whimsical and curious things men and women have done in what is still wild-river country.

It is these things I wish to share with you in this book.

In *Wild Rivers of North America* my emphasis is upon wilderness rivers, not whitewater of and for itself. A number of famous sporting runs, flanked by road, railroad, or both, have been omitted; some relatively quiet rivers such as the Suwannee and the Yukon are included.

13

When planning a voyage down one of the rivers featured in this book, I would suggest you send away for maps and other supplemental information listed in the Bibliography and Appendices.

Although there are still a great many rivers or sections of rivers that have retained their wilderness characteristics, their number diminishes yearly. Even as this is being written, wild rivers are being polluted, dammed, or developed by those who feel outdoor recreation is enhanced by scenic loop roads, marinas, and motels with a television set in every room.

Beautiful things are often fragile. A travel writer has a lingering guilt that were his book to be read widely, the exposure may hasten the destruction of his subject. Already a few wild rivers face the ironic problem of overcrowding.

In spite of this, I feel our wild rivers will be preserved only to the extent that people experience them—in person or vicariously—and understand how they are threatened. There is not much time. Within a decade this book may well be regarded as less of a celebration than a requiem.

CHAPTER ONE

River Running

Throughout history rivers have been considered an easy means of getting from one place to another. They offer passage through forests, mountains, and jungle growth; following them across deserts, the traveler is assured he will not perish of thirst. It is only in recent times that river floating has come to be considered a fine thing to do just for itself, without, necessarily, other motives, such as fishing, hunting, or carrying trade goods, the Flag of Empire, or the Word of God.

People have run rivers in a variety of craft, ranging from galvanized bathtubs to elegant houseboats that could be set down, without looking seedy, on the best residential street of any town. Children often take to the water on whatever is lying around. One sweltering afternoon in a bar near the Santa Fe rodeo grounds, I heard a bull-rider reminiscing about his childhood in West Texas for anyone who was close enough and cared to listen.

"We'd wait for a storm. Get a gully-washer shootin' down the arroyo. And ride it? I mean to tell you. In big washtubs, old boards, most anything we could lay hands on. Wonder we all didn't drown."

He set his beer down with a soft clunk. "Most fun I ever had. . . ."

Canoes, especially east of the Rockies, are the most popular outing craft for rivers and lakes. A basic proficiency is not hard to acquire, and most models are lightweight for easy portaging. It has been remarked that the best canoe for an individual is the largest one he can gracefully carry.

Rubber rafts are a favorite in the West, where some of the finest rivers have bigwater rapids that are attempted only by the most skilled or foolhardy canoeists. A good raft, capable of bouncing over or off rocks, is

15

more forgiving of mistakes than a canoe. It does, however, have the disadvantage of being sluggish to paddle over any distance of flatwater.

Kayakers are somewhat of an elite group among boaters. Their trim craft are so maneuverable that slalom races are held in them, amid the crash and boil of some of America's wildest rapids. An expert kayaker with nerve can follow a raft almost anywhere, darting like a dragonfly while the rubber boats bull their way through. Of the three types of craft, the kayak is the most difficult to master, and carries the least gear.

When buying a boat for river running, as with most other purchases, you generally get as much quality as you care to pay for. This is especially true of some bargain-rate rafts, which begin to leak copiously after the first few rock abrasions. The emergency patches and goop that come with the cheap rafts are undependable—it is best to take along a monkey-grip tube patching kit. A number of the most reliable boat companies will, upon request, send literature on their products. You will find a list of these concerns in Appendix VII.

It is, of course, preferable to try different kinds of boats before purchasing one. There are canoe rental concessions scattered across the country, and at some places, such as the Boundary Waters Canoe Area on the Minnesota-Canada border, one can outfit for an extensive journey. The Hudson's Bay Company has established a U-Paddle canoe rental service, patterned after the U-Haul trucking idea, by which the craft can be left at designated destinations.

"Kayakers are somewhat of an elite group among boaters"

Battling the whitewater of "The Slot" in an inflatable raft on the Rio Grande, between Pilar and Embudo

One of the best ways to learn about river running is through contact with whitewater organizations, of which there is probably one not far from where you live (see Appendix VI). A number of universities and colleges have outing clubs that engage in float trips, and a few Explorer Scout troops have focused on this activity. An Explorer post in Los Alamos, New Mexico, has voyaged down some of the roughest water in America, including the Middle Fork of the Salmon and Cataract Canyon of the Colorado. Not surprisingly, these youths are in great demand as river guides.

There are, in addition, a number of good books and other materials on the how-to-do-it aspects of river running, and some of these are listed in the Bibliography and other Appendices.

Inflatables have been used for a long time. In the British Museum there is a stone plaque some 2500 years old which portrays figures swimming a river supported by air-filled animal skins. Yet it was not until the close of World War II, when large neoprene rafts were auctioned as war surplus, that inflatables became an important factor in American river running. Bus Hatch, of Vernal, Utah, was one of the first to use them, taking friends through the wild, rapid-strewn canyons of the Green and Yampa rivers, which lay practically in his back yard. Soon, when he felt he knew the rivers well enough to assure a certain degree of safety, he began piloting paid passengers.

During the lean years of the Depression, an unusually self-reliant woman named Georgia White pedaled a bicycle from Chicago to Los Angeles. She liked the West. Most of all she liked Grand Canyon. Never one to ooh and aah from the edge of things, she hiked down into the gorge, strode up and down it, later swam portions of the lower river with a companion, and by the 1950s was guiding parties through on rubber rafts. For stability, Georgia lashed three 27-foot neoprene rafts together, using an outboard for control. In 1955 she guided fifty people through the canyon, introducing an era of mass whitewater pilgrimage.

Georgia White still runs tours through the canyon, although these days she has a host of competition. One of the most interesting outfitters is the American River Touring Association (A.R.T.A.). This organization not only conducts tours on more famous American runs such as Grand Canyon, the Middle Fork of the Salmon, and the Rogue, but also schedules river trips ranging from the Copper River of Alaska to the Amazon, and a shoreline cruise off the Great Barrier Reef of Australia. A.R.T.A. is a nonprofit organization which works closely with the Sierra Club and other conservation groups in efforts to preserve wilderness rivers.

The growth of guided float tours in recent years has been phenomenal. It allows people with little or no whitewater experience to savor the excitement and scenic values of bigwater canyons formerly accessible only to the handful of expert river runners capable of challenging them.

Although fine equipment and well-trained boatmen reduce danger to a minimum, there is always a taste of fear for everyone at the lip of a large thundering drop like Lava Falls in Grand Canyon. The boatman, after surveying his route from the rocks above, and saying something like "Let's truck on through," or "Move 'em out," is probably tenser than anyone. He has the responsibility. Boats have gone over. Men have drowned.

The Middle Fork of the Salmon River in Idaho was unusually high in the early weeks of summer 1970. Four men "bought it," as the rivermen say, in a single week. A professional guide and one of his passengers were drowned when their boat capsized in Weber Falls, a wild tumble of current in high water. A kayaker in another party was swept away and, at a different location, a Stanford professor was dragged under a torrent while attempting to cross the river attached to a rope.

Yet, considering the number of guided parties who float the great canyons of the West, upsets are remarkably few, and drownings even rarer. Statistically, one is in a great deal more danger driving to and from the rivers. Should you get dumped in a rapids, try to face forward and keep your feet and arms in front of you to fend off rocks. In most cases it is better not to fight the current—let it carry you into an eddy or slower section below the rapids and then swim to shore.

As with most activities, river running offers a richer experience to those who do it on their own, with friends, rather than depending upon the services of a guide. As with any sport, be it skiing, rock climbing, tightrope walking, or river running, you want to start out gradually, working up to more difficult things as your ability increases.

Rock climbers depend heavily upon difficulty ratings which have been assigned to various routes up a particular peak. Most major river rapids in the United States have been rated as to difficulty on a scale of I to VI. The hazards of a rapids, however, may vary greatly depending upon volume of water. A stretch of whitewater rated Class IV in moderate water may be impossible during high water (equivalent to what rock climbers whimsically refer to as Class VII—an overhanging sand dune). The scale of difficulty presented below is given for periods when water level is average, or generally favorable to river running.

Scale of Difficulty

Approximate Difficulty		*Approximate Skill Required*
CLASS I	Easy	Practiced Beginner
CLASS II	Requires Care	Intermediate
CLASS III	Difficult	Experienced
CLASS IV	Very Difficult	Highly Skilled
CLASS V	Exceedingly Difficult	Team of Experts
CLASS VI	Utmost Difficulty—Near Limit of Navigability	Team of Experts Taking Every Precaution

On some Western rivers that are rafted extensively, river charts may rate rapids on a scale of 1–10. Conversion from one system to the other is not difficult: a rapids rated 5 on this Western system would be a Class III, and so forth.

When you have decided to run an unfamiliar river, send for all available material on it, and obtain maps. It will be noted that in some instances the mileages by river, from point to point, in the text of this book will seem greater than indicated on the maps in the book, most notably with the Rio Urique, Grand Canyon, Upper Yukon, and Green River and Canyonlands. This is largely due to numerous river meanders, all of which are impossible to portray on maps of these scales.

Arriving at the river, inquire locally as to water conditions. In arranging your car shuttle, carefully memorize the take-out point. If hard to spot from the water, you may want to mark it with a strip of sheeting or a bandana tied to a tree branch or other conspicuous place.

The object of packing for a wilderness voyage is to carry as little as possible while ensuring safety and comfort. There are regional considerations. Whether to carry insect repellent and how much depends on where you are going and at what season. A good rule of thumb is to bring some just in case—those few extra ounces may save you a lot of misery. Hammocks are desirable for jungle travel or swamp boating. When voyaging through the vast backcountry of northern Canada and Alaska, some people carry firearms for camp meat and bear protection (although it can be argued that more people have got into bad bear trouble by using guns on them rather than climbing the nearest tree). One imaginative party, cruising rivers of the sub-Arctic Barren Lands where there are huge grizzlies and no trees to climb, brought along firecrackers to frighten off any ill-tempered bears.

Some backcountry manuals and every sporting-goods dealer advocate sending you into the wilds with enough gear to homestead out there—so much steel, canvas and leather it would take a string of pack horses to carry it all. Portable showers and camp toilets are obviously aimed at the Land-Rover Safari set; yet a number of items frequently fobbed off on river runners should be carefully considered with regard to boat space and weight if portaging or flatwater paddling is involved.

A lantern and camp stove are indeed convenient, but are bulky and fuel must be carried. I prefer to take along a flashlight, candles (for seeing your supper if served up after dark), and a lightweight grill. I feel the virtues of hauling an ax (or hatchet, or saw) into the outback are likewise overrated. On the majority of my wilderness voyages I have neither taken nor missed any of these weapons (as surely the greenwood victims of overanxious, overgrown Boy Scouts must view them). On all but the most frequented rivers a bit of prowling will lead to driftwood that will fit into your fire-ring of stones, or at least you will find dry, dead wood that can be broken into manageable sections by bashing it against a hard surface or stomping on it with your boots. If you must take a wood-cutting tool, I would suggest a small folding handsaw.

The notion that one should *always* bring a tent when camping is a myth. On many wild rivers discussed in this book—the Colorado and the Rogue, for example—rainfall is slight during the season (usually summer) when they are customarily run. A good water-repellent sleeping bag and a poncho will shield you from what brief showers might occur. Regions blitzed by mosquitoes and other biting beasts of the air are another matter. During their peak season (early summer in most places) a tent or mosquito netting will seem worth its weight in gold.

Careful waterproofing, especially on whitewater rivers, is essential. Probably the finest containers are neoprene boat bags which have overlap lips. Unless defective or improperly closed, these will keep your gear bone-dry through the wildest mayhems of tumbling water. They can be purchased at a number of sporting goods or surplus stores, or ordered from the Ski Hut (1615 University Avenue, Berkeley, California), or Louis Matacia (7414 Leesburg Pike, Falls Church, Virginia 22043). Watertight ammunition boxes, available at many surplus stores, are excellent for storing camera gear, film, and other valuables. Make sure the gaskets are watertight, line the boxes with sponge rubber, and paint them white to cut down on heat absorption. Lash them to the boat with a short strand of rope. Plastic sheeting, while not as effective as boat bags or ammo boxes, will help, in lieu of them, to keep your gear dry. It also can be used to rig a shelter in times of violent weather.

Equipment checklists are invaluable. Many a rueful river runner has driven hundreds of miles to the banks of an exotic waterway—only to find he has forgotten the paddles.

Checklist

Boat and equipment: Paddles. There should be Coast Guard-approved life preservers for each member of the party if whitewater is to be encountered, and for weak swimmers on any kind of water. Buying a cheap life preserver makes as much sense as purchasing a car whose steering mechanism is dubious.

Take a repair kit for whatever kind of craft you are using. It can be

Bivouacked overnight beside the Rogue River, this camper uses a lightweight shelter and a sleeping bag

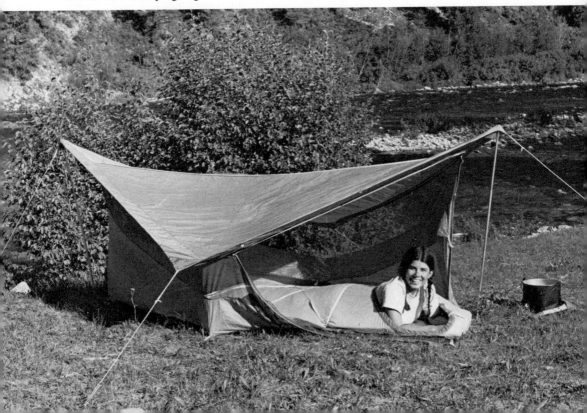

extremely dangerous to have a leaking boat that wallows through rapids, and most unpleasant to observe that your boat has become a kind of floating bathtub. ("Honey, the snake-bite kit and our freeze-dried lobster newburg just floated off into that eddy.")

Sleeping bag: This is the most important item of wilderness equipment you will ever buy. One can go virtually anywhere in the world—and survive— with a good bag, a sharp knife, and an understanding of how to set up a figure-4 trap and find hidden water. Own the best bag you can afford (best does not necessarily equate to price). Until the last decade, down bags were the only way to go first class, but the recent introductions of remarkable synthetics—such as polyurethane foam and Fiberfill II—have completely changed the picture. Selection of a quality sleeping bag is as complex, if not more so, than purchasing an automobile.

Tent: Lightweight back-packing model. If you want to travel lighter (and with less expense) lay the head of your sleeping bag next to a spruce or another tightly branched tree when it rains; a poncho or sheet of plastic can be an adequate shelter for the rest of your bag.

Grub: On most extended wilderness trips, you will periodically have to hoist the weight of your food onto your back over portages, or, at times, paddle that weight across flatwater. Fresh steaks are a wonderful first-day-out tradition—from there on one should travel light. Use freeze-dried dinners, dehydrated eggs and bacon. Most sporting-goods stores carry entire lines of lightweight foods with everything prepackaged from morning chocolate or coffee to tapioca pudding for supper dessert. Bargain-minded outbackers can find all they need at their local supermarket: dried fruit, soups to which you have to add only water, Lipton Ham Chedderton and other delicious dinners; the list is as long as the aisles of the store. Canned goods are bulky, heavy, have most of their nutriments cooked out of them, and the empties should be buried (add a camp shovel to the equipment list), or carried out. Scratch them from the shopping list. On a prolonged wilderness voyage bring fishing tackle. Angling may not be your cup of tea—but freshwater fish browned in bacon grease tastes mighty good, and can spare you the effort of packing extra beans.

Clothing: Travel light. Make sure you always have a dry set of clothing in a waterproof container. If you get spilled in a rapids, have no dry clothing, and the sun has set, you can shiver yourself halfway to Antarctica and back before the campfire really takes off. Ponchos for rain, broad-brimmed hats for harsh sunlight, are highly recommended. Bring tennis shoes for travel on the river, sturdy boots for hiking around camp or up side canyons.

Packs: A must if portages are required. If there are no portages on your route, but you plan hikes up side canyons, a rucksack should suffice.

Rope: A sufficient supply of nylon or Manila for lining boats, hanging food packs out of the reach of wild animals, and whatnot.

Miscellaneous essentials: First-aid kit (snake-bite kit should be included except in the Far North, where there are no snakes); cooking grill; cooking and eating utensils; flashlight (with spare bulb and batteries); waterproof match supply; candles; maps (see Appendix IV); compass (if travel across large bodies of water is involved); water containers (if river is too muddy to drink without settling); insect repellent; hunting, fishing, travel or fire permits (where applicable); toilet tissue; personal items—soap, washcloth, towel, knife, sunglasses, spare prescription glasses, toilet kit, Chapstick, sunburn lotion.

Optional items: Fishing and hunting gear, camera equipment, lantern, camp stove, fuel, sewing kit, binoculars, notebook and pencil, books about the area, smoking paraphernalia, reflector or Dutch ovens, folding bucksaw, ax, hatchet, folding camp shovel, a little rum or whiskey for medicinal purposes.

The backpacker's wilderness is a broad expanse of country, with numerous trails and campsites to choose from. The wild-river environment, on the other hand, is compressed, a mere strip of outland that must bear the full traffic of its visitors, and its comparatively few campsites the full weight of their passing. Therefore, along the rivers, a special meaning and accent hone the saying: "Take nothing but photographs, leave nothing but footprints."

There is something infectious about river running. A few years back, several citizens of Aspen, Colorado, shoved their raft into Roaring Fork for a trip down into the Colorado River, and thence through the canyon country of Utah to the confluence of the Green River. A large group of well-wishers had gathered to see the party off. As the raft approached the bridge where many of them were gathered, a bank clerk (who was already late for work) became so agitated that he yanked off his tie and jacket. While onlookers cheered, he leaped off and down into the water, swimming to the raft. Pulled aboard, he thus joined the expedition at the last possible moment.

And, although he naturally lost his job, he never looked back—he was yelling and singing like a kid on his first recess even as the raft started to buck through the first sharp drop, a boil of whitewater.

CHAPTER TWO

The Irascible Rogue

The Rogue River begins in snow-melt and springs in Crater Lake National Park, in the Cascade Mountains of southwestern Oregon. In its upper reaches, the Rogue is a clear and turbulent stream, superb for fishing, with fine campsites along its banks. State Highway 62 parallels it in much of this portion. Once into the Rogue Valley, the river, enlarged by the flow of numerous tributaries, placidly meanders through farming and apple-orchard country. Smoke from lumber mills smudges into the sky, but water pollution is minimal. Several miles beyond Grants Pass, commercial hub of the valley, the Rogue begins to cut its way through the Coast Range. The current quickens: the country becomes wilder. Eighty-four miles of the Rogue, the entire Rogue River Canyon, has been designated as a component of the Wild and Scenic Rivers system; 33 miles, from Grave Creek to Watson Creek near Illahe, are virtually roadless and without settlement of any kind.

There is a paradox to the Rogue River where it breaches the Coast Range. Most western rivers boil furiously over rocks on their upper reaches, then flow gently through valleys that open toward the sea. The Rogue saves much of its fury for the final leg, churning falls and chutes, as if to hurl back ascending salmon and steelheads, as if to reach the ocean as spray rather than current. Yet even its rapids are subtle; green water squiggling quietly through sun-struck forest until a man, relaxed and perspiring, gets to water fighting with people on another boat or swimming for a while. Then, suddenly, there is a low steady roar up ahead. Around an elbow of rock, the river beats down through boulders as if to rip them into sand.

It is as though the Rogue were less an entity than a superb actor: here

Reading the water of the turbulent Rogue River is a skill which takes considerable practice to develop

it portrays the choppy doglegs of the Middle Fork of the Salmon River in Idaho, there a deep incision into rock such as you would expect in the Big Bend Country on the Rio Grande, and then again, the kind of easy, wide drift associated with the Buffalo in the Ozarks or the South's leisurely Suwannee. Even the foliage along the Rogue, like a costume, varies greatly. Most summers the trees and undergrowth are thick and green, satiated with groundwater. Other years, by August the manzanita, live oak, and ponderosa are so dry it seems they might ignite if a man merely scratched his eyes across them. The Rogue is a river that during flood has stacked itself 80 feet high through narrow clefts in the canyon, flung aside high bridges of the best steel and stone—yet in lowwater it is a strand of emerald pools, threaded by faster water tumbling across shallow shoals.

Two hundred miles from where it begins close to Crater Lake, the Rogue passes into the Pacific Ocean at Gold Beach.

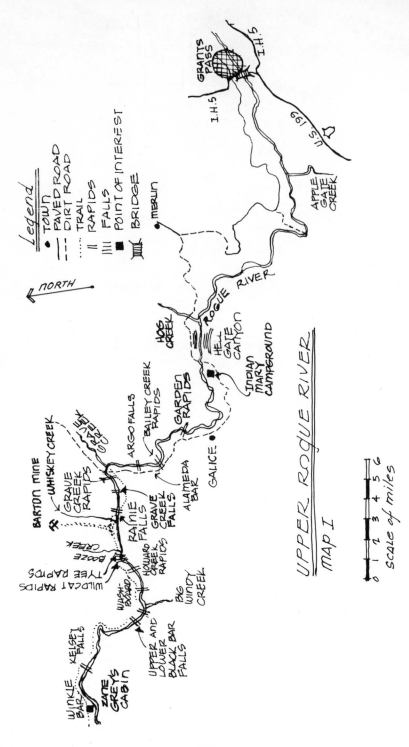

Legend

- • TOWN
- ‾‾‾ PAVED ROAD
- --- DIRT ROAD
- ⋯ TRAIL
- ‖ RAPIDS
- ⫼ FALLS
- ■ POINT OF INTEREST
- ⟏ BRIDGE

← NORTH

GRANTS PASS

I.H.5

I.H.5

U.S. 199

APPLE GATE CREEK

• MERLIN

ROGUE RIVER

HOG CREEK

HELL GATE CANYON

INDIAN MARY CAMPGROUND

GALICE

BAILEY CREEK RAPIDS

ARGO FALLS

GARDEN RAPIDS

ALAMEDA BAR

WHISKEY CREEK

GALICE ROUTE 00

BARTON MINE

GRAVE CREEK RAPIDS

RAINIE FALLS

GRAVE CREEK FALLS

BOOZE CREEK

HOWARD CREEK RAPIDS

TYEE RAPIDS

WILDCAT RAPIDS

WASH BOARD

BIG WINDY CREEK

UPPER AND LOWER BLACK BAR FALLS

KELSEY FALLS

WINKLE BAR

ZANE GREYS CABIN

UPPER ROGUE RIVER

MAP I

0 1 2 3 4 5 6
scale of miles

26

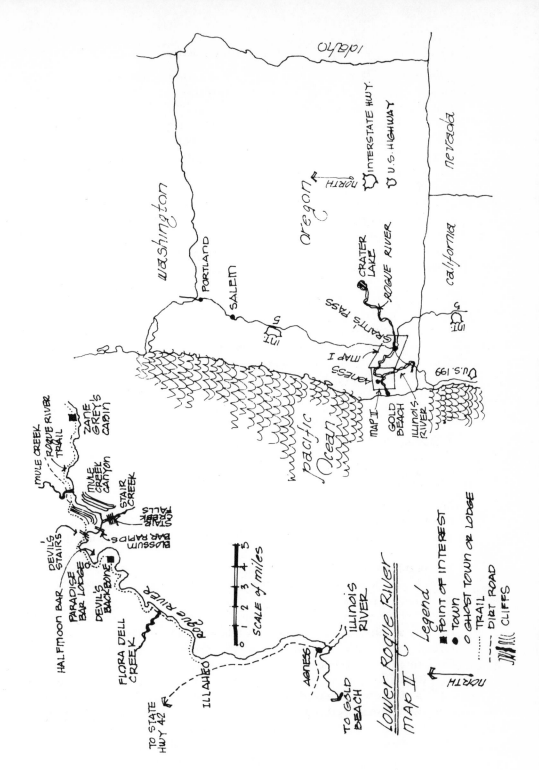

Idaho

Washington

Oregon

Nevada

California

NORTH

INTERSTATE HWY.

U.S. HIGHWAY

CRATER LAKE

ROGUE RIVER

GRANT'S PASS

PORTLAND

SALEM

INT

Pacific Ocean

AGNESS

MAP I

GOLD BEACH

Illinois River

U.S. 199

101

101

MULE CREEK

ROGUE RIVER TRAIL

ZANE GREY'S CABIN

MULE CREEK CANYON

STAIR CREEK

STAIR CREEK FALLS

HALFMOON BAR

DEVILS STAIRS

BLOSSUM BAR RAPIDS

PARADISE BAR LODGE

DEVIL'S BACKBONE

FLORA DELL CREEK

ROGUE RIVER

ILLAHEO

AGNESS

ILLINOIS RIVER

TO GOLD BEACH

TO STATE HWY 42

0 1 2 3 4 5

SCALE of miles

Lower Rogue River
Map II

Legend

■ POINT of INTEREST
● TOWN
○ GHOST TOWN or LODGE
...... TRAIL
- - - DIRT ROAD
⋀⋀⋀ CLIFFS

NORTH

27

Christmas Week 1964. It was raining in the town of Grants Pass. Not the endless, gray drizzle that keeps the entire western side of the Cascades puddled all winter and makes it green as God's own country club when the sun finally does break out in the spring. This was a hard rain that rattled on roofs and hats, a downpour, and people watched the swollen river with concern. In houses close to the banks, everything not nailed down or too heavy was carried up to the second story, while drapes were tied up high, away from what water and mud might come.

Over steaming coffee mugs in the cafés and in stripped living rooms, everyone turned weather prophet: some speculated the river would rise to the flood crest of 1962 (27.23 feet), and a few dourly predicted that unless Someone turned the taps off Up Above there might be a repeat of the great flood of 1955 (30.16-foot crest). Not many could take that seriously.

But miles away, on the volcanic slopes that cup Crater Lake and give birth to the river, something unusual was happening. A warm rain was falling upon a 90-inch snowpack, eroding it into torrents of chill water.

On Wednesday, December 23, Ed Trickey, a printer whose home sits high above the river, was watching television when his wife walked in and commented with rather bemused detachment: "Honey, there's a tree floating up our driveway."

And in a high-ground tavern just outside town, where men, mostly loggers, were drinking Olympia Beer and shooting eight ball, an old timer gazed out the window at the town, which was now half filled with river. "Damned old Rogue done it again," he muttered.

Down by the filtration plant, the gauge read 34.15 feet.

The Rogue is not the only Oregon river prone to flood—the Umpqua, McKenzie, Santiam, and Willamette have all rolled houses, cattle, and people toward the sea. Yet while macadam was being laid out beside these other rivers and tourist courts snuggled into the side hills, the ruggedness of the Rogue River Canyon deflected captains of industry, tourism, and transportation to gentler places. Even today most of the canyon is accessible only by boat or foot trail.

There has always been an aura of the wild, the unpredictable, in Rogue River country. Around glowing stoves of logging-camp bunkhouses on rainy evenings there is sometimes talk of Bigfoot, a mysterious giant or race of giants that men claim to have seen prowling lonely draws along the California-Oregon border.

Back in the 1880s an immense, wily grizzly acquired a taste for the cattle and sheep that grazed in the Siskiyou Mountains, south of the Rogue. One awed herder, perched in a tree, watched the bear kill a calf and then slap its mother to the ground when she charged. A nearby bull rammed the grizzly, knocking it off its feet. Before the bull could ready itself for another charge, the bear was upon it, clawing and snapping. The bull dropped, its backbone crushed by the powerful jaws.

In about the year 1875 the grizzly had been caught in a powerful steel beartrap but had managed to pull away, leaving three claws and a part of its paw in the locked teeth. For some fifteen years thereafter, Reelfoot, as he was called because of his distinctive track, continued to slaughter cattle and elude the ranchers and professional hunters who stalked him. Dogs he outwitted—or simply whipped around and killed. Few men ever got a clean shot at him, and those who did usually swore and pondered the supernatural, for a .38-55 slug seemed to do no more damage to Reelfoot than a flung pebble. A stockman's reward of $2700 went begging.

When the 1800 pound grizzly was finally downed for good in 1890, it took a barrage of bullets to do it and the bear crumpled only 15 yards from the rapid-firing hunters.

On October 9, 1855, a disheveled, mud-spattered rider galloped into the mining settlement of Jacksonville, five miles southwest of the Rogue, and shouted hoarsely: "The Indians have broken loose and are killing everybody!" About twenty armed men mounted hurriedly and headed toward the river. Near a burned wagon they found the bodies of two teamsters who had been transporting provisions; beside a wagon full of apples were two more dead men, and the remains of a settler named Jones sprawled next to his cabin, already half devoured by wild hogs.

Chief John of the Rogue River tribe, long restless at seeing miners and settlers occupy ancestral lands while his people were shoved back onto the Table Rock Reservation, had led his warriors on a search for scalps.

The Indians threw burning brands onto the roof of the J. B. Wagoner homestead, igniting it and trapping Mrs. Wagoner inside. The last person to glimpse the woman alive claimed she stood before a mirror, calmly arranging her hair as flames billowed up the walls. A mail carrier and two other white men witnessed the inferno from hiding places in the woods, but were helpless to intervene as it was surrounded by Indians.

Other homesteads were attacked. George Harris was shot on the stoop of his cabin. His wife pulled him inside, barred the door with shaking fingers, and followed the dying man's instructions for loading a revolver, rifle, and double-barreled shotgun. It was the frequency, rather than the accuracy, of her gunfire that held the Indians at bay and eventually caused them to withdraw. When the woods were silent and without movement, the woman fled her cabin with her wounded and sobbing daughter, hiding in a willow thicket until rescuers arrived.

The volunteers from Jacksonville caught up with the war party at Hellgate on the Rogue. Most of the Indians had already crossed the river in canoes, but several stragglers were fired upon and killed. Chief John fought for almost a year before surrendering. He and his people were placed on the Siletz Reservation on the coast, where the tribe was rapidly decimated by disease.

There are, of course, quieter memories of the Rogue River Canyon. Mrs. Ella McFarlane, a soft-spoken, white-haired woman who lives in Grants Pass, spent her first ten years on the Big Bend Ranch near Illahe without ever once taking the path or a boat all the way "outside." So isolated was the region in that era, the 1890s, that mail would sometimes take weeks to arrive. Prospectors entrusted to carry letters had a penchant for working promising gravel bars en route. The Indian who stands out in Mrs. McFarlane's recollections was a tireless fiddler, who provided the music at the schoolhouse when settlers waltzed and danced the quadrille.

Today the big whoop-up in the town of Rogue River, about 10 miles east of Grants Pass, is the Rooster Crow Contest, possibly because more obvious traditions on which to base civic festivities—such as pioneers, Indians, grizzlies, logging, and apple growing—had already been staked out by other towns. The Grants Pass event features a parade; beef barbecue; arts, crafts, and antique automobile exhibits; sack races, bingo, darts, cotton candy, a princess, and *the contest*. Each rooster entered in this headline attraction has an individual judge who qualitatively scores each crow emitted by the fowl during a half-hour period. Winning birds are awarded cash prizes and, presumably, a permanent reprieve from the stewpot. The 1971 winner, Super Chicken, crowed 85 times in championship style in half an hour.

The crowing rooster contest at Grants Pass still retains a smalltown, rural Fourth of July, church-cakewalk kind of flavor that has been lost in the commercialized mob scenes of larger, more spectacular festivals. It is great fun. The contest is staged on the last Saturday in June, and that is a good season for starting down the river. The Rogue can be run from early summer until October. Heavy rains in late October and November make the trip uncomfortable and the water level dangerous.

Unless you are traveling with a guided party, the Rogue should be attempted only by experienced river runners. Due to the rocky, turbulent nature of its rapids the river is more suited to rafting and kayaking than to canoeing. During the summer months temperatures in Rogue River country climb into the 90s and rain showers are infrequent. When scrambling about on shore, be cautious where you put your feet and what plants you grab for support or let tickle your face. Rattlesnakes like to coil in hollows of rock and poison ivy flourishes as if planted by the black-sheep brother of Johnny Appleseed.

Unlike most wilderness river runs, the Rogue River Canyon has some substantial towns in the valley above it. While the rapids provide excellent aeration, it is nevertheless prudent to drop purifying tablets in drinking water taken from the river itself, or to fill canteens at side streams.

One can put into the Rogue at several places along the 34-mile stretch from the city park in Grants Pass to the Grave Creek Bridge. However, until one reaches Hell Gate Canyon (16 miles below the city park), the Rogue is still wandering through its valley, a placid innertube float with the works of civilization cluttering its shores on every hand. Better to shove off at Hog Creek, head of Hell Gate Canyon; Indian Mary Campground, Galice store, Alameda Bar or Grave Creek—where the wilderness river begins.

At Indian Mary Campground a rustic signboard catches the eye:

HISTORIC INDIAN MARY PARK

Smallest Indian Reservation ever created, granted to Indian Mary by U.S. Government in 1885 in recognition of gratitude to her father, Umpqua Joe, who gave the alarm which saved white settlers of this area from a planned massacre.

At the time of the 1855 uprising, Umpqua Joe had married a woman of Chief John's Rogue River tribe. She had brothers who had bloodied their scalping knives during the outbreak. Northwestern historians, ranging from cracker barrel to professional, differ in their interpretations of how Umpqua Joe spread an alarm of the impending massacre and thus probably saved some forty lives on Grave Creek. Some see him as a western Paul Revere; others assert he merely left hurriedly, afoot, with his wife, and the rumor-haunted, edgy settlers simply correctly read the lay of the cards. Most historians, in any case, do point out that the miners along Grave Creek were conspicuously absent when the Indians arrived to massacre them, and that though Umpqua Joe's wife had conflicting loyalties between her tribe and her husband, Joe resolved her confusion by calmly threatening to slit her throat should she contact her brothers or Chief John.

While the beaten Rogue River tribe was dying out at the Siletz Reservation from venereal diseases and smallpox, Umpqua Joe remained on the river, operating a ferry that transported supply mules to the mines. His daughter, Mary, lived beside the Rogue for many years, and in 1885 President Grover Cleveland gave her title to her home and the acreage around it.

Between the historic mining settlement of Galice and the confluence with Grave Creek, 7 miles downriver, the Rogue twists down a deepening canyon, riffling over numerous shoals. Garden and Bailey Creek rapids, as well as Argo Falls, can be lively when the water is up.

Where Grave Creek tumbles into the Rogue, the road swings across the river, then away from it, up onto piney slopes. Once under the bridge, as if to celebrate its plunge into wilderness, the river breaks into white-water. Grave Creek Rapids are followed immediately by Grave Creek

Falls. The falls can be wicked (a 6-foot drop with a big backwave) and one suffers no loss of face from a portage. Look them over carefully.

A little more than a mile beyond Grave Creek Falls the Rogue really shows its teeth, rolls out the Big Cannon, C.O.D. package from the God of Fear, the boat breaker, the widowmaker—Rainie Falls. The river thunders over a 10-foot drop with such force that drift logs sometimes shatter against rocks beneath the foaming pool under the falls. Expert river runners have taken rafts over Rainie Falls without mishap, but it is a gamble nevertheless.

Most people use ropes to line their boats down the fish ladder, a tight, rocky chute used by salmon ascending to spawn. Running the ladder has its own excitements, besides inflicting wear and tear on the boat and one's body. It's rather like sitting on a jackhammer or being dragged across a brickyard.

After the fury of Rainie Falls, the Rogue smooths out and slows for a

A 12-foot Avon Redshank raft successfully negotiates Rainie Falls. This was the first time, to the author's knowledge, that so small a craft has gone over the falls

Running the Rogue River below Rainie Falls

spell, like a person apologetic after a fit of anger. There is time to lay aside paddles and oars to dangle one's hands in the cool, green flow, head canted back into the sun. Try to pick out the overgrown trail to the Barton Mine up Whiskey Creek, or watch for raspberry patches, bald eagles, or great blue herons. Then, just about the time the drift is so soft and lovely you begin to forget what whitewater is, the old Rogue kicks loose again. Boulder-blistered Tyee Rapids are considered as rough as Rainie Falls at some water levels. Wildcat Rapids, just beyond, will scratch your eyes out if you don't keep to the left of the island, threading a needle between it and a submerged boulder. And then, suddenly, you are back onto water so gentle it might have been pressed with a flatiron. You can clearly see polliwogs twitching in side pools overhung with ferns. Here and there, from the water, one catches through thick foliage a glimpse of the Rogue River trail—a path used for centuries by coastal Indians for trading in the interior. In places it is enjoyable to beach one's boat and amble a section of the trail. The vegetation is profuse and varied: rhododendron, ferns,

American River Touring Association boats on a peaceful stretch of the Rogue

manzanita, huckleberry, Oregon grape, and dogwood blanket the sloping canyon sides. Oak, maple, ash trees, and golden chinquapin sprawl out thick, informal limbs not far from the ground, while Douglas fir and ponderosa pine lift with stiff-backed formality into the sky.

Upper and Lower Black Bar rapids (4 miles below Wildcat) are both fine stretches of whitewater. Upper Black Bar is littered with boulders except on the extreme right, the best route. Lower Black Bar is an unobstructed chute with high waves—an exciting ride. Four miles below Lower Black Bar Rapids the Rogue tumbles through the delightful confusion of Kelsey Falls—boulders, small islands, and gaps through which the river spurts. This is a dangerous rapids—look it over carefully.

A couple of miles beyond Kelsey Falls, you come to Winkle Bar, where Zane Grey wrote many of his novels. His cabin is now owned by the president of the Levi Strauss Company, whose blue jeans are another durable commodity. It is a greenly beautiful, isolated retreat.

On any great whitewater river, most individual rapids tend to blur into a generality, like too many interesting people met at a brief and intoxicating party. One remembers a feeling about all the rapids, rather than the nuances of a particular rapids. Yet probably everyone who has run the Rogue retains a special image of Mule Creek Canyon, 5 miles below Winkle Bar. Here rock walls 40 to 50 feet high jam against the river as if to pinch it out entirely, force it into caves and the very pores of the stone. In places the Rogue is only 15 feet wide. There are strange eddies and cross-currents, sudden eruptions of current. River guides always scout Mule Creek Canyon afoot from the rims in spring—a log wedged in that cleft of pushing water could prove fatal. Midway through is the Coffee Pot, aplty named, for here indeed the waters do percolate in a manner to confound the unwary.

In the vicinity of Mule Creek Canyon there are some sportive places. The waterfall on Stair Creek invites a concentrated and invigorating shower. There is a fine jumping rock in the canyon. During a memorable voyage down the Rogue, the author had a go at it.

From a cliff ledge 50 feet up, the river seems surprisingly distant and stiff. It resembles a strip of blue-green sheet metal with tiny rafts and smaller upturned faces of the rafting party at one edge. There is no way to back down now, not so much because of the potential loss of face as the fact that the cliff is too steep to descend without breaking at least a leg. (It is always easier to find handholds on the way up.) Besides, a companion, giddy with macho and confident that the pool is deep enough, has already made the leap without dismembering himself. Just keep your arms against your side, he said; otherwise you might dislocate a shoulder. Legs together. Otherwise—rupture city!

You peer over the brink again and the river, if anything, is receding. No way to psych it closer. Drive everything out of your mind. Zen concentration. Simply step out into space. Falling, one's instinct is to windmill madly as if to catch one's balance in midair. Near the bottom of the plunge, the velocity seems more than a body will endure—bolts shearing off and rivets pulling out. Then comes the impact and you are rushing deeply downward, to the green core of the river itself. Swimming up slowly, you break through the surface and are dazzled by sunlight.

Blossom Bar Rapids, below Mule Creek Canyon, is what older boatmen call a rock garden, their youthful, long-haired counterparts a rock festival. There's a lot of whitewater, lots of dodging between boulders. This is followed by the Devil's Stairs—a stretch of huge, easy waves that give you a roller-coaster ride. As you slide past Paradise and Halfmoon bars, you can look to starboard and see the jagged ridge called the Devil's Backbone pushing up beside the river.

A diving rock on the Rogue

Paradise Bar Lodge has overnight accommodations for hikers and river runners. A sign over the front desk proclaims: "The World is Coming to an End. Please Pay Now So I Don't Have to Look All Over Hell for You." Roy Gervais, who runs the lodge, usually has a fair amount of company during the warm season, yet for six months of the year he is frequently snowbound and the river is too high for boat travel.

While drifting through the canyon, you will probably see duck and heron, perhaps an eagle or osprey. Wildlife ashore includes deer, bobcat, and black bear. Be on the lookout for rattlesnakes, especially in late summer when they shed their skins. Blind and irritable, they may strike with little or no provocation.

Flora Dell Creek, about 9 miles below Paradise Bar Lodge, is a magical place, full of odd promontories of rock sculpted by countless floodings of the Rogue. The clear water of the creek drops from pool to pool over waterfalls, and the sandy beach makes a fine campsite.

At Illahe, not far below Flora Dell Creek, there is a possible take-out point as a forest road runs 41 miles out to State Highway 42 at Myrtle Point. Agness, 7 miles downriver, is a pleasant hamlet which has changed little over the years. Resident Larry Lucas, who is seventy-three and collects hornets, commented: "People were more prolific in the old days. There were twenty kids in Agness school when I was there. Now there's only ten. Same school." Perhaps the biggest difference between the Agness of today and that of yesteryear is the content of the mailboats. Around the turn of the century a mail run was started from Gold Beach. Gradually, local people began taking the 32-mile trip as an excursion, and the word spread.

Today a number of "mailboats" bring passengers to Agness. After lunching on beef or chicken in Lucas' 10-room turn-of-the-century house or in the garden of Singing Springs Lodge, they return to Gold Beach.

Between Agness and Gold Beach there is very little whitewater, although the country remains wild and scenic. Since a 5-mile dirt road connects with the forest road at Illahe, many river runners take out here rather than continuing on to Gold Beach. For those who have made charter-plane arrangements at Grants Pass, there is a primitive airstrip, a short and bumpy dirt track bisected by a country road, where an incautious pilot may find himself propellering into a pickup truck or an unagile Hereford steer. While waiting for a plane here, one can feast on the local profusion of wild raspberries.

Looking back at the river, it seems calm and gentle as it sweeps in a wide bend around Agness—yet high upon the canyon slopes linger signs of its irascible character: flood-uprooted trees and a huge twist of metal that was once a steel road bridge.

At the bow paddle of an Avon Redshank raft on the Rogue

Guide Notes for the ROGUE RIVER

LOCATION—Southwestern Oregon.

LENGTH OF TRIP—The roadless wild-river section, Grave Creek to Illahe, is 33 miles. The more popular run from Galice to Agness is 47 miles and the average party runs it in four or five days. (Add a couple of extra days if continuing on down the river to Gold Beach on the Pacific Coast.)

FAVORABLE SEASON—June through September.

DEGREE OF DIFFICULTY—Gentle stretches alternate with a number of fast, dangerous drops. Should be attempted only by experts or skilled boaters who are willing to portage in places (and know just where to get out and look things over). Those with less experience should enjoy the run with a guided party (see Appendix).

RECOMMENDED CRAFT—Raft or kayak. Possible for expert canoeist (craft should be decked) who knows where to portage.

ACCESS POINTS—Although there are several possible put-in points, the most popular is at Galice, 20 miles west of Grants Pass on a forest road. Other good put-ins are within 10 miles of Galice, up or downriver. Grants Pass, commercial center of southwestern Oregon, is at the junction of U.S. Highway 199 and Interstate 5. One can take-out at Illahe or Agness, connected by over 40 miles of forest road to State Highway 42 near Myrtle Point, or continue to Gold Beach on U.S. Highway 101.

CAMPING—Numerous fine campsites. It is good to camp close to a side stream, of which there are many, as it is not advisable to drink the river water. There are also a handful of fishing lodges scattered along the river for those disinclined to rough it.

FISHING—Excellent. A vast number of Chinook salmon and steelhead ascend the river in May and early June. The run dwindles as the summer progresses, although there is a resurgence of steelhead in late August.

CHAPTER THREE

River of No Return: The Salmon

1. Salmon River Lore

In the winter, the Sawtooth Range of Idaho tilts upward out of vast snow-fields—a serried fortress of raw slabs, buttresses, arêtes, and pinnacles that stab at the sun and the stars. The slopes and crags are rock too steep in most places to hold the snow, but in the high meadows white drifts gather 30 feet deep and more.

Ceaselessly winds scour the summit rocks. Lower down, the tightly branched spruce are burdened with snow; now and then a limb that has bent too far releases a shimmering, disintegrating package of crystals with a soft hiss and plop in the stillness. On high, dizzy ledges of rock and grass, mountain goats paw at fodder under the crusted snow.

But mostly, the winter here is hushed and silent except for the sounds of the wind and trees and the shifting snow.

In late spring, by the time the sun has peeled away the snow to expose new grass and flowers in the lower meadows, and Basque herders are working their sheep up through them, the dominant sound is water. Water. Moving. Ripping out the foundations of snowfields, seeping through grass. Trickles that join, meander through high basins, gathering force and width from the melt of other divides, then plunging as clear waterfalls into the gorges.

The headwaters of the Salmon River are like this. Loon Creek, Pistol Creek, Rapid River, Panther Creek, Cache Creek, Big Squaw Creek, Horse Creek—all have their own wild movements, shaped by ledge and rock and logjam. Their sounds are as constant as the earth turning on its axis.

The waters of the main Salmon River rise in the Sawtooth Mountains and the Bitterroot Range in the east, on the Idaho-Montana border. The Middle Fork, major tributary of the main Salmon and almost its equal in length and volume of water, draws most of its strength from the snow-melt and springs of the Sawtooth Mountains. The combined flow pounds its way through a tangle of high mountains to merge with the Snake River beyond Hell's Canyon.

So far as we know the first white men to investigate the swift waters of the Salmon were the explorers Meriwether Lewis and Captain William Clark. In the spring of 1804 they started up the Missouri River from St. Louis, headed for the Pacific Ocean. The mountains that lay beyond horizons of buffalo prairie were largely unknown, mysterious as the dark side of the moon. The United States had just acquired the vast Louisiana Purchase from France, and if little was known about its geography, even less was known of the Indians who inhabited it.

As the party moved upriver, through the country of the Omahas, the Sioux, and Mandans, Lewis and Clark made extensive notes on the terrain, and, with extraordinary instincts for diplomacy, made amiable contacts with a number of diverse tribes. In only one area did this well-organized expedition fail—through no fault of their own. The dream of a Northwest Passage was still very much alive at the turn of the nineteenth century. President Jefferson, and indeed, most of the nation, waited with anticipation for news from the expedition indicating that the upper Missouri would connect by easy portage to a river flowing to the Pacific.

Once the continental divide had been crossed, however, and the expedition encamped on the Lemhi River, a tributary of the Salmon, a Shoshone chief gave Lewis scant encouragement as he spoke of the country ahead.

> . . . here he placed a number of heaps of sand on each side which he informed me represented the vast mountains of rock eternally covered with snow through which the river passed; that the perpendicular and even juting rocks so closely hemmed in the river that there was no possibil[it]y of passing along the shore; that the bed of the river was obstructed by sharp pointed rocks and the rapidity of the stream such that the whole surface of the river was beat into perfect foam as far as the eye could reach. . . . (From *The Journals of Lewis and Clark,* edited by Bernard De Voto, Boston: Houghton Mifflin Co., 1953.)

Three days later, Captain Clark, not a man to be thwarted by mere hearsay, proceeded for several miles down the watercourse which was known to later nineteenth-century frontiersmen as the River of No Return, and now is called the main Salmon. In his Journal for August 23 he reports:

The River is almost one continued rapid, five verry considerable rapids
. . . the passage of either with Canoes is entirely impossible, as the
water is Confined between huge Rocks & the Current beeting from one
against another for Some distance below . . . my guide and maney
other Indians tell me that the Mountains Close and is a perpendicular
Clift on each Side, and Continues for a great distance and that the
water runs with great violence from one rock to the other on each Side
foaming & roreing thro rocks in every direction, So as to render the
passage of any thing impossible. those rapids which I had Seen he said
was Small and trifleing in comparrison to the rocks & rapids below, at
no great distance & The Hills or mountains were not like those I had
Seen but like the Side of a tree Streight up. . . .

And so the first white men to see the canyon of the Salmon River
turned their backs on it, to toil over Lost Trail Pass to the Bitterroot River,
then over Lolo Pass to the Lochsa River, down which they would pass to
the Clearwater and the Columbia. The beautiful, contorted realities of the
Rocky Mountains and the violent rivers draining them were becoming
known. Dreams of an easy water passage to the Pacific were fading.

There were other dreams. Gold was one of them. It was a central
feature of the American dream. You could be the immigrant son of the
rawest peasant, illiterate, a drape of ragged odor in from the creeks one
moment—and in the next, if your deerhide pouch bulged with true color,
the toast of the town. It was, after all, a form of money, and most who
found it blew it quickly on a sky-wheeling drunk, or women who smiled
shyly after unhooking everything but the ivory lockets around their necks.
Others parlayed their pokes into more wealth and power. In a land where
every man had a chance of scrabbling gold from ledges of an unnamed
creek, where prairie and forest seemed to stretch almost to the Orient, the
carefully nurtured class systems of Europe had no validity. For frontier
Americans, money, not family lineage, established Society.

The Salmon River country is extremely rugged. As one longtime resident put it: "Seems like the Creator chopped it out with a hatchet." Which,
naturally, did not deter early-day miners, who would have followed a vein
of wire-gold or horn silver right into an erupting volcano if they figured the
color wouldn't pinch out. In the 1860s, the '70s, they started to swamp in,
panning mostly, axing out crude sluice-boxes, blasting loose promising
ledges with dynamite. Their towns—Bonanza, Custer, Leesburg, Yellow-
jacket, Forney, Yellow Pine—boomed briefly, with their smell of whip-
sawed pine and their bearded men striding dusty streets that were soon
abandoned to wind and drifting leaves.

The Thunder Mountain Mining District, south of the Salmon River,
was a strange place to be during electrical storms. Somehow the structure
of the mountains, maybe the underlying rock, seemed to hold the rumble

"Seems like the Creator chopped it out with a hatchet," said one oldtimer of the rugged Salmon River country

incessantly, rolling the sound back and forth long after the initial burst. Certain Indians held that the thunder came not from the sky but out of the earth. The mining camp of Thunder Mountain lasted only a few years, but long enough for the local newspaper editor to declare it was "bounded on the north by the Aurora Borealis, on the east by the rising sun, on the south by the vernal equinox and on the west by the Day of Judgement."

Roosevelt, a town not far from Thunder Mountain, went out with a bang rather than a whimper. Loosened by heavy rains, a sizable chunk of mountain roared down into the canyon, damming a flood-swollen creek. Backup soon began lapping up the sides of the log buildings. Most residents fled in panic, fearing additional landslides. One bawdy-house madam, however, wrestled ineffectually with her upright piano, attempting to get it out of her establishment and to the safety of higher ground. It had, after all, been brought in piece by piece on muleback. Her pleas for help went unheeded, as miners splashed past her up the street, arms filled with clothing and provisions. Her remarks, directed at departing backs, are said to have been extremely colorful.

When the sun again shone at Roosevelt, only a couple of buildings poked out of the water. Beaver later lived in the attic of one of them. People soon drifted away to other camps. Prospectors, camped by the lake, would sometimes strip and dive down into submerged saloons, fumbling in the dark chill for whiskey bottles.

Although there was rich gold ore in high country above the Salmon River Canyon—certain pockets yielded as much as $100 per shovelful— most of the settlements were in isolated locations. In 1861 word of a strike drew numerous prospectors into mountains north of the river. Wooden tent frames soon lined Baboon Gulch—"hotels," saloons, and stores where flour sold for $75 a sack and bacon for $3 per pound. By December, the settlement, now christened Florence, had a population of more than ten thousand.

It was a winter of heavy snows. Snow lay 10 feet on the level, and higher in drifts, burying trails and making prisoners of those miners, who, with the obdurate optimism of their breed, had lingered to work frozen claims. Hopes would kindle at a couple of days of weak sun—"Looks like someone's bound to snowshoe in with some grub." Then the sky would seal off again, gray, merging with the land. Flakes drifted down in silence, the kind of silence that makes a trapped and slowly starving man want to run outside shouting, beating a pan, as though that could break the spell, instead of huddling without words next to cast-iron stoves. Some men, incredibly, survived for weeks on what they could cook out of flour and water, and by boiling the inner bark of pine trees.

It was May before packers could get a mule train within 10 miles of the camp. When the animals floundered, men loaded the supplies onto their own backs and pressed on. Before Florence was reached, several of them were snow-blind, and had to be guided by their companions with shovel handles. They made it. The gaunt citizens of Florence, loquacious after a little medicinal whiskey, were alternately overjoyed at their salvation, profane at the delay. It was quite a celebration.

Not far away, in the bottom of the Salmon River Canyon, winter temperatures are milder than in any other place in the northern Rockies. While the hapless miners of Florence, with little else to do, wagered gold dust on how much snow would fall the next day, down in the canyon, bunchgrass was already several inches high. Currant bushes were leafing out, and wildflowers—yellow bell, sagebrush buttercup, and spring beauty —were in full bloom.

Yet, here too, prospecting had its perils. A man with the curiously prophetic name of Swim discovered a ledge of quartz honeycombed with gold near the mouth of Yankee Fork. The claim was staked, vaguely as it turned out, and recorded at Challis. The ore assayed $18,000 to the ton.

Swim spent the following winter raising money to develop the claim. When he started down the canyon in the spring, he was followed at a distance by other gold-seekers who had heard rumors of the strike. By alert tracking, they discovered where his horse had entered the water. There were no signs of it on the other side. Later, bones of the animal were found in a logjam.

No trace of Swim, nor his ledge of gold, have been discovered to this day.

For three decades, from the 1860s to the 1880s, the Salmon River country saw mining camps prosper and decline. Often, abandoned placers were worked by Chinese who had helped construct the Central Pacific Railroad. But eventually they, like most of their predecessors, moved on to other strikes, other places. A few hardy souls lingered in the country to homestead. To survive, they had to raise gardens and orchards, run cattle and sheep, be hunters and guides, and sometimes distill moonshine or pack mail. Harsh winters got to them in big meadows of the high country; in the canyons, where it was mild enough, there were almost no toeholds.

Oldtimers tell a story of a silver-tongued Boise real estate man who somehow lured two wide-eyed easterners into the precipitous canyon of the Middle Fork of the Salmon. He was going to sell them a ranch. Walking along a goat path beside the river, they halted abruptly when an immense boulder came crashing down from above and shattered at their feet. A few more paces and another great rock thundered into the river behind them. As the greenhorns eyed the sky and surrounding cliffs apprehensively, an apple tree plummeted downward, bursting into a million splinters. A moment after, it was followed by a pig, seven chickens, and a team of mules. Then a man in bib overalls, who landed with a tremendous whack on his backside.

"Confound this country!" he roared. "This is the third time today I have fallen out of my ranch!"

Homesteaders in the Salmon River country, at least those who stayed, mostly died violently or lived to a ripe old age. History tells us that Sam Hopkins, mistaken for a bear, was shot near Copper Camp. And that Jake Grosclose was killed by Indians, "Boozer" Elliot expired of Rocky Mountain spotted fever, Jack Shafer drowned in the South Fork, Bob Smith froze to death carrying mail over Elk Summit, and "Sheepherder" Bill was lamented when his moonshine still blew up.

Most of the early settlers in the Salmon River country were bachelors. One chap, who despised housework and owned a dog named Water, was fond of remarking to his infrequent dinner guests that the plates were as "clean as water could make them." If a man got tired of his own indifferent

A hard pull around an unexpected rock on the Middle Fork of the Salmon

cooking, and longed for a bit of conversation, he could plod out to the occasional roadhouse, such as the one at Dry Lake, whose menu was a masterpiece of brevity: *Meals* . . . 50 cents; *Gorge* . . . 75 cents; *Royal Gorge* . . . $1. The entree was made from whatever animal had most recently drifted in front of the proprietor's rifle sights. If a man's loneliness had a sharper edge to it, he might trek on into one of the larger mining camps, where he could have companionship aplenty—over a bottle, around a card table, or on the bed of an upstairs room—for as long as he cared to slap down the price.

Before long, some men were raising families in the backcountry. Some say that Charles Bemis won his Chinese wife, Polly, in a poker game at Warren; others claim this is untrue, that a mutual attraction developed while she was nursing pistol wounds he received from a feisty card dealer. At any rate, they got married, and together developed a ranch in the depths of the Salmon River Canyon.

Idaho settlers began to have problems with the Indians in the 1850s, when some ranches, wagon trains, and an army fort were attacked; Idaho Indians had had problems with the settlers since they first pushed into the country, righteously putting down roots on tribal lands, confident the Indians, like gentle ghosts, would fade to those places deemed unsuitable for farming and barren of minerals. Most did. Others, like Chief Joseph of the Nez Percé, and Chief Buffalo Horn of the Bannock, led their people into warfare, angered to desperation by a pattern of broken treaties. They were defeated, but not with ease. General Howard of the U.S. Army pursued Chief Joseph's band through the piney, corrugated country of the Salmon and Clearwater rivers, usually outnumbering the Indians two to one, or better. Many of the Nez Percé were women, children, and old, toothless sages of visions and dreams, who could no longer pull back a bow, and had never held a rifle. Chief Joseph and what able-bodied men he possessed, time and time again held up their foes with fierce fighting, pitting knowledge of bush and shadow against superior firepower, luring the troopers onto dead-end trails with a cunning that Coyote, who stole fire from the gods, would have admired. Chief Joseph and his people worked their way up the Lolo Trail, attempting to reach Canada. They almost did. At the battle of Bear Paw Mountain, a few miles from the border, the outnumbered, weary, and outgunned Nez Percé were forced to surrender. General Howard and his troops had bogged down long ago, telegraphing army units in Montana to intercept the determined band. The defeated but defiant Indian leader lashed out at his captors with bitter, ironic dignity.

"From where the sun now stands, I shall fight no more!"

In retrospect, it appears that with a few more guns, or people to fire them, Chief Joseph might have bestowed upon General Howard the same sort of immortality accorded to General Custer for his overconfident death in the windy grass.

The Tukuarika, a branch of the Shoshone tribe, more commonly called the "Sheepeaters," were living in the Salmon River country long before pyramids were lifted above the sands of the Nile Valley. Their descendants were still living there until the last quarter of the nineteenth century—gatherers of berries and other edible plants, skillful hunters, particularly adept at tracking mountain sheep. The tribe might have remained in their rugged homeland to this day had not Indian attacks on ranchers and Chinese placer miners led to the "Sheepeaters' War," in which, after bitter pursuits through the wilderness, U.S. regulars at last effectively separated the Tukuarika from their mountain habitat of several thousand years. They were exiled to the Fort Hall reservation, more than 200 miles away, to live in shacks in a strange territory alien to their traditional knowledge and myths.

Ironically, historians now believe that the initial violent incidents that precipitated the war were actually committed by Bannock living on the fringes of the Salmon River country, not the Tukuarika.

Legend has it that the Salmon River rapids were first navigated in the 1820s by a bearded giant named McKay, who is said to have encountered the Devil himself stroking a boat upriver near Chamberlain Creek. The touchy Scot, who had been known to uproot cottonwood trees when irritated, became enraged when Lucifer demanded right-of-way.

"Go to hell!" McKay roared, smacking his antagonist's face with a bow sweep so vigorously that teeth were scattered across the raging water. The site of the altercation is still known as Devil's Teeth Rapids.

A Hudson's Bay trapper, lacking, perhaps, the stature of McKay, but little of his audacity, somehow managed to keep afloat through almost half the canyon—plunging through bigwater rapids in a small bullboat, fashioned from willow poles and buffalo hides. He left his name, T. Flapper, and the date, 1827, chipped onto a rock that loomed out of the river.

During the gold booms of the 1860s, '70s, and '80s, a good deal of freight was floated down the upper part of the Salmon River to miners, some of it arriving rather waterlogged, and a considerable amount never arriving at all. The waters that William Clark had described as running "with great violence from one rock to the other on each Side foaming & roreing thro rocks" were a rude shock to several freighters, who came West thinking to carry cargo down another Ohio, Missouri, or Mississippi, where the principal dangers were snags, sandbars, or the navigator falling overboard out of boredom or too much bourbon. The River of No Return did not treat them all gently.

Harry Guleke was one of the early freighters. His boat designs, evolved through experience, soon became good—shallow-drafted, sturdy craft guided by large sweeps fore and aft. In rapids of the upper river—Long Tom, Horse Creek, Rainier, Devil's Teeth, Salmon Falls—he trained his eyes and reflexes. He almost never lost cargo, though a heavy rapids might leave his goods, passengers, and himself drenched in an eddy below. With a splintered sweep. No matter. Tie up. Shoot some camp meat—lots of deer, duck, and mountain sheep if one wanted to climb up for them. Chop down a likely pine and carve out another paddle.

Onto the river again. Drifting and careening to the destination, usually a couple, perhaps three, slake-roof cabins, where the male occupants were already hunkered down on the beach when the boat prowed in and they would stand up, dignified, waiting to catch a line. Whatever of their faces was not hidden by hair—upper cheeks, eyes, forehead—had been worn into wrinkles by wind and sun, sorrow and a kind of basic, backcountry humor about it all.

There would be coffee, dynamite, sugar, flour, tobacco, bacon for the men; a bolt of cloth, maybe, if there was a woman around. Sometimes, if there were children scampering barefoot along the beach or round-eyed toddlers clutching mother's dress, Guleke would pass out oranges—exotic, edible treasures from distant fairy tales.

During his freighting, Guleke learned to respect the river, knowing an error in judgment or timing could be fatal. Yet he did not fear it. He once ripped down the wild Middle Fork on a slapped-together raft, commenting later, "I knew I wouldn't get into a place I couldn't get out of. Sometimes I was on the raft and sometimes I was under it. But I wasn't afraid. And until a man is afraid, he'll be all right."

Guleke was not afraid when a group of sportsmen urged him to take them down the length of the Salmon in 1896, but he considered the proposal a spell, knowing there are men who, for the sake of adventure, would row over Niagara Falls. Other people had already attempted the canyon; a few had made it—most had not. Although the boatman had never run the formidable rapids of the lower canyon, he was confident of his skills.

The timing was what bothered him. It was late autumn. He had completed his last freight run, carrying supplies to miners at Indian Creek. Upset in summer, if he didn't drown, a man could walk out, eating berries and catching rabbits and grouse in figure-4 traps. A mishap in winter could mean starvation against the slippery cliffs.

Guleke decided to make the run. There was no time to go back upriver to the boatyards at Salmon City. He would have to make a boat on the spot. From dry timber on an island near the mouth of Indian Creek, planking was cut for a flat-bottomed scow 32 feet long. Green, tough wood to stand the shock of submerged rocks.

By the time the double-decked vessel was completed, the river was icing at the edges, congealing in eddies. Snow-winds howled off mountains. As the boat slid along polished sections of water, and then plunged downward through rapids, Guleke and his mate, George Sandiland, became familiar with their craft, the feel of it in current.

They entered rapids unknown to them, and for that matter, unknown to almost anyone—and passed through them, several times averting capsizing by precision handling of sweeps at the right instant, the water-drenched boulders falling behind them.

Guleke and his mate made it seem almost too easy, in spite of the roar and bursting of water across the deck in the more severe rapids. It was almost too easy—like watching a good matador caping a strong bull. Yet both are illusions created by skill—hair-trigger timing and an ability to read the characteristics of dangerous adversaries. Sandiland was later drowned running the River of No Return.

At Lewiston, end of the run, the Guleke party was cheered, dined, and toasted with a substantial portion of the town's best booze. The festive atmosphere was not lost on Harry Guleke. He soon made a full-time career of guiding whitewater pilgrims down the Salmon River. "Cap," as he was commonly called, carried passengers down the canyon for almost forty years—yet never drowned one of them, a record some of the modern outfitters, with much better equipment, have somber reason to envy.

There were, nonetheless, some lively times. Like the night a party decided to sleep aboard above Big Mallard Rapids. Somewhere around the witching hour, a beaver gnawed through both tie-ropes, and the boat plummeted through that wild chute, bouncing off dark rocks, emerging below wet but right-side-up. And with no one, miraculously, missing.

In the evenings, after supper (like as not consisting of a Guleke Dutch oven specialty such as wild duck, onions, and potatoes baked in layers) when the campfire had dropped to changing caves of glowing coals, there might be stories, a song, or just quiet listening to things without sound. As out there, just beyond the flicker of light and murmur of voices, there was the river running: water and gravity pressing a sure, slow knife through mountain ribs.

At the west end of the Salmon City cemetery is a tombstone:

Captain Harry Guleke

1862–1944

RIVER OF NO RETURN

2. Running the Middle Fork

The Middle Fork of the Salmon River is famous among fishermen, renowned among whitewater enthusiasts. The water is both clear and chill, and when not plowing through rapids, one can watch the changing contours of the rocky bottom, and sometimes see salmon, steelhead, or trout slipping through the currents. It is a fast river, dropping an average of 27 feet per mile in the 100-mile stretch, from Dagger Falls to Cache Bar, that is most frequently run. During the spring highwater period, usually late May through much of June, the river is often a destroyer of boats, and an occasional killer of the incautious—inexperienced and experienced alike.

At any stage of water, the Middle Fork is not recommended for novices unless as members of a guided party.

The Middle Fork begins about 20 miles northwest of Stanley, Idaho, beneath Cape Horn Mountain at the confluence of Marsh and Bear Valley creeks. It flows 106 miles to the northeast, emptying into the main Salmon below Long Tom Rapids. Dagger Falls, reached by a dirt road which branches off State Highway 21, is the most popular put-in point for a float trip. After July, the water is too shallow on the upper river, and float trips must begin at Indian Creek or below. Stanley, on the main Salmon, is the customary gathering place for Middle Fork boaters—an uncluttered village surrounded by grassy meadows and some of the most spectacular mountains in America. The rustic Sawtooth Hotel offers memorable meals.

The Chinook, largest of the salmon family, migrate up the Salmon River in late summer. Nearly a third of the Chinook spawning nests of the Salmon River drainage are in the Middle Fork and its tributaries. Spawning season usually occurs during August and September, and salmon can be seen leaping through the fish ladder beside Dagger Falls.

Most river runners take from five to seven days to float from Dagger Falls to Cache Bar on the main Salmon, a popular take-out place. A U.S. Forest Service map shows over sixty campsites beside the river, most of them at junctions of side streams.

American River Touring Association boatmen and river guides in high spirits after a hard day's work on the Middle Fork

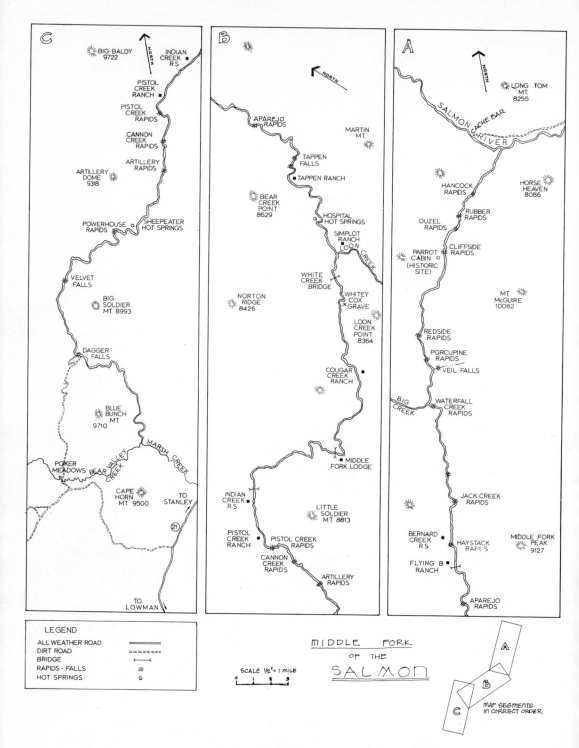

MIDDLE FORK
OF THE
SALMON

SCALE 1/2" = 1 MILE

LEGEND

ALL WEATHER ROAD	─────
DIRT ROAD	═════
BRIDGE	⊱─⊰
RAPIDS - FALLS	≡
HOT SPRINGS	Q

MAP SEGMENTS
IN CORRECT ORDER

The first rapids of any real consequence, Velvet Falls, is about six miles downstream from Dagger Falls. There are eighteen named rapids on the Middle Fork, and a number of other drops of fast water—many of which have been given profane and unofficial names by boatmen who have come to grief in them. The roughness of individual rapids varies from week to week, depending upon fluctuations of water level. A hair-raiser in high-water may seem but some glorified riffles in low-water, or vice versa. Veteran river guides consider the following rapids (listed in order of passage downstream) to be trickiest: Velvet Falls, Pistol Creek Rapids, Tappen Falls, Haystack, Redside, Ouzel, and Hancock Rapids.

Sheepeater Hot Springs is a couple of bends beyond Powerhouse Rapids, which comes after Velvet Falls. For those heady souls so moved, a close-to-scalding bath in the hot springs, followed by a plunge into the chill river, is reputed to be a great cure for almost anything. Except pneumonia. Those who hesitate have another chance some 40 miles on downriver, at Hospital Hot Springs, where warm water spills down a rocky slope.

There is no margin for error on the Middle Fork. Here and there beside the river, wrecked wooden river boats lie broken and deformed against rock and sand. For some time, the deflated remains of a yellow rubber raft stirred in an eddy beneath Velvet Falls like some gaunt, dying water creature. On the north side of Pistol Creek, some eight miles beyond Sheepeater Hot Springs, the crushed fuselage of a small aircraft lies where the plane was unable to lift above the tall pines when banking for a turn.

Yet tragedy is the exception. Almost all experienced river runners and guides have had tight moments in rapids when a stroke was missed, an oar broken or pulled from their hands—yet they somehow plunged through intact. There are a half dozen "cornfield" landing strips at Forest Service stations or private ranches beside the river, where planes land and take off without mishap. Usually they are piloted by men who, if they had to, could make a three-point landing on a lily pad or the back of a running tiger.

Although there are a few private ranches beside the river, most of the Middle Fork is within the Idaho Primitive Area. Here mechanized transportation—campers, jeeps, trail bikes, power boats—are prohibited. To get from here to there you guide a boat, sling saddle upon a horse, or walk. The Middle Fork itself was designated in 1968 a part of the Wild and Scenic River System.

A point of interest near the river, some 15 miles below Pistol Creek, is the grave of Whitey Cox, marked by a stack of deerhorns next to a warm pond full of squirming polliwogs. Cox, a miner, was killed by falling rock. Not far beyond the Cox grave the river is spanned by the White Creek Pack Bridge, where professional river guides and occasional intrepid passengers sometimes take leaps from the railing, some 50 feet up. The

Looking over a rough section of the Middle Fork before attempting a descent

river passes through a narrow gorge at this point and is very deep. Nothing to worry about if you hit the water right. A bit scary, though.

Down around a bend, Loon Creek comes sweeping in from the east. Captain Reuben Barnard, U.S. Army, in 1879 led his troopers down Loon Creek to the Middle Fork with orders to seek out and capture the Sheep-eater Indians. In his diary he commented that "within a distance of ten miles we have come from ten feet of snow to roses and rattlesnakes." Loon Creek, like a dozen other streams rushing down into the Middle Fork, is fast water out of high snows, bouncing from rock to rock, twirling slowly in deep pools where rainbows feed at twilight.

Historic Simplot Ranch, situated on meadowlands at the junction of Loon Creek and the Middle Fork, now belongs to the owner of Harrah's gambling casino at Reno, Nevada. Every so often, he flies entertainers in from Reno for a day or two of quiet fishing.

Along the river, they still talk about the Chinese placer miners who purloined some $300,000 of placer gold from payroll shipments up in the

Sawtooths. Knowing there would soon be men waiting with cocked carbines at every bend of the stage roads running between Idaho City and the Montana border, the robbers shoved off onto the raging Middle Fork on a raft of lashed logs. No trace of the Chinamen or their loot has been found to this day.

The fishing is still good on the Middle Fork, though not what it used to be. Today one has to sight a trout and then covertly pursue it, slipping over rocks and damp tree roots, whipping, always sinuously whipping, various artificial flies over stillwater wedges, in a kind of predatory seduction—*get hungry, damn you.* It was easier in the Good Old Days. A chap named Rusty Gates of Palm Beach, Florida, hooked 280 trout on a five-day run down the Middle Fork a couple of decades ago. Most of them he released from a barbless hook.

As the river winds deeper into its canyon, the slopes become steeper and more arid. Falls can be readily seen—the cascades of Waterfall Creek and Veil Falls. The stretch of river from Big Creek to the main Salmon is

Singer Glenn Campbell finds the fishing on the Middle Fork of the Salmon a rewarding experience (*Michael Jenkinson Photo*)

what Captain Barnard called "Impossible Canyon." Granite slabs lift from 2000 to 3000 feet above the water. Here one is most likely to spot bighorn sheep or mountain goats, impassively staring down from narrow ledges.

The placer camp and riverside cabin of Earl Parrot are a few miles beyond Redside Rapids. Parrot also had another cabin high above the river and accessible only by using the crude ladders he had constructed and laid against sheer bands of rimrock. There, in the winter, a thousand feet above one of the wildest canyons in America, the old hermit would hibernate—sleeping as much as twenty-two hours out of a twenty-four-hour period, stirring only to eat something or stoke up the fire. Twice a year he would hike out some thirty miles to a mining town where he would exchange gold dust for those few products not provided by the wilderness or his garden—salt, ammunition, matches, tools. He estimated his expenses to average about 8 cents per day, which was fortunate, since his placers apparently did not yield much color. When away from his high cabin he would post a sign over the unlocked door:

EVERYTHING IN THIS CABIN IS POISON

A number of years ago, a party of river runners toiled up the faint, steep trail to Parrot's upper cabin, assuring their welcome by bringing salt, which the old fellow could always use, and half a box of cigars, which he enjoyed. After a bit, one of the boaters asked him how he came to live such a solitary life.

"Well," the hermit replied, firing up a cheroot, "the answer to your question is very simple. You see I went to the Klondike in 1898, leaving behind a girl who had promised to marry me when I returned a rich man. When I finally did get back she had got tired of waiting and had married another man. After I heard of the Salmon River gold rush I came here and panned gold on the river. I had very good luck and put my money in a bank in town. It was only a short time until the bank went bust. What with having lost confidence in both women and men, I hunted out this place and I've been here ever since. It suits me fine and no one can ever make me move."

Earl Parrot has been dead a good many years now. But his cabins remain, windowless, facing the piled rock and tumbling water and the eagles slowly swinging as they ride the air currents.

A couple of miles from the junction of the Middle Fork with the main Salmon is Cache Bar, customary take-out point for one of the most challenging and scenic river runs in America.

Guide Notes for the MIDDLE FORK, SALMON RIVER

LOCATON—North-central Idaho.

LENGTH OF TRIP—The run from Dagger Falls to Cache Bar on the main Salmon is about 100 miles. Figure about 5-6 days.

FAVORABLE SEASON—June to September.

DEGREE OF DIFFICULTY—As with all rivers, difficulty depends upon the amount of water flowing. During spring run-off this stream is strictly for experts. In the reduced current of mid to late summer boaters of intermediate skills should be able to take it. But in all seasons it is a swift, strong river capable of flipping your boat around any bend where you relax too much. Inexperienced boaters should truck down it with a guided tour (see Appendix V).

RECOMMENDED CRAFT—Raft, kayak. Although decked canoes have run the Middle Fork, this craft is not recommended: there is too much heavy water coming at you too fast.

ACCESS POINTS—Best place to put-in is Dagger Falls, reached by forest road out of Stanley, Idaho. Stanley, with its dirt streets, moosehead-hung saloons, boardwalks, and jagged mountains, has the flavor of a remote Alaskan village, in spite of the fact it is on U.S. Highway 93, major vehicular route between Sun Valley and Missoula. Favored take-out point is Cache Bar on the main Salmon, west from the village of North Creek on a forest road.

CAMPING—A number of fine, maintained campsites. Rangers run the rapids to pick up trash.

FISHING—The Middle Fork is one of the most legendary trout streams in America. Action has slacked somewhat in recent years as the result of its being considered an ultimate by sportsmen. Yet for those who fly-fish up the side streams, the legend will remain intact.

3. Down the Main Salmon

The main Salmon River, which drops over 7000 feet in 425 miles, is the longest river located entirely within a single state. Traditionally, the head of any sort of navigation has been Salmon City, although there are interesting stretches of water for the sportsman both higher up on the Salmon and on its tributary, the Lemhi.

In the early days, there was a goodly amount of freighting down from Salmon City to mining camps that lay between there and the junction with the Middle Fork. One enterprising soul even launched a paddle-wheel steamer from below the Salmon City bridge. Those who brought celebrative champagne aboard barely had time to drain their magnums before the river, ripping over rocks, had reduced the boat to little more than kindling. Everyone apparently managed to flounder ashore safely.

This part of the river is still frequently run by kayakers and rafters. U.S. Highway 93 parallels the river on its southward run to North Fork, and a gravel road then hugs the river for 46 miles, as it abruptly swings westward. From the end of the road, at Cunningham Bar, to Vinegar Creek, 28 miles above Riggins, the river slashes through 79 miles of roadless canyon where fishing lodges and homestead cabins are few and far between. For much of the summer season, however, one's sense of wilderness adventure tends to be a bit blunted by the sheer number of rafts heading downriver, and jet boats powering upriver.

Between the village of North Fork and Cunningham Bar there are a number of minor rapids that are excellent for acquiring a feel for the river—and a couple which should not be taken lightly. Pine Creek Rapids, a little below the atrophied mining town of Shoup (named for Idaho's first governor, who was a pioneer in the area), are deceptively tough. Veteran boatmen consider them potentially as dangerous as any rapids on the Salmon. Long Tom Rapids, just above the junction with the Middle Fork, offers exciting water.

On the river, between rapids where the water glides slow and smooth, you can see changes as the river cuts down to new climates. Lodgepole pine and Douglas fir higher up on the slopes give way to yellow pine as the canyon drops, while in the cleft itself Engleman spruce are predominant. There is time, as your boat drifts, to watch wild duck beat off the water in a wedge, dropping to float with sudden dignity in an eddy below. Tail-feather-twitching grouse, locally called "fool hens" for their insensitivity to danger, bob about in brush beside the river. They can be killed with a well-thrown rock, photographed by the slowest photographers, or simply observed.

If fortunate, one may see deer, cougar, bighorn sheep, mountain goat, bear, otter, beaver. Or eagles, which, when mating, sometimes fold together and plunge down more than 1000 feet in ecstasy before breaking apart to feather up from death upon the rocks.

Voyagers down the main Salmon River should stock up on supplies at Salmon, if not sooner. Vending at North Fork is geared to the riverbank fisherman, and other towns marked on the map, such as Shoup, offer little more than tinned sardines.

At a number of places along the river are remnants of old Indian

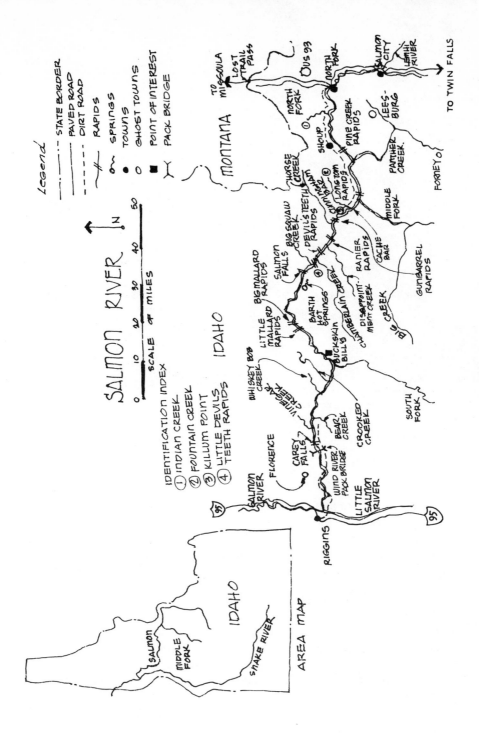

SALMON RIVER

Legend
------- STATE BORDER
———— PAVED ROAD
– – – – DIRT ROAD
〜 RAPIDS
〜 SPRINGS
● TOWNS
○ GHOST TOWNS
■ POINT OF INTEREST
X PACK BRIDGE

N

SCALE OF MILES
0 10 20 30 40 50

IDENTIFICATION INDEX
① INDIAN CREEK
② FOUNTAIN CREEK
③ KILLUM POINT
④ LITTLE DEVILS TEETH RAPIDS

IDAHO

MONTANA

TO MISSOULA
LOST TRAIL PASS
NORTH FORK
SALMON CITY
LEMHI RIVER
TO TWIN FALLS
US 93
NORTH FORK
LEESBURG
PINE CREEK RAPIDS
SHOUP
PANTHER CREEK
FORNEY
HORSE CREEK
CUMINGHAM
LONGTOM RAPIDS
MIDDLE FORK
DEVILS TEETH RAPIDS
BIG SQUAW CREEK
SALMON FALLS
BARTH HOT SPRINGS
RANIER RAPIDS
CACHE BAR
GUNBARREL RAPIDS
DISAPPOINT-MENT CREEK
BIG CREEK
BIG MALLARD RAPIDS
LITTLE MALLARD RAPIDS
BUCKSKIN BILLS
CHAMBERLAIN CREEK
SOUTH FORK
WHISKEY BOB CREEK
BILLS CREEK
BEAR CREEK
CROOKED CREEK
FLORENCE
CAREY FALLS
WIND RIVER PACK BRIDGE
LITTLE SALMON RIVER
95
SALMON RIVER
RIGGINS
95

AREA MAP

IDAHO

SALMON
MIDDLE FORK
SNAKE RIVER

Relics of the mining era can be seen along the Salmon

camps, some of which archaeologists estimate to be 8000 years old. All of the early Salmon River explorers remarked upon the profusion of fresh mussel shells in the vicinity of native river villages. Today there are still mussels to be dug out—feel with your toes, claw with your fingers—and you come up with tasty meat that is about as chewable as sliced saddle-horn.

At a number of locations along the main Salmon, as on the Middle Fork, there are Indian pictographs. The rock paintings, many of them done with red ochre—earth stained with iron oxide—represent animals, birds, and other, more mysterious shapes. It is assumed that they, like many pictographs found in other parts of the continent, were associated with religious, magical ceremonies directed toward assuring a good hunt, or with more complex, forgotten ritual.

Unfortunately, much fine rock art, some of it hundreds of years old, has been badly vandalized over the past fifty years, and so to pinpoint exact locations in a book such as this would be a great disservice to an extraordinary form of fading communication. Those seriously interested in seeing the pictographs of the Salmon River country should speak to Forest Service personnel or local residents.

Below Long Tom Rapids, the Middle Fork enters the Salmon from the south, clear water spilling into green. Cache Creek, about three miles downstream, is where most Middle Fork rafters take-out and where many Salmon River runners put-in. Fountain Creek, close to Cache Bar, shoots down a spectacular waterfall during spring thaw. Cunningham Bar, on Corn Creek, is the end of the road—from there one travels on foot, horse-back or boat. Around a couple of bends is Killum Point, which must seem sardonically named to those voyagers dumped in nearby Gunbarrel Rapids, one of the wildest on the river. Only Pine Creek Rapids and Salmon Falls are considered as formidable.

Emerging upright from Gunbarrel Rapids, one will probably want to stop at Horse Creek, a short distance below. This is an old Indian camp-site. A packbridge, sturdy if inclined to sway, crosses the river here. In the early days, one crossed the Salmon by raft, swimming, or an oc-casional short-lived ferry. Those who camp at Horse Creek can shove off into the river with more than a touch of excitement the next morning. It will be Whitewater Day by proclamation of the river. You're coming to Rainier Rapids, Devil's Teeth Rapids, Little Devil's Teeth Rapids, and Salmon Falls—a whole lot of water moving fast through boulders that don't move at all.

Above Salmon Falls there is a fine 30-foot-high "jump-off" rock with a deep pool beneath it. (Before leaping off any tall bridge or rock it is prudent to be with someone who knows the water depth from previous experience, or to sound it by diving. Dropping 30 feet onto a submerged rock can be rather debilitating.)

Salmon Falls itself, really more of a rapids, is an exciting rush of water that should be given a careful once-over from the bank before making the run. Two miles below the falls one can beach beside Barth Hot Springs, where the water, issuing from granite cracks, is 134 degrees Fahrenheit. Creek names in the area tend to reflect the unquenchable optimism and setbacks of prospectors (Lucky, Disappointment, Fortune, Thirsty, Cold, Blowout, No Man's), or to be named for animals (Bear, Panther, Deer Park, Raven, Elkhorn). Very few refer to people (Big Squaw, Whiskey Bob).

Shoshone Indians called the Salmon River *Tom-Agit-pah,* or "Big-fish water," and big fish there are—Chinook and sockeye salmon, steelheads, eastern brook and rainbow trout, Dolly Varden, smallmouth bass, white-fish, and an occasional sturgeon. A Chinook was reeled out of here weigh-ing 45 pounds.

Most operators of the scattered lodges and ranches along the river cater to fishermen and hunters for a livelihood. Sylvan Hart, more commonly known as "Buckskin Bill," who has been living at the confluence of Five Mile Creek and the Salmon since settling on a placer mining claim in 1932, depends on himself for just about everything. Game, fish, a large and varied garden, and wild plants such as squaw cabbage, dandelion, currants, rose hips, and brodiaea roots provide most of his diet. He makes his clothing from buckskin and other animal hides, and favors elkskin for bedding.

Before moseying up to the Salmon River, Hart picked up a degree at the University of Oklahoma. Intelligent and industrious, he soon mastered the basics of survival in his wild environment, and turned to other projects, such as constructing several buildings of rock and homemade cement, learning to mine, smelt and refine copper—then fashioning cooking utensils and tools. Today his shop is filled with tools for hide-tanning, copperworking, silverworking, woodworking and blacksmithing—virtually all of them either home-smelted or fashioned from old mining machinery or moonshine stills abandoned in the canyon by earlier settlers.

Hart's carefully hand-crafted flintlock rifles are not only extremely functional (he uses them for his own hunting, including bear), but also objects of considerable beauty. Hart recalls a Los Angeles collector who was so taken with one of them that he offered a blank check for it. The collector was not pleased when the check was refused.

"Dammit, you need the money," he fumed. "You *do* use money, don't you?"

"No," responded Hart, "not where I live."

About three miles downriver from Buckskin Bill's is Mackay Bar, an early-day ranch that is now a resort. The South Fork pours into the Salmon around a short bend from Mackay Bar. There were a number of early-day placer claims and homesteads on the South Fork in the later years of the nineteenth century.

Several miles down the Salmon from Mackay Bar, at Crooked Creek, is the historic Sheep Ranch whose two proprietors, Charlie Williams and "Four-Eyed" Smith, once raised produce which they packed out to mining camps in the high country. A barn, built of fitted logs and handmade wooden pegs almost a century ago, is still standing. Across the river from it lies the former ranch of Polly Bemis, who won the affections of her husband-to-be in classic western style—while patching him up after a spirited poker-table dispute in a Warren saloon.

A dirt road follows the river up-canyon from Riggins to Vinegar Creek, a couple of miles above Wind River Pack Bridge. This is a popular take-out point for float trips. Be sure to take-out just above Vinegar Creek, as the rapids below are extremely rough due to debris brought down by a flood five years ago.

After the rubber rafts are deflated, kayaks loaded upon car tops, and one has stopped to gas up, have a hamburger and cold beer, and then has driven across the mountains to the flatlands or cities, he will find that the sounds of turbulence will linger in his memory for a long time.

Guide Notes for the MAIN SALMON RIVER

LOCATION—North-central Idaho.

LENGTH OF TRIP—79 miles of roadless canyon from Cunningham Bar to Vinegar Creek. Most parties average about a week.

FAVORABLE SEASON—June through September.

DEGREE OF DIFFICULTY—The main Salmon, whose whitewater is not as constant as that of Middle Fork, nevertheless has a number of abrupt drops. For experts only, unless as part of a guided party (see Appendix V).

RECOMMENDED CRAFT—Rafts (10-man or better), or kayaks.

ACCESS POINTS—Cunningham Bar is on a forest road west from North Fork on U.S. Highway 93. It is a good put-in point. Drive south from Missoula, Montana, or north from Twin Falls, Idaho, to reach North Fork. Vinegar Creek is close to Riggins, Idaho, on U.S. Highway 95.

CAMPING—Numerous fine campsites.

FISHING—Excellent. Salmon, trout, Dolly Varden, smallmouth bass, whitefish, sturgeon.

CHAPTER FOUR

Treasure of the Sierra Madre:
The Rio Urique

The Rio Urique of Mexico begins near the village of Norogachic, some 100 miles southwest of Chihuahua. The river, which soon enters one of the deepest canyons on the North American continent, flows west and then south, merging with the current of three other rivers to become the Rio Fuerte about 150 miles from its source. The Rio Fuerte passes to the southwest, entering the Gulf of California close to Los Mochis in the state of Sinaloa.

1. The "Barrancas" of the Tarahumara Indians

In the Sierra Madre of northwestern Mexico there is an Alice-in-Wonderland sort of region, where the mountains rise so gently as to seem almost flat and bottomlands are perpendicular; where four creeks have carved canyons deeper than Grand Canyon of the Colorado; where running Indians leave tire-treads upon dusty trails; where fruit trees have houses and there are owls no bigger than sparrows.

Much of it is wild country, known only to the Indians who inhabit it. Anthropologists were startled when, in the 1930s, members of the Warihio tribe were discovered in a remote pocket of the sierras. They had long since been considered extinct, and were so solitary in their habits that one clan did not know of the existence of another clan less than a day's walk away.

Years after the warriors of Cochise and Geronimo had laid down their rifles and been herded onto reservations, bands of nomadic Apache roamed the Sierra Madre, skirmishing with Mexican soldiers who ventured into their wilderness stronghold. By the time the last of the Apache was annihilated by *Federales,* a former paperhanger with a Charlie Chaplin mustache and a gift for oratory was rising to power in Germany, while in America shabby men sold apples outside of theaters featuring Hollywood versions of Geronimo's last stand.

The final tie for the Chihuahua al Pacifico railroad, which crosses the Sierra Madre, was spiked in 1961. The terrain yielded to roadbed grudgingly: in the short drop from continental divide to coastal plain, engineers were forced to blast 89 tunnels and construct 48 bridges. And so now self-propelled Fiat passenger units, and old Pullman cars from the Southern Pacific line sway through the heart of the Sierra Madre, bearing tourists who like as not are middle-aged or elderly and wear lapel name tags provided by their tour directors, and who look up from canasta and conversation to see wild country rolling by the windows.

The trip is a curiously insulated experience, both for them and for the *moscas* (flies), which is what trainmen call the Mexican transients who cluster on the slow freights—in gondolas, boxcars, even under the smooth steel bellies of tank cars.

Few know when they pass within a few miles of Cusihuirachi, a 300-year-old ghost silver-mining city where silent, hollow buildings face each other for more than a mile down a narrow canyon. Or realize that at the logging town of San Juanito, a trainstop, they are but a day away from Basochiachic Falls, highest waterfall in North America. More tourists visit Niagara Falls in a day than have ever seen the awesome 980-foot plunge of Basochiachic. Not even the *moscas* know of the cliffside cave where a Chinese was killed for buried gold; or the house of an old Yaqui woman who is said to cure rabies with herbs. These, and other places—a cave of glittering crystal, an ancient, remote church where a human skull and a headless doll lie behind a row of votive candles—are not far from the railroad, but are reached by axle-breaking dirt tracks or mule trail.

The tour directors, teeth flashing in lighted dining cars, tell their clients which restaurants in Los Mochis and Chihuahua have really safe water, and don't just put city water into *agua pura* bottles. They don't talk about the man who raged through the Sierra Madre with forty hard-riding *Pistoleros* at his back, pillaging, wiping out an army outpost, threatening to attack trains. Some say he was a revolutionary; others say just a bandit. The tour directors don't speak of him, even if they have heard, because the events are not reminiscences of the Pancho Villa era: they happened less than five years ago. The band was finally hunted down after they had shot a government helicopter out of the sky.

It is still wild country away from the tracks. The trains, hurtling through it, hardly touch it.

For some 70 miles west of Chihuahua the landscape is one of dry hills where cattle browse between cactus clusters, and low stone walls, used in lieu of barbed wire, recede into the distance. In scattered mud villages, men in straw hats squat in the shade before small stores, smoking, talking softly, gazing into the distance. In places, where the hills fall back and there are large areas of tilled land, one might see a buckboard or spring wagon driven by a man with blue eyes and straw-colored hair in bib overalls. The woman beside him will be in a black dress with a black shawl upon an upright head. They are Mennonites, emigrants from Poland by way of Canada. There are more than eighty thousand of them in this part of Mexico. They live in numerous adobe-walled, tin-roofed villages, *colonias,* where they farm and produce delectable yellow rounds of cheese. Automobiles, as well as most gadgets of modern civilization, are prohibited.

So gradual is the slope of Mexico's great central plateau that the mountains are announced by forests rather than pronounced foothills or distant peaks. Scrub oak gives way to tall ponderosa pine, live oak, and gnarled madroño, whose bark is the color of burgundy wine. Granite boulders push up between the trees. Where there are cleared farms, young fruit trees are protected from scavenging goats by logs piled around them like so many small roofless huts.

In the highlands there are several logging towns, most of them astride the railroad. They are evocative of towns on the American frontier West— dusty streets, log or frame buildings, horsemen and wagons, the smell of freshly cut lumber. Law enforcers wear boots, western hats and shirts, Levi's, and carry guns at their hips. Most other males who can afford pistols also own and sometimes carry them, tucked in pants' waists and covered by a shirt or jacket. The favored caliber is .45: they are not infrequently used. Next to the ubiquitous tequila, the most popular tipple in these towns is *Ron Batopilas,* a locally distilled white lightning of considerable potency. The real *caballeros* of these places jockey two-and-one-half-ton Chevy trucks over impossible wagon tracks, hauling logs. They wrap their gear-shifts with psychedelic masking tape, drape cloth fringes on rear cab windows, and can fix anything short of a dropped transmission with a rock and a pair of pliers.

It is the canyons, the *barrancas,* that dominate the landscape of the Sierra Madre. It appears certain that the canyons of the Rios Urique, Batopilas, Verde (or San Miguel, as it is sometimes called), and Chinipas are all deeper than Grand Canyon of Arizona. Precise depths are still unknown, for the region has never been thoroughly explored or mapped. Many deeply cut tributary canyons that would warrant a national monument in the United States are not even named.

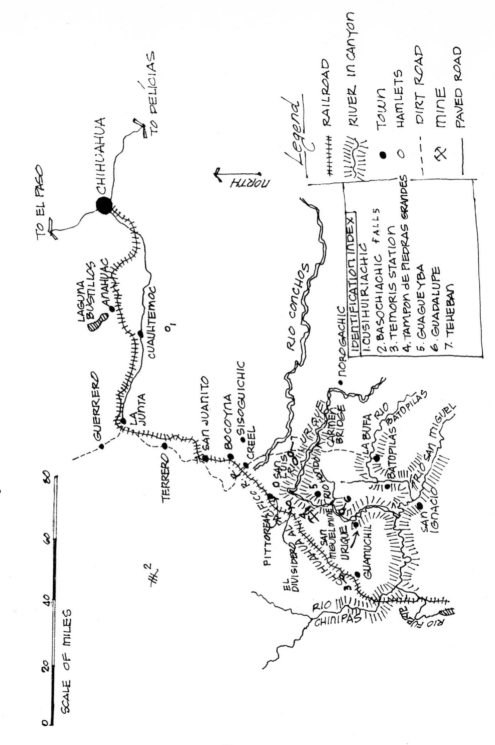

Barrancas of the Tarahumara

SCALE OF MILES
0   20   40   60   80

TO EL PASO

CHIHUAHUA

TO PELICIAS

LAGUNA BUSTILLOS
ANAHUAC
CUAUHTEMOC

GUERRERO

LA JUNTA

TERRERO

SAN JUANITO

BOCOYNA
SISOGUICHIC
CREEL

PITTOREAL

EL DIVISIDERO

SAN MIGUEL MINE

URIQUE

GUAMUCHIL

RIO CHINIPAS

RIO FU

SAN IGNACIO

BATOPILAS

RIO SAN MIGUEL

RIO BATOPILAS

LA BUFA

RIO URIQUE

CARTHEY BRIDGE

SAN LUIS

NOROGACHIC

RIO CONCHOS

NORTH

Legend

|⊢⊢⊢⊢⊢| RAILROAD
RIVER IN CANYON
● TOWN
○ HAMLETS
--- DIRT ROAD
✗ MINE
——— PAVED ROAD

IDENTIFICATION INDEX
1. CUSIHUIRIACHIC
2. BASOCHIACHIC FALLS
3. TEMORIS STATION
4. TAMPON DE PIEDRAS GRANDES
5. GUAGUEYBA
6. GUADALUPE
7. TEHERAN

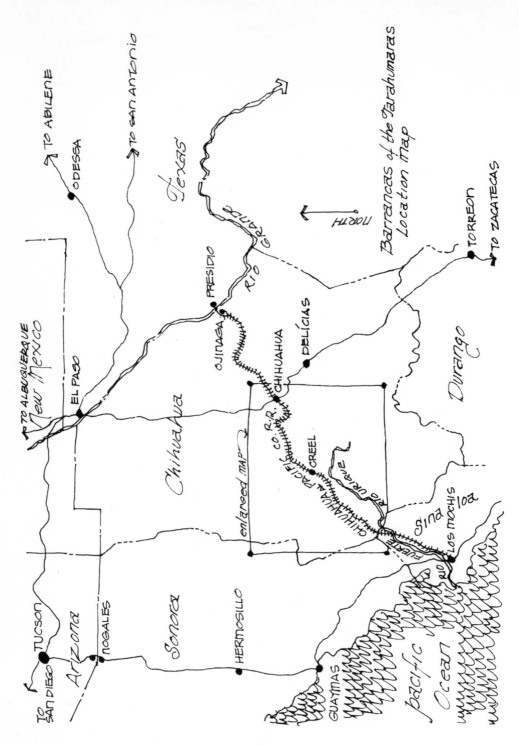

A Tarahumara Indian, Blas Morales, in his back yard—the Barranca Urique, or
Barranca del Cobre, near Divisidero

On the rims, ravens croak through pine forests, and there is sometimes
snow as late as May. By May, in the bottoms of the *barrancas,* the sun
beats off of cliffs and immense boulders, and when the wind dies they
are like open forges. Flocks of parrots sweep over bamboo thickets and
orange trees. Yellow butterflies jiggle between trees whose bark is silver on
one side, bottle green on the other. On the side hills, century plants, kapok
and tamarind trees, sotol, tree and ball cactus, stand in the heat.

In the dry season, wooden plows are pulled by hand or oxen across
dusty fields in the high country, and smoke from unchecked forest fires
hazes the canyons. In the *barrancas* the jade rivers are shallow, trivial, out
of all proportion to the deep trenches they have cut. In most places they
can be waded. From late June through September, however, thunderheads
build in the heat of late morning, to explode in storm during the afternoon.

Dry arroyos become sizable creeks, creeks swell quickly into rivers, and everywhere waterfalls plummet over ash-gray cliffs. In the bottom of the major *barrancas,* roiling masses of water pound through barricades of gigantic, polished boulders. Rocks the size of two-story buildings grind and shift with rumbles that cut through the incessant roaring of whitewater.

There are two old Spanish mining towns deep in the *barrancas:* Batopilas and Urique. They are self-contained, isolated places. Supplies are mostly brought in by burro trains from towns near the rims, thousands of feet above. Both villages have landing strips, and when the infrequent visitor arrives by aircraft—a government official or perhaps a mining engineer—the reception, especially among excited children, is rather like that given a ship docking at a seldom-visited South Seas island. A lack of air travel to these places, except for pressing business, is understandable. The airstrip at Urique, for example, is a narrow, rocky track that pitches down a hill at a slope only slightly modified from that of a barn roof. An ancient walled cemetery conveniently flanks the base of the strip.

When the villagers of Urique or Batopilas do make a journey, it is almost invariably up the switchbacking trails to the canyon rim, and then possibly by train to Chihuahua. For them, most of the *barranca* country is unknown, a wilderness.

Occasionally backpackers head down into the canyons, following Indian trails, but this can be tricky, as the paths are faint and fork frequently. One tequila-belting group of Chihuahua students lost their path in the dusk and ended up dozing fretfully all night astride weird tropical trees that grow out almost horizontal from precipitous slopes.

There are others who have come into the *barrancas* for a time and then passed on: priests seeking souls, prospectors seeking gold, or men who, for reasons of their own, wish to be isolated.

A while back, one such man was observed plodding down the railroad track near the rim of the Barranca Urique. Gary Anderson, a towheaded, easygoing native of Utah, watched the ragged figure's slow progress from the porch of his ranch house. Anderson, who is married to a Mexican woman and has become a Mexican citizen, was not used to seeing Americans trudging down the ties. And the approaching stranger was undoubtedly an American, although his clothes were in flaps and the soles of his shoes, all that remained of them, were secured to his feet with baling wire.

The man drew within speaking distance.

"Where you from?" Anderson has a soft, easy voice.

The man looked up and regarded Anderson guardedly. "Back there." He jerked a thumb over his shoulder.

"Where you headed?"

The stubbled chin lifted, indicating the tracks ahead.

"Down there."

"How about some coffee and a bite to eat?"

"Why not?"

After a breakfast of *huevos rancheros,* eggs enlivened with chile sauce, onion, and tomatoes, the men rolled Indian tobacco in corn shucks, as Anderson was out of cigarettes. It turned out that Bob Jones or John Smith—whatever his name was—knew a bit about mining, knew how to set a jackleg drill and claimed to have a nose for high-grade. Anderson had a mine in a remote bend of the *barranca* and needed someone to manage it, to oversee the Indian workers. Lonely job. Supply burros would be driven down from the rim periodically. Accommodations would be simple: a dirt floor shack with an oil-drum wood stove and kerosene lamps. Not much company. A few Indians. One loses touch with the outside world.

Perfect. Bob Jones, John Smith, or whoever, headed down into the wilderness—and may be there yet.

The Rio Urique, which passes through what many consider the most spectacular of the *barrancas,* begins as a docile gathering of streams in the vicinity of Norogachic, a Tarahumara Indian village. It soon drops into a deep boulder-strewn gorge, often referred to as the *Barranca del Cobre* (Copper Canyon). Although the Rio Urique is relatively short, little more than 150 miles long, very few people have attempted to run it.

Naturally, there are reasons for this. Until the Chihuahua al Pacifico Railroad was completed, the *barrancas* region was fairly inaccessible. Today, trains pause at El Divisidero so that passengers can gape down at a thread of the river more than a mile below. Yet the narrow, precipitous paths that twist into the gorge make the comfortably graded Grand Canyon trails seem escalators by comparison. Packing boats and equipment into or out of the *barranca* is a major undertaking. In contrast to the terraced sides of Grend Canyon, Barranca Urique is V shaped, and whereas the flow of the Colorado is drawn from much of the western United States, in the much shorter Urique there is simply not enough volume of water to carry away boulders that have tumbled down to jam sections of the river.

There are many trails leading down to the Rio Urique, some of them rough but passable for burros or mules; others scarcely more than goat paths that traverse harrowing ledges and thorny slopes. Over these the Tarahumara Indians, thirty-five thousand of whom inhabit the *barrancas* region, stride easily in sandals whose soles are made from discarded truck tires. Frequently the journey is to the *gari,* log and stone hut, of a relative or friend. Or perhaps to a cave. There are many caves and overhangs in this rocky terrain; they are used by the Indians as dwellings, goat pens, and burial sites. Eventually, if the right turns are made, the path will lead to a high country trading post or a Mexican village. Sometimes the Tarahumara will bring things out of the canyons—drums, violins, calcite crystals, coati

skins, bearded ceremonial masks, bamboo flutes—hoping to sell them to tourists where the train stops. The violins are carved with great care and ritual from native woods, and there is a Tarahumara word for each part of the instrument.

On occasion, an Indian will approach a trader he trusts with some gold dust tied up in a bandana or bit of rag. The traders know better than to ask where it comes from: the Indian would merely mumble "from the *barrancas*," and his face would become expressionless. In the past, Tarahumara have shown Spaniards and Mexicans the sources of gold, and have ended up being killed or slaving out their lives in dim tunnels.

Sometimes whole families go to the railroad villages just to look. Women and girls wearing bright red dresses, men in cotton pullovers, headbands, and a sort of cloth diaper, peer through the open doorways of *tiendas,* modest shops, where canned goods are stacked in rows of bright cylinders. Food is hard to come by in the *barrancas. Pinole,* a cornmeal mush, is the main staple. As well as corn, the Indians grow beans and squash in small plots that are sometimes on slopes so steep that it would appear difficult to stand upright on them, much less engage in cultivation. The diet is supplemented by an occasional feast of goat meat or wild game.

Although domestic plants make up the bulk of his diet, the Tarahumara is a constant, sharp-eyed forager. Numerous wild plants and roots are gathered for food, seasoning, medicine, and ceremonial purposes. Wild onions and mustard greens, for example, are welcome additions to a family's meal. The soft center of ball cactus is squeezed into the ear of a person afflicted with earache or deafness.

With a frail bow and wooden arrows with sharpened tips, the Indians occasionally hunt deer or peccary. More frequently, rabbits, pack rats, squirrels, skunks, chipmunks, duck, quail, and other small game are brought down with a well-thrown stone. A strong throwing arm is also good for knocking honeycombs out of cracks in the cliffs. Snares are set for gophers, rock deadfalls for mountain lions. Lizards, considered delicacies, are caught by hand, and rattlesnakes are also eaten.

Snakebite cures include blowing smoke into the victim's face, giving him peyote buttons to eat, and holding the snake while he bites it back.

There are trout in the high country ponds, and the *barranca* rivers contain bullhead, catfish, mountain sucker, squawfish, and other species, some of which are found nowhere else. The Tarahumara use several of the

Camped beside the Rio Urique in the bottom of the *barranca,* Blas Morales carves a flute from cane

some twenty-five narcotic plants that grow in the region to stun fish. A substance is stirred into a quiet pool with a stick, and soon groggy fish float to the surface where they can be grabbed with the hands. Certain plants, such as a type of agave and poison hemlock, are used only in running water, as they are potent for as much as 300 yards downstream. When they can obtain dynamite sticks from Mexican miners, the Indians "fish with thunder." The sticks are lobbed into larger pools, and if the timing is right, an explosion sends a column of water into the air and may tear slabs of rock loose from the cliffs above. The dead and dying fish are scooped up, split down the backbone for cleaning, and either roasted over coals on the spot or dried on rocks for later consumption. The "thunder sticks," of course, kill fingerlings as well as larger fish, and their continued use will eventually doom any sort of river life in the *barrancas*. Ecology, however, is not a prime concern of a man who may not have eaten for the past twenty-four hours.

Blas's one-room house is typical of the Tarahumara. His life, like that of the Navajo, is centered between a native culture, not poor, but close to the earth, and a dominant European culture, in this case the Mexican. Blas and his wife raise three children here

Virtually the only animal life not considered potential food by the Tarahumara are bears and bats. Except for those few Indians who own old Mauser rifles or have been fortunate enough to get hold of newer ones, the hunter's weapons are inadequate to kill a bear. More importantly, a bear is considered to have ancestral ties and power, and elderly Indians refer to it as "grandfather."

Also, among Tarahumara it is believed the dead awaken at night and may swoop about in the form of bats. In daylight, the dead may take the form of butterflies, and, from the wing markings, a shaman can sometimes interpret the identity of the human or animal spirit thus liberated.

Tarahumara wealth is measured in cattle, sheep, and goats, but most Indians are poor and possess only small flocks of goats. These animals are rarely sold and are generally eaten only at special feasts occasioned by a house raising, a major footrace, a church fiesta, or a curing ceremony. Curing ceremonies are conducted by shamans who may be called upon to exorcise the spirits that cause illness or drought or to drive away evil influences at the time of crop planting, death, or birth.

Spaniards penetrating the *barranca* country early in the seventeenth century sought both silver lodes and Catholic converts. Jose Pascual, a Jesuit priest, established the first Tarahumara mission in 1639. Today there are Catholic churches scattered throughout Tarahumara country, some of them dating back more than two centuries. In remote areas that have not been visited by outside priests for decades, church services are conducted entirely by Indians, with an amalgam of Christian dogma and native beliefs. Undoubtedly, there are theologians who must muse unhappily at the irony of Tarahumara shamans periodically conducting ceremonies to purify the churches themselves.

The Tarahumara occupy a region of approximately 35,000 square miles. Because game and edible plants are sparse, crop failure often means starvation. Only one out of five Tarahumara babies lives to age five; the rest succumb to malnutrition and disease.

The Tarahumara who do survive in this harsh yet bewilderingly beautiful landscape are short, wiry, and possessed of incredible endurance. Women frequently walk from the *barrancas* to Chihuahua or even Ciudad Juarez, infants in shawls on their backs. The Juarez trek is roughly equivalent to a hike from Phoenix to Los Angeles, and the Chihuahua desert presents almost as sere a landscape as the Mojave. Tarahumara hunters literally run deer into the ground. Once on the track of a deer, a man or several men will continue to jog after it for hours, rarely in sight of the prey, skillfully reading the most minute signs. By the second day of steady chase, the fleet animal usually drops, exhausted, and the hunters kill it with knives or rocks.

Recently a Tarahumara courier was dispatched from the Jesuit Mission center of Sisoguichi to ascertain food supplies in several Indian hamlets. He is said to have covered 50 miles of rough mountain trails in six hours—including the stops at each hamlet. Forty years ago a Tarahumara chief was invited to send runners to a marathon race in Kansas. Upon learning, to his great surprise, that the course was to be a mere 26 miles, the chief sent three girls.

The Tarahumara may be the finest natural distance runners in the world. Yet, when taken out of their natural environment, performance pales, as with the gifted high jumpers of central Africa, who achieve their altitude potential only when leaping from rounded, cement-hard little anthills. Although there were some Tarahumara runners on the 1928 Mexican Olympic team, and others have been persuaded to try out for international competition in more recent years, the results have not been dramatic. To begin with, there is a matter of diet. The Tarahumara lives mostly on corn gruel in the mountains. When he comes to an Olympic training camp, they keep plopping beefsteaks on his plate and filling his gaunt gut with eggs and milk and other strange food. His metabolism begins to run crazy. He doesn't sleep much and when he does, he has weird dreams.

Then there is the matter of where he runs. In the mountains he is always loping up rocky hillsides and then plunging down again; there are logs to be hopped and flocks of goats to be skirted. Here, at the training camp, one just runs around in a circle. Nice grass inside, but still a circle. Round and round. It soon gets boring.

There are always people watching. At the important races, concrete mountainsides of people, shrieking as if bitten by mad dogs. For a Tarahumara, who has a doelike shyness with any but his own people, it is terrifying.

Finally then, the matter of footwear. A Tarahumara's feet are splayed out from constant unconfined use, broad, with deep permanent cracks in brown soles. All his life he has worn sandals; tire tread lashed to bare feet with thongs. At Olympic track meets he is expected to push his feet into confining leather shoes; some even have spikes, like hard shiny cactus spines, on the soles.

No. Running in shoes has about as much appeal to a Tarahumara as competition in a raincoat would have for American or European athletes.

But back in the mountains, without medals and with a few weird dreams still lingering, the Tarahumara runners again compete in tribal games, running for miles through wild country where birds dart up against the sun and canyons drop away into haze and grandeur.

The most popular and elaborate Tarahumara sport is called *rarijipari,* a sort of marathon kickball race. The top runners from one district, or *ejido,* compete as a team against the best competition another *ejido* can put up. The *ejido* chiefs determine the course, marking it with crosses cut into

A *rarijipari* on the rim of the Barranca del Cobre

the bark of trees. (The cross was used as a symbol by Tarahumara long before Jesuits arrived with crucifixes: to the Indians it signified the Tree of Life.) Individual laps may vary from 3 to 12 miles, while the entire contest may last for three days and cover up to 200 miles. At night, the runners carry pine torches to light their way.

On occasion, short races—of 50 miles or so—have been staged for anthropologists or other outback travelers. At one such abbreviated affair, it was discovered that two quarts of tequila promised by the sponsor had been overlooked in a flurry of barbecue preparations. One of the runners made a brisk loping beeline over the hills for 8 miles to the nearest source, returned with the bottles and, after throwing back a couple of stiff ones, was ready for the race.

Major *rarijiparis* are not taken lightly. As the event draws near, spirited wagers are made, sometimes with money, but more often involving cattle, sheep, goats, drums, flutes, clothing, or other personal effects. Since most Tarahumara are poor and the betting may be heavy, the outcome of a race can drastically deplete or increase a bettor's assets. For a period of two to five days before a contest, runners avoid contact with women, and do not eat fat, eggs, potatoes, or sweets. *Tesguino,* a drink made from fermented corn sprouts, is forbidden, although gallons of it are brewed for the upcoming festivities. The runners' legs are rubbed with smooth stones and oil, then brushed with herbs and boiled cedar branches.

Magic is used. Once the kickballs, which are about the size of a grapefruit, have been carved from madroño wood, a shaman takes them to a burial cave. The shinbone of a man's right leg is exhumed. The bone, the wooden balls, bowls of food, and a jar of *tesguino* are set before a cross, and the spirit of the dead man is asked to cast a spell that will weaken the opponents. Other bones may be taken and secretly buried at certain places along the *rarijipari* course. Runners of the shaman's *ejido* are advised of those places, so that they will not pass near them; hopefully, runners of the other team, unaware, will become fatigued. It is believed the relics can exert a powerful influence for a short distance.

The night before the race, candles are lighted on either side of a small wooden cross. The runners arrive, many with the fetishes they will wear in the race to make them strong: eagle feathers, hawk and vulture heads, glowworms, rattles made of deer hooves and bamboo. The shaman chants and sings "The Song of the Gray Fox." The runners make ceremonial turns around the cross and candles, the exact number of laps they run during the *rarijipari*. Then the runners wrap in their blankets and are soon in deep, untroubled slumber, next to the food and water they will take at intervals throughout the race. Here, the magic of their opponents cannot touch them, for the shaman will remain with them until dawn. A shaman, it is believed, can see clearly on the darkest night, even if asleep.

On the day of the race, excitement is at fever pitch, as more and more Indians surge in from the backcountry. There are a number of small fires for cooking and for warmth. A certain amount of sly flirtation goes on (most Tarahumara girls have informally but permanently acquired mates by the time they are fourteen or fifteen, whenever they grow into a strong physical urge for a man), but generally the men tend to gather around different fires from those of the women. Gourds are dipped into cut-off oil-drums filled with *tesguino*. Old friendships are renewed. Bets are made. There are flocks of goats everywhere, herded by tiny barefooted girls who keep strays in line by lobbing stones at them with amazing accuracy.

Before the *rarijipari* gets underway, the governor of the home *ejido* gives some final instructions, in which he may note that any runner who throws his kickball by hand will not only be disqualified but will wind up in hell. The Tarahumara do believe in a nasty place where wrongdoers emerge after death. (When pressed for physical details about this place, they profess ignorance, saying no Tarahumara has ever gone there. All they claim to know is that there is a devil who has a bitchy wife, and that their numerous offspring are Mexicans.)

The teams start off. Only one runner at a given time kicks the carved globe; others carry bladed sticks with which they can feed the ball toward him. Rather than actually kicking the wooden ball, which even for a Tarahumara's leathery foot would soon become toe-shattering, the runner slips his toes under the ball and flips it with his foot. Each team is accompanied by six referees, who make sure no shortcuts are used, no tripping or other foul play occurs, and that no runners are chewing the dried leaves and seeds of the *riwerame* plant. It is believed that the breath of a *riwerame* chewer, blown into an opponent's face, will cause that unfortunate to have the blind staggers within half a mile. Drunks, naturally, must be kept off the race course, and pregnant women, considered bad luck when it comes to matters like this, are kept from watching the runners. The life of a *rarijipari* referee is no easier than that of his counterpart in baseball.

The runners, jogging through darkness or through the heat of high noon, often chew peyote as a stimulant. At certain specified places they stop for warm water or *pinole,* rest briefly, then continue on.

Along the course, people sleep, talk, and play violins and flutes. Fires glow in the night, and one must reach deep into the oil barrels to scoop out *tesguino.* Life's hardships, the struggle for survival, are briefly forgotten in laughter, music, and the mingling of people who share the same thoughts and places.

At the end of the race sometimes only one man is left, the others have fallen away in exhaustion. He receives no prize—only a small percentage of the bets.

Yet he will know, even when very old and half-dozing in lost dreams, that he once did something better than anyone. It is enough.

2. Running the Rio Urique

Water level is a crucial factor in running the Rio Urique. During most of the year the river does not carry enough flow to make boating practical. One would be better off hiking beside it. On the other hand, during the rainy season (July and August), when the river is in flood, it is the author's opinion that even the most expert whitewatermen would find themselves portaging or lining most of the way. A river map could be more practically marked with occasional "tranquils," with the rest assumed to be rapids, rather than the other way around.

Generally, the best time to attempt to run the river is in late February or early March, when there is a certain amount of snow-melt in the highlands. There will still be a few portages necessary, and a fair amount of lining—but the river can be floated. Probably the best craft for such a voyage is an inflatable kayak or a foldboat (see Appendix VII). Any rigid-construction craft such as a conventional kayak or canoe would be immensely difficult to get into or out of the canyon, and next to impossible to portage across certain rockpiles. Any inflatable wider than a kayak will be thwarted at numerous boulder piles that allow a narrow shape to slip through.

Since the completion of the Chihuahua al Pacifico Railroad, the west rim of the Barranca Urique, or at least a brief section of it, is now accessible. One can drive south from El Paso, Texas, to Chihuahua on a major highway, even if the road is hazardously narrow in places. Railroad and airplane service between El Paso and Chihuahua are also available. At Chihuahua one buys a ticket to El Divisidero on the Chihuahua al Pacifico and takes the train westward into the mountains. '

When you detrain at El Divisidero with your packs and inflatable boats, don't look around for a Mexican Holiday Inn for a hot bath before heading into the backcountry. The only structures at El Divisidero are the shacks from which Indian vendors shyly wheel and deal when the train stops. Once the train pulls out, El Divisidero's doors are locked, the Indians leave, driving their flocks and goats ahead of them, and the traveler is left alone with the magnificent emptiness of mountains and canyon.

Tarahumara Indian porters can be hired at reasonable rates, and are well worth every peso of their fee. Not only are they tireless packers, but valuable as guides on the faint and branching trails of the canyon country. Like the Sherpas of Nepal, they make trustworthy and interesting companions on a wilderness adventure. You can leave bread, biscuits, and the like on the grocery shelves if you arrange with a Tarahumara porter to cook up a batch of fresh tortillas each evening. They are delicious with dehydrated chili, stew, eggs—even peanut butter!

As the *barrancas* are a true wilderness, not a designated "primitive" recreation area in the American sense, there are no agencies to contact for hiring a guide or porter, no outfitters who send out brochures (though the people at a couple of small lodges back up above the rim might drive you to an Indian village in a station wagon). The people at the Hotel Nuevo in Creel (a trainstop) can be helpful in securing guides, as can the Posada Barranca close to El Divisidero. Mostly you have to do it on your own. Being able to speak some Spanish (or to fake it with a dictionary and gestures) helps a lot.

In the *barrancas* one wants to travel as light as possible. Take along dehydrated foods and lightweight but warm sleeping bags. Although the days may be blistering hot, it can get bitterly cold through the wee hours of the morning. Bring a good first-aid kit. You will be in snake country, as much as two weeks away from medical help should you be bitten, contract dysentery or fever, sprain an ankle, or break a leg.

Halazone tablets are recommended for the trip into the canyon but Rio Urique water is fine. Take along also some sort of sunburn lotion and a wide-brimmed hat, as the sun really booms down on you in the canyon. You will want waterproof bags for all equipment, long strands of rope for lining, and plenty of patching material for the rips that will inevitably be inflicted on your boats. If you want to knock a Tarahumara's head off with your generosity, or swap for drums, masks or blankets, don't bring merely needles, fishhooks, or colored beads. Throw a couple of multiple-attachment pocket knives into your pack.

Establishing a first ascent of a mountain is fairly easy to record; either the climber makes it or he doesn't. "Conquest" of a river like the Urique is somewhat more elusive. It is known that at least three parties have passed down the upper section of Barranca Urique, from Carmen Bridge to El Divisidero, with boats. To what extent they hiked rather than floated remains a moot question. As does, of course, the distance one can portage beside a river and still claim to have run it.

All of which is immaterial to those of us who do not have an arm cocked toward History, but merely wish to travel a beautiful canyon which, were not Man a cunning fashioner of things, could be enjoyed only by an animal combining the best physical attributes of the seal and mountain goat.

A dirt road leads from Creel to La Bufa, an old mining camp. En route, it enters the Barranca Urique and vaults the river at Carmen Bridge. The only written records we have of a run on the upper Rio Urique recounts how a 1963 exploration party, headed by John Cross, a Utah river guide, came to grief. (See Bibliography, "Lady on a River of Rock," *Sports Illustrated*.) Mostly what they did was drag 400-pound neoprene rafts up and down immense rockpiles. Finally Tarahumara Indians were sent down to guide them out. Later in the year a Cross expedition used inflatable kayaks to voyage as far as El Divisidero.

In spring of 1971, Cross and two of his sons, Jim and Jerry, were back at the rim of the Barranca Urique at El Divisidero, hoping to complete their exploration of the canyon down to the village of Urique, and then on to Temoris Station, where the railroad again joins the river. A film crew from Albuquerque was on hand to make a documentary of the voyage. Ed Smart, a mining engineer from Aspen, Colorado, an investor in the film, was a member of the expedition, as were his son Kevin and a mining *compadre,* Fred Baker. Dr. Luis García, Karl Kernberger, and I filled out the party.

Following are some excerpts from my bedraggled and water-stained notes.

March 19—The train paused at El Divisidero about half an hour. Lots of time for the passengers to peer into the abyss, bargain for Indian drums, or eat a goat-meat taco. The half hour was a galloping nightmare for us, as we had to unload several hundred pounds of movie cameras, film, kayaks, packs, food, and other gear. The train pulled away, leaving us wondering what we'd left in the baggage car.

Here we are at the edge of emptiness, with a long ridge of silvery waterproof bags, all bulging and heavy. The Indians, gathering up their wares, look at us curiously, perhaps wondering if we plan to set up a prefabricated city on the spot. There is a sort of wagon track that spills down through the trees, over rocky humps, and after a bit a battered Ford pickup bounces down toward us. Approaching a formidable drop-off, a young Mexican leaps out of the passenger side and skillfully bowls a large rock under a front wheel. The pickup stops—fortunately, as it turns out, for as we learned later the vehicle's footbrake has not worked for some time and the handbrake has just burned out.

Turns out the driver and the rock-bowler are the sons of Donato Loya, who is making arrangements for Tarahumara porters to accompany our expedition. In the Ford we nervously shuttle up from the railroad to Loya's house and trading post. It is a log structure behind which a stubble-chinned mare relaxes as much as possible without collapsing, and a lone tom turkey struts and blows like a drum major who somehow pranced away from his parade. There is much red jerky drying on a shed roof—it seems to be shingled with it. Inside the store Donato, whiskery and of a sharp, humorous eye, leans over the rough plank counter, seemingly as patient as the Tarahumara who perch on flour sacks or peek in the doorway. His stock is meager—beans, canned milk, sardines, farina, Pepsi Cola—yet one soon realizes he is an important man in this part of the world.

Tarahumara have been wandering in all afternoon, squatting on the sloping rock between the log trading post and a listing chicken house. These are to be our porters. A lean young Mexican in a blue baseball cap, Lupe, is their *jefe*, or chief. As our party included a documentary film crew with heavy cameras and other paraphernalia, fifteen porters were engaged at the then going wage of $2 a day. John Cross, organizer of the expedition, also agreed to provide the porters' lunch. This meant that Cross would supply them daily with a five-pound bag of corn meal for *pinole*, a broth, or tortillas. He also promised that while we were in the canyon he would buy some goats and a side of beef for the porters from Indians in the area.

In the gathering dusk, some of the Indians began to kick balls around in the road outside Donato Loya's house and trading post. I noticed that the balls were of wood and later learned that the Tara-

The Rio Urique has carved a vast, V-shaped gorge into the Sierra Madre Occidental

humara carve these balls regularly. I watched the ball games and Donato's chickens climbing a slanting pole into their chicken house. One Leghorn couldn't seem to make it; she repeatedly lost her balance near the top of the slanting pole and fluttered foolishly down. I wondered if the foxes would get her.

Some of us will sleep in a back room of Donato's house, others out under the stars.

March 20—Long before dawn those of us who slept outside are wide awake, sitting around a fire to ward off the chill. In the interests of efficiency, the Crosses are providing boats, supplies, and even sleeping bags. Unfortunately, some huckster in Salt Lake City has sold them disposable bags—thin layers of paper in plastic sheaths—and after the first night most of them are in shreds. The cheap space blankets are little help. It is like trying to gift wrap yourself in tinfoil. The fact that the Crosses brought their own, nondisposable bags does not bring the party any closer together.

John Cross estimates the trail down to the river to be 15 to 18 miles. Heavily burdened as we are, it seems more like 30. The trail is not hesitant. After passing through a side canyon, it cuts across cliff-ledges and corkscrews down steep spurs. The bottom of the canyon never seems far away; it just continues to recede down from you, a vertical mirage. The sound man with the film crew passed out from sunstroke, but revived after a bit.

It's beautiful country, with its endless cliffs and changing vegetation as we descend to ever lower altitudes. In a side canyon we pass a few Tarahumara huts. In the shade of one of them an old man squats, peering down toward the main *barranca*. He nods at us affably, conversing with some of the porters. At times we hear a rather haunting, repetitive melody which one of our porters plays upon a bamboo flute. The porters, all of whom have heavy loads, set a blistering pace. Striding behind one of them on a steep upgrade, I notice that he periodically blows like a horse.

After crossing a divide, the trail plunges down to the river, twisting through a rocky canyon and then above a gorge where there are hot springs, orange and banana trees. At last we reach the river and note the water is low and falling rapidly. Two weeks earlier it might have given us a wild ride, but at this stage we may have to do a lot of lining through shallow, rocky shoals. [This assumption proved to be woefully correct.]

Packs are laid down and camp is set up on a wide sand beach. Our porters are mostly young. They range in age from fourteen to forty-five. Kevin Smart breaks out a frisbee. Tarahumara are usually portrayed as guarded and solemn around outsiders, but some of the young Indians soon master the techniques of the spinning disk, and the porters are soon grinning, laughing and conversing with animation.

Tomorrow we head into the unknown. The river has not been

mapped in detail, nor scouted from the air. Few of our Tarahumara porters have been all the way to Urique by way of the river.

March 21—The first day is rough going. We may have made two miles in all. Several times we were forced to line the boats. The boulders in the river are immense. In places we paddled through tunnels of leaning rock. The porters must ford the river frequently as we find cliffs on all sides. Many of the Indians seem a bit uneasy in the water, glad to reach the other side, although they casually carry 100-pound packs across cliff faces where conservative rock climbers would want to hammer in pitons. The bright orange kayaks fascinate the Indians; they like to hunker below fast chutes to see if anyone will spill, and are greatly amused when one of us does. In this low-water level, the principal danger is that of breaking a leg while lining down through slippery rocks.

Lining an inflatable kayak through a rapids on the Rio Urique

We make camp. To the west, a waterfall that we estimate to be about 200 feet high drops off a high cliff. The frisbee comes out again, and some of the Indians have knife-throwing contests, at which they are very adept. There is a stone house back up toward the waterfall and some of the porters climb up to it and purchase a hindquarter of beef. A feast.

March 22—Cold! The boulders throw off heat until about two in the morning, then those of us whose sleeping bags are in the worst shape get up and doze around a fire until dawn. By now my bag is merely shreds of paper in a plastic shell—it is like climbing into a wad of crepe paper, and not much warmer. Fred Baker and I both throw our bags away in disgust. From now on we will curl up next to the fire, coverless, as do most of the Indians. (Fred, Ed Smart, Dr. García, and Ned Judge, director of the film, are all first-rate raconteurs, and we pass many a frigid night huddled next to driftwood blazes, swapping anecdotes.)

After dawn I climb some giant rocks behind camp. There are some kapoc trees growing between the boulders, and I gather up some of the white tufts for a mock snowball fight. A flock of green parrots wing overhead. The cliffs here, as in much of the canyon, are volcanic, with slanting bands of conglomerate between them. The conglomerate slopes bristle with thorny trees.

We name the waterfall Vulcan Falls, and a high promontory behind it, Vulcan's Throne. Once on the river we come to several places where lining is necessary. We make about 5 miles before setting up camp. Traveling light, one could make much better time, but the filming takes time, and that is, after all, a major objective of the expedition. During the afternoon some of the porters push on ahead of us. We hear a dull boom, and when we arrive they are cleaning fish beside a deep pool. The dynamite explosion has killed some forty fish, ranging from sardine size to about 7 inches long. We camp on a small beach across from two ancient prospect holes. Mineralization in the canyon is fantastic. Fred comments: "Can you imagine if someone had stumbled onto this up in Colorado or Nevada?" In his broad, sweeping gesture one sees frantic stampeders, tent cities, streets lined with false-front buildings. Down here on the Urique, next to the prospect holes, the buzzing of a single bee stands out clearly against the silence of the canyon.

Tarahumara are tireless. After toiling all day under heavy packs, three of them now jog up a steep mountainside behind the camp. Within half an hour we estimate them to be perhaps 2000 feet above us. We assume they are heading for an Indian *ranchito*.

March 23—During the night we heard distant drums, high on the mountain which our porters had ascended. There seemed to be an immense fire burning up there, at times illuminating the entire face of a cliff that we later, in the daylight, estimated to be 3000 feet high and 2 miles long. A brush fire seemed to be a logical explanation; yet there was little smoke. Most curious. Another, unscientific, possibility was that some sort of ceremony was taking place around a fire that threw out a light vastly disproportionate to its size. As anthropologist Carlos Castaneda indicates in his book, *The Teachings of Don Juan,* there are things that happen among the Indians of northern Mexico that are outside the rules of physics as we know them. Our three porters, on their return the next morning, would make no comment about the incident.

We make fairly good time today until in late afternoon we arrive at a place where the canyon is filled with gigantic boulders from wall to wall. The great rocks are white, black, red, veined, striped, polished, rough, lumpy—looming high above the river which spurts through a labyrinth of cracks and deep tunnels. Crystalline geodes gleam in sunlight, torn open by the summer torrents. There is no way anyone will ever run this rockfall in any level of water. There is a fairly good trail on the right-hand cliffs that can be used for portaging. An Indian tells us there is a mine, the San Miguel, that is being worked a short distance ahead.

The mine manager, a soft-spoken Texan, greets us at his hut. He rarely sees non-Indians, and when he does, they have come down the rough mule trail that winds up to the rim—his link to civilization. He shows us his vegetable garden and the mine. In addition to himself, a foreman and a jackhammer operator, the mine employs about ten Tarahumara laborers. They receive 24 pesos ($2) per day.

The monumental rockjam, which John Cross names *Tampon de Piedras Grandes* (Plug of Giant Rocks), extends all the way around a large horseshoe bend. Two major side creeks enter the river from the right on this bend and we camp in a bamboo thicket at the mouth of the second one. In the dusk we watch a small Indian boy work a herd of goats up what appears to be an almost vertical cliff. We are entranced—it is like watching a high trapeze act without nets. Goats and boy all make it safely.

March 24—After breaking camp we wrestle the boats and equipment around the rest of the Tampon de Piedras Grandes. Ahead of us there is a high, detached white peak, which I call the "Hound's Tooth" on my sketch map. When someone actually does get around to making detailed maps of the Barranca Urique, I hope they will rely mostly on Tarahumara names. Today's run is more open. The current is fast; there are some entertaining chutes, and we make our best distance thus far—perhaps 9 miles. We stop in the morning to examine an ancient Spanish *arreste,* where a waterwheel once revolved a massive stone which ground silver or gold ore. Not far beyond this is a rusted cable across the river. A trail from the left bank leads up to the Tarahumara village of Guagueyba, a good-sized settlement. We camp next to a cliff that is covered with tree-root tentacles.

March 25—We made fairly good time again today—I would ven-

Jim Cross shooting a rapids on the Rio Urique

ture another 9 miles. Early in the day Jim Cross catches a poisonous vine snake. It is long, incredibly thin, and pale yellow in color. John Cross is collecting reptiles for a zoologist in Utah. We pass through an impressive gorge where the walls overhang both sides of the river. There are huge polished boulders in the current, but the stretch is passable. In high water it would not be. We ferry the Indians through this cleft, in the kayaks. After some initial hesitation, they find this great sport.

By late afternoon we reach the most awesome gorge of the entire run. Fortunately, the water is quiet and the boats run it without difficulty. Wishing to take some pictures from above, I follow the porters up a path that is only inches wide with a drop of several hundred feet down to the river. In trying to hop across an eroded place, I grab wildly at the brush and come up with a palm full of cactus spines. Well, O.K. At least I didn't fall. We camp above a jumble of boulders that will have to be portaged in the morning.

Running one of the awesome gorges of the Rio Urique

March 26—We continue in this inner gorge, from which we cannot see the upper cliffs of the *barranca,* for several miles. The water, however, is more open than on any stretch we have thus far encountered on the voyage, and we make about 12 miles. We pass a major canyon coming in from the left, in which there is a good running stream, the Rio Hondo. At this time of the year most of the watercourses are dry. We camp below a stone house, the first structure we have seen since leaving San Miguel Mine, and learn that the village of Guadalupe is around the next bend in the river. We are only about 6 miles from Urique.

We have decided to leave the river at Urique. The water level has continued to fall and the kayaks are so battered and leaking it is doubtful any of them can stand much more punishment.

March 27—Dawn. I waken to the calling of doves. Once underway, we can again see the upper cliffs: we are out of the gorge. In the village of Guadalupe there is a fascinating old church with notched logs leading up to various levels of the roof. Behind a row of votive candles on the altar stand a human skull and a headless doll.

Three of us push ahead on foot, eager to see what Urique is like. The path finally opens onto a single, clean-swept, cobbled street lined with whitewashed adobe houses. Birds chatter in shade trees. Some men nod at us from the doorway of a small *tienda* where they are listening to an old battery-operated phonograph. There are no cars and we see no wagons; just a horse or burro here and there, heads drooping in the low afternoon sun.

We feel ourselves a thousand miles and a hundred years away from the cities we have known outside, up there beyond the cliffs that rise for more than a mile into a cloudless sky.

Guide Notes for the RIO URIQUE

LOCATION—Sierra Madre Mountains of northwestern Mexico.

LENGTH OF TRIP—The entire river is perhaps between 150 and 175 miles long, although it cannot be said for sure at this time, as the region has never been accurately mapped. The run from the point on the river below El Divisidero to Urique, perhaps 45 miles, can be done in 4–6 days, although this may vary greatly according to water level. My field notes, given in "Running the Rio Urique," are of one of the first, if not the first, voyage through this section, and hence it is hard to say just how long the average party would take. As far as river runners go, much of the rest of the river is unexplored, an intriguing mystery.

FAVORABLE SEASONS—It would seem the optimum time for running the Urique is in March, when water level is sustained at a good level by snowmelt in the high country. By late March and April the water level has dwindled so that one must expend much energy dragging one's boat over rocks. July and August are the rainy season in the *barranca* country. From looking at highwater marks and various monumental rock piles in the river, I would venture to say that even for the most expert whitewaterman, an attempt at the river during this season would be suicide or a lot of walking, lugging a boat. Fall and winter have no stable highwater periods.

DEGREE OF DIFFICULTY—In high water, the Urique may be the most violent river in America. During rainy season, some Urique rapids seem like science fiction. But most of the year, water levels are low, and a Urique trip means some portaging and lots of lining. A sure footing on slippery rocks is perhaps more important than whitewater expertise.

RECOMMENDED CRAFT—Inflatable kayak is best, but a small rubber raft (2-man) will do. The fact that everything has to be packed several thousand feet down into and then out of the canyon renders hard-shell craft such as kayaks or canoes impractical. Water gushes through narrow clefts between boulders in this canyon; large rafts will be repeatedly bottled up.

ACCESS POINTS—Carmen Bridge on the La Bufa road (steep, hard struggle down to the river); Teheban, also close to the La Bufa road; El Divisidero, where a trail of sorts drops over 6500 feet down to the river; Urique, equally profound, where there is a rough airstrip; Temoris, where the combined waters of the rios Urique, Batopilas, San Miguel, and Chinipas—the four greatest *barranca* rivers—sweep back to the railroad. This country is reached by driving south from El Paso, Texas, to Chihuahua, Mexico, then taking the Chihuahua al Pacifico Railroad to Creel, situated high in the mountains, about halfway to the coast. The La Bufa road, a winding dirt affair, takes off from Creel. El Divisidero and Temoris are stations on the railroad south of Creel.

CAMPING—Numerous good campsites. It is recommended that one boil drinking water, or use Halazone, although I never have. Try to camp well before dark, as there are several sections where the canyon walls are vertical and one is hard pressed to find a good sleeping nook.

FISHING—Poor. There are many species of fish in the Rio Urique, including catfish, squawfish, and perch, but the Tarahumara Indians, driven by hunger, keep the aquatic population at a low level.

CHAPTER FIVE

River of the Shining Mountains: The Colorado

1. "A Thing Much to Be Marveled At"

Up a side canyon of the Colorado River, where a flow of cool turquoise riffles over reefs of deposited minerals, is the Sipapu, where, Hopi Indians believe, man first emerged from the underworld. The Sipapu is a great blister of dark rock, hollow inside where there is a spring, open at the top to the sky. Deep under the concave rim, where it appears no man could descend, there is a feathered prayer stick thrusting out of a minute crack in the stone.

It is fitting that the Sipapu, sacred and mysterious, should be close to the Colorado, feeding water into it, for the river itself is unique; an unpredictable flow whose twin sources are the Wind River Range of Wyoming and the Never-Summer Mountains northwest of Denver, and whose delta is in the Sonoran Desert, where the world's highest temperatures have been recorded. Between source and ocean the 1700-mile river has cut awesome canyons through the most sparsely populated region of America—eastern Utah, northern Arizona, the Mojave and Sonoran deserts. In an age when most great American rivers have become little more than strings holding together grimy necklaces of industrial cities, for hundreds of miles along the Colorado there are only a handful of hamlets and bridges. Here the land, not man, is dominant—an immensity of raw and delicately carved rock.

Early geographers, who could judge only by the currents swirling at their feet, often erred in guessing which river was lord and which flow was merely giving tithe. Thus it is that we must refer to our longest watercourse as the Missouri-Mississippi, and also cannot speak of the Colorado without equating the Green, a tributary which is actually longer. The Green rises in Wyoming, the Colorado in what is now Rocky Mountain National Park. Merging in southeastern Utah, the combined flow of the two rivers has cut its way through rock at the rate of less than an inch in ten centuries, exposing fossils of the earth's earliest life and the mud and molten rock that preceded it. After writhing its way through southern Utah and across northern Arizona, the Colorado slips placidly through desert country, forming the boundary between California and Arizona. Finally it passes south through Mexico to wash into the Gulf of California.

The Colorado is a dry-lands river, whose strength and cutting power come from melting snowfields in the complex of sawtooth crests and forested ridges that early Spanish explorers called the Shining Mountains, and subsequent, more material-minded Yankee prospectors referred to as the Rockies. Prior to the dam-building era, the spring thaw brought incredible torrents through the canyons. Such a flood has been recorded as raging with more than a hundred times the volume of water that might constitute the dry-season flow. Even today one can find driftwood deposited on ledges 50 feet and more above the river.

Generally speaking, a chart of the internal commerce of a nation will coincide with a map of its river systems, roads, railroads, and communication lines following the paths of least resistance. An exception to this is the perverse Colorado. Its numerous boulder-strewn rapids render commercial navigation impossible. There are several hundred miles of monolithic cliffs, many of them rising right out of the water, more than enough to appall the most swashbuckling civil engineer. Yet, rather astoundingly, a man once conceived of constructing a railroad from the Rockies to the Pacific Coast—via the canyons of the Colorado. Frank Brown, a Denver financier, was bullish on the prospects of his Denver, Colorado Canyon, and Pacific Railroad. Shortly after personally driving the first stake at Grand Junction in March of 1889, he cast off on a survey expedition, accompanied by an engineer, a photographer, some roustabouts, a couple of cronies out for a lark, and two Negro servants to provide the comforts of nineteenth-century civilization.

There was, as it turned out, little comfort to be had in the deep, turbulent gorges of the Colorado. Two of their light cedar boats were lost in the rapids of Cataract Canyon, along with most of their supplies. By sheer luck no one was drowned, although Brown had neglected to bring life preservers. Somehow the party managed to struggle into Lees Ferry where food could be purchased. The expedition entered Marble Canyon.

By now, much of Brown's buoyancy had leaked away. Above Soap Creek Rapids he was "lonely and troubled" and begged Stanton, the engi-

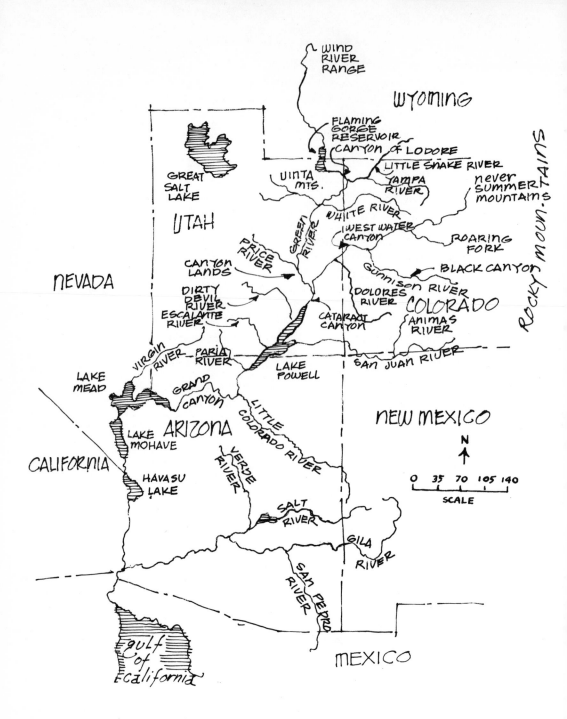

Colorado River Drainage

neer, to stay and talk with him late into the evening. That night, Brown, who had not dreamed of the river during the entire voyage, saw rapids in his sleep, and spoke of them with concern upon awakening. The river took him that morning, a little below Soap Creek. A member of the party, Peter Hansbrough, carved an inscription into the rock:

> F. M. Brown
> was drowned
> July 10 1889
> opposite this
> point

Five days later Hansbrough himself was thrown into the river and died in the water. The Denver, Colorado Canyon, and Pacific Railway was never built.

Like Brown, most Europeans who visited the Colorado between the sixteenth century and the twentieth century believed the river would conform to their particular obsessions, and were doomed to frustration. In 1539 Francisco de Ulloa commanded three ships that sailed up the west coast of Mexico, seeking a point from which an overland march could be made to the fabled Cities of Cibola. They were thwarted by the tidal bores of the Colorado: "We perceived the sea to run with so great a rage into the land that it was a thing much to be marveled at; and with a like fury it returned back again with the ebb . . ."

The following year the search for Cibola continued, with more ships, footsoldiers, and *conquistadores*. Hernando de Alarcón came to the place Ulloa had discovered: "Where we found a very mighty river, which ran with so great a fury of a storm, that we could hardly sail against it." He managed to get above the mouth of the Gila River before retreating.

Some of Coronado's soldiers reached the rim of Grand Canyon after Hopi Indians guided them for twenty days across a country so dry that women carried water gourds that were cached for the return trip. García Lopez de Cardinas, leader of the party, found the canyon hard to put into perspective. He thought it 8 to 10 miles wide, the river a mere 6 feet across. Men dispatched to the river found they could not even get close to it; their descent was halted by smooth, unbroken cliffs, and rocks that from above had seemed no more than head-high were in truth taller than the 300-foot tower of Seville. Clearly, this was not the way to the cities of gold.

Later, Franciscan missionaries such as Francisco Graces and Silvestre Escalante made monumental journeys through the unknown country of the Colorado River drainage basin, where they found the proportion of heathen souls to be depressingly small in relation to the harsh and sprawling landscape. As Father Graces was to comment about Grand Canyon: "I

This is the chasm that stopped the early explorers who tried to cross northern Arizona. Gazing into the depths of the Grand Canyon, they grossly misjudged the distance to the Colorado River, and estimated the river to be a mere stream 6 feet wide. This photo was taken at Toroweap Point on the North Rim, above Lava Falls

am astonished at the roughness of this country, and the barrier which nature has fixed therein."

The first Yankees to encounter and write of the river, wandering fur trappers, were not rhapsodic in their observations. James Ohio Pattie, plodding along the rim of Grand Canyon in 1826 through snow 12 to 18 inches deep, reduced to eating the bark of shrubs, later recorded: "We arrived where the river emerges from these horrid mountains, which so cage it up, as to deprive all human beings of the ability to descend to its banks, and make use of its waters. No mortal has the power of describing the pleasure I felt, when I could once more reach the banks of the river." The year before, another trapper, William Ashley, had started down the Green River, major tributary of the Colorado, with some companions in two hastily constructed bullboats—cottonwood frames over which buffalo hides had been stretched. His diary states: "These mountains present a most gloomy scene. They are entire rock generally of a reddish appearance, they rise to a height of 2 to 4000 feet. . . . the rocks that fall in the river from the walls of the mountain make the passage in some places danger-ous—windy unpleasant weather. . . ."

Although both Pattie and Ashley appear to have been more vexed at the obstacles of the river than awed by its grandeur, they continued to follow it, lured by the prospect of pelts and a restless urge for the unknown that had brought them to the Shining Mountains in the first place. From Grand Canyon, Pattie worked his way through the rimrock country to the northeast, still paralleling the general course of the river; fought off Shoshone, then crossed the continental divide to the Platte and swung north to the Yellowstone. He arrived there in May of 1826, having plodded across hundreds of miles of country no other white man had yet seen.

Ashley's frail bullboats were flung through the rapids of Red Canyon and Flaming Gorge; then the river slowed and the mountains fell back. This was Brown's Hole, where bands of Indians gathered; it would soon become the major fur rendezvous for trappers throughout the mountain West. Ashley could have left the river here, and perhaps should have, for ahead the river veered headlong into the almost unbroken wall of the Uintah Mountains. The river enters a crack in this range and thunders its way through the very heart of it. Ashley pressed on, through Lodore Canyon, Hell's Half Mile, Disaster Falls, Whirlpool and Split Mountain canyons—much of it without food or chance of escape other than down the raging river. Finally emerging from the canyons, he was able to pur-chase horses from Ute Indians and rejoin his associates on the other side of the mountains.

The Colorado may not have washed the feet of golden cities or been ideal for beaver trapping, but by 1857 the United States government, dreaming its own dreams, decided the great waterway might make a fine supply artery for its western forts, and then—the commercial possibilities were boundless. Accordingly, a 58-foot steel-hulled steamboat, the *Explorer,* was constructed in Philadelphia, dismantled, and put back together again at the mouth of the river. Her commander, Lt. Joseph Christmas Ives, was instructed to probe the mysterious canyons of the river, blazing the way for subsequent navigation.

The expedition got off to an inauspicious start, as the *Explorer* ran aground almost immediately after leaving Fort Yuma on January 11. Once afloat again, the sternwheeler steamed northward into what became increasingly a navigator's nightmare. The boat ground to a halt on mudbars, was dragged from anchorage by a howling sandstorm, battered while forcing its way up through rapids, and, in one particularly trying piece of whitewater, the current would repeatedly catch the *Explorer's* bow, whirling it back downstream. After several harrowing tries, the stretch was finally ascended.

By the time the expedition reached the mouth of Black Canyon, in March, even the dogged persistence of a man such as Lt. Ives had been sorely tried. As he was to comment: "The lines have become almost worn out by hard service; the skiff is badly battered, and scarcely able to float, and all the oars are broken." Nevertheless, the expedition pushed through the high, chopped portals of Black Canyon, and were

> eagerly gazing into the mysterious depths beyond, when the *Explorer,* with a stunning crash, brought up abruptly and instantaneously against a sunken rock. For a second the impression was that the canyon had fallen in. The concussion was so violent that the men near the bow were thrown overboard; the doctor, Mr. Mollhausen, and myself, having been seated in front of the upper deck, were precipitated head foremost into the bottom of the boat; the fireman, who was pitching a log into the fire, went half-way in with it; the boiler was thrown out of place; the steam pipe doubled up; the wheel-house torn away; and it was expected that the boat would fill and sink by all, but Mr. Carroll, who was looking for an explosion from the injured steam pipes. (From *The Grand Colorado,* T. H. Watkins and contributors. Palo Alto, Calif.: Ame. West Pub. Co., 1969.)

The *Explorer,* as it turned out, was not mortally damaged, and after repairs, returned to Fort Yuma under its own steam. Yet not for more than a century, until after the invention of the jet boat, would anyone attempt to ascend the canyons of the Colorado.

Lieutenant Ives, along with half of the expedition members, continued his reconnaissance overland. After climbing up onto and crossing the Colorado plateau, Ives was confronted by Grand Canyon:

> The extent and magnitude of the systems of cañons . . . is astounding. The plateau is cut into shreds by these gigantic chasms, and re-

A pontoon raft is buffeted in the rapids as a guided tour party runs the Colorado

sembles a vast ruin. Belts of country miles in width have been swept away, leaving only isolated mountains standing in the gap.

Struggling eastward out of the convoluted Grand Canyon country, the Ives expedition lingered at the Hopi Pueblos and finally finished their journey at Fort Defiance in May of 1858. Ives' report did not mince words:

Ours has been the first, and will doubtless be the last, party of whites to visit this profitless locality. It seems intended by nature that the Colorado River, along the greater portion of its lonely and majestic way, shall be forever unvisited and undisturbed.

Eleven years later the Colorado would, however, be visited by an extraordinary, one-armed naturalist who would mold his life's work around a study of the river and the "profitless locality" surrounding it. John Wesley Powell came to the Colorado without visions of what *should* be there: it would be his calm and patient passion to observe and record what actually was there. And although he had little time for adventure as such, it would be his destiny to carry out one of the greatest voyages in the annals of exploration.

Powell grew up in the Midwest. His father, a part-time farmer and Methodist circuit rider, had hopes that the youth would become a minister—but from an early age it became increasingly apparent that his interests were in the area of the natural sciences. Things seen and found in the woods elicited his curiosity and questions; for answers he went to books wherever he could find and borrow them. Most of his education was makeshift. Between bouts of teaching school and working the farm, he made numerous excursions—hiking across the state of Michigan, making river voyages down the Ohio, Illinois, and Des Moines, and floating the Mississippi all the way from St. Paul to New Orleans.

When the Civil War broke out, Powell, whose family were staunch abolitionists, was among the first to enlist in the Volunteer Army of the North. He returned from the war a major, missing an arm that had been shattered by a minie ball at Shiloh. He was now also married, having taken a brief leave to wed his cousin, Emma Dean. For a time he taught natural history at Illinois Wesleyan College, then at Illinois Normal University—but his intense, restless nature demanded something more. Powell was a persuasive man, and had soon talked various institutions into contributing to the establishment of a natural history museum at Bloomington. As curator, he then promoted funding for an expedition to collect specimens in the Rocky Mountains.

The three-month expedition, which included an ascent of Pikes Peak, was a success, and Powell might well have rested awhile on his laurels. But rather, it was as if in having sipped he grew more thirsty. The lure of the unknown soon tugged him West for another, far more extensive trip—up across the Front Range into Middle Park, a first ascent of Long's Peak, out of the high Rockies by way of Cedar Canyon and Rabbit Ears Pass, down the White River and out across rolling sagebrush country to Brown's Hole, then up to the town of Green River on the Union Pacific Railroad. True to his sponsors, the young naturalist diligently collected plants, animal skins, barometric readings—but he was also conditioning himself for the great project now shaping in his mind: the exploration of the Colorado River.

The nine men who joined Powell at the town of Green River in May of 1869, jump-off for a voyage into the unknown, were neither scientists

nor skilled in river running. Five of them had accompanied Powell's wide-
ranging journey of the year before. The major's brother, Walter, an expert
boatbuilder, and two drifters completed the party. They stood to personally
gain no more than the experience itself, although there was some hope that
gold might be panned en route.

Several people have written of Powell's voyage, a few of them quite
well—but no account is more exciting than the diary of Powell himself.

> May 24, 1896.—The good people of Green River City turn out
> to see us start. We raise our little flag, push the boats from shore, and
> the swift current carries us down.
>
> Our boats are four in number. Three are built of oak; stanch and
> firm; double-ribbed, with double stem and stern posts, and further
> strengthened by bulkheads, dividing each into three compartments.
> Two of these, the fore and aft, are decked, forming water-tight cabins.
> It is expected these will buoy the boats should the waves roll over them
> in rough water. The fourth boat is made of pine, very light, but 16 feet
> in length, with a sharp cutwater, and every way built for fast rowing,
> and divided into compartments as the others. The little vessels are 21
> feet long, and, taking out the cargoes, can be carried by four men.
>
> We take with us rations deemed sufficient to last ten months, for
> we expect, when winter comes on and the river is filled with ice, to
> lie over at some point until spring arrives; and so we take with us
> abundant supplies of clothing, likewise. We have also a large quantity
> of ammunition and two or three dozen traps. For the purpose of build-
> ing cabins, repairing boats, and meeting other exigencies, we are sup-
> plied with axes, hammers, saws, augers, and other tools, and a quan-
> tity of nails and screws. For scientific work, we have two sextants,
> four chronometers, a number of barometers, thermometers, compasses,
> and other instruments. (From *Canyons of the Colorado,* John Wesley
> Powell, Flood & Vincent, 1895.)

For some 60 miles below Green River City the river flowed through
eroded badlands. There were no rapids, but the current pushed along at a
good clip, which allowed the men to get a feel for their boats and the river
before entering the dangerous waters of the canyons. Then, slipping between the high rock walls which Powell named Flaming Gorge, the expedition got its first taste of whitewater, and found the fast ride exhilarating.
During the next six days, while passing through Flaming Gorge and Red
Canyon, the roar of tumbling water was often in their ears. Many of the
rapids required lining, an arduous task with the heavy, loaded boats.
Portaging one falls, Powell noted an inscription: "Ashley 1825"—although it was difficult to make out the third numeral.

The expedition arrived at Brown's Hole without major mishap. Gone
now were the vast Indian encampments that Ashley had spoken of; gone,

too, the last wild echoes of the fur rendezvous. It was, as it is today, an isolated, peaceful valley.

> June 6.—At daybreak I am awakened by a chorus of birds. It seems as if all the feathered songsters of the region have come to the old tree. Several species of warblers, woodpeckers, and flickers above, meadow larks in the grass, and wild geese in the river. I recline on my elbow and watch a lark nearby, and then awaken my bedfellow, to listen to my Jenny Lind. A real morning concert for me; none of your "matinees"!

In Brown's Hole the expedition dined well on fish and wild duck, relaxing a little. Powell's thoughts, however, were on the deep cleft before them. He had heard vague stories of Ashley's attempt to run the river; that somewhere in the canyon he was now preparing to run, a boat had been swamped and several men drowned.

The canyon they entered was deep and turbulent. Several times during the first day one boat or another would capsize in rapids, throwing the occupants out into the water. Waterproof compartments prevented the boats from sinking, and their crews clung to them as best they could until a quiet eddy would stop the headlong, helpless rush.

> June 9.—One of the party suggests that we call this the Canyon of Lodore, and the name is adopted. Very slowly we make our way, often climbing on the rocks at the edge of the water for a few hundred yards to examine the channel before running it. During the afternoon we come to a place where it is necessary to make a portage. The little boat is landed and the others are signaled to come up. . . . I walk along the bank to examine the ground, leaving one of my men with a flag to guide the other boats to the landing place. I soon see one of the boats make shore all right, and feel no more concern; but a minute after, I hear a shout, and, looking around, see one of the boats shooting down the center of the sag. It is the "No Name," with Captain Howland, his brother, and Goodman. I feel that its going over is inevitable, and run to save the third boat. A minute more, and she turns the point and heads for shore. Then I turn downstream again and scramble along to look for the boat that has gone over. The first fall is not great, only 10 or 12 feet, and we often run such; but below, the river tumbles down again for 40 or 50 feet, in a channel filled with dangerous rocks that break the waves into whirlpools and beat them into foam. I pass around a great crag just in time to see the boat strike a rock and, rebounding from the shock, careen and fill its open compartment with water. Two of the men lose their oars; she swings around and is carried down at a rapid rate, broadside on, for a few yards, when, striking amidships on another rock with great force, she is broken quite in two and the men are thrown into the river.

The Gate of Lodore as pictured in Major John Wesley Powell's official report, *Exploration of the Colorado River of the West and Its Tributaries* (Washington, D.C., 1875)

After some harrowing moments during which the three men were tumbled through a second rapids, all managed to scramble onto a rocky island, bruised but alive. Their situation was still hazardous, as the river raced by on both sides and below was a falls. With superb rowing and a dash of luck, one of the other boats was propelled to the island; the stranded men were picked up and the boat was rowed back to shore without further mishap.

Powell, anticipating just such a disaster, had distributed provisions, clothing, and scientific gear among all four boats. Yet there was one exception: all the expedition's barometers were in the *No Name*, whose wreckage was scattered for half a mile down the river. The largest section of the boat, where the instruments were thought to be, was lodged against a rock,

Wreck of the *No Name* at Disaster Falls. Illustration from Major J. W. Powell's narrative of his journey down the Colorado

unreachable in midtorrent. Powell brooded through the night, debating whether or not to strike out overland for Salt Lake City to order new barometers from the East.

In the morning, the wreck had been carried farther downstream, and two men volunteered to attempt to reach it in another boat. Their return was greeted with cheers, for they had not only salvaged the barometers but a keg of whiskey that had been smuggled aboard without the major's knowledge. Powell affably allowed them to keep it for medicinal purposes, to combat the chill water.

The 20-mile run through Canyon of Lodore continued to be eventful. Rampaging current tore the *Maid of the Canyon* loose from the men who were lining her down a rapids. Miraculously, the boat ended up drifting undamaged in an eddy. A sudden gust of wind sent campfire sparks whirling into dry willow and cedar, which ignited so rapidly that several men had their clothing burned and hair singed before they could shove the boats into the river. Once on the water, they were unable to pull upstream against the current, and were swept through an unscouted rapids.

On June 17 the expedition reached Echo Park, where the Yampa River flows in from the east, and the smooth red bulk of Steamboat Rock rises from the water. During his voyage of exploration, Powell was constantly climbing, scrambling up cliffs to calculate elevations and observe the lay of the land. His agility was greater than that of most men with two arms. Powell, accompanied by a crewman, Bradley, laboriously worked his way up precipitous Steamboat Rock to take barometric readings. Close to the summit, Powell found himself in a perilous situation.

> Here, by making a spring, I gain a foothold in a little crevice, and grasp an angle of the rock overhead. I find I can get up no farther and cannot step back, for I dare not let go with my hand and cannot reach foothold below without. I call to Bradley for help. He finds a way by which he can get to the top of the rock over my head, but cannot reach me. Then he looks around for some stick or limb of a tree, but finds none. Then he suggests that he would better help me with a barometer case, but I fear I cannot hold on to it. The moment is critical. Standing on my toes, my muscles begin to tremble. It is sixty or eighty feet to the foot of the precipice. If I lose my hold I shall fall to the bottom and then perhaps roll over the bench and tumble still farther down the cliff. At this instant it occurs to Bradley to take off his drawers, which he does, and swings them down to me. I hug close to the rock, let go with my hand, seize the dangling legs, and with his assistance am enabled to gain the top.
>
> Then we walk out on the peninsular rock, make the necessary observations for determining its altitude above camp, and return, finding an easy way down.

And thus it was: the beauty and solitude of unnamed canyons, endless bone-wrenching work of lining and portages, Powell's unfaltering curiosity and painstaking measurements.

The expedition pressed on—into Whirlpool Canyon, the narrowest gorge yet encountered, where an inane, swirling current swung the boats from one side of the river to the other; through aptly christened Split Mountain Canyon; and then suddenly the cliffs dropped away, the river glided gently around islands and past meadows where herds of antelope grazed. They beached at the mouth of the Uinta River, and hiked upstream to the Uinta Indian Agency, last contact with the outside world from the river. Beyond this point, where Ashley had terminated his adventure, they would be on waters no man had ever voyaged.

Once more on the river, they floated the long, lonely aisles of stone which, lacking the whitewater drama of Lodore, the prodigious scale of Grand Canyon, and the accessibility of either one, are even today rarely visited, although beautiful in their own rights. Ninety-seven miles through the Canyon of Desolation; 36 through Grey Canyon. Southward, passing through the folds of Labyrinth and Stillwater canyons, the rocks were becoming ever more wildly colorful, split and carved into every imaginable shape and form. *"Toom'pin wunear' Tuweap"* the Indians called it—Land of the Standing Rock.

By the time the expedition reached the junction with the main Colorado on July 18, provisions were dangerously low, a fact which failed to quench Powell's enthusiasm for the hallucinogenic landscape, which he viewed from the vantage of a high rock.

And what a world of grandeur is spread before us! Below is the canyon through which the Colorado runs. We can trace its course for miles, and at points catch glimpses of the river. From the northwest comes the Green in a narrow winding gorge. From the northeast comes the Grand, through a canyon that seems bottomless from where we stand. Away to the west are lines of cliffs and ledges of rock—not such ledges as the reader may have seen where the quarryman splits his blocks, but ledges from which the gods might quarry mountains that, rolled out on the plain below, would stand a lofty range; and not such cliffs as the reader may have seen where the swallow builds its nest, but cliffs where the soaring eagle is lost to view ere he reaches the summit. Between us and the distant cliffs are the strangely carved and pinnacled rocks of the Toom'pin wunear' Tuweap'. . . . Wherever we look there is but a wilderness of rocks,—deep gorges where the rivers are lost below cliffs and towers and pinnacles, and ten thousand strangely carved forms in every direction, and beyond them mountains blending with the clouds.

Now we return to camp. While eating supper we very naturally speak of better fare, as musty bread and spoiled bacon are not palatable. Soon I see Hawkins down by the boat, taking up the sextant—rather a strange proceeding for him—and I question him concerning it. He replies that he is trying to find the latitude and longitude of the nearest pie.

Both the Green and the Colorado are smooth-flowing and quiet for a good many miles above their confluence; below it, the combined waters pound through rapids that Powell considered the worst he had yet attempted. The major named this Cataract Canyon. But by now he was more skilled in reading whitewater, his crews in navigating it, than had been the case when the *No Name* had shattered in distant Lodore. The boats all emerged intact on the quiet waters of Glen Canyon below, although broken oars had to be replaced with new ones sawed from driftlogs, battered hulls pitched with pine resin. Some of the more eventful moments in Cataract Canyon took place off of the river. Major Powell, caught in a violent storm while climbing, observed a flash flood gathering up a side canyon and barely managed to outrun the roiling mass of red mud and water. The camp was moved to higher ground just before the torrent swept over the site and passed into the Colorado. No less dramatic to men who had been living on bread, beans, and dried apples, was the killing of two bighorn sheep, and the feast that followed.

For a week the expedition drifted through Glen Canyon, which was unlike any other place they had seen on the Colorado, or would see farther on. Here the river was peaceful, and the brilliant rock formations somehow seemed closer, more intimate. Each bend of the river brought some new revelation: walls of orange, vermilion, purple, and chocolate; arches and monuments; oak-set glens and fern-hung alcoves. Finally they reached the mouth of the Paria River, which was soon to be known as Lees Ferry. This marked the end of Glen Canyon.

> August 5.—With some feeling of anxiety we enter a new canyon this morning. We have learned to observe closely the texture of the rock. In softer strata we have a quiet river, in harder we find rapids and falls. Below us are the limestones and hard sandstones which we found in Cataract Canyon. This bodes toil and danger.

Major Powell called the new gorge Marble Canyon. It quickly deepened and there were many rapids. Powell and his brother climbed the canyon walls to view an eclipse of the sun, but clouds covered the sky. During a storm, they lost their way in the dusk and were forced to spend a wet and miserable night on a high ledge. The next day the expedition reached Red Wall Cavern, an overhang carved by the river on the outside of a bend. Powell speculated that if used as a theater, the vast interior should hold fifty thousand people. "Objection," he wryly added, "might be raised . . . for at high water the floor is covered with a raging flood."

> August 9.—The river turns sharply to the east and seems inclosed by a wall set with a million brilliant gems. What can it mean? Every eye is engaged, every one wonders. On coming nearer we find fountains bursting from the rock high overhead, and the spray in the sunshine forms the gems which bedeck the wall. The rocks below the fountain are covered with mosses and ferns and many beautiful flowering plants. We name it Vasey's Paradise, in honor of the botanist who traveled with us last year.

The next day the party reached the mouth of the Little Colorado, which enters from a gorge almost as impressive as that of the main river. This is rattlesnake country. While out hiking, Powell killed two; another

An American River Touring Association party visits Vasey's Paradise in the Grand Canyon

was killed at camp. At the junction of the Little Colorado, Marble Canyon becomes Grand Canyon.

August 13.—We are now ready to start on our way down the Great Unknown. Our boats, tied to a common stake, chafe each other as they are tossed by the fretful river. They ride high and buoyant, for their loads are lighter than we could desire. We have but a month's rations remaining. The flour has been resifted through the mosquito-net sieve; the spoiled bacon has been dried and the worst of it boiled; the few pounds of dried apples have been spread in the sun and re-shrunken to their normal bulk. The sugar has all melted and gone on its way down the river. But we have a large sack of coffee. The lightening of the boats has this advantage: they will ride the waves better and we shall have but little to carry when we make a portage.

We are three-quarters of a mile in the depths of the earth, and the great river shrinks into insignificance as it dashes its angry waves against the walls and cliffs that rise to the world above; the waves are but puny ripples, and we but pigmies, running up and down the sands or lost among the boulders.

We have an unknown distance yet to run, an unknown river to explore. What falls there are, we know not; what rocks beset the channel, we know not; what walls rise over the river, we know not. Ah, well! we may conjecture many things. The men talk as cheerfully as ever; jests are bandied about freely this morning; but to me the cheer is somber and the jests are ghastly.

The expedition proceeded cautiously down the canyon, which by the second day was cut into a layer of hard granite. This meant, as Powell well knew, that there would likely be rapids. There were.

Hearing a "great roar ahead," Powell found himself above a "descent of perhaps 75 or 80 feet in a third of a mile," where "the rushing waters break into great waves on the rocks, and lash themselves into a mad, white foam." Cliffs dropped sharply into the water on either side—there could be no portaging or lining. The boats were tossed like chips on high backwaves, spun by whirlpools—but all made it through, cockpits filled with water.

In the following days they would hurtle through scores of rapids, many of them easy—others raging giants like Grapevine, Horn Creek, Hermit, Dubendorff, and Lava Falls. In places, cliffs looming directly out of the water prevented lining or even adequate scouting, and the rapids had to be run blind.

"Running a Rapid."
Illustration from Major
J. W. Powell's
*Exploration of the
Colorado River* . . .

And now we go on through this solemn, mysterious way. The river is very deep, the canyon very narrow, and still obstructed, so that there is no steady flow of the stream; but the waters reel and roll and boil, and we are scarcely able to determine where we can go. Now the boat is carried to the right, perhaps close to the wall; again, she is shot into the stream, and perhaps is dragged over to the other side, where, caught in a whirlpool, she spins about. We can neither land nor run as we please. The boats are entirely unmanageable; no order in their running can be preserved; now one, now another, is ahead, each crew laboring for its own preservation.

There were quieter times also: long stretches where the current still pushed strongly but was smooth, and a man could look upward and marvel at the gigantic terraces of stone reaching skyward above him. Places like Bright Angel Creek, where a clear, cold stream tumbled over rocks and there were ancient Indian ruins. Places where there were cascades and shallow, fern-draped caves. Powell was still entranced by the natural phenomena around him. On August 25, after examining a volcanic layer, he wrote:

What a conflict of water and fire there must have been here! Just imagine a river of molten rock running down into a river of melted snow. What a seething and boiling of the waters; what clouds of steam rolled into the heavens!

And then added: "Thirty-five miles today. Hurrah!"

Beautiful as the canyon was, it began to seem endless. Provisions were down to flour and coffee. On the evening of August 27, O. G. Howland attempted to persuade Powell to abandon the river, and to try to reach one of the Mormon settlements by climbing out of the canyon and traveling overland. The major refused, feeling the overland course was potentially as dangerous as sticking with the river, and perhaps more importantly, he calculated their position to be within 50 miles in a straight line from the mouth of the Virgin River. Even though this might mean 90 more miles on the winding Colorado, he would not give up so close to his goal. Howland, his brother, and another crew member decided to leave the river. Powell awakened the remainder of the party, and they agreed to remain with him.

The next morning Howland and his two companions watched the boats swing downriver from an overhanging ledge. The parting had been emotional; both courses of action were desperate gambles. Powell's remaining crew ran several rapids that day, one of which trapped a boat in a whirlpool and capsized the major's vessel. No one was drowned, the boats still floated: they continued on.

August 29.—We start very early this morning. The river still continues swift, but we have no serious difficulty, and at twelve o'clock emerge from the Grand Canyon of the Colorado. We are in a valley now, and low mountains are seen in the distance, coming to the river below. We recognize this as the Grand Wash. . . .

Now the danger is over, now the toil has ceased, now the gloom has disappeared, now the firmament is bounded only by the horizon, and what a vast expanse of constellations can be seen!

The following afternoon they reached the mouth of the Virgin River, where they were greeted by three Mormon colonists. A messenger from Salt Lake City had asked the colonists to be on the lookout for floating wreckage or other relics of the expedition, which had long since been given up for lost.

Powell had no reason to proceed farther: Lt. Ives had explored the Colorado up to the Virgin River. Provided with fresh provisions, the four remaining crew members continued down the river to Fort Yuma, two of them even going all the way to tidewater. The major and his brother traveled toward Salt Lake City, anxiously inquiring at each Mormon settlement for news of the three men who had left the expedition at what is now known as Separation Rapids. Church authorities sent riders to outlying ranches and Paiute camps, but by the time Powell reached St. George there was still no word. Finally, two days up the Mormon trail that skirts the eastern edge of the Great Basin, they learned that Howland and his companions lay next to a waterhole in the forested plateau above the canyon, their bodies stripped and filled with Shivwits Indian arrows.

Powell had spent a hundred days in the wilderness of the Colorado River country. Over the next eight years he would return to it many times accompanied by trained scientists, mapping, determining the geologic structure and history, gathering material on the Indians. His work along the River of the Shining Mountains was just beginning. Man's last great voyage of exploration was over.

Two years before Major Powell made the first documented run of the Colorado canyons, a cottonwood raft was pulled out of the river at Callville, Nevada. The half-starved, sunburned, and delirious man who sprawled upon it identified himself as James White. When he had recovered sufficiently, he had a remarkable story to tell. He and two companions, Capt. Charles Baker and George Strole, were prospecting in the vicinity of the lower San Juan River when a band of Ute Indians attacked them. Baker was killed, and the other two men ghosted their way down to the Colorado River under cover of darkness, where they hastily built a raft.

For four days the river was smooth, but then they began crashing through rapids that repeatedly overturned the raft. Strole was swept off and drowned. White lashed himself to the raft and drifted on, over falls he was later to describe in a letter as "10 to 15 feet hie." For a week his only nourishment came from gnawing on his rawhide knife sheath. Finally he was able to obtain some mesquite bread and the hindquarters of a dog from Indians.

White's tale sparked a controversy that is argued to this day. It would appear he had entered the Colorado in Glen Canyon and floated the entire length of Grand Canyon. Most men who voyaged the canyon over the next few decades viewed the feat as impossible, and noted that the prospector's geographical observations were vague. Robert Stanton, who had surveyed the canyon for Frank Brown's ill-fated railroad venture, concluded that White's anguished voyage had started below Grand Canyon, at Grand Wash Cliffs.

Yet until his death White steadfastly maintained that he had entered the river in the San Juan country. Not until the advent of neoprene rafts in the canyon did rivermen begin to realize that a raft, wide, and of shallow draft, conceivably might have spun its way through rapids which demolished more conventional boats.

No one will ever know for sure.

White had found himself on the Colorado by accident; Powell and others of his generation voyaged the canyons in the interests of natural science and surveying. By the turn of the century, Grand Canyon's fame as a scenic spectacular had begun to spread. Stagecoaches brought tourists up from Flagstaff and many an adventurous lady whose derriere was more accustomed to porch swings than a saddle found herself astride a mule, being guided down into the canyon by affable "Captain" John Hance. The first purely recreational run of the canyon was made by Julius Stone, an Ohio manufacturer, in 1909. His guide was Nathaniel Galloway, who had previously floated parts of the canyon while trapping beaver. Whereas Powell's crews had rowed bow first through rapids, Galloway pointed his stern into the fast water: a technique that allowed a better view of where he was going, as well as more control by rowing against the current. Most river runners up to the present day have followed his ingenious example.

Galloway and Stone made the run from Green River City, Wyoming, to Needles, California, without a single upset. Most early-day float parties were not so fortunate. Ellsworth and Emery Kolb set out to film a voyage of the river in 1911. Their boats capsized several times and much valuable film and equipment were lost. Nevertheless, the trip was a resounding success. They scrambled ashore at Needles with the makings of a movie and numerous fine still photographs.

Clyde Eddy, a member of the Explorers Club of New York, headed up a 1927 Colorado River expedition whose members included several college youths, a tramp they had met at Green River City, a dog, and a bear cub. They were not experienced river runners and generally had a woeful time of it. The tramp and three others called it a day at Lees Ferry, but the remaining adventurers, including the dog and bear, struggled on to Needles.

Mr. and Mrs. Glen Hyde tried the river in 1928, using a scow with end sweeps. It was their honeymoon. Less than a month after leaving Green River, Utah, they arrived at Bright Angel Creek and hiked up to the south rim to ask Emery Kolb about the rapids ahead. Kolb tried to give them life preservers, but Mr. Hyde refused them as unnecessary. Mrs. Hyde may not have shared her husband's optimism, for shortly before leaving she glanced down at her muddy boots and softly mused: "I wonder if I shall ever wear pretty shoes again."

That was the last anyone saw of them. Their partially swamped boat was later found downriver.

There is a counterpoint to the dangers, hardships, and tragedies of the river. Haldane ("Buzz") Holmstrom made the first solo run through the Colorado canyons in 1937. A service station attendant from Coquille, Oregon, he built his 15-foot boat from scratch, sawing the boards out of a Port Orford cedar tree. Seven weeks out of Green River, Wyoming, approaching the end of his voyage, he wrote:

> I find I have already had my reward, in the doing of the thing. The stars, the cliffs, and canyons, the roar of the rapids, the moon, the uncertainty and worry, the relief when through each one . . . the campfires at night . . . the real respect and friendship of rivermen I met. . . .
>
> This may be my last camp where the roar of the rapids echoed from the cliffs around and I can look at the stars and moon only through a narrow slit in the earth.
>
> The river and the canyons have been kind to me. . . .

Today some of the canyons that Powell passed through have been buried under gigantic reservoirs. Flaming Gorge, Red Canyon, and Glen Canyon are gone. Much of Grand Canyon and the Canyon of Lodore would also be driftwood-littered sheets of slackwater had not vigorous public opinion forced the dam-builders to back down.

2. The Canyon of Lodore

Some of the most scenic whitewater canyons in the United States have been carved through the Uinta Mountains where the upper corners of Colorado and Utah join. In Dinosaur National Monument, the Green River cuts down through the Canyon of Lodore, the Yampa through Bear Canyon, to unite at Echo Park. The combined flow then rushes through Whirlpool Canyon and Split Mountain Canyon.

A superb 90-mile trip begins at Dutch John, Utah, below Flaming Gorge Dam, with a take-out point near Dinosaur National Monument Headquarters. This is a bigwater trip, with tough and frequent rapids. Although Leslie Jones of Herber, Utah, in 1957 ran solo from the Gates of Lodore to Jensen in a single day with a decked aluminum canoe, virtually all voyages are made with rafts or kayaks. To put Jones' voyage into perspective, it is to be noted that he has also canoed Grand Canyon and the Frazier of British Columbia; probably he is the only man to have done so. A boating permit must be obtained at the National Monument Headquarters near Jensen. Life preservers are required. To reach Dutch John, one can drive north on Highway 44 from Vernal, Utah; or south on Highway 530 from Green River, Wyoming.

The trip begins on lively, clear water that winds through the lower end of Red Canyon. There are a few sportive riffles, but no real rapids until the Gates of Lodore are passed. This is a fine trout river. Seven miles downriver, George Creek tumbles in from the right, marking the start of Little Hole, a small valley where the bandit Butch Cassidy had a cabin in the 1890s. This stretch of the Green River was highly regarded by outlaws of the period as a remote, relatively inaccessible place to lay over until the enthusiasms of posses and Pinkerton agents might cool. Red Creek, not far below, was the home of Jesse Ewing, who became known as the ugliest man in South Pass after a grizzly clawed his face. He was killed by a young gunslinger named Duncan who then eloped with his wife. There is a minor rapids at Red Creek.

At Brown's Hole, 13 miles below the put-in point, the current slackens. Butch Cassidy's Wild Bunch were not the only badhats to frequent this area. One passes the Jarvie Ranch on the left bank of the river. Jarvie, an early settler and storekeeper, was robbed and murdered in 1909. His corpse was sent downriver in a skiff, and found a year later in the Canyon of Lodore by two men drilling test cores at a dam site. Toliver Creek, which washes in from the right, was named for Joe Toliver, who expressed his displeasure at being pinned in a wrestling match by knifing his opponent to death. After various other brawls of one kind or another, the former marshal killed himself while playing Russian roulette in a Vernal barbership. Flynn Bottom is named for Mike Flynn, a rustler who was gunned down by a hired professional.

About a third of the way through Brown's Hole, the river swings against a spur of the Uinta Mountains and enters Swallow Canyon. Today, as in Powell's time, the walls of the short canyon are plastered with thousands of swallows' nests. The bulk of Brown's Hole lies within Colorado

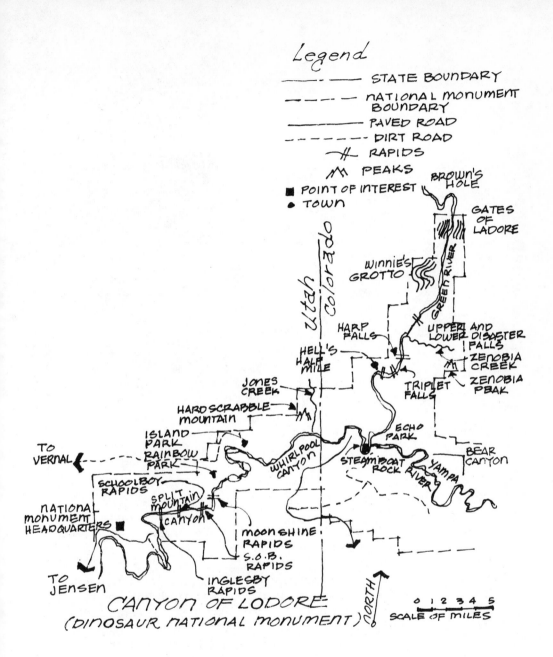

Legend

—————— STATE BOUNDARY

— — — — NATIONAL MONUMENT BOUNDARY

—————— PAVED ROAD

- - - - - DIRT ROAD

⊬ RAPIDS

ᨓ PEAKS

■ POINT OF INTEREST

● TOWN

BROWN'S HOLE

GATES OF LADORE

WINNIE'S GROTTO

GREEN RIVER

Utah / Colorado

HARP FALLS

UPPER AND LOWER DISASTER FALLS

HELL'S HALF MILE

ZENOBIA CREEK

ZENOBIA PEAK

JONES CREEK

TRIPLET FALLS

HARD SCRABBLE MOUNTAIN

ECHO PARK

ISLAND PARK

RAINBOW PARK

WHIRLPOOL CANYON

STEAMBOAT ROCK

YAMPA RIVER

BEAR CANYON

TO VERNAL

SCHOOLBOY RAPIDS

SPLIT MOUNTAIN CANYON

NATIONAL MONUMENT HEADQUARTERS

MOONSHINE RAPIDS

S.O.B. RAPIDS

TO JENSEN

INGLESBY RAPIDS

NORTH

0 1 2 3 4 5
SCALE OF MILES

CANYON OF LODORE
(DINOSAUR NATIONAL MONUMENT)

Boaters camped at Brown's Hole

and is a wildlife refuge. Canada geese nest here, as do a variety of ducks, including mallard, redhead, gadwall, and cinnamon teal. Great blue heron, snowy egret, coot, grebe, and killdeer wade shallow waters, while hawks, falcons, bald and golden eagles soar overhead. Deer live in Brown's Hole throughout the year and are joined by elk in the winter.

There is nothing left of Fort Davy Crockett, a fur post that was visited by Kit Carson, Jim Bridger, and other mountain men in the late 1830s. Close to the Gates of Lodore Canyon is a Ranger Station with a nearby boat ramp. Fishermen and inexperienced boaters not wishing to tangle with the whitewater ahead can take-out here, or one can put-in at this point, shortening the voyage to Park headquarters by some 47 miles.

The entrance to Lodore is awesome, abrupt. One minute you are gently drifting through the flatlands of Brown's Hole, and 10 minutes later are deep in a chasm of the mountains, where high, pinched cliffs allow only a few hours of direct sunlight a day, and the rumble of plunging water is ceaseless. Three miles into the canyon one passes, on the right, Winnie's

Grotto, a tall, narrow, side canyon, which, were it not open to the sky, would more resemble a gigantic keyhole than a gorge. Here Powell found the abandoned boat of a group of trappers who had attempted Lodore in the 1840s. The canyon had so unnerved them that they scaled its cliffs to get out, digging steps with their rifle barrels. Three miles beyond Winnie's Grotto are Upper Disaster Falls and Lower Disaster Falls, where Powell's expedition lost the *No Name*. Here the river drops 35 feet in 0.6 of a mile—one of the most challenging rapids in the entire Colorado River system.

Below the falls Zenobia Creek comes in from the left. "Queen Ann" Bassett, an early-day Brown's Hole resident who was prone to slapping her brand on any steer that was handy, reputedly once drove a herd of cattle over a cliff near the junction of the creek and the river in order to destroy evidence before a posse, hard on her trail, could catch up.

Big rapids now follow each other in close succession. Harp Falls is sheer delight—a series of haystacks, giant white-topped waves. In most

Taking a small raft over Disaster Falls, where Powell's expedition lost the *No Name*

water levels it should present no problems. Triplet Falls, little more than a mile further on, is rocky and dangerous. It should be scouted carefully. Only half a mile beyond, where the river veers to the west, is Hell's Half Mile. This is a long boulder garden that is a great deal easier to run if boats are lined through the first drop. Except for minor rapids, it is clear sailing from the end of Hell's Half Mile to Echo Park. The river drops an average of 15 feet to the mile in the 18 miles of the Canyon of Lodore.

The Yampa River joins the Green at Echo Park, where the smooth, 1000-foot cliffs of Steamboat Rock loom above the mingling waters. It was in attempting to scale this monolith that Major Powell almost fell to this death. Echo Park is well named: from the right places a shout may be repeated ten times or more. There are petroglyphs in the area, drawn by Indians of the Fremont Culture between A.D. 400 and 800. They were a cave-dwelling people who hunted bison and other animals of the region.

The river hairpins around Steamboat Rock and then enters Whirlpool Canyon, which is narrow and deep. About midway down the canyon, Jones Creek washes in at the foot of Hardscrabble Mountain. Although it has been heavily fished in the last few years, there are trout in the stream. A 2-mile hike beside the creek, where willow, poplar, dogwood, birch, and mountain maple shade the water, brings one to more Indian petroglyphs. The river drops about 10.5 feet per mile through the 10 miles of Whirlpool Canyon. There are some eleven rapids, all of them minor.

Between Whirlpool Canyon and the entrance to Split Mountain Canyon, the river idles across the flats of Island Park and then Rainbow Park. This is a good place to troll for catfish. In Powell's time the Green yielded Colorado River white salmon ranging up to 6 feet long and weighing as much as 80 pounds—but they are scarce and smaller today. Entering Split Mountain Canyon the pace of the river quickens: for the next 7 miles it drops an average of 25 feet to the mile. There are four rapids—Moonshine, S.O.B., Schoolboy, and Inglesby—which are lively but do not present the challenge of some of the whitewater in the Canyon of Lodore, such as Disaster or Triplet falls. A road from the take-out point at the mouth of Split Mountain Canyon leads to Dinosaur National Monument Headquarters and Jensen, Utah.

Guide Notes for the CANYON OF LODORE

LOCATION—In Dinosaur National Monument in northwestern Colorado and northeastern Utah.

LENGTH OF TRIP—90 miles from Dutch John, Utah, to Dinosaur National Monument Headquarters. 4- to 5-day trip.

FAVORABLE SEASON—June through August.

DEGREE OF DIFFICULTY—Disaster Falls, Triplet Falls, and Hell's Half Mile are for experts. If these are lined or portaged, boaters of intermediate skills should be able to make the run in most water levels.

RECOMMENDED CRAFT—Raft or kayak.

ACCESS POINTS—Flaming Gorge Dam, by the village of Dutch John, Utah, is a good put-in point. Dutch John is 43 miles north of Vernal, Utah, on State Highways 44 and 260. The take-out point is at Dinosaur National Monument Headquarters, 5 miles northeast of Jensen. It is necessary to obtain a boating permit from the rangers at National Monument Headquarters before beginning a voyage. It is also possible to shorten the trip by putting-in at Gates of Lodore, but in doing so one will miss some beautiful country and save little time, as this alternative involves lots of back-road driving or a car shuttle.

CAMPING—There are a number of good campsites in the canyon—Gates of Lodore and Echo Park are among the favorites.

FISHING—Fair, for catfish and some whitefish.

3. Mountain Tributaries of the Colorado

Outside of Alaska and Hawaii, only three states have mountains over 14,000 feet high: Washington, California, and Colorado. Washington has one, Mt. Rainier; California less than a dozen, and Colorado well over fifty. From the slopes of these fifty-some peaks and the ridges that connect them, hundreds of chill streams feed the upper Colorado and its tributaries. The tributary rivers—the Williams, Blue, Eagle, Roaring Fork, Frying Pan, Gunnison, Uncompahgre and Dolores—tumble down narrow canyons where cascades alternate with deep, green trout pools.

Some improbable characters visited the upper Colorado during the middle of the last century. Sir George Gore, an Irish baronet, for whom Gore Canyon of the Colorado is named, passed beside the river in 1855. The nobleman's obsession was hunting, and during a jaunt that ranged over three states his party slaughtered 3000 buffalo, 40 grizzly bear, and numerous deer and antelope. One of the party is reputed to have found gold. Gore's response was one of outrage. "This is gold, but I did not come here to seek gold! I don't need it. This is a pleasure hunt!" Gore swore the men to secrecy and hastily broke camp, fearing his forty hired hands would desert en masse if they learned of it.

Samuel Adams arrived at the mining camp of Breckenridge on the Blue River in 1869 with a vision somewhat more elevated than laying waste to the fauna of the region. As he had enthusiastically written to the 42nd Congress: "The Colorado must be, emphatically, to the Pacific Coast what the Mississippi is to the Atlantic." Adams' momentous announcement came after he had voyaged up the Colorado from Fort Yuma to Black Canyon on a steamboat commanded by Capt. Thomas Trueworthy.

Unlike many a Colorado river visionary, Adams was willing to back up his contention with a voyage of exploration. With Adams at the helm, eleven men left Breckenridge in four rowboats: destination, the Gulf of California. After descending 4000 feet in ten days, the party was missing five men and two boats. After a layover, Adams and five companions continued, more cautiously, lining boats down most of the rapids. Notwithstanding that the men's boots were worn through with the constant scrambling over rocks, by August 8 the last boat was in splinters and nearly all of the supplies in the river.

Adams, an optimist of rare persuasiveness, talked two of the men into constructing a raft, and the three of them once again maneuvered out into the raging waters of the canyon. When that raft broke up, they built another one. After the wreck of the third raft, all they managed to salvage was a frying pan and a soggy chunk of bacon. When the fourth raft struck a rock, it was all over.

As Adams wrote to Congress: "Worn out by excessive fatigue and constant exposure in the cold water, I confess that it was with no ordinary feelings that I was compelled to yield to the force of circumstances."

The major roads and railroads of western Colorado slip through the canyons carved out by the river and its tributaries. In places this has changed the character of the flow, as between Glenwood Springs and Rifle where fill from recent highway construction has constricted the channel, creating rapids where formerly the water was smooth. There are a number of interesting runs in the upper Colorado drainage which, because of proximity to roads, do not fall within the scope of this book. Four wilderness runs, however, are worth noting.

Black Canyon of the Gunnison is one of the more spectacular gorges in America. In the canyon's deepest part, the depth ranges from 1730 to 2425 feet, while the width narrows to 1300 feet at the rim and as little as 40 feet at the bottom. Lichen grows in places of perpetual shade. Beaver, muskrat, and mink live along the river, and large trout that have thrown many a hook feed in deep pools. Three-and-a-half-pound rainbows have been taken from Black Canyon.

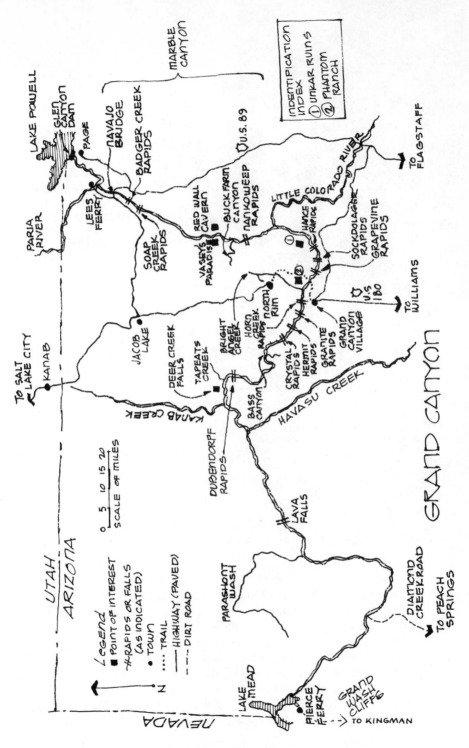

GRAND CANYON

The Gunnison River run is definitely for the experienced (*Cradoc Bradshaw Photo*)

The best run is an 18-mile trip from Cimarron to the East Portal of Black Canyon of the Gunnison National Monument. At East Portal a 6-mile diversion tunnel bleeds off much of the river's flow to irrigate crops around Montrose. The entire voyage is definitely for experienced river runners, but only one rapids, Crystal Creek Falls, is a heavyweight. Unless deaf, one has ample warning before reaching it—the thunderous roar is amplified by towering cliffs. In certain water levels, this drop can be as tough to run as any in America, including Lava Falls of Grand Canyon, Big Drop of Cataract Canyon, Rainie Falls of the Rogue, or Disaster Falls of Lodore. Appraise it as carefully as you would a route up Everest.

Because of the glorious abruptness of the gorge, one should be cautious of where camp is set up. Rockslides can happen at any time, especially after heavy rainfall. A storm upriver may bring sudden rises in water level. In 1955 a catskinner working beside Cimarron Creek unexpectedly found himself standing upon the seat, knee deep in swirling water, his machine inundated except for the breather stack. When such a flood hits the narrow slot of the main gorge, it is nice to have your tent pitched well above normal water line.

In the author's opinion, this is one of the finest short wilderness whitewater runs to be found anywhere.

A few miles below Grand Junction, the Colorado begins cutting down into Westwater Canyon, a scenic gorge whose rapids are as challenging as they are unheralded. This run is for experts. A few years back, four deer hunters attempted to float through with their dressed game aboard a rubber raft. It flipped in a rapids, and only one of them made it out of the canyon alive. Another party was spun in a whirlpool for days before being rescued by helicopter.

The challenging rapids of scenic Westwater Canyon (*Bob Krips Photo*)

Westwater Ranch is the customary put-in point. Boaters should write the owners of the ranch for permission to pass through their property. One quickly enters a canyon with high sandstone walls. The first rapids of consequence are several miles downstream. Just past the mouth of the Little Dolores River there are four steep chutes in succession. The gorge deepens. One of the trickiest whitewater sections is called Skull or Whirlpool Rapids. It features an immense whirlpool in most water levels. One float party discovered a human skull beside the rapids and laid it upon a knob of rock. It remained there for some time until someone either buried it or took it home to put on the mantel.

The voyage from Westwater Ranch to the first ranch below the canyon is about 26 miles—a beautiful trip.

The Dolores River brawls its way out of the San Juan Mountains of southwestern Colorado and then swings north to cut through a series of spectacular canyons, joining the Colorado River in Westwater Canyon. A 46-mile run, from Slickrock near Highway 80 to Bedrock on Highway 90, is one of the most scenic floats in the state. There are no rapids of any consequence, although in places a lively current demands the skills of canoeists with at least moderate experience. This is a fine run for novice rafters.

The Dolores does not have a large flow, and trips down the river are usually made during the peak of spring run-off, before June 1. Memorial Day weekend has long been popular with aficionados of Dolores River floats. A 3- to 4-day trip allows ample time for prowling interesting canyons. Below Slickrock, the river pushes through a short canyon, then meanders across Big Gypsum Valley. As there is a dirt road into the valley, it is possible to put in here and thus shorten the trip. On the north side of the valley the river twists through Slickrock Canyon, a wilderness defile whose walls average about 1000 feet in height. Bull Creek Canyon, a mile and a half from Big Gypsum Valley, is a pasture of wildflowers in the spring. It is good hiking country. There is a spring about a mile up Bull Creek. The Dolores runs through cattle country, and therefore river water is suspect. Bring your own drinking water, or carry Halazone tablets. Below Bull Creek the river begins to writhe its way through colorful rock formations. A hike up the "Gooseneck" known as the Cloverleaf is well worth the perspiration. From there, much of the astounding contortions of the canyon can be observed. Muleshoe Bend, near the end of the run, offers a similar vista over psychotic geography.

Upstream from Slickrock the canyon is rocky and drops 50 feet per mile in certain stretches. This section, which horseshoes around Dolores River Overlook, has been run by experts when water levels are favorable.

Like the Dolores, the Animas rises in the mountains of southwestern Colorado, but instead of flowing north into the upper Colorado River it has cut its way south to join the San Juan, which enters the Colorado River at what is now Lake Powell, and was Glen Canyon. The country that gives birth to these rivers certainly ranks high among the most beautiful regions in America. Its 14,000-foot peaks abruptly give way to dry piñon coun- try—wind-tortured rock rising in weird and awesome shapes, with deep arroyos sculpted over countless centuries. Early Spanish explorers, who were less interested in scenery than in gold, silver and pagan souls, attempted to march up the river that rushed, cold and clear, out of the mountains. They were thwarted by a sheer-sided canyon and raging water. Turning back, they called it the *Rio del Animas Perdidas,* River of Lost Souls.

The Spaniards had been spoiled. In Mexico and in Peru, the Indians had mined and fashioned precious metals into objects that could be simply picked up, like apples under a tree. They were not prospectors.

Much later, real prospectors—Spanish, Irish, Indian, who knows what—climbed the high peaks and found silver near the summits, close to the sky. Mining camps—Eureka, Animas Forks, Cunningham Gulch, Silverton—sprang up at the headwaters of the Rio del Animas Perdidas, now usually called the Animas. Somehow, bed for a narrow-gauge railroad was blasted out of the cliffs of the canyon.

The steam trains still run between Durango and Silverton, carrying tourists, mountain climbers, and boats, for those who wish to tackle the gorge. This is live, whipping water—with an average drop of 80 feet per mile. The Animas rips right along. From Silverton to Elk Park is a fast stretch, Class III on a scale of six. Between Elk Park and Needleton (a ghost town), the river picks up speed. Two and one half miles below Elk Park is a boatbreaker rapids, and there is another one 2 miles beyond that. Good places to portage. The runnable chutes range from Class II to Class IV. The Animas has few stillwater eddies; it is one long whitewater carni- val. This is a cold river to get dumped into—42 degrees Fahrenheit in the mornings and 48 degrees Fahrenheit in the afternoon when the sun pokes on down through tall towers of rock.

Two miles downstream from Needleton there is a wild stretch of river, just beyond a steel footbridge, and about a mile below is more heavy water. If skilled, you will enjoy this stretch. If not, you may drown. There are Class III and IV rapids. One can run a bit beyond Ah Wilderness camp, but one has to take-out at the steel railroad bridge which leaps the Animas 25.6 miles below Silverton.

Beyond that, the canyon has never been run. Its sheer, slab sides offer no way to portage or line. This is the Rio del Animas Perdidas. Here topographical charts show the river drops 250 feet to the mile.

The mountain tributaries of the Colorado offer difficult whitewater runs as well as smooth-flowing river cruises; they pass from jagged peaks where the snow never melts in some ravines down through high desert country where the most striking colors are not of the vegetation, but of the rock itself. They are a delight to the river runner.

Guide Notes for the
MOUNTAIN TRIBUTARIES OF THE COLORADO

Black Canyon of the Gunnison

LOCATION—Western Colorado, northeast of Gunnison.

LENGTH OF TRIP—18 miles from Cimarron to the east portal of Black Canyon of the Gunnison National Monument. Can be done in a single day but most people prefer to camp overnight.

FAVORABLE SEASON—May through September.

DEGREE OF DIFFICULTY—This is fast water, for experienced boaters only. Crystal Creek Falls, about midway down the trip, is for experts only and should be portaged by everyone in high water.

RECOMMENDED CRAFT—Raft or kayak.

ACCESS POINTS—Cimarron, on U.S. Highway 50 east of Montrose, is the put-in point; the eastern portal of the Gunnison National Monument, reached by spur road off the main highway, is the take-out place.

CAMPING—Several benches beside the river make fine campsites. Since the Gunnison is prone to sudden rises in water when a storm hits upriver, try to pitch camp well above water level.

FISHING—Good to excellent for trout.

Dolores River

LOCATION—Drains the La Plata Mountains of southwestern Colorado, and flows into the Colorado River over the Utah border.

LENGTH OF TRIP—46 miles from the small towns of Slickrock to Bedrock, both in Colorado. 3- to 4-day trip.

FAVORABLE SEASON—Peak of spring run-off, May to the first week in June.

DEGREE OF DIFFICULTY—Easy run for rafters and kayakers. Canoeists should be experienced.

RECOMMENDED CRAFT—Raft, kayak or canoe.

ACCESS POINTS—Slickrock, or Gladel (as it is alternately referred to), is the customary put-in point for running the Dolores. It is 22 miles north of Dove Creek on State Highway 141. Bedrock, the take-out point, is on State Highway 90 southwest of Uravan.

CAMPING—Several good camping spots, except in Big Gypsum Valley, which is fenced-off rangeland. It is a good idea to boil water or add Halazone, except for that gathered at seeps or springs, such as the clear welling of water up Bull Creek Canyon.

Animas River

LOCATION—Southwestern Colorado, draining the La Plata Mountains on the west and the San Juans to the east.

LENGTH OF TRIP—25 miles from Silverton to the take-out point at a railroad bridge that many miles south of the put-in point. A 2-day trip.

FAVORABLE SEASON—Spring run-off. Late May and most of June.

DEGREE OF DIFFICULTY—Extremely fast water, with a drop of 80 feet to the mile. For experts only, and even they should be prepared to portage or line in places. The run from Silverton to Elk Park can be taken by skilled and experienced boaters; it gets rougher between there and the railroad bridge. Beyond the railroad bridge one gets into a sheer-walled canyon which topographic charts show to drop 250 feet to the mile. There is no way properly to scout it, to line bad places or to portage. It is pure suicide. *Get out at Elk Park or at the 25-mile railroad bridge.*

RECOMMENDED CRAFT—Raft or kayak.

ACCESS POINTS—Put-in point is at Silverton, mining camp on U.S. Highway 550 (the "Million Dollar Highway") and terminus of the narrow-gauge Denver and Rio Grande Southern Railroad spur up from Durango, perhaps the most spectacular run any steam train makes in America. It runs daily throughout the summer months (write the Durango Chamber of Commerce for details). The take-out point is at the railroad bridge 25 miles south of Silverton or at Elk Park, several miles upriver. The steam train is the only way out of the canyon. Flag it down on its afternoon return from Silverton.

CAMPING—Beautiful campsites with rushing river and jagged peaks for a backdrop. If you enjoy scrambling up peaks as much as bouncing down rivers, there are some fine, high fangs of rock in the vicinity.

FISHING—Good trout fishing.

Westwater Canyon of the Colorado

LOCATION—On the Colorado-Utah border near Grand Junction, Colorado.

LENGTH OF TRIP—26 miles. A 2-day trip for the average party.

FAVORABLE SEASON—May through September.

DEGREE OF DIFFICULTY—For experts only. Some very tough rapids.

RECOMMENDED CRAFT—Raft or kayak.

ACCESS POINTS—Westwater Ranch, a few miles east of Grand Junction, Colorado, is the put-in point. Take-out points are on ranches in the vicinity of Cisco, Utah. All of these access points are on private property, and one must secure permission from the owners before making the trip.

CAMPING—Several good spots. Camp well before dark, as there are some sheer-sided sections.

4. Canyonlands

For many people, myself included, no region of North America contains more elemental and varied beauty than southeastern Utah. Here there are high forested mountains, where snow-water meanders through aspen glades. Up remote canyons ancient stone dwellings perch on shelves beneath overhanging cliffs; and over hundreds of square miles the rock has been exposed and carved into wild extremes of color and shape. During the summer months, transient, seasonal cities spring up in our more popular National Parks and automobiles clog highways leading to beach and mountains. Fortunately for those who like their outdoor neighbors to be more than a camper-truck away, much of the canyon country of Utah is accessible only by extremely rough roads, unmarked trails, or down the rivers.

The Green and Colorado rivers form a giant V in the heart of Canyonlands, converging at the entrance to Cataract Canyon. The 117-mile run down the Green River from the town of the same name to the confluence is both immensely scenic and smooth-flowing. There are no rapids. Arrangements can be made with powerboat operators for a rendez-vous at the confluence and transportation up the other side of the V, the Colorado, to Moab. Cataract Canyon should be attempted only by experts, unless one is a member of a guided party. A cruise from Green River to the confluences averages a week; then, by jet-boat, one can be back to the highway (at Moab) within a few hours.

Green River, a farming community, is situated at the site of one of the most historic river fords in the West. No one knows when Indians first

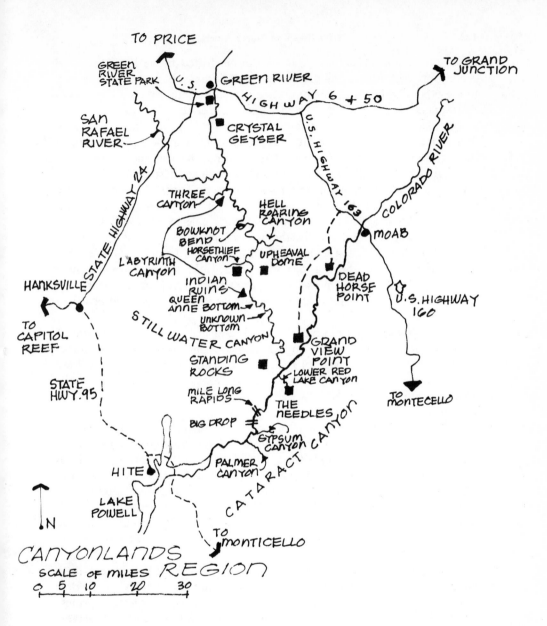

TO PRICE

GREEN RIVER STATE PARK

GREEN RIVER

TO GRAND JUNCTION

U.S. HIGHWAY 6 + 50

SAN RAFAEL RIVER

CRYSTAL GEYSER

U.S. Highway 163

COLORADO RIVER

STATE HIGHWAY 24

THREE CANYON

HELL ROARING CANYON

MOAB

BOWKNOT BEND

HORSETHIEF CANYON

UPHEAVAL DOME

LABYRINTH CANYON

INDIAN RUINS

DEAD HORSE POINT

U.S. HIGHWAY 160

HANKSVILLE

QUEEN ANNE BOTTOM

UNKNOWN BOTTOM

TO CAPITOL REEF

STILL WATER CANYON

GRAND VIEW POINT

STATE HWY. 95

STANDING ROCKS

LOWER RED LAKE CANYON

TO MONTECELLO

MILE LONG RAPIDS

THE NEEDLES

BIG DROP

GYPSUM CANYON

CATARACT CANYON

HITE

PALMER CANYON

LAKE POWELL

N

TO MONTICELLO

CANYONLANDS REGION

SCALE OF MILES

0 5 10   20   30

129

began crossing the river here, but as Powell drifted by in 1869 he noted crude rafts and other signs that a band had recently passed from one side to the other. Throughout much of the nineteenth century the ford was used by trappers, explorers, traders, gold-seekers, and settlers.

Green River State Park, close to town, is a good place to launch. Some four miles downstream, the iron oxides of Crystal Geyser have stained the terraced rock of the riverbank into vivid red, brown, and yellow hues. The "geyser," actually an unsuccessful oil and gas test drilled in 1936, spouts up a column of warm water about once an hour. It was somewhere along this stretch of the river that a member of Powell's second Colorado River expedition (1871), jerked at his fishing pole in irritation, assuming he had hooked a snag. Up came the head of an enormous Colorado River salmon which was boated with "barely a wiggle as if he did not know what it was to be caught." Several fish were landed, the largest estimated at 3 feet long. As the whopper was being prepared for supper, its heart was observed to pulsate twenty beats to the minute for half an hour after it had been removed.

It is characteristic of rivers to wind, and it appears characteristic of rivers in the Canyon Country to twist twice as much as rivers elsewhere. Sand deposited on the inside of sweeping bends often gives rise to willows and tamarisks; sometimes there are cottonwoods. These bottoms make good campsites. As the river water is quite muddy, it is advisable to use saucepans and the like to settle out the grit overnight.

The country is mostly flat, or consists of broken cliffs and massive buttes, above the mouth of the San Rafael River. Some four miles below this side stream, where people from Powell's day to the present have been picking arrowheads out of the sand, the Green River enters Labyrinth Canyon. The walls rise quickly from 50 feet high to 300 . . . 600 . . . and 1000 feet. At some bends in the river the water has undercut the rock faces so that they lean overhead. During storms, cascades plunge off these rims and, pulled apart by the winds of their long fall, reach the river as fine spray.

Bring your boots. This is hiking country. That is, if you have a taste for canyons that are wagon-wide with walls rising higher than a cathedral spire—for pinnacles, gargoyles, arches, cliff dwellings, unexpected springs, curling jigsaw puzzles of dried mud, petrified wood, fresh tracks of beaver, deer and coyote, ancient treads pressed by dinosaurs, Indian petroglyphs, and abandoned uranium mines where careless nests of tin cans and stove lids are already rotted with rust. Such are the signs of water and life, which come and go.

Some of the cottonwoods up Three Canyon were well rooted when Powell walked here. There is usually fresh water within half a mile of the river. A few miles downriver, there are scratches in red sandstone that were made while European knights were setting out on the Crusades. They depict bighorn sheep and horned gods or shamans. The narrow neck of Bowknot Bend, farther on, is a good place to reflect on these figures. Here the river rolls out for 7½ miles before returning to within 1200 feet south of itself. From the crest, this edge of naked stone, the slashed landscape is basic and powerful. Here one witnesses the primordial struggle of water to escape from rock, and in summer, a fire hanging in the sky with nothing to burn.

About a tenth of a mile up Hell Roaring Canyon there is an inscription:

> D. Julien
> 1836
> 3 mai

History tells us that Denis Julien was a beaver trapper operating out of the Uinta Basin in the 1830s; it tells us nothing about the strange boat and what appears to be a winged sun that are carved next to his name.

A little more than 10 miles downriver from Hell Roaring Canyon is Upheaval Canyon coming in from the left. A 4-mile walk up the canyon brings the hiker to Upheaval Dome, one of the most striking geological features of the entire Colorado plateau. The dome is a sharp, circular uplift about 2 miles in diameter, encircled by a syncline, or what might be described as a gigantic waterless moat. Some 5 miles beyond the mouth of the canyon are the ruins of crude, circular towers believed to have been built by the Fremont People who farmed nearby Fort Bottom 700 to 1000 years ago. Perched on a bluff, they are a short steep scramble from the river. The walls are extremely fragile; were people to climb on them, what has stood for centuries might well collapse. There is an old cabin in Fort Bottom, thought to have been built by Butch Cassidy, the outlaw whose Wild Bunch ran cattle, rarely their own, all through the Robbers' Roost country.

About 85 miles down from the town of Green River, one enters Queen Anne Bottom, then Anderson Bottom, lowlands which were once loops of the river. Powell, observing breaks in the canyon walls, marked an end to Labyrinth Canyon, and when high red slabs once again squeezed a narrow sky, he called the next section Stillwater Canyon.

Botanists have remarked upon the profusion of prickly pear cactus and jimson weed in Unknown Bottom of Stillwater Canyon. Since there are several Fremont Culture ruins close by, the patches may have been seeded intentionally by Indians centuries ago. Like a number of tribes of the southwestern United States and northern Mexico, it is believed these people ate prickly pear as food and jimson to induce shamanistic visions. There are numerous spectacular rock formations, such as Turk's Head and Candlestick Tower, visible in the final 30 miles to the confluence.

Wild burros live in Stillwater Canyon. Back in the 1880s, a large grizzly was thought to have hibernated there. A rust-coated animal, he was known, unaffectionately, as Red Robber by ranchers from Robbers' Roost to Book Cliffs. It seems the bear liked to kill cattle, and not just for food, as he often left the carcasses untouched. By the time two prospectors came upon Red Robber tearing up their cabin and killed him, stockmen estimated he had done in better than 150 head of longhorns, not to speak of several horses. During his wanderings in the Canyon Country the bear once panicked a herd of cattle into a disastrous stampede and, on another occasion, demolished a Ute Indian camp. When he was dressed out, two old rifle bullets and an arrowhead were found in his flesh, and his hide was a welter of scars from duels with longhorns.

The confluence of the Green River from the north and the Colorado heading west (*Bob Krips Photo*)

The confluence of the Green and the Colorado is a fine place for a layover day, whether one is returning to Moab or continuing on into Cataract Canyon. It's a good spot to swim and laze around a sandbar, and this is magnificent hiking country.

Early-day explorers, prospectors, trappers, and adventurers referred to Cataract Canyon, below the confluence, as the "graveyard of the Colorado." In a distance of just under 50 miles the combined flows of the Green and Colorado formerly dropped 405 feet, mostly in short, abrupt plunges. At least twelve men are known to have drowned in this deep, boulder-strewn gorge.

Today, back-up from Glen Canyon Dam has inundated the lower end of Cataract, and one of the wildest rapids, Dark Canyon, is no more. Yet the most challenging whitewater still roars unchecked; splendors of carved rock still rise on every side. About 4 miles below the confluence there is a fine campsite: a sandbar backed by groves of willow and cottonwood. A 3-mile hike up Lower Red Lake Canyon leads up into the Needles, a fantasy of strange and beautiful rock formations.

The rapids begin. Between here and the flatwater of Lake Powell, river-mappers have delineated forty-two of them. Several are awesome in moderate water, impossible in high water. Mile Long Rapid, actually six rapids laid out head to tail, is 11 miles below the confluence. If one is dumped in the first one, the life-jacket ride will be long, bruising, and scary. A little more than 2 miles beyond this is Big Drop, where the river crashes down through giant boulders at a pitch that has been aptly described as a tilted waterfall. River guides consider this one of the toughest rapids in America.

One gets an idea of the temper of a river from the condition of its driftwood. Frederick Dellenbaugh, staff artist with Powell's second Colorado River expedition, wrote of Cataract Canyon:

> There was a vast amount of driftwood in tremendous piles, trees, limbs, boughs, railroad ties; a great mixture of all kinds, some of it lying full fifty feet above the present level of the river. There were large and small tree-trunks battered and limbless, the ends pounded to a spongy mass of splinters . . . (From *A Canyon Voyage*, Frederick Dellenbaugh, New Haven: Yale University Press, 1962.)

The river pounds and roars its way through this spectacular gorge whose rock formations are varied and beautiful. Several side canyons are well worth hiking. Gypsum Canyon, where Powell outran a flash flood on his 1869 expedition, is a steep-walled cleft. Four miles up the canyon a 100-foot waterfall drops into a shaded pool. A higher basin lies above the falls, apparently inaccessible. One-armed Major Powell climbed up to this

Running a rapids in Cataract Canyon (*Bob Krips Photo*)

level, gathered pitch for fixing his boats, and then somehow descended without breaking his neck.

Three miles below Palmer Canyon the river winds through a lovely 2000-foot-deep gorge—one of the most scenic stretches of Cataract. A little below this one encounters the upper end of Lake Powell. There are some 20 miles of stillwater on into Hite Crossing, the take-out point.

Guide Notes for CANYONLANDS OF THE COLORADO

LOCATION—Southeastern Utah.

LENGTH OF TRIP—Labyrinth and Stillwater Canyons are 117 miles long;

Cataract Canyon 47 miles long. From the town of Green River most parties average about a week floating down the Green to the confluence with the Colorado. From the confluence it is just a matter of hours back up the Colorado to Moab by jet-boat. Cataract Canyon is generally a 3- to 5-day trip.

FAVORABLE SEASONS—May through October.

DEGREE OF DIFFICULTY—Labyrinth and Stillwater canyons contain no rapids and should pose no problems even for boaters of limited experience. Unless expert in whitewater, *be sure to take-out at the confluence with the Colorado.* Cataract Canyon, just beyond, has some of the roughest rapids in America. If not continuing into Cataract, arrange for a pick-up by jet-boat out of Moab.

ACCESS POINTS—The only put-in point for this trip is the town of Green River, Utah, on U.S. Highways 6 and 50. If you are only running Labyrinth and Stillwater canyons, take-out at the confluence with the Colorado. Take-out place after a run through Cataract Canyon is Hite Marina on Lake Powell, from which State Highways 95 and 24 lead back to Green River.

CAMPING—Numerous fine campsites, especially upon wide, sandy beaches. There is lots of driftwood. The river water is potable but should be settled as it is muddy. Clear water can be found in some side canyons. Plan to camp early and hike up the magnificent side canyons.

5. Grand Canyon

Lees Ferry, a short distance downriver from Glen Canyon Dam, is the jump-off point for Grand Canyon voyages. The Mormon farming settlement was named for John D. Lee, its first resident, who was later shot while seated on the edge of his own coffin at the site of the Mountain Meadows Massacre.

The year 1857 was a troubled time in Utah. A federal army was en route there, supposedly to put down a Mormon "rebellion." It was said that an emigrant party, camping out at Mountain Meadows, had poisoned springs and might attack Mormon settlements. Brigham Young instructed church elder John Lee to "waylay our enemies, attack them from ambush, stampede their animals, take their supply trains . . . to waste away our enemies." Paiute Indians agreed to do the bloodletting; the Saints were merely to advise.

But the Paiute, although they inflicted a number of casualties, were beaten back by the emigrants. William Bateman, a Mormon, then approached the wagon train under a flag of truce. He told the emigrants that if they would surrender their weapons, the Mormons would escort them to the safety of Cedar City, where they could attend to their wounded and then proceed to California. This was agreed to, and the arms were placed in a wagon. Lee went to the emigrant camp, and as he later recalled:

"As I entered the fortifications men and women gathered around me in wild consternation. Some felt the time for their happy deliverance had come, while others though in deep distress and all in tears, looked upon me with doubt, distrust, and terror. . . ."

The unarmed men, with their women and children, started down the trail flanked by their Mormon escorts. At a signal, the Indians, who had been waiting in ambush, and the Mormons, attacked the emigrants with such violence that within five minutes the entire party of some 130 people had been killed. Only infants, who would not later be able to tell of the grisly incident, were spared.

The participants were sworn to secrecy. But word leaked out, and soon Lee and other principals were sought by federal authorities. For years Lee hid out at the lonely Colorado River crossing which bears his name. He was finally captured and taken to Mountain Meadows for execution.

In the early days Lees Ferry was just a good place to whoop and whip your animals across the river. Later there was a flatbed ferryboat, hooked to a cable contraption so you wouldn't get shoved all the way down to Fort Yuma by the current. In 1928 the ferryboat flipped over, spilling two Model-T's and some people into high and no-nonsense water. The Model-T's and four of the people were snatched off by the River God, and nobody bothered to put in another ferryboat, since Navajo Bridge, a few miles to the south, was abuilding.

There is a lot of activity on the beach of Lees Ferry of an evening, mostly boatmen getting their rigs together for departure, salting their chores with considerable lying and cutting up. Great people. Most of the pilgrims they guide through the canyon soon became very involved with it, sensitive to wilderness no matter what their backgrounds. They do, of course, occasionally get someone who has a hard time adjusting. Such as a city gent a couple of seasons back who brushed a stinging nettle downriver and insisted he had been zapped by a diamondback rattler. White-lipped, he was whisked out by helicopter.

The majority of people who run Grand Canyon do so with outfitters. Yet expert river runners can apply for a permit from the Park Service to do it on their own (Box 129, Grand Canyon, Arizona 86023).

Until the construction of Glen Canyon Dam, river runners used to settle the mud out of river water before drinking it. These days one can

Indian ruins in the cliff above Nankoweep Rapids in the Grand Canyon

usually dip clear water right out of the flow. The fact that the water level in the canyon is now, as one boatman phrases it, "regulated by the Bureau of Reclamation rather than the Lord," will obviously affect the nature of river running in the canyon. Already there is a scarcity of driftwood. Most Grand Canyon rapids are formed where boulders and other debris have washed out of side canyons. The annual spring floods used to grind up and wash away much of this material. It is safe to assume that over the years most of the rapids will now become more boulder-strewn, dangerous, and perhaps even unrunnable.

Lees Ferry, the beginning of Marble Canyon, is usually mile zero on river maps, and mileages given in parentheses in this guide will be from that point. See map on page 121.

After passing beneath 467-foot-high Navajo Bridge (4 miles) the only way out of the canyon is up a few rough and little used trails until Phantom Ranch is reached (87 miles). An early explorer described Marble Canyon as having "marble enough to build forty Babylons, walls and all." The first real rapids, Badger Creek (8 miles) is rated 4–6 on a difficulty scale of 1–10. From Badger Creek to Vasey's Paradise (32 miles) there are ten sizable rapids within the same general range of Badger Creek. The limestone walls of Marble Canyon are high, magnificent—and arid. At Vasey's Paradise, however, green plants seem to burst out from the rock. Here, spring water issuing from a cliff flows through a thick growth of flowering bushes, grass, ferns, and vines.

Along this stretch of the river there are a number of exquisitely carved natural features, both on the river and up side canyons: Silver Grotto up Shinumo Wash (29 miles), Red Wall Cavern (33 miles), Buck Farm Canyon and Royal Arches (41 miles), and Triple Alcoves (47 miles). One can hike some distance up Buck Farm Canyon, whose smooth, twisting walls are only a few feet apart in places. Part of the way one wades through clear spring water.

There are Indian ruins in an overhang high above the river at Nankoweep Rapids (52 miles), on the delta of Unkar Creek (72 miles), and in numerous other locations throughout Grand Canyon. Although nomadic hunters used caves in the canyon as early as 4000 years ago, leaving figurines of split willow twigs in some of them, most ruins close to the river were occupied by Pueblo Indians for a mere century (A.D. 1050–1150)—and then abandoned.

The three most formidable rapids on the run to Phantom Ranch boil through the granite gorge beyond the Unkar ruins; they are Hance Rapids (76 miles), Sockdolager Rapids (78 miles), and Grapevine Rapids (81 miles).

Downstream navigation in Grand Canyon is difficult enough, but in 1960 an attempt was made to run upriver in jet-boats. Four 18-foot fiberglass craft were launched at Lake Mead. The pumps of the marine jet-propulsion units were able to throw back as much water as four fire department pumper trucks. They were manned by some of the most knowledgeable rivermen in the world, who came from as far away as New Zealand.

The run, considered impossible by many observers, took its toll. At least one hole was punched into the tough fiberglass hulls each day. One man broke a leg when his boat plunged over a 10-foot wave and he lost control. He was lucky to get out alive, as was the driver of the *Wee Yellow,* which sank in Grapevine Rapids. Expedition members communicated with their wives on the rim by means of mirror signals and messages like "O.K." drawn massively in the sand. Eventually, the three remaining boats reached Lees Ferry after an epic journey of 350 miles.

Phantom Ranch (87 miles) is a tree-shaded resort, reached by mule trails from both the north and south rims. The north-rim trail spans the river over the Kaibab Suspension Bridge. Beyond Phantom Ranch the current continues to wind through the inner gorge, and soon thunders through four of the biggest rapids on the river: Horn Creek Rapids (90 miles), Granite Rapids (93 miles), Hermit Rapids (95 miles), and Crystal Rapids (98 miles). Granite and Hermit rapids feature huge standing waves that are awesome as they crash over your raft, drenching you. But Crystal Rapids, though not quite as photogenic, is more dangerous. Crystal Rapids and Lava Falls are generally considered to be the toughest whitewater on the entire Colorado.

Until 1967 Crystal was a modest rapids, dwarfed by many others. But in that year a cloudburst sent flash floods careening down Bright Angel and Crystal creeks, sweeping away some of the Phantom Ranch buildings and washing great boulders into the river. Overnight Crystal became a major rapids.

Hermit Rapids and Hermit Canyon are named for Louis Boucher, a prospector who lived at the head of the canyon, around the turn of the century. Boucher planted fruit trees—orange, peach, fig, pomegranate— and grew tomatoes, chilies, melons, grapes, and miscellaneous vegetables in an extensive garden. He grazed sheep, pick-and-shoveled out a trail which he called the Silver Bell, and had goldfish in his watering trough.

Prior to his capture by federal authorities, the Mormon John Lee reputedly buried a large amount of gold somewhere in Grand Canyon. This interested William Bass, a former railroad dispatcher from New York who, hankering for a little excitement, headed west in 1883. In the frontier town of Ashfork, Arizona, Bass met one of Lee's widows, who gave him a map which purported to show where the gold was hidden. Bass failed to uncover the gold, but he became entranced with Grand Canyon. Before long he was guiding parties of tourists and hunters down a trail he had constructed. Bass played the violin and perhaps it was inevitable that one of his lady wayfarers, a graduate of the Boston Conservatory of Music, would fall in love with him. They married and raised a family on the south rim.

The bride found the view from her new home magnificent, although there were drawbacks. During dry spells, doing the laundry involved a three-day muleback ride down to the river. In 1908 Bass built a cable across the river at the canyon mouth which now bears his name (108 miles). The suspended cage was large enough to carry men and even horses. Hoping to build up his herd of pack animals, the guide released a number of burros in the canyon. Today their descendants gaze at passing river runners with the wistful curiosity of their breed.

The trail up Tapeats Creek (133 miles) is one of the most beautiful in Grand Canyon. For much of the way the path traverses a ledge high above the stream, as sheer walls rise directly out of the water. Three and one-half miles upstream is Thunder River, a large cascade which bursts out of a smooth cliff face. From here, you can hike over to the next canyon, rejoining your boating party at Deer Creek Falls, a couple of miles down-river from the mouth of Tapeats Creek.

The Colorado at Tapeats Creek

There are not many pools where one can catch both trout and catfish. Yet where the cold waters of Havasu Creek fall into the Colorado (157 miles) both species will fight for your bait (even if it be no more than canned corn on a drop line). The Havasupai Indian Reservation, several miles up the canyon, contains one of the most beautiful and isolated Indian villages on the continent. The blue-green waters of the creek have created an oasis of green surrounded by scorched red cliffs. The Havasupai plant crops, graze cattle, and are noted as rodeo performers. Above their village the rimrock of the outer canyon looms; below it the creek drops over four spectacular waterfalls, one of which, Mooney Falls, plunges down some 200 feet. The village can be reached by trail from the rim or the river.

By the time you reach Havasu Creek, most of the Grand Canyon whitewater is behind you. The river is smooth except for minor rapids that can be floated in a lifejacket. Then one hears a deep roar in the distance. It is Lava Falls (179 miles), biggest rapids on the river. Eons ago an outpouring of lava completely blocked the canyon here. Today the river

Thunder Falls, reached by hiking from the river in Grand Canyon

cascades over the rubble of this ancient natural dam. The holes and back-waves are enormous, capable of flipping a raft of any size if one should break an oar, have an engine die, or simply miscalculate the best route through.

Lava Falls is a fitting climax to Grand Canyon, one of the finest whitewater runs to be found anywhere. One can take-out at Diamond Creek (225 miles), reached by rough dirt road from Peach Springs, or continue on to Lake Mead, where there are several possible take-out points.

Guide Notes for the GRAND CANYON

LOCATION—Northwestern Arizona, extending from Lees Ferry to Lake Mead. See maps on pages 94 and 121.

LENGTH OF TRIP—From Lees Ferry to Phantom Ranch is 87 miles (5-day trip); Lees Ferry to Diamond Creek is 225 miles (10-day trip); Lees Ferry to Pierce Ferry on Lake Mead is 280 miles (14-day trip). The length of time one will take to make these runs will vary, depending upon whether power is used on slow stretches, how many hours per day one is on the water, and how much time one allows for exploring side canyons. The days given above are average.

FAVORABLE SEASON—April through October.

DEGREE OF DIFFICULTY—The most famous whitewater canyon in the world, with numerous major rapids. For experts only (who must register with the Park Service and convince them of their ability) unless going through with a guided party (see Appendix V).

RECOMMENDED CRAFT—Raft (10-man or larger).

ACCESS POINTS—Lees Ferry, on U.S. Highway 89 north of Flagstaff, is the customary put-in point. The south to north rim trail crosses the river at Phantom Ranch, but equipment must be packed all the way to one of the rims (mules can be rented at Phantom Ranch). Diamond Creek, reached by rough road 25 miles out of Peach Springs on the Hualapai Indian Reservation, is a more practical take-out place. Four-wheel vehicles are recommended for the last few miles of the road. A gravel road leads into Pierce Ferry from the vicinity of Hackberry on U.S. Highway 66, or a connecting road which takes off from U.S. Highway 93 between Boulder City and Kingman. Better than 50 miles of backcountry in either case.

CAMPING—Numerous sandy beaches make excellent campsites. River water is chill and delicious. Upriver dams block out the silt so there is no need to settle water as in Canyonlands. Leaving a clean campsite is of prime importance on any wild river. In Grand Canyon, the volume of people voyaging through it (most of them with outfitters) would soon destroy the quality of the environment were this practice not scrupulously followed.

FISHING—Fair for catfish in the Colorado; trout up several side canyons such as Havasu and Tapeats.

CHAPTER SIX

River of the Trembling Earth:
The Suwannee

1. Okefenokee Swamp: Headwaters of the Suwannee

The Suwannee River rises in the Okefenokee Swamp of southeastern Georgia, and winds south through Florida to empty into the Gulf of Mexico. The Okefenokee is not a true swamp, as there are currents moving through it, the flows of which come together to make up the Suwannee.

The Suwannee is slow and crooked, molded by banks of gray sand in low water, spilling out through miles of eerie, moss-hung forests during flood. Large, pencil-legged heron and egret stand motionless in the shallows, as if waiting for something. Sometimes a bull alligator will bellow in the night, a deep anguished sound that carries for miles. The dark waters of the river come from a place where tall forests and fields of flowers lie awash in what could be the drift of an enchanted sea, where on certain islands the ground trembles and trees lean if a man passes close to them.

Creek Indians told an eighteenth-century traveler that deep within this curious place was an island considered the most blissful spot on earth. Hunters in pursuit of game had seen the island, but attempts to reach it had been thwarted by a labyrinth of passages. Lost and on the point of perishing, the hunters were hailed by several indescribably beautiful women, who gave them corn cakes, dates, and oranges, then told them to flee before their husbands, fierce and cruel to strangers, should find them there.

After great hardship the hunters managed to return to their own village. Hearing about the island of beautiful women, young warriors of the tribe desired to see for themselves, and headed into swamp country. They poled dugouts along narrow channels that twisted endlessly through roots

Out of the mysterious fastness of the Okefenokee Swamp flows the legendary Suwannee River. Here boaters explore Okefenokee Swamp Park near Waycross, Georgia

and trunks of trees whose foliage stitched together tightly overhead, making a twilight of high noon. They paddled across empires of water lilies where it was open, only to come against impenetrable clots of drowned trees.

None were ever able to find their way back to the blissful island.

The Okefenokee Swamp, headwaters of the Suwannee River, is an ideal setting for such a story. Located in the southeast corner of Georgia, south of the town of Waycross, the swamp extends some 38 miles from north to south and is 25 miles wide in places—a wilderness of close to half a million acres. Although most of the interior is covered with water—1 to 4 feet deep in most places—there are a number of islands, ranging in size from Billy's Island, more than 4 miles long, to sandy hummocks scarcely large enough to spread a blanket over. Some islets are actually detached, floating masses of vegetation. An early visitor to the Okefenokee, Maj.-Gen. G. A. McCall, wrote of an experience in *Letters from the Frontier,* published in 1868:

> As the sun rose the following morning . . . I looked out upon the lake, when, to my no little surprise, the island I had observed the previous day had disappeared, and on further examination the water of the lake seemed to have receded from the shore nearly one hundred yards. It was not until I had walked down to the shore of the lake that I discovered that the island I had discovered the day before had drifted with the wind against the shore where I stood.

This is deceptive country. From a boat, the groves of cypress, gum, and slash pine could be on dry land, or pushing up through a couple of feet of water. Until one is actually hard against them there is no way to tell. There are vast "prairies" in the swamp, where acres of water lilies, floating hearts, pickerelweed, and other plants cover the water so thoroughly that a canoe seems oddly out of place, as if one should be hiking rather than boating.

The pitcher plant is common on the prairies, a green, hooded stalk that rises a foot above water level, graceful as a cobra. Insects buzz into its mouth. Deep within the sheath of the plant they alight on what they take to be pollen, where they drown in digestive fluids.

A bewildering network of "runs," threads of open water, wind through the forests and across the prairies. Many are ancient Indian trails. Pioneer trappers, alligator hunters, and moonshiners have used them. In places the runs widen into round 'gator holes only a few boat lengths across, or narrow, long lakes such as Big Water.

In all the runs, through all the lakes, there is current, often surprisingly strong. For the Okefenokee is not your classic swamp, a malarial slackwater. It is a watershed, where rains and the flow of swamp springs move out of the north and west into the Suwannee, and, to a lesser extent, into St. Marys River. The water, although stained by tannic acid, is potable. The Swampers, early settlers, drank it all their lives without ill effect.

During Pleistocene times, roughly a half million to a million years ago, the Okefenokee was a shallow reach of the ocean. Over centuries, wave action built up a 100-mile-long sandbar, a feature now called the Trail Ridge. A large body of water was trapped, cut off from the sea. Gradually rains flushed out the salt water, and the lake became fresh. Sandbars scattered behind the Trail Ridge were now islands. Aquatic plants flourished in the warm shallows, then decayed, dropping onto thickening layers of peat. As these deposits approached the lake surface, sedges and other marsh plants took root; later a great forest grew through

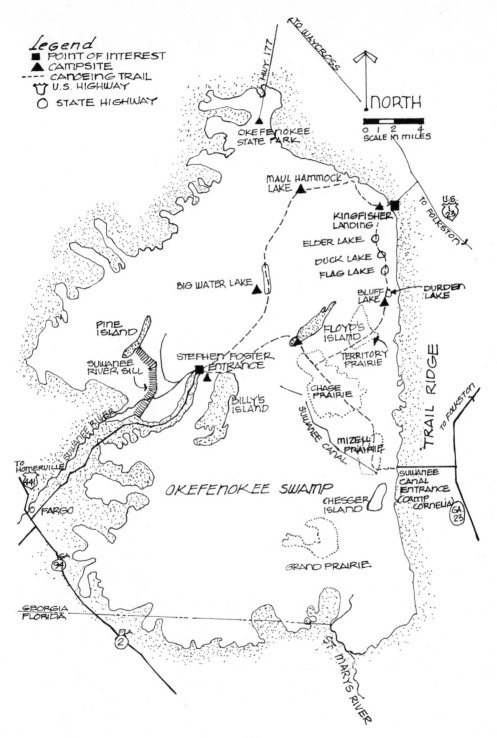

and over the waters. The swamp prairies of today are the sites of ancient forest fires.

One gets into the swamp very quickly, very thoroughly. A couple of twists down some run and the swamp closes gently behind you, offering only the most subtle of landmarks. It is easy to get lost; even the old Swampers would find themselves lost on occasion, sleeping in their dug-outs, poling down unfamiliar runs until they could regain their bearings. Sounds—splashing, rustling, croaks, bird-cries—are prehistoric, except for the burr of an occasional plane, or, on the swamp's eastern edges, the deep hum of a fast freight on the Seaboard line. These seem set away more in time, perhaps, than in space—as indeed, they would be were one's boat to sink.

The open water ranges in color from umber to pitch, depending upon place and time of day, but nearly always it acts as a dark mirror, yielding a flawless image—moss dangling from solemn trees, the tints and cloud shapes of the sky. Persons lost in the swamp have been known to leap frenziedly into the water, thinking it the reality, and all above merely reflection.

The swamp is filled with living things. If there were an urban center, a New York or London, of frogs, this would be it. Frogs of all sizes and voices. Zoologists tell us there are over twenty species here, including such exotics as the ornate chorus, bronze, southern leopard, eastern narrow-mouth, and barking treefrogs. During the daytime one usually hears rather than sees them—constant plops and splashes—movement at the edge of vision. After dark, apparently more at ease in moonlight and starlight, they are less timid.

Memory: a night deep in the swamp. Trying with a companion to sleep in an overloaded canoe, mosquitoes whining in persistent greed. Surrounded by water and floating plants. Lightning from drifting thunderstorms mirrored on black waters. Large splashes close to the boat. Scales or hide? Alligator, bass, or cottonmouth? At the burst of illumination from my flashlight, sounds abruptly cease. Nothing there, except a green frog, squatting on a lily pad a few inches from the canoe. Protruding eyes yellow and watchful in the glare. Snap off the light, doze fretfully for an hour or two, snort abruptly awake as a mosquito bites the inside of my left nostril. Long night. Stars have changed, the sky has wheeled a bit, but no lip of ash-blue to the east; dawn seems to have died somewhere—perhaps has been buried under the sands of the Sahara.

An owl shrieks back among dim trees, trying to frighten its prey into blowing their cover. Heavy splashes. I flick on my flash. The green frog is there, on the same pad, watchful. I begin to wonder what its role is. Is it a protector, or ritualizing an elaborate curse?

Even in the vivid slashes of dawn, the yellow, patient eyes linger in the mind's eye.

There are innumerable birds in the swamp, but perhaps the most striking are the egrets. You see them in the prairies, standing motionless beyond lilies and iris, tall and white, the quintessence of the kind of dignity striven for by college presidents. When they fly it is usually not far, an indolent, lazy flap of long, beautiful wings. Cranes and herons stay mostly close to the water. Buzzards perch in the highest trees, where the winds are. Sometimes they fill the upper reaches of a tall cypress like clumps of old, unpicked fruit.

In the swamp, as everywhere else, there is a hierarchy of survival—strong, agile entities feeding upon the weak and the slow. In Okefenokee country, a large alligator is hunted by nothing except poaching humans; the alligator, in turn, eats virtually anything smaller that moves, including its own offspring.

We have given an aura of undeserved horror to the alligator, imagining him to be a cunning capsizer of johnboats, dugouts, and canoes; we see him digesting the bloody limbs of incautious adventurers. Were someone to wade a section of the swamp, thrashing through slippery shallows, quite likely after a time he would see the glide of a nubbly head in lazy pursuit; pale amber eyes with pupils scarcely more than slits slipping just above the water. The attack comes not so much in a slashing fashion, but with the great teeth snapping together in a lockjawed clamp, unbreakable as a beartrap. Swampers affirm that 'gators like to pull large prey, such as razorbacks or dogs, underwater to drown them.

There is no doubt that an alligator would as soon eat a man as anything else, but like the shark, he has survived eons; he is cautious. The underbellies of boats are big, and give no signs of fear. Moreover, some of them emit horrible noises. Alligators mostly leave them alone, watching from mudbars with the heavy-lidded indolence of a species that has waited centuries for other creatures to reveal their weaknesses. Documented attacks are rare—yet they have occurred.

A few years back for example, a game-management man stepped out of his skiff onto what he took to be an old log. The alligator swung its ponderous, warty head around and nipped a few ounces of flesh from the startled official's posterior.

Here and there in the swamp, usually close to open runs, one finds mounds of grass and mud. A female alligator will lay forty to sixty eggs in such a nest. Heat from decaying vegetation incubates the eggs and they hatch in two to three months. When the mother hears a chucking sound within the mound she claws it apart, and young alligators come wriggling out. They grow about 1 foot per year for the first six years of their childhood, and then growth becomes more gradual.

"There is no doubt that an alligator would as soon eat a man as anything else, but . . . he is cautious"

Some alligators live more than half a century and are 15 feet or more in length. They become jowly, with wide, saggy midriffs, and yellow teeth that hook over their lower jaws. Watching such a patriarch stretched immobile on a sandbar, one wonders if motion can still be possible for it, with those ridiculously stumpy legs twigging out of such a great gray mass. Yet if motivated, these old veterans can move—quickly, with motions a belly-dancer could envy.

There are other big animals in the swamp. Black bear inhabit most of the islands. Swampers used to hunt them with dogs, and perhaps here, in the Okefenokee, the bear had more of an even chance with their hunters than anywhere else in the country. The strong, tough-hided animals could crash through thickets impenetrable to man or dog alike. Bear would splash through sections of water leaving the hounds that pursued them baying with frustration at the edge of solid ground. Some legendary bear were so cunning at wading and lousing up scents that Swampers were convinced they could walk across water.

Most of the old Swampers would just as soon have stood up to a mad she-bear with a clasp-knife, or wrestled an alligator with his bare hands, as to come, gun or no gun, onto a pack of piney woods "rooters." The rooters were wild pigs thought to have been ranging through the swamp country since they escaped from Spanish explorers more than four centuries ago. Long enough for boars to develop 6-inch, daggerlike tusks and evolve bristles almost as tough as porcupine quills. Time enough for the red-eyed, furious animals to generate such a reputation for roguery that even today a mere mention of them will cause a knowing man to glance uneasily into the blackness beyond his campfire.

Lots of places, including the Okefenokee, have some razorbacks—hogs more recently gone wild—but as any Swamper will tell you, a razorback, compared to a piney woods rooter, is docile as a Jersey cow waiting to be milked.

All of which is not to say that those who venture out into the swamp in canoes or homemade, flat-bottom johnboats are running a good chance of being torn up by a boar rooter. Or stepping onto an alligator, being mauled by an angry bear, or attracting the strike of a cottonmouth moccasin. One's chances of falling afoul of one of these creatures is considerably less than that of being struck by lightning. Most people who venture into the swamp will be attacked by nothing more vicious than a mosquito or a deer fly. They have as good a chance of seeing an ivory-billed woodpecker, one of the world's truly rare birds, as stumbling onto a pack of hungry rooters. In the dark, the unseen, mysterious rummaging down by the boat is more likely a raccoon than a bear or an alligator.

It is just that in the swamp you are very much on your own; too many mistakes can be uncomfortable or even fatal. There is no place to phone for a map, a prayer, or an oxygen tent if in trouble. This gives an edge, a dimension, to all wilderness experience. One's pores open to fears and exaltations almost forgotten in our cocoons of steel, glass, concrete, controlled temperatures, and instant foods.

As befits the illusionary world of the Okefenokee—where forests thrust from stillwater, flowers are floating, and open runs turn the sky upside down—the origin and nature of the early swamp dwellers are obscure, the subjects of legend. The Seminole, last Indians to fish and hunt the region, spoke not only of an enchanted island but also of a race of giants who once lived there. A Spanish map, dated 1542, portrays the swamp area as ringed by forts. Yet who built them, or if they actually existed at all, remains as much of a mystery as what enemy they surrounded.

The early dwellers of the rockless swamp pushed up sand and soil to form huge mounds, burial sites where pottery and tools have been found along with bones. Some of the human remains have been quite large. When a 7-foot, 2-inch skeleton was unearthed in the 1920s, old legends were reconsidered.

In the first half of the sixteenth century, Spanish explorers floundered their way into the marshy fringes of Okefenokee country, ever gullible to Indian tales of gold and other riches. The strangers, with their great ships, horses, muskets, and other wonders, were taken for gods by many tribes. The Indians soon concluded that—deities or not—there was more misery than benefit to be derived from prolonged association with the fair-skinned *conquistadores,* and were only too happy to concoct stories that would excite them into charging off toward distant lands—the more distant the better.

Ponce de León sighted mainland Florida in 1513 and got as far north as the St. Marys River, a minor outlet of the Okefenokee. Although he was well aware of the West Indian legend of the Fountain of Youth, history indicates that he was far more interested in soft yellow metal than in clear magical water. Like any *conquistadore* worth his stirrups, he regarded eternal youth without wealth to be a prize of dubious value.

One-eyed Panfilo de Narvaez, a great shock of red hair under his helmet, landed at Tampa Bay in 1528. The gold, he was informed, as well as silver and pearls, was in the land of the Ocali—powerful warriors whose very shouts could fell a bird on the wing. The Narvaez expedition, banners whipping in the ocean breeze, started inland. After a long, difficult haul across sawgrass marshes and through jungle patches, Narvaez was greeted by the chief of the Ocali, who would shortly inform him that no, the rich kingdom, the fabled warriors, lay off to the north and west. And so the expedition, with an air of grim determination to it now, plodded toward what the Ocali had called the River of Reeds, where lazy currents glided over sandy ribs gleaming with gold—the waters we now call the Suwannee. This was the southern boundary of the kingdom of Apalacheen, whose opulence was even more lavish than described by the misguided coastal Indians.

There was, of course, no gold in the Suwannee, and Apalacheen seemed to recede like a damp mirage deeper into the swamplands. The Ocali guides had slipped away. Horses thrashed until immobile in dark, viscous mud. Soldiers reeled from fever and stragglers were filled with arrows from Indian ambushes deep in palmetto thickets, or in the gloom beneath blackgum and cypress groves. Now there was little talk of treasure; every man struggled to get back to the sea alive. Two-thirds of them made

it. In makeshift boats whose very nails had been forged from their spurs
and crossbows, sails from their shirts, they moved erratically westward
along the coast. Some died of thirst when water containers, made from
entire skins of horses' legs, became rotten and opened. Others perished in
storms.

Only four men ever reached Mexico again. It took them eight years.

The misfortunes of the Narvaez expedition, far from discouraging the
search for gilded cities, seemed if anything to stimulate it. Eleven years
after Narvaez retreated from the swamp country, Hernando de Soto arrived
at a place which the historian of his expedition was to describe as a "great
morass bordered by forests of huge and lofty trees with a dense underwood
of thorns and brambles and clambering vines, so interwoven and matted
together as to form a perfect barrier." De Soto may have breached the
barrier, and entered the Okefenokee, but if so he found nothing he considered of value, and continued on, trekking across the entire Deep South.

It is small wonder that the Spaniards became a bit giddy after walking
into the treasure houses of the Aztecs and the Incas almost right off the
bat, and assumed their luck was limitless; yet years of desperate search
would bring them little more than new lines on their maps. The luck of De
Soto ran out on a bank of a great river he discovered, the Mississippi, for
there he died of fever.

The tall, graceful Timucuas, "children of the sun," lived in the swamp
country at the time of the Narvaez expedition, and quite likely were among
those who drove arrows at the hapless party. Perhaps there was a prophetic
knowledge to their hostility, for within time Spaniards hunted them down
and brought captives back to the settlement of St. Augustine to "civilize"
them, which generally meant enslavement. A few apparently drifted back
to the Okefenokee, for a Spanish map of 1765 carries the annotation:

> Lagoon and Island of Ocone, in which there is a village of Indians of
> the Nation of Timuquantos, whose forebears were all Catholics. In the
> first years of the present century, when the British attacked St. Augus-
> tine, these Indians moved to the lagoon area where they have since
> lived without Catholic communion. All that is known of them is that
> they retain the Catholic faith, wearing large Rosaries around their
> necks.

Few of the Seminole, who all but eradicated the remaining Timucuas
in swamp country, took to wearing rosaries, and indeed, such was their
resistance to outside influences and pressures that some bands never sur-
rendered to the U.S. Army. After losing some 1500 men and expending
forty million dollars waging the Seminole Wars, the government prudently
let them be. Cattle were one of the few European introductions the Seminole could relate to. Bartering breed stock from the British, the Indians
eventually built up fine herds, which in turn was to cause envious white

settlers to grab the grazing lands on the edges of the swamp for themselves.

Back before the Civil War, Clyde Ross, an alligator trapper, was following an unfamiliar run in the northern Okefenokee that suddenly opened into a pond. It was high noon of a summer's day, a time when there seems to be as much moisture in the air as below one's boat, when sweat stings corners of the eyes, and things are hushed and bright as in a fever. The bleached cow skulls—perhaps a dozen of them, hanging head high from stubs on the looming blackgum and bay, some laid upon mangrove roots—were not what frightened him. It was more the feeling of having blundered into a ceremonial place, where, if caught, death would be violent and slow. He poled out quickly and kept moving until the pond was far behind.

The still pool was, indeed, a sacred place to the Seminole for many years. At an appropriate time, somehow a cow or steer would be driven through a mile or so of drowned landscape. At the pond, the animal's throat would be slit, and naked men then bathed in the mingling of blood and water; a ritual cleansing. The severed heads were placed on trees.

No. It was not healthy for a Swamper to witness such a ceremony. In the early days, about the only Seminole a white man saw close up (unless he was ducking an arrow) were the chaff—outcasts, drunks, lickspittles. It was presumably of such motleys that the British, one of seven countries who raised flags over Florida, attempted to form a small army at Pensacola in 1814. Of the Seminole drilling in the public square, a bystander was moved to write: "Such scenes of preposterous costuming, tripping over swords, and mad marching can hardly be imagined. The British might as well attempt to drill the alligators of the Florida lagoons."

But back in the lagoons of the Okefenokee, and in the forests beside the Suwannee, the Seminole were masters of a difficult environment. In the swamp, they could pole a boat straight into what appeared to be a solid wall of trees—and pass right through it. They knew which crushed berries dropped into a 'gator hole would stun fish and turtles, which herbs were good for what, how to track larger game with the quietness and persistence of wraiths.

As the thin soils in their Appalachian hollows began to wear out, many Scotch-English settlers in Tennessee and the Carolinas moved south or west, looking for level patches to fence and crop, grasslands for cattle, trapping and hunting country. The new people took land by force. The Seminole could understand this, as did most Indians displaced across our nation—they themselves had gained their lands at one time or another by warfare. What was novel, largely incomprehensible to the Seminole or any other Indian mind, was that the invaders could solemnly meet under truce, draw up a treaty—and then within a few months or years break it as though the words had had no more meaning than the clatter of two gossiping squaws.

The Seminole whose cattle cropped close to the swamp found their lands dwindling, their "wild" cattle run off to someone's log barn for butchering. Formerly they had only hunted, fished, and trapped in the wetlands; now they made semipermanent camps on some of the sandy islands. There was nowhere else to go. As settlers erected cabins on hummocks right within the swamp itself, some Indians remained friendly with them, trading and even advising them on the best ways to plant crops. Other Seminole, proud and still anointed with fresh blood and dark water, wondered if this were the way.

Typical of the pioneer Swampers of English stock was one ill-fated family named Wilde, who lived in the Okefenokee near Wilkinson Settlement. One evening when Mr. Wilde returned from gathering firewood and reported signs of Indians, his wife implored him to take the family to the collective safety of the settlement. Wilde, a brave or foolish man, refused. After dark, there were an uncommon number of bird calls close to the cabin.

At dawn the attack came, suddenly. The strongest and weakest died as quickly, parents shot and baby brained with a club. Three other children were killed, but four managed to escape into the swamp, where they hid until long after the Indians had left. Then they made their way to the safety of a neighbor's house.

Such Indian attacks grew more frequent, and retaliatory raids against the Indians met with little success. Then, in 1838, Gen. Charles Floyd marched into the Okefenokee with 250 dragoons. Chief Blue King of the Seminole (or Billy Bowlegs, as the whites called him) was shrewd and knew every trail and run in the swamp. Floyd, however, led his troops along Indian trails and over quaking bogs to the forested sandspit now called Floyd's Island, deep in the swamp. The Seminole had fled their encampment there, and the dragoons destroyed it.

This ended Indian attacks in Okefenokee country, for the Seminole moved south to the Everglades, where they would make a defiant and successful stand.

The Swampers who displaced the Seminole in the Okefenokee proved to be almost as insular and independent as the Indians. Few of them, for example, fought for the Confederacy; to them, everything beyond the edge of the swamp was foreign. Until fairly recent times, when the last Swampers died or moved out, much of their speech, folklore, and songs retained an Elizabethan character. Archaic words like *fixment, rookus, scoggin, betwixt, fitified,* and *blowzy* were commonly heard. Trapping for fox, otter and other pelts, as well as shooting alligators for hides, was the hard cash mainstay of the Swampers. For those who knew its ways, the wetlands were bountiful. On sandy islands like Chesser and Billy's, corn, beans, pumpkins, melons, and other crops could be grown. Wild swamp honey could be gathered, pecans crushed into oil. Any boy or man who wasn't able to bring in a brace of 'coons or squirrel had to be blind in one eye and mosquito-stung on the other. The fishing was (and still is) incredible. In 1925, from a swamp pond about ¼ mile long and some 30 feet wide, forty thousand fish were taken—mostly warmouth, catfish, jackfish, and largemouth bass.

Moonshining was one of the more respected callings in the swamp. A good craftsman with a copper kettle, coils, and a healthy stack of hardwood could distill 80 to 100 gallons a day. Green corn liquor, swamp style, demanded a robust constitution. Old moonshiners affirm that if an outsider, palate mollycoddled by too much weak store-bought whiskey, could somehow down a pint of swamp green within twenty minutes and then walk a hundred yards without the ground coming up to smack him in the face, he would be immunized against poisonous snake bites for five years.

The Swampers traveled through their watery domain in long shallow-draft *bateaux* which one of them described as having "just enough room for two men, dogs, guns, blankets, sweet potatoes, and a side of bacon." The boats were poled from the stern. Some Swampers carried spears for "striking"—skewering fish attracted to the light of pine-knot torches. One oldtimer kept a pole with a bayonet attached to it for jabbing at alligators that got after his dogs, which they apparently considered a tasty morsel. Meals were often cooked right on the *bateau*. A board was laid over one end, muck piled upon it, and a fire lighted on top of that.

While the Swampers were quite content and adapted to their wet wilderness, a wealthy Atlanta visionary, Capt. Harry Jackson, decided the region could be put to more profitable use. In 1889 his Suwannee Canal Company purchased the Okefenokee from the state of Georgia for 14½ cents per acre. His plan was to drain the swamp, creating farmlands and access to timber. At an immense cost, some 22 miles of canal were trenched out. Yet the swamp remained invincibly swamplike, and when Jackson died in 1893 the project was abandoned.

Dan Lee, a crusty settler living on Billy's Island with his wife and various of his fourteen children, viewed the canal project with a mingled skepticism and apprehension. Billy's Island, in the heart of the swamp, offered a man about as much solitude as could be found east of the Mississippi River, and Lee liked it that way.

Yet Billy's Island was not likely to be left alone for long—not with all those tall stands of cypress, and loggers just itching to let in some daylight. The Hebard Lumber Company purchased the Okefenokee in 1908. It soon had 35 miles of rail laid in over pilings, trees falling everywhere, and a town built on Billy's Island that boasted a population of six hundred, a school, movie house, commissary, "jug" (for refreshments rather than retainment), and the inevitable Baptist church. It was all too much for Dan Lee, who moved out to quieter corners; but later got homesick for the island and returned. Travel to the logging camp was by boat or train, although a doctor would occasionally make professional visits via a Model-T Ford from which the tires had been removed, enabling it to chug down the railroad track.

Occasionally a Swamper would reluctantly take a job at the sawmill, and one of them, so the story goes, used to carry a club when walking to work through the early morning mists as a protection against bear and "h'ants." One day a rattlesnake struck savagely at the club. The Swamper killed it and hung it over a gallberry bush, noting that the huge snake dangled for more than a yard on either side. He proceeded on his way. The club grew ever more swollen and heavy, filled as it was with the powerful venom.

By the time the Swamper arrived at the sawmill, he was dragging the biggest cypress log ever to come out of the Okefenokee. The lumber buyer had it cut into railroad ties, which he reckoned would line more than a mile of track. The Swamper anticipated good money, but during the night it rained on the ties, weakening the poison, so by morning they had shrunk to the size of toothpicks, and all he got was a dime.

By 1927 Hebard had axed down most of the best timber and ceased operations. The logging settlement later burned, and all that remains at the site today are the railroad embankment, some bricks and other rubble, and some wooden headboards in the Lee family burial plot.

The swamp was once again a wilderness. In 1937 most of it was set aside as a wildlife refuge. Thus it remains today.

2. Way Down Upon the Suwannee River

It is often said that Stephen Foster, one of America's most hummable composers, put the Suwannee River on the map. Which is appropriate, since Foster selected the name he made world famous in "Old Folks at Home" from a map, or more precisely an atlas, while residing hundreds of miles north of Old Dixie. During Foster's time, there were plantations scattered along the river for which slaves may have harbored sentimental affections; yet there were also remote colonies of runaway slaves, who, along with the Seminole to whom they paid tribute, would have cheerfully thrown up their old rifles and ventilated white interlopers.

Then, as now, much of the Suwannee ran through wild, uncultivated country.

The entire 250-mile length of the river, from where it gathers at the edge of the Okefenokee to its flow into the Gulf of Mexico, is scenic and navigable for small boats. It is the headwaters, however, the swamp, which offers a truly unique wilderness experience. Three recreation areas—Camp Cornelia, Stephen Foster State Park, and Okefenokee Swamp Park—feature exhibits and short guided tours, but until recently a trip into the interior meant a guide and leaving the swamp by sundown. The Bureau of Sports Fisheries and Wildlife, which administers the big swamp, has now established several marked canoe trails which penetrate remote areas that are off limits to power boats. Canoeists must camp at designated spots, usually open-plank platforms elevated above the marsh.

The first step in preparing for a canoe voyage through the swamp is to write the Okefenokee National Wildlife Refuge (Box 117, Waycross, Georgia) for information on which trails are open and how to apply for a permit. They're good people there, very helpful.

On all backcountry trips, compact, light foods have merit; and especially here, where you may inadvertently end up sleeping in your canoe. A pocket compass is essential. In places it will be needed to get from one trail marker to another, and it gives one a sense of security. The swamp, beautiful as it may be, is a miserable place to be lost in. Although mosquitoes are more numerous at the edge of the swamp than within it, and are relatively inactive while the sun is up, netting or a tent is highly recommended. June through September is considered the rainy season, although showers may occur throughout the year. Some sort of portable stove should be carried: campfires on wooden platforms make for restless sleep.

One of the more interesting swamp trips is from Camp Cornelia to Kingfisher Landing. Camp Cornelia, where there is a museum and a store with picnic and fishing items, is on the east side of the swamp, and can be reached by driving some 7 miles southwest of Folkston, Georgia, on State Highway 23. Currently, Camp Cornelia is the only Okefenokee access with canoe rentals.

One begins by paddling down the Suwannee Canal, the financial fiasco of almost a century ago. The channel is lined with low banks of mud and brush, much favored by fishermen with bamboo poles close in to the boat docks, and by sunning alligators farther out. At Mizell Prairie the canoe trail leaves the canal and winds off into the distance, a thread of water scarcely 3 feet wide surrounded by acres of floating greenery.

The trails are marked by small signboards thrusting out of the water,

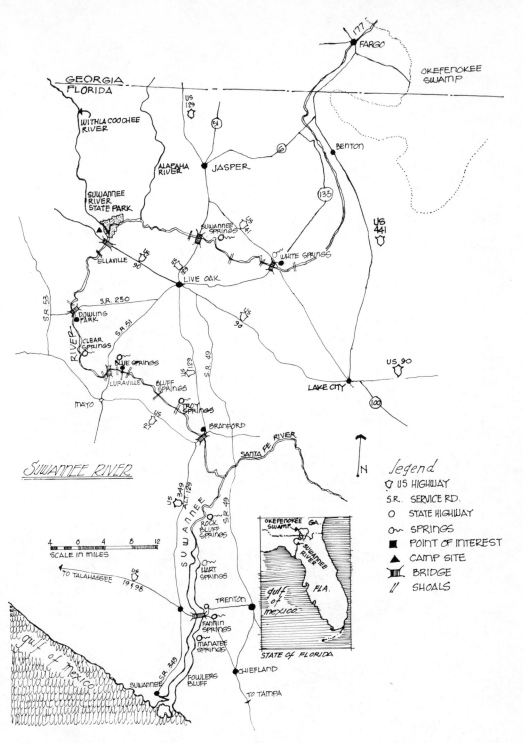

SUWANNEE RIVER

Legend

US HIGHWAY
S.R.   SERVICE RD.
STATE HIGHWAY
SPRINGS
POINT OF INTEREST
CAMP SITE
BRIDGE
SHOALS

SCALE IN MILES

STATE OF FLORIDA

spaced approximately a mile apart. Between these mileage markers, posts without signs have been placed for additional guidance.

The first day's run is a long one—some 14 miles—across Mizell Prairie and up the length of Chase Prairie. Numerous clumps of trees promise islands that do not exist. Close to Floyd's Island the trail twists its way into a swamp forest so dense it is like boating through a tunnel. For a stretch, rotted pilings parallel the passage, mementos of logging days. The island itself, sandy and wooded, offers one of the few dry-land campsites on the canoe trails.

There were burial mounds here, now dug over and scattered countless times, and it was a favored hideaway of the Seminole. Back in a clearing hulks an old building, probably once a logging company bunkhouse, with thick cobwebs like so much dusty frost over the windows and oddments of furniture inside. The water pump around back works if you prime it. Huck Finn would have liked Floyd's Island.

The second day's paddle is shorter, only 8 miles, but it can seem like 20. Much of the going is easy, across prairies where the trail seems but a crack in a vast green tabletop and stands of trees, lacking solid ground beneath them or substance behind them, are scattered with surrealistic abandon. Between Chase Prairie and Territory Prairie the route plunges into a thick forest. Tree branches and vines mingle overhead, diffusing the sunlight. The underlying peat has blistered up along much of this stretch, retarding one's progress with its soft, spongy resistance. Paddling gets one nowhere; the blade must be pushed hard against the peat—the canoe edges forward a couple of feet, then you reset the paddle. It is hard work. And no place to be if squeamish about ducking under spider webs and having occasional strands swing against your face as their proprietors drop into the boat.

But there are compensations. Here one feels within the fabric of the swamp itself. Above the massed heads of the cypress, maple, blackgum, and bay trees, clear and stormy skies alike seem remote. One watches the scuttle of a raccoon across a tangle of honeysuckle and chokeberry. A baby alligator, scarcely longer than a man's forearm, lies motionless on a mossy bank. Strange plants crowd against the narrow run.

The camping platform at Bluff Lake is out in more open country, close to a good fishing hole. Sleeping thus right *on* the swamp is quite an experience. A great place for listening. It is 8 miles from Bluff Lake to Kingfisher Landing, mostly prairie and easy going—lots of egrets and other

The tunnel-like canoe trail through the dense swamp forest near Floyd's Island

wildlife, some ponds for fishing: Durden, Flag, Duck and Elder lakes. Kingfisher Landing is located at the end of a short spur road veering off of U.S. Highway 1 some 9 miles north of Folkston.

Another fine three-day trip is from Kingfisher Landing to Stephen Foster State Park. The first camping platform is at Maul Hammock Lake, the second at Big Water Lake. Whereas the accent of the Camp Cornelia–Kingfisher Landing trip is upon prairies, here much of the trip is through forests. South of Big Water Lake the trail twists for miles beneath tall cypress draped with Spanish moss.

Most of the trails follow natural runs and old Indian routes. The Bureau of Sport Fisheries and Wildlife plans to mark 115 miles of trail, providing only the minimum development and maintenance necessary to keep the runs open and prevent people from becoming lost or polluting the swamp. Quality-control policy has stipulated that only one canoe party (maximum of twenty people) may use any trail at a given time. Therefore, it is wise to make early application for permits.

After crossing the swamp one can, of course, pass into the main channel of the Suwannee and strike out for the Gulf of Mexico 250 miles away. It is necessary to portage over the Suwannee River sill, a dike constructed in 1960 at the edge of the swamp to prevent excessive loss of water during drought periods. The Suwannee is a languid river, with an overall drop of less than ½ foot per mile, but scenically it is one of the finest canoe runs in the South.

Once free of the swamp, the coffee-colored waters, some 100 feet wide, glide between limestone cliffs and high sandy banks which are lined with thick stands of live oak and palmetto. During highwater, the river pushes far back into the forest. This first segment of the Suwannee— swamp to White Springs—is little frequented. Powerboats rarely venture above White Springs, since many a sheer pin and entire kicker have been shattered in the rapids close to town. During low-water, canoeists should look these shoals over before running them.

White Springs is the locale of the Stephen Foster Memorial; a carillon bell tower, a museum constructed like an antebellum mansion, hoop-skirted hostesses, and flowerbeds galore set amid well-trimmed expanses of grass. For those who, like myself, prefer less landscaped nostalgia, there are some fascinating old spa hotels nearby, abandoned and warping into decay. As well as springs, there are a number of "wet sinks" in the vicinity,

The languid Suwannee River offers one of the most scenic canoe runs in the South

deep holes which appear to be connected to the river by subterranean channels. A rise on the Suwannee fills them with water. A cave-in caused a barn and two trucks to tumble into one of these sinks a while back.

Beyond White Springs the river swings to the west. Its valley begins to broaden and with the addition of the Alapaha and Withlacoochee rivers its volume increases. Between White Springs and Branford there are a number of shoals (see map, Appendix IV), most of which are troublesome only during low water-levels. A little below the U.S. Highway 129 bridge there are rocks in the center of the stream that can be tricky. Just beyond Blue Springs is a potentially dangerous rapids. Pass on the southwest side of the island and hold close to the bank.

Branford was once quite a river town. Over the years between 1886 and 1914 some thirty paddlewheelers slapped water between Branford and Cedar Keys. Most measured about 200 feet long and had twin stacks and double decks. Cargo—cotton, peanuts, lumber, tobacco, naval supplies—was stored down below with piles of pine fuel, while passengers rode on the top deck. The 110-mile run was generally made in a single day.

Probably the most flamboyant character on the river was Capt. James Tucker, who once declared he would take his vessel, the *Madison,* all the way up to White Springs even if he lost his superstructure in the process. Wharf rats nudged each other knowingly: above Branford the river was narrow with overhanging trees in places, there were mudflats, shoals, and shallows, and a man might just as soon spur his horse into an uncovered well as try to navigate a steamboat up there. The *Madison* arrived with both her stacks and the pilot cabin gone, ripped away by tree limbs, the structure battered and paddles half in splinters—it looked as though it had come through a battle zone. Yet the irrepressible Captain Tucker strolled ashore, nodding affably to the gaping locals; he had made it.

The *Madison* actually did see battle later on, during the Civil War. Union forces had blockaded the mouth of the river. For several months Tucker hauled Confederate troops up and down the Suwannee either on attack or retreat from one skirmish after another. Finally, to avoid capture, he ran the *Madison* above Branford to Troy Springs. After pulling the plugs, he leaned against a bankside tree and watched a big part of his life slip beneath the dark slow current.

Below Branford the Santa Fe River joins the Suwannee. From the confluence to the Gulf the main channel broadens; it is 150 to 300 yards wide. The country becomes wilder. Still living back among the palms and sawgrass, wild orchids and magnolias, are descendants of the runaway Negroes who made up the 19th century colony of King Nero, a statuesque Ethiopian who took to chopping someone else's cotton as a cat takes to water.

As on the upper portions of the river, there are several springs—Rock

On the bank of the Suwannee near White Springs, Florida, an old home recalls plantation days

Bluff, Hart, Fannin, Manatee, pushing clear, cold flows into the river. Close to Old Town, across the river from Fannin Springs, the sternwheeler *City of Hawkinsville* sank in 1923, ending the riverboat era on the Suwannee. The fishing village of Suwannee, on an estuary close to the mouth, is a practical terminus for voyages down this fine river.

Guide Notes for the SUWANNEE RIVER

LOCATION—Begins in the Okefenokee Swamp of Georgia and flows through northwestern Florida to empty into the Gulf of Mexico.

LENGTH OF TRIP—The Suwannee is 250 miles long. A run of the entire river would take from 2 to 3 weeks in a canoe or kayak.

FAVORABLE SEASON—Winter months (mid-October to early March). The river can and is run at other times of the year, but the weather tends to be hot and muggy and the insects more voracious.

DEGREE OF DIFFICULTY—Gentle. Although there are several shoals on the upper Suwannee (above Branford), none of them should give a boater of moderate experience much trouble if reasonable caution is taken.

RECOMMENDED CRAFT—Canoe or kayak. Slow going for rafts.

ACCESS POINTS—One can put-in at the southern edge of the Okefenokee Swamp, reached by spur road northeast of Fargo, Georgia, on U.S. Highway 441. One can take-out (or put-in) at a number of places between the Okefenokee and the Gulf of Mexico.

CAMPING—Start looking for a campsite well before dark, as high banks and a lot of privately owned land make good sites few and far between. Good area to bring a hammock for sleeping. The wildest country, and hence the best camping, is between the Okefenokee Swamp and White Springs, and also between Branford and the Gulf. There is a developed campsite at Suwannee River State Park west of Live Oak. Boil water, or use Halazone tablets.

FISHING—Good. Bass, catfish, perch.

Okefenokee Swamp

The Okefenokee Swamp, headwaters of the Suwannee, offers 3- to 6-day canoeing adventures. The Department of the Interior maintains several lonely swamp "trails," along which some campsites are on islands, and others are wooden platforms elevated above the swamp. Best access points are at Kingfisher Landing and Suwannee Canal, a few miles northwest and southwest of Folkston, Georgia, respectively; and Stephen Foster State Park, north of Fargo, Georgia. Excellent fishing for bass, warmouth, jackfish, perch, and catfish.

CHAPTER SEVEN

River of Gold: The Yukon

1. Gold Rush Days

In several respects the Yukon is a river of ironies. It begins in the glaciers and snow pockets of the St. Elias Mountains, less than 15 miles from the Pacific Ocean, yet wanders for 2300 miles up through the Yukon Territory and across most of Alaska before emptying into the Bering Sea. For most of its length the great river is crossed by neither bridge nor ferry nor dam, yet in recent years there has been considerable legislative clamor to plug its flow with a mammoth hydroelectric project that would back up a reservoir forty times greater than Lake Mead, 10 percent larger than Lake Erie. Although any atlas will show a scattering of place names along the river, they are mostly ghost towns or small Eskimo and Indian villages—yet for a time the biggest western city north of Seattle and perhaps the gaudiest city anywhere sprawled upon its banks. Swarms of steamboats once plied the river: today one can drift for 100 miles and more without encountering another vessel of any sort, and ornate luxury packets warp on wooden skids back amid the willows.

Possibly the greatest irony was economic. Both the Russians, who began trapping along the lower river in the 1830s, and the Hudson's Bay Company, which established a fort on the upper river in 1848, held to an unswerving faith that the wealth of the northlands lay in beaver pelts. Archdeacon Robert McDonald casually commented to his friends at Fort Yukon in the 1860s that he had found a place where gold could be scooped up with a kitchen spoon. To Rev. Mr. McDonald it was no more than a geologic curiosity; his work was in translating prayerbooks for the

Crooked-Eye Indians. The tale stirred little excitement among the other inhabitants of the lonely outpost; their trapping afforded little time to chase a will-o'-the-wisp such as gold.

Alexander Baranov, who ruled what was known of Alaska from a bastion of Old World comfort at Sitka, was likewise unmoved by reports of the precious metal. Were such tales allowed to spread unchecked, who knew what hordes of penniless men would make their way into his fiefdom, squabbling over minerals worth a fraction of his fur trade, and begging supplies that had been shipped thousands of miles from Russia. It is reputed that he once had a man shot who babbled of a gold discovery while in his cups.

Yet the demand for beaver pelts was in a decline. The Hudson's Bay Company would soon withdraw from the Yukon drainage, over the Mackenzie Mountains. And Russia would sell Alaska to the United States for a pittance.

It would be gold, hundreds of millions of dollars' worth of gold from the Klondike and other diggings that for a few frenzied years would make the Yukon a thoroughfare for paddlewheelers and Dawson City the "Paris of the North."

For some two decades prior to the Klondike strike, prospectors had prowled the banks of the Yukon River, panning up side streams. In places they found color, and mining camps sprang up—log villages where pickle jars chinked with moss served as windows and the principal diversion was to sit around the glowing wood stoves of a saloon drinking forty-rod whiskey and devising tales of astonishing implausibility.

It was rough country, hundreds of miles from civilization and largely unexplored. In places, insect swarms were so thick as to plug up the nostrils of pack animals, suffocating them. During the long winter, temperatures ranged between −20 degrees and −70 degrees. At Circle City cold snaps were judged by bottles of quicksilver, whiskey, kerosene, and Perry Davis Painkiller set out in front of McQuesten's trading post. They froze in ascending order.

On an August afternoon of 1896, a frontiersman named George Carmack ambled into Bill McPhee's saloon at Forty-Mile. Carmack was something of a puzzle to the prospectors whose lives were hinged around the dream of finding a fortune in the frozen soils. Although Carmack panned a little now and then, he seemed to prefer hunting and salmon fishing with his Indian wife and her relatives.

Carmack downed two whiskeys neat, and then turned to the other men in the room.

"Boys, I've got some good news to tell you. There's a big strike up the river." He poured out a Winchester shell of gold onto some scales.

By dawn Forty-Mile was a ghost town. The Klondike rush had begun.

House at Forty-Mile, the settlement where George Carmack announced his discovery of gold on the Yukon

News of Carmack's strike swept down the Yukon Valley. Prospectors sitting by campfires on remote creeks or frying bacon in the log huts of scattered settlements left in a matter of hours for the Klondike hills. Most of the men who slogged into the expanding village of Dawson, nucleus for the goldfields, found the pickings rich. As fall chilled into winter, the miners set fires to burn their way through frozen muck to bedrock, where the gold rested. From ridges overlooking the creeks, countless flickering fires seemed like glowworms, while overhead Northern Lights rippled in banners. Many of the toiling men would soon be millionaires, but they lived in poverty, for supplies were at a premium. Salt was literally worth its weight in gold, and a small charred keg of bent nails salvaged from a fire was sold for $800. Eggs fetched $1 apiece; a bargain, for there were only two hens in Dawson. Numerous sled dogs were killed, as there was not enough food for them.

Gold could purchase little—but there was no lack of it. One miner's wife, when she needed some household change, simply broke apart frozen clods with a stick on her husband's dump, and picked out the nuggets.

Dawson was isolated from the world that first winter. To the west, the jumbled ice of the Yukon River wound 1700 miles to the Bering Sea; eastward lay hundreds of miles of unexplored forest and muskeg. South of the Yukon, steep and blizzard-lashed mountains rose in a great wall to cut off routes to the sea. But as spring thawed into summer, Dawson's long months of obscurity were numbered. In the crude shacks and lean-tos on the Klondike creeks, miners watched the level of gold rise in fruit jars and canvas bags, waiting for the ships that would take them to the outside world.

On a mid-July morning of 1897, the steamer *Portland* nudged up to Schwabacher's Dock in Seattle. Five thousand people jammed the waterfront, pressing for a glimpse of the Klondike miners aboard. Newsboys yelled their way through the mob: "Gold! Gold! Gold! *Portland* carrying a ton of solid gold!"

The pulse of America, dulled by the depression of the not-always-so-gay Nineties, suddenly quickened. Here, it seemed, was a place where nuggets could be picked up like pebbles, and the names Bonanza, Yukon, and Dawson were soon mouthed from Manhattan to the Golden Gate, were shouted in saloons and whispered in the back pews of churches. Men and women from all walks of life abruptly dropped whatever they were doing and headed for the Pacific coast, jump-off for the Klondike. Two thousand New Yorkers attempted to buy tickets to the goldfields within twenty-four hours after the news broke. The mayor of Seattle, attending a convention in San Francisco, immediately wired his resignation and set about buying a steamer for Yukon trade. Whaling in the Canadian Arctic ground to a halt as officers and crewmen deserted en masse, and a group of Chicago clairvoyants pooled to send a medium to dig where the spirits dictated. Within two months after graduation from medical school, half of California's fledgling doctors had departed for the goldfields.

The rush was on. Seattle, Tacoma, and Vancouver were swarming with stampeders, many of whom had arrived on transcontinental trains replete with "gold rush cars," where jars of nuggets, gold pans, maps of the Yukon, and other paraphernalia whetted their desires. Hotels were overflowing, and men slept in stables, washing at fire hydrants. Mounds of equipment and supplies lay upon the wharves. Animals from all over the country were driven onto Alaska-bound vessels, and streets near docks were a bedlam of grunts, barks, whinnies, and bleating. Not only were horses, mules, burros, and oxen sold as beasts of burden; but dogs, sheep, reindeer, and Washington elk. Most stampeders bought vast quantities of easily portable foods: evaporated eggs, onions, and split-pea soup, milk tablets, peanut meal, and pemmican. They purchased tons of hardware and staples like flour, beans, and sugar. Woolen blankets and heavy clothing passed over store counters faster than the mills could produce them.

Some, however, had less conservative ideas of what was a suitable outfit for the Klondike. A middle-aged spinster set out with a maid, cook, horse, parrot, three canaries, piano, two St. Bernard dogs, and a sealskin suit. One dashing gentleman outfitted himself for the rigors of the Far North with thirty-two pairs of moccasins, a case of pipes, a case of shoes, two Irish bull setters, a bull pup, and a lawn-tennis set.

Vessels of every description churned north from Seattle that summer and the following fall and winter, filled with gold-seekers, animals, and supplies. All were greatly overcrowded, many were scarcely seaworthy. There were converted ferryboats, coal barges, sloops, and scows; there was the former yacht of an Indian rajah, the steamer that had brought Livingstone's body back from Africa, and an ancient side-wheeler which for years had been stationary at the Seattle waterfront where it was used as a saloon and gambling hall.

Predictably, there were many mishaps on the ragged storm-lashed coast of British Columbia and Alaska. Some ships floundered because their captains were unfamiliar with northern waters, others piled onto rocks because their pilots could not see clearly over mounds of freight on the decks. One vessel, crammed with an illegal combination of passengers and dynamite, blew up between Juneau and Skagway at the northern end of the Inland Passage. Only a dog survived.

Many a cramped and ill-nourished argonaut, seeing the port of Skagway rise into view over the ice-shelled sides of his ship, felt a wild exhilaration and relief. Here was the gate to the promised goldfields; fortune was only a stone-fling away.

Few realized their ordeal had only begun.

Until William Moore built a mile-long wharf out into the deep water of Skagway Bay, most of the debarkations of the stampeders were like scenes out of Dante. Horses, pigs, and other animals were simply shoved overboard to sink or swim their way to shore. The stampeders' outfits were transported to the beach in skiffs, as well as the men who could afford to ride. The rest, like people fleeing a doomed ship, joined the terrified, noisy animals in the chill water, struggling toward shore.

The action on the tidal flats was almost as macabre. Men swore and fought amid supplies stacked there, while 30-foot tides ebbed and swirled in. When dropped by the ship crews, often the supplies were hopelessly mixed, the labels torn off. Among them moved con men, cutthroats, and prostitutes, as well as luckless stampeders who had lost their outfits on the trail, returning to Skagway now desperate.

Before long, Skagway was a city of ten thousand, most of it in the

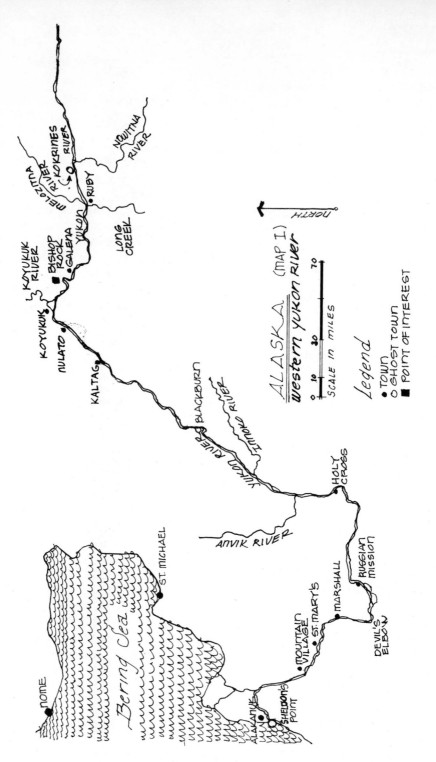

ALASKA (MAP I)
Western Yukon River

NORTH

SCALE IN MILES
0   10   30   70

Legend
• TOWN
○ GHOST TOWN
■ POINT OF INTEREST

Bering Sea

Nome

St. Michael

Anvik River

Holy Cross

Russian Mission

Marshall

St. Mary's

Mountain Village

Sheldon's Point

Alakanuk

Devil's Elbow

Yukon River Blackburn

Innoko River

Kaltag

Nulato

Koyukuk

Koyukuk River

Bishop Rock

Galena

Yukon

Long Creek

Ruby

Kokrines River

Melozitna River

Nowitna River

172

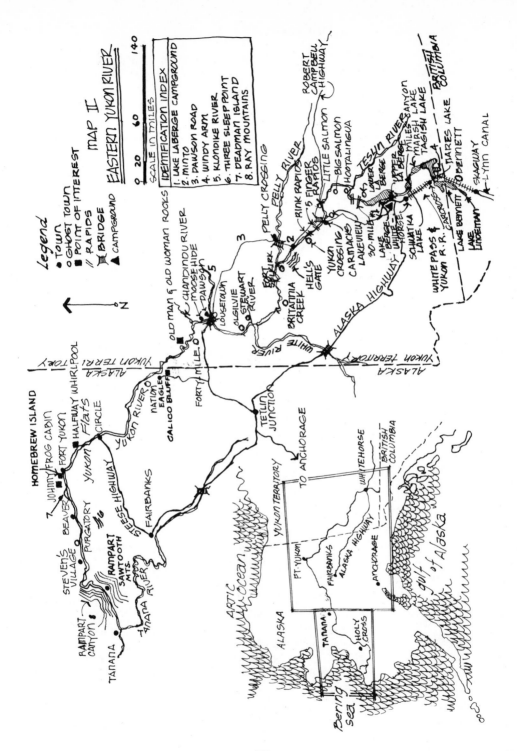

Legend

- Town
- Ghost Town
- Point of Interest
- Rapids
- Bridge
- Campground

MAP II

EASTERN YUKON RIVER

SCALE IN MILES

0   20   60   140

IDENTIFICATION INDEX

1. Lake Laberge Campground
2. Minto
3. Dawson Road
4. Windy Arm
5. Klondike River
6. Three Sleep Point
7. Deadman Island
8. Ray Mountains

173

process of passing through to the goldfields. The set-up was perfect for a shrewd con man with a flair for organization. Jefferson ("Soapy") Smith was just such a person.

Smith, who affected the manner of a southern planter, perfected his nefarious talents in the gold camp of Creede, Colorado. He came to Skagway accompanied by men like "Reverend" Charles Bowers, who often masqueraded as a minister and was known among the initiates as a "gripman," or one who has mastered the secret handshakes and signs of fraternal organizations to gain the confidence of potential victims. Smith and his cohorts planned to take over Skagway.

It fell into their hands like overripe fruit.

Soon Smith's men were everywhere, in a bewildering variety of roles. Some toiled up the trail as stampeders, luring their unsuspecting companions into rigged gambling tents. If this failed, a rock to the head or a bullet on a lonely stretch would suffice. Fake information bureaus were set up to inveigle newcomers into Smith's web; members of the gang posed as gold buyers to fleece those returning from the Klondike. It is estimated that Smith's gang ran to two or three hundred men at its peak, including such strong-arm types as Yeah Mow Hopkins, whose name means wildcat in Chinese, and who had been a bodyguard during San Francisco's tong wars, and Big Ed Burns, who relished chewing up whole cigars.

Smith passed himself off as a pillar of respectability. On the surface, he was merely the proprietor of an oyster house. He befriended widows, contributed to church funds, and, as numbers of abandoned dogs began to haunt the town, started an "Adopt-a-Dog" compaign. He strictly forbade his gang to prey on citizens of the town, only on those who were passing through. Often enough, when a stampeder who had been cheated or robbed on the trail returned to Skagway destitute, it was Jefferson Smith who benevolently paid his passage home. These things could hardly escape the notice of the citizenry, for the newspaper was constantly extolling his virtues. Small wonder: the editor was also in Smith's employ.

Of course, the onetime Colorado cardsharp was unable to bamboozle everyone. A vigilante committee was formed for the express purpose of driving out the many-tentacled gang. Smith retaliated by forming a vigilante committee of his own, whose rallying cry was protection of the established businesses and citizens against ferment caused by "outsiders." He was strongly supported, which is not surprising when one considers that in Skagway at that time there were seventy saloons, which, if not all on Smith's payroll, were at least in sympathy with his activities. The decent citizens were further confused by Smith's pledge to drive out the undesirables that plagued the town. The con man's propaganda was too skillful, and the first vigilante committee was forced to back down for lack of support.

Eventually, however, Jefferson ("Soapy") Smith came to his end in the grand western manner. He and Frank Reid, unflinching man of law and order, shot it out on the Skagway wharf. When the smoke cleared Smith was dead and Reid dying.

As Reid, slowly expiring, was borne away on a stretcher, he uttered a phrase that has left its echo in almost every horse opera ever made: "He may have got me, boys, but by God I got him first." With their leader vanquished, Smith's gang wavered, then broke. Skagway was again relatively safe. But while the Colorado con man had been in power, Skagway was as much a peril for the stampeder as the icy passes and savage rapids on the trail ahead.

Behind Skagway, the White Pass Trail wound up and over the mountains to lakes Linderman and Bennett, headwaters of the Yukon River. Blizzard-lashed in winter, incessant rains made it a nightmare of slippery mud in summer. Men and packhorses toiled up it in a plodding column of misery.

Of five thousand men who attempted it in the fall of 1897, few made their goal—Lake Bennett—before freeze-up. Of three thousand packhorses that labored up the trail, almost none survived.

Lake Bennett, site of the town of Bennett, where over 10,000 souls spent the winter and built boats in 1897–98

As Jack London was to write:

The horses died like mosquitoes in the first frost and from Skagway to Bennett they rotted in heaps. They died at the rocks; they were poisoned at the summit, and they starved at the lakes; they fell off the trail, what there was of it. . . . men shot them, worked them to death and when they were gone, went back to the beach and bought more. (From *Klondike,* Pierre Burton, Toronto: McClelland & Stewart, 1962.)

At the onset of the stampede, a score of cities and transportation companies began clamoring for gold rush trade; advertising that the only sensible route was the one for whom they were the springboard or vehicle.

For those who could afford it, the all-water route seemed to be the most practical. To be sure, it was the long way around—3000 miles on the ocean rim from Seattle to St. Michael on the Bering Sea, then 1700 miles upriver to Dawson—but competitive steamship lines made it sound like a pleasure cruise. As their ships steamed gaily away from the Seattle docks in the summer and fall of 1897, few realized the all-water route would be made a lie by the Arctic winter; that they would spend the following Christmas far from the goldfields, half starved and huddled like animals in makeshift shelters on banks of the frozen Yukon River.

Merchants of Vancouver lauded the Ashcroft Trail, which wound for 1000 miles through the interior of British Columbia. Although fifteen hundred men and twice as many horses attempted this route, only a battered remnant reached their goal. All along the trail were the signs of defeat: rotting trunks and rusted tools that had been flung aside, dead horses under swarms of mosquitoes, the graves of men who had hanged themselves rather than return without gold.

Edmonton advertised itself as "the back door to the Klondike," and boasted several good trails. In point of fact there were no real trails at all, and the Klondike routes from Edmonton ranged from a torturous 1700-mile-long trek by way of the Peace River, to a 2500-mile circuit which followed the Mackenzie River to the mountain divides, near the Arctic circle.

Lured by pamphlets and articles, stampeders poured into Edmonton equipped with all manner of contrivances designed to whisk them to the Klondike. There was a steam sleigh christened the *I Will,* consisting of a locomotive and freight cars, powered by a great spiked drum. Its owners assured the awed townspeople that it would have no trouble traversing rocky canyons, snowfields, mudflats, or any other obstacles nature might throw in the way of such an indomitable machine. On departure day, smoke billowing from its stack and drum spinning, the *I Will* belied its name by digging a deep trench in the frozen mud and not budging forward a single foot.

There was the "duck," a vehicle made of wine barrels topped by a sleeping platform. This device lumbered for about 4 miles before the hoops came off and it collapsed. Other gaudy failures included a "boat-sled," built for the rigors of both water and ice, and a sort of gigantic lawn mower husked with sheet steel.

The stampeders themselves were often as colorful as their contrivances. There was a party of English aristocrats, replete with servants and grooms, headed by Lord Avonmore, soon nicknamed Lord "Have-one-more." Supplies for the Avonmore party included tinned turkey, a hundred pounds of toilet tissue, and seventy-five cases of vintage champagne. Perhaps predictably, this exquisite company faltered long before reaching the Promised Land.

Of all the routes used in attempts to reach the gold country, none was more sinister than across the Malispina Glacier. Sprawling across an area of southwestern Alaska larger than the state of Rhode Island, it is a maze of crevasses and blinding glare. Behind it, the ragged peaks that give it birth rear 4 miles into the sky.

A party of nineteen New Yorkers started across this frozen waste in the spring of 1898, undaunted by the fact that all their supplies save meat and flour had been ruined by saltwater.

None reached his goal.

Almost a year later, seven survivors stumbled back to the coast where they had started from. There they were found by a revenue cutter—three were dead in their sleeping bags and two others completely blind from the incessant dazzle of the ice.

And thus on a score of rapids-torn rivers, the slopes of impossible mountains, and in the depths of endless forests, men and women toiled and cried out, died, dreamed, and struggled on.

To the gold-fevered men planning their dash to fortune, no path seemed more forbidding than Chilkoot Pass. So steep no animals could get over it, avalanches thundered down onto the path from above and the wind was like a devil's rake across bare slopes.

By a stroke of irony, it was through this inhospitable notch that most of the men who finally reached the Klondike were to pass.

A few miles northwest of Skagway, the town of Dyea sprang up at the end of a fjordlike inlet. This was the beginning of the Chilkoot Trail. There was an air of grim fantasy about the trail as it snaked upward; the straining men and women, the shell game tents, sheep and goats packed like mules, a group of Maoris from New Zealand camped in wattle huts, a middle-aged woman towing a glowing stove on a sled, stopping often to warm her hands or cook a meal . . .

The final pitch before the summit of the pass was the hardest. One man claimed it was like "scaling the wall of a house." Each stampeder had to carry a ton of supplies up this slippery, 1000-foot barrier, for the red-coated Mounties guarding the summit would not allow anyone into Canada they felt would not be able to provide for himself in the harsh land ahead. Most packed up 50 pounds at a time, a back-breaking six-hour struggle. Once at the summit, they deposited their loads, and then, with laughter and a sense of joy that was rare on the gold trail, took a fast slide to the bottom on their backsides. As the frenzied days progressed, steps were chopped in the ice.

Slowly an unbroken chain of stampeders moved up to the notch: from the beetling crags above they seemed a line of ants ascending a mound of sugar.

If a man had money enough, he could hire a packer, usually a stolid Indian who thought nothing of shouldering a 100-pound pack for the ascent. Among the packers, feats of strength became legendary. One man made the summit with a 350-pound barrel on his back. Anderson, a Swede, challenged a Siwash Indian named Jumbo to a contest. Each staggered to the summit bearing 300 pounds, and returned to the base in a photo finish. Anderson calmly hoisted a second 300-pound load upon his massive shoulders, at which Jumbo gave up in dismay.

Up they trudged like pilgrims doing penance, bearing illegal whiskey concealed in false-bottomed boxes and bales of hay; carrying dismantled pianos, live chickens, silk for the dance-hall girls, bacon, and flour. Over the mountains that winter a man and his wife moved two small steamboats in bits and pieces on their backs.

On they came, driven by a lust for gold; a prizefighter, a bagpiper blowing Scottish airs, a gnarled and proud German lady in full-length dress with a lace apron, a man heaving himself forward on crutches. . . .

At Lake Bennett, end of the mountain trails and headwaters of the Yukon River, the largest tent city in the world was growing by leaps and bounds. Briefly, it would have over ten thousand population.

In tents men paid to bathe and gamble; under canvas they ate, slept, worshiped, and dallied with dance-hall girls. As winter passed into spring, snow loosened its grip on the peaks, crashing into the valleys below. Water splashed greedily, hungrily, over and under the snow, as if intoxicated with gravity and the sun. The pulse of men, too, was quickened with the tilt of the earth.

All along the shore the rasp of whipsawing came from raised platforms where green logs were cut into lumber. Boats of every imaginable design were being thrown together on the beaches, and men frequently tested the lake ice with their boots, speculating and wagering on when the waters would be clear for travel.

On May 29, 1898, ice began to grind out of Lake Bennett. Within 48 hours after the first ungainly craft had nosed into the slushy water, 7124 vessels had entered a wild race to the Klondike goldfields. There were scows and trim canoes, rafts of hastily lashed logs, outriggers and kayaks. In them, along with the stampeders, were goats, hogs, sheep, horses, dogs, and haystacks. One man balanced on a single log, using his coat for a sail; two women on another craft had sewn their undergarments together to catch the wind.

Bobbing across the deep blue waters of Lake Bennett, the bizarre fleet might have been engaging in a sportive regatta. Faces blackened with charcoal to prevent sunburn, stampeders bantered with each other from boat to boat or played concertinas, Jew's harps, and mouth organs. Others were intent, silent, eyes riveted upon the horizon as if they could already make out outcroppings of gold there.

It was a race in which many of the participants had staked all their resources, and indeed, their very lives, for a chance to enter.

On they swept, through the narrow channel that separates Lake Bennett from Nares Lake, called Caribou Crossing for the great herd, as much as 1 mile wide and 5 miles long, that swam this gap on their annual migrations; through Windy Arm, where sudden squalls came howling down from icy crags; into Marsh Lake, rimmed by thick, dank forests and willow bars.

The Yukon proper slips out of the lower end of Marsh Lake hesitantly, as if undecided whether to bunch into a single channel or spread out into another shallow lake. Swift stretches walled by cutbanks alternate with sluggish, swampy channels that meander in a maze of thickets and mud. Here, in early summer, there is no real night, only a few hours of deep twilight. Swarms of mosquitoes and black flies jiggle over pools of still water, and tatters of mist drift across spongy ground. One often hears the lonely cries of a loon.

Rather suddenly, the marshes give way to higher ground, river channels come together, quicken, then plunge into the cleft of Miles Canyon. The river is squeezed into a third of its former size by sheer cliffs that in places rise 100 feet from the water. Great whirlpools spin out from dark, protruding columns of basalt. Huge boils erupt in midstream.

The first boats of the argonauts' strange armada swept down Marsh Lake and entered the river, their occupants jubilant at being in the forefront. They reefed their sails and drifted down slow meanders that bristled with snags, boisterously waving broad-brimmed hats at unfortunates who had picked the wrong channel and were now sludging knee-deep in gumbo, towing their boats into better water.

The stampeders had heard of the perils of Miles Canyon; that the water was so swift and volume so great that a 4-foot hogback was pushed up in midstream, of the two Swedes who three years before had been accidentally swept into the gorge and were spun dizzily for five hours in an immense whirlpool before breaking free—that those who successfully navigated the canyon would then face the rocky chutes of Squaw and Whitehorse rapids. But most stampeders were confident, excited to the edge of mania, and probably would have walked barefooted through a forest fire to be first at the goldfields.

The gorge was announced by a distant rumble of water, then a strip of red calico hanging from a bank, and a board upon which had been scrawled a single misspelled word—CANNON. Few paused to reconnoiter even though for many of them, prior to their present adventure, knowledge of water had been largely limited to that contained within a glass. Typical of the prevailing attitude was that of a Norwegian who drifted toward the maw of the gorge on a bateau, waved cheerfully at the handful of beached, anxious souls at the entrance, and disappeared downriver squeezing out a lively tune from a concertina. He was soon swamped by a large wave. At that, he was luckier than some. In the first days ten men were drowned and one hundred and fifty boats wrecked.

Now men began to hesitate as word filtered back. Boats were jammed against each other above the canyon, and some stampeders began erecting tents, planning to pack their gear around; others milled aimlessly, eyeing the swift water with uncertainty. Two partners disagreed violently as to what should be done, and each decided to go his separate way. After carefully dividing up their outfit, they then sawed their boat in two.

Downstream, things were even more chaotic. Wherever there was a toehold—shelf of rock or beach—stampeders attempted makeshift repairs on battered boats, and spread out what gear they could salvage to dry in the sun. Others, whose boats had been smashed to kindling, and whose entire outfits were now at the bottom of the river, cursed, wept, clutched the coatsleeves of strangers to explain their disasters, or sat quietly staring at the water in a daze.

As was so frequently the case during the Klondike era, order was restored by the Northwest Mounted Police. Superintendent Sam Steele, tall, affable, and incorruptible—prototype of fictional Mounties—arrived on the scene and, as the stampeders crowded around him, described how things would henceforth be done:

> There are many of your countrymen who have said that the Mounted Police make the laws as they go along, and I am going to do so now, for your own good. Therefore the directions that I give shall be carried out strictly, and they are these: Corporal Dixon, who thoroughly understands this work, will be in charge here and be responsible to me for the proper management of the passage of the canyon and the rapids. No women or children will be taken in the boats; if they are strong enough to come to the Klondike, they can walk the five miles of grassy bank to the foot of the White Horse, and there is no danger for them

there. No boat will be permitted to go through the canyon until the corporal is satisfied that it has sufficient freeboard to enable it to ride the waves in safety. No boat will be allowed to pass with human beings in it unless it is steered by competent men, and of that the corporal will be the judge. (From *Klondike,* Pierre Burton, Toronto: McClelland & Stewart, 1962.)

Steele put teeth into his decree by declaring a $500 fine for anyone who broke the rules. Few did. Knowledgeable whitewater pilots began guiding well-constructed boats through the canyon and the rapids. Inadequate vessels—ranging from a brace of lashed logs to unwieldy, ornate boats that appeared to have been conceived during a nautical opium dream—were emphatically discouraged from passing into Miles Canyon. Few boats floundered in the wake of Sam Steele's proclamation.

Those thwarted from running the fast water soon had another alternative. A tramway, whose crude but serviceable rails were merely poles spliced end to end, was constructed around the rough water. For 5 cents per pound a stampeder could pile his equipment and boat (if it were a small one) onto a miniature flatcar which would be pulled by a horse to the bottom of White Horse Rapids.

Below the rapids the river calmed, gliding through hills where swallows' nests clung to high clay banks like honeycombs. Hundreds of the small birds wheeled and fluttered above drifting boats. Beyond lay Lake Laberge, where a young wanderer named Robert Service would later cremate Sam McGee in verse, which eventually was to make him wealthier than almost any of the men who moiled for gold.

Sails again stretched in mountain breezes, as the stampeders maneuvered down the length of Lake Laberge, dodging great chunks of drift ice. Then once again onto the river—blue, chill water winding between poplar-covered hills. In the meadows, wildflowers were pushing up through new grass: forget-me-nots, shooting stars, magenta fireweed, lupins, and bluebells; while bear, gaunt from hibernation, stuffed themselves with raspberries, blueberries, and cranberries. The river runners, their homemade vessels burdened with hundreds of pounds of provisions and tools, had little time to enjoy the scenery, for this was the fastest stretch of water on the Yukon. The Thirty-Mile, as it was called, was soon a boneyard of wrecked boats. On July 8 the remains of twenty wrecks were counted on a single rock.

As in Miles Canyon, partners sometimes argued bitterly as to whose error had caused disaster. Two such men, whose skiff had smashed into a hump of granite in midchannel of the Thirty-Mile, vented frustration by throwing wild haymakers at each other, oblivious to the plunging water around them.

Yet for every boat that caught upon a rock or was swamped, a dozen

Lake Laberge, of Sam McGee fame

more lunged through the fast water without mishap. On every stretch of the river from Lake Bennett to the mouth of the Pelly River, there were now drifting boats. Hundreds of campfires flared in the night, and ragged Stick Indians wandered from bivouac to bivouac, offering to swap dried salmon for whatever they could get.

Captain Goddard, the man who with his wife had packed two steamboats over Chilkoot Pass, had successfully plowed through Miles Canyon, and Squaw and White Horse rapids in one of them, and was now working his way downstream. Aboard were a pair of comely sisters, the Oakleys, who were soon to enthrall the Klondike miners with duets of songs such as "Break the News to Mother" and "A Bird in a Gilded Cage."

Most of the wild assortment of drifting vessels carried men intent upon the goldfields, and their outfits reflected this: flour, beans, candles, bacon, dried fruit and vegetables, coffee, gold pans, tools, clothing, cooking utensils, and tents. Other canoes, skiffs, barges, and scows were piloted by men who had shrewdly packed merchandise over Chilkoot Pass, hoping to sell to those who had already struck it rich. One man's cargo featured a crate of live chickens; another's a milk cow. There was a youth with a stack of outdated papers, a man with fifteen hundred pairs of boots, another with a load of feathery women's hats; yet another whose scow was literally crawling with kittens. One barge bore a huge banner: "Happy Hooligans." It carried forty dance-hall girls, numerous gamblers, and others of the sporting element.

On the Teslin River, which flows into the Yukon below the Thirty-Mile, there were also boats carrying goldseekers. These were the men and women who had managed to plod the length of the Ashcroft Trail—a 1000-mile route which led through the interior of British Columbia. An estimated fifteen hundred people with three thousand horses had optimistically set out on the trail early that spring; few even came close to their goal. Clouds of blood-feeding insects had weakened their pack animals and caused some to go berserk; incessant rains turned much of the path into a continuous bog in which horses floundered belly deep; there were steep ridges of loose rock and immense forests so dense that sunlight only touched the ground in pale, scattered patches; and mountain torrents swept horses, dogs, and stampeders away as if they had been chips of wood.

Below its confluence with the Teslin River, the Yukon broadens out and pushes to the northwest with a strong, steady current. The fore-running stampeders found the river full of ice floes, many of which had been brought down by the Teslin. Some of the more fragile boats had to be constantly maneuvered back and forth to avoid being crushed by the ice. Four men, tiring of the struggle, dragged their canoe onto a substantial chunk of floating ice, relaxed and lit their pipes, and then watched with considerable satisfaction as the current pushed them ahead of their hard-paddling neighbors.

After the upsets at Miles Canyon, White Horse Rapids, and the Thirty-Mile, the stampeders were prepared for a rough go at Five Finger Rapids. Beyond that, it was felt, an easy float of a day or two would bring them to Dawson and the goldfields. They were wrong on both counts.

At Five Finger, conglomerate plugs rise from the water like giant stepping stones, forcing the river into five swift, narrow channels. Here the ubiquitous Mounties had set up camp. They politely pointed out that only the extreme right-hand channel was navigable, instructed the argonauts on how to approach it, and fished out those who had the misfortune of capsizing. Thus guided, few of the stampeders had trouble with Five Finger Rapids or with Rink Rapids a short distance below.

The elation of having conquered the final obstacles quickly subsided downstream at the mouth of the Pelly River, where grinding slabs of ice barricaded the Yukon from shore to shore. Men paced the banks, spat tobacco juice at the malevolent ice, and anxiously looked upriver to see who was catching up. Tempers began to fray. So many partners began to have second thoughts about their associations that an island just above the Pelly became known as Split-up Island. A man from Worcester, Massachusetts, was elected mayor, and his principal duties were to adjudicate arguments. As a badge of office he sewed a heart of red oilcloth onto the seat of his trousers.

But even as men paced and swore, snow-melt waters of a thousand rushing tributaries were pushing at the ice, pulling it from underneath. Soon, with sharp cracks and a muffled roar, the ice jam fragmented and was spun away by a deep, swift current. The stampeders followed, past the old fur trading post of Fort Selkirk on its high, grassy bank; past the mouth of the silt-laden White River, which discharges a tawny flow that for miles runs side by side with the green of the Yukon before mixing; past the mining camp of Stewart River, where the river becomes still broader and there are numerous islands and sloughs where a boat can be lost for hours or days.

And finally, where the Klondike River tumbles its blue waters into the Yukon, the stampeders saw the place that had obsessed them, awake and in dreams; the goal toward which they had struggled for months while suffering incredible hardships. On a marshy flat beside the river were countless tents, lean-tos, cabins, and false-fronts: this was Dawson, the city of gold.

The first arrivals were greeted by hundreds of excited men and women who crowded at water's edge. During the previous winter stocks of provisions had dropped so low that people had been forced to flee the Klondike in droves or face starvation, and many a miner whose cabin contained a fortune in gold dust had nourished himself for months upon an unvaried diet of salt pork and beans, with resultant scurvy. The first boat to beach with eggs aboard was mobbed. Its occupant, a Seattle merchant, sold his entire load of two hundred dozen at $18 a dozen in less than an hour. Within a week so many competitors had arrived on the scene that the price fell to $3 a dozen, yet the man with the crate of live chickens created quite a stir, and the first egg his hens laid in Dawson went for $5. Women's hats, newspapers, and rubber boots were all snatched up by eager buyers. The man with a scowload of kittens created a sensation among lonely miners and dance-hall girls, and his unusual cargo sold briskly at an ounce of gold per animal.

A small steamer, the *May West,* was the first arrival from downriver, where it had been locked in the ice all winter. A throng of some five thousand people were on hand to welcome the boat.

"Has she whiskey aboard?" someone bellowed from shore.

She had, some sixteen barrels of it, and the news provoked prolonged cheering as rifle bullets were discharged gleefully at the sky.

Few of the stampeders found much gold. The good claims had already been staked, and there was scarcely a place anywhere in the Klondike hills that had not been probed with shovel, pick, and gold pan. Some immediately booked passage downriver for home; others stayed on, taking whatever jobs they could get, mining, cutting wood, building cabins and stores. Many of the argonauts just wandered about the boardwalks of Dawson, mesmerized by the carnival atmosphere.

The sandbar that stretched between the river and the town was like a vast Oriental bazaar, with the smells of cooking food drifting between tents where men ballyhooed the virtues of their goods. One could buy a prehistoric mammoth tusk from a miner, or moose hides from an Indian. There were tents where dentists softly malleted gold into cavities, tents where lawyers expostulated with vigor, and tents where fortune-tellers gazed earnestly into open palms. Everywhere there were pathetic 1-ton mounds of equipment that stampeders had packed over Chilkoot Pass, and floated down the Yukon. Now they were for sale at any price. The vendors needed money to book passage home.

Steamboats were now arriving almost daily from downriver, disgorging passengers and unloading an endless stream of whimseys for the Kings

One of the many
abandoned steamers
that once plied
the Yukon River

of the Klondike—opera glasses, pink lemonade, ostrich feathers, and paté de foie gras which would later be served by candlelight in uptown eateries where string quartets played chamber music. Nothing was too good for the men who only a few months before had watched their legs blacken with scurvy as they pulled nuggets out of frozen gravel with their fingernails.

One diminutive dance-hall girl offered her services as paramour and housekeeper, and got the price she asked—her weight in gold.

It was a never-never land, where birds, dyed every color of the rainbow, flapped on false-fronts, a transformation reportedly perpetrated by the volunteer fire department. Gold was everywhere—the mainspring. It flowed into town in tobacco cans and moose-hide pouches; was poured onto scales in saloons where bartenders sometimes put treacle on their mustaches to pick up a little dust for themselves.

Every third door in Dawson's business district opened into a saloon. Here the fiddles constantly sawed, dance-hall girls in satin gowns were whirled about the floor by men in boots caked with mud from their diggings, and the champagne corks popped by way of celebration. A sport treated the house to champagne in the Monte Carlo one night: his final bill was $1,700. Another filled a bathtub with champagne for a dance-hall thrush to bathe in. He was not, as he had hoped, allowed to scrub her back. Diamond-toothed Gertie danced in the saloons of Dawson, as did Nellie the Pig, so named because she once bit off the ear of a bartender who offended her.

And in the saloons, the cafés, drifting through muddy streets, were as strangely a mixed bag of people as have ever been gathered anywhere—let alone a thousand miles from the nearest outpost of civilization. There were men and women from more than a dozen countries—farmers, politicos, Oxford dons, priests, migrant fruit pickers, poets, prostitutes, outlaws, and clairvoyants. Calamity Jane and Buckskin Frank Leslie, once the deadliest shot in Tombstone, were there, fading into historical obscurity; as were Alexander Pantages, Tex Rickard, Sid Grauman, and Jack London, who were beginning careers that would bring them fame and fortune.

The stampeders watched Silent Sam Bonnifield lay down four kings in a poker game one evening—and calmly rake in a pot of $150,000. They gaped at a saloon show where a man mounted a scaffold, hands tied, as a noose was placed around his neck. The platform was then shoved out from under him and he dropped into space. As his face purpled, a curtain was drawn. Just to what degree this was staged was never known, for a different "victim" was used every night.

By 1900 Dawson was a substantial place, where women wore Paris fashions and encouraged their children in piano lessons. Most of the productive claims had been bought up by corporations who replaced pick-and-shovel miners with steampipes, large water flumes, and gold dredges.

A street scene in Dawson today

Some of the thirty thousand people who had scaled Chilkoot Pass and floated the Yukon in 1898 were still there, men mostly drawing a salary of some sort and trimming their beards before arriving at the office, women nursing infants born in this distant place where bright fences of color undulated at noon of winter nights, and the low summer sun washed over midnight gardens.

But most had left. After a couple of days, weeks, months, years, they had gone on to other places, where rock or river sands had folded over gold; where paystreaks were waiting to be discovered.

And many simply went back to the places from which they had come. As losers—with no gold. But as they went back hundreds of miles to sling corn seed into dark Kansas furrows or splint broken arms in Baltimore, or portray Hamlet for road companies—they carried with them a knowledge that their will power had not broken on the snow-packed trails or the rapids of the river. They had not only endured, but prevailed.

The Klondike gold rush was over.

Today Dawson is a quiet place, with the population of a village. Old wooden buildings, long abandoned, sag and lean toward the streets, the heat from their foundations having thawed, over decades, the underlying permafrost. Willow trees have made tall nests around the hulls of decaying steamboats. A rusty engine waits upon a stretch of track that goes from nowhere to nowhere. Broken windows admit wind and snow to swirl over floors polished by the feet of a thousand vanished dancers.

At Bennett there is an abandoned church, whose pews have known only ghosts; a few weathered headboards, dated 1897 and 1898; some broken bits of unfamiliar bottles. Scattered along the Yukon are window-less cabins, mushrooms sprouting from the roofs, that face the swirling current of what was once the River of Gold.

2. A Yukon Float Trip

For its entire 2300-mile length the Yukon is a wilderness river. There are three roads which parallel the river, the Alaska, Robert Campbell, and Dawson highways; each of these follows the river's winding course for no more than a few miles. Roads lead away from only four river settlements. From Dawson, Eagle, and Circle, gravel roads lead back to the Alaska Highway; from Ruby, a road curls back through forested hills, passing through old placer-mining villages until it finally dwindles away into a grassy path. Towns marked on the map often turn out to be a scattering of empty, sagging cabins.

Obviously then, a Yukon float trip requires a good deal of advance planning. A good first-aid kit, accurate maps, and adequate provisions are a necessity. The first part of the trip is through Canadian territory, and maps of the Canadian portions can be obtained from the Canadian Department of Mines and Technical Surveys. The United States Geological Survey sells maps of the sections in the state of Alaska. (For addresses, see Appendix IV.) Snake-bite kits are not necessary as there are no snakes along the river. Kayaks or canoes are more practical than rubber rafts. Most trips involve a long paddle down Lake Laberge, as well as occasional flatwater. Anyone who has attempted to stroke a raft down a mountain lake, especially water prone to breeze up into high, choppy swells, will appreciate a trimmer craft.

Although there are only two rapids of any consequence on the Yukon

(Five Finger and Rink), other hazards should be noted. In many places banks have caved in, throwing trees out across the water. Care should be taken when putting into shore above such "sweepers," for the current is swift and strong. The water is very cold. A veteran Yukon river runner has commented: "Two or three minutes in the water numbs you, five to ten kills you."

Float parties are required to register with the Royal Canadian Mounted Police at Whitehorse, Carmacks, or Dawson, giving their trip route and estimated time of arrival at destination.

The river ice usually breaks up in late May or early June. The most enjoyable river running is from mid-July until early September. Temperatures are generally warm, sometimes hot, during the day, although evenings can be brisk. By midsummer, mosquito activity has already peaked. As reputed, mosquitoes in the northlands are large, numerous, and conscientious about their work. They attain a whining crescendo of gluttony during late spring and early summer, and boaters planning trips from July on will be plagued more camping beside the Alaska Highway on the way up than on the river trip itself. One is rarely troubled on the water, as the Yukon is wide and breezy. If tent netting is in good shape, insect repellent carried, and boggy campsites avoided, mosquito misery can be largely prevented.

A recommended addition to any expedition's gear is a book on edible plants of the region. Such items as boletus mushrooms, wild strawberries, raspberries, rose hips, and Hudson Bay tea grow in profusion, delectable supplements to a diet of dehydrated fare. Caribou moss and willow bark, when boiled, are nourishing in an emergency situation, although hardly gourmet dishes.

Fishermen can find action anywhere along the river. There are trophy lake trout in the headwater lakes, and huge pike lurk in weedy, slow stretches of the upper river. As tributary rivers, laden with glacial silt, begin thickening the Yukon's flow, river fishing falls off. Yet innumerable clear side streams continue to tumble and slide into the river, all of them teeming with grayling, which are similar to trout in size, flavor, and fight. Many of these creeks are rarely, if ever, fished. Each summer millions of salmon work their way upriver to spawning grounds. Sportsmen can get them to hit spoons or other bright lures in the side streams; Indians scoop them out of the river with fishwheels, huge revolving nets. In eddies of the lower river, whitefish will fight each other for a crack at your bait.

Camp meat, too, is easily obtained. Float parties carrying a shotgun or .22 should have some memorable meals of spitted grouse, duck, and honker, as well as rabbit stews. This is bear country—black, brown, and grizzly. Some boaters feel more secure with a rifle in their gear; others hold to the theory that if you don't bother bear they won't bother you, which is usually the case. At any rate, extra care should be taken with food scraps,

The author's boat near Little Salmon on the Yukon

and it is not being overcautious to rope one's food pack up to a tree branch.

The rewards of a Yukon trip are bountiful. From early June to mid-July there are more than twenty hours of daylight. There is a profusion of wildlife everywhere; one floats past moose gazing blandly from willow thickets, bear scrambling up side hills, foxes prowling the shoreline. Sometimes one goes to sleep to the distant howling of timber wolves, and awakens to the honking of wild geese wedging their way southward overhead. Here and there one pauses at shapes of the past: ghost towns; solitary, windowless cabins; decaying steamboats; abandoned Indian graveyards; an ancient Russian Orthodox church . . .

Lake Lindeman and Lake Bennett, headwaters of the Yukon, are blue deep lakes that probe like long fingers back into snow-crusted mountains. Paddlers who wish to retrace the route of the Klondike gold stampede can ship their boats over the White Pass and Yukon Railroad from Whitehorse or Skagway to Bennett, once a tent city of thousands, now marked only by the station (where passengers are served moose steak and berry pie), a deserted church, and some ruins and relics scattered back among the brush.

The railroad hugs the eastern shore of Lake Bennett to the picturesque village of Carcross, named for the thousands of caribou that used to swim across the narrow channel leading to Nares Lake. The railroad bridge that now spans the gap is favored by local Indians as a place for fishing and serious tippling. Not long ago an old fellow, mellow from Guinness Stout in the summer sun, fell off into the chill water. He was rescued by friends, and accepted the pulls of whiskey offered as a means of restoring numbed circulation. He soon felt better, and ambled up onto the bridge to point out how the accident occurred, promptly falling in again.

The chain of mountain lakes feeding into the mouth of the Yukon River proper—Bennett, Nares, Tagish, and Marsh—are all blessed with spectacular mountain scenery and superb fishing. An industrious angler could fill a wheelbarrow with whitefish in an afternoon if he dropped bait in the right places. Lake trout shorter than a man's forearm are usually released with disdain. An 87-pound giant was landed from the Carcross railroad bridge. Like all proper treasures, the legendary whopper fish of the headwater lakes are guarded by a demon—wind. Although lakes Nares and Marsh are fairly calm, sudden, violent winds can transform both Lake Bennett and Lake Tagish from placid surfaces to a mass of foaming white-caps within a matter of minutes. Good-sized boats have capsized here.

Below Marsh Lake the Alaska Highway crosses the river, and the beginning of Miles Canyon is not far beyond. Backup from the hydroelectric dam at Whitehorse has tamed much of Miles Canyon and obliterated Whitehorse and Squaw rapids, but it is still a swift and interesting run. Schwatka Lake is a tree-rimmed body of water created by the dam. There is a road along the south shore over which boats may be portaged around the dam.

Whitehorse, capital of the Yukon Territory, is a mixture of old and new. A street address is as likely to be a sod-chinked log cabin as a modern apartment building. Women wearing fashionable pants-suits, bearded sourdoughs, and Indian women in bright print dresses wheel carts down the aisles of supermarkets. Floatplanes carrying loggers and hunters buzz over the abandoned steamboats that rest high and dry beside the river. At Whitehorse, McBride Museum, which houses relics of the gold rush era, is well worth a visit.

The most popular float trip on the Yukon River is from Whitehorse to

Dawson, a distance of 435 miles. The trip usually takes about ten days. One can put-in at Whitehorse, or drive down the Dawson Road to a campsite on Lake Laberge.

Here one shoves off into wilderness. Less than twenty thousand people live in the Yukon Territory, which is about the size of New York and California combined. Maps show a number of river settlements, but this is deceptive. Upper Laberge and Big Salmon are deserted Indian villages; Lakeview and Britannia are only a couple of rotting cabins; Lower Laberge, Hootalingua, Fort Selkirk, Ogilvie, Stewart River, and Little Salmon are ghost towns. Only at Carmacks, where the river and the Dawson road rejoin one another for brief companionship, can one count upon obtaining supplies, and these are limited.

Like the headwater lakes, Lake Laberge is narrow and long. Mounds of granite rise up from the shorelines. The extreme north end of the lake is heavily silted. The steamboats that formerly ran from Whitehorse to Dawson often had to spend hours probing for the shallow channel that opens into the river, the stretch called the Thirty-Mile. The bleached hull of a wrecked steamboat, the *Casca,* juts from the river's edge here. Beyond is the deserted town of Lower Laberge.

The Thirty-Mile is a beautiful stretch of blue water, first gliding through poplar-covered hills, then bounding over short, rocky rapids. Midway through, the current whirls around the point of land called Cape Horn, the water rising into choppy "haystacks." Modern river runners are usually puzzled that the Thirty-Mile was regarded as presenting such a formidable obstacle to the Klondike stampeders; yet it is to be remembered that few of the argonauts knew how to handle a boat properly, and that most of their boats were overloaded and many ill designed.

The former steamboat stop of Hootalingua lies at the junction of the Yukon and Teslin rivers. In the tongue of the Athapascan Indians of Alaska and the Yukon Territory the name means "the place where the blankets are spread." Between the abandoned buildings there is a cover of green, deep grass and wildflowers—lupins and bluebells.

Some 40 miles farther downriver, where the Little Salmon River joins the Yukon, there is another ghost town. Faded lettering over the principal log structure reads: "Little Salmon Anglican Mission." An overgrown path leads to a nearby Indian graveyard with its rows of miniature wooden houses. The Athapascan Indians build these houses for the dead to live in until it is time for the spirit trail to be taken to another world. In them they place food and favorite belongings of the deceased.

At Little Salmon the Robert Campbell Highway reaches the river; it is a fairly short float of only 35 miles on into Carmacks, the only point between Whitehorse and Dawson where provisions may be purchased.

Five Finger Rapids, located 25 miles below Carmacks, should be scouted prior to running. Conglomerate bluffs break the river into five swift channels, of which the right-hand, or north, channel is the least dangerous. There is a good view of the rapids from a high overlook on the north side of the river. Here one can also see the remains of the cables that were once used to winch steamboats through the fast water.

Rink Rapids is a few miles beyond. From the water it appears more spectacular than Five Finger—a line of breaking waves that seem to stretch across the entire river. Yet hard against the right-hand bank is a narrow avenue of calm water over which one glides serenely.

The abandoned sod-roof roadhouse of the Yukon Crossing Station has stood beside the river since the presidency of Theodore Roosevelt, when stagecoaches with leather springs stopped there, as well as horse-

Scouting Five-Finger Rapids before running it

drawn sleighs in the winter equipped with buffalo robes to keep passengers warm. For several miles one can see segments of the stage road which once linked Whitehorse with Dawson by way of Yukon Crossing. In places it has entirely vanished, buried by rockslides and rampant undergrowth; elsewhere it is clearly discernible under a light cover of grass.

Beyond Hell's Gate, a section of reefs and sloughs, the Pelly River flows into the Yukon. It is one of the Yukon's largest tributaries. Close to the confluence, the well-preserved ghost town of Fort Selkirk is located on a wide, grassy meadow.

In 1848 Robert Campbell established a Hudson's Bay trading post at the site where Fort Selkirk now stands. He was alone at the post when a war party of Chilkat Indians attacked it. In a bizarre, lopsided struggle, he managed to escape in a canoe, but not before his clothes were torn from his back.

Later he assembled a band of friendly local Indians, and they poled upriver in birchbark canoes to a point opposite the fort, which was in smoldering ruins. His companions refused to go farther, and for a time prevented Campbell from crossing the river, so great was their fear of an ambush.

The trader managed to allay their fears, however, by gravely and ceremoniously peeling two willow sticks. Crossed before his chest, he assured them, the twigs would deflect any bullets or arrows shot in his direction. Satisfied with this magical protection, they allowed him to cross to the fort. Almost everything of value had been plundered or burned.

By 1892 a large settlement sprang up around an Anglican mission at Fort Selkirk. Trading again became active. Within a few years, over $50,000 worth of raw fur was hanging from the rafters of one storeroom alone.

During the Klondike era, Fort Selkirk's isolation was broken by the proliferation of steamboats on the river. In 1898 the first steamboat to travel round-trip from Dawson to Whitehorse almost bogged down at Selkirk for lack of oil. Fifty pounds of moose tallow, purchased from Indians, saved the day.

The last regular Yukon River steamboat run was made in 1956. When the paddlewheeler had churned past Fort Selkirk, headed for slow rot on the skids at Whitehorse, the final remaining residents of the settlement moved away, leaving behind furniture, books, tools, a pump organ in the Catholic church. . . .

The run from Fort Selkirk to Dawson is one of the most enjoyable on the entire Yukon. This is wooded, highland country, with the Dawson Range to the south and the Klondike hills rising to the north. Occasionally, there are impressive palisades beside the river. There is a great deal of wildlife in the area. Cow moose, especially, frequent the numerous islands in the river, since they can raise their calves there with little danger of wolves swimming out to them.

Although there are towns on the Yukon which one could float by without knowing it, if in the wrong channel, the buildings of Dawson can be seen from some distance away, crowding against the waterfront on the right-hand side of the river. Just above Dawson, the clear blue flow of the Klondike River sweeps into the muddy current of the Yukon. About five hundred people now live in Dawson, a far cry from the ten thousand population it boasted during the gold rush prosperity around the turn of the century. By the time you reach Dawson, you will likely be ready for a meal at a café, a beer in an oldtime bar, or a hot bath in a hotel. For camping I would suggest crossing the river to the unpopulated western side, if for no other reason than to keep the numerous village dogs from raiding your grub supply. The current is surprisingly strong here—start a good distance upriver from where you wish to land on the other side. Once your camp is set up, you can cross back over on the ferry which carries cars to the highway leg at regular intervals.

Several major fires swept through Dawson during the gold rush era, yet there is still much to see in the City of Gold. One prized relic is, appropriately, a gleaming hand-drawn fire pump that was responsible for the preservation of a number of old buildings. A particularly fierce holocaust, which the hose team was not able to extinguish, started when a dance-hall girl heaved a lighted lamp at a rival during a fit of pique. Since several raging fires had originated on Paradise Alley, Dawson's red-light district, certain dance-hall performers and other fallen doves were banished to quarters across the Klondike River at Lousetown.

Few of Lousetown's buildings remain today, but there is an old steam engine rusting back among the trees. And in Dawson there are still steamboats—the completely restored *Keno* close to the main section of town, and the "steamboat graveyard," where a number of old vessels lie upon skids. The graveyard is reached by crossing the Yukon River on the ferry (an interesting diversion in itself), and then hiking north along the river for perhaps a mile. There is a well-defined path.

Dawson's Palace Grande Theater was built in 1899 by Arizona Charlie Meadows, a flamboyant entrepreneur and entertainer who could shoot the spots off a playing card at 30 feet. The theater, once falling into ruin, has been restored. Plays and gold rush skits are now performed there during the summer months. Among other structures that have been preserved are the cabin of Robert Service and the imposing old Canadian Bank of Commerce Building on the waterfront. One should allow at least a couple of days to explore Dawson and the surrounding country—there is much to be seen.

Two miles below Dawson one comes to the Indian village of Moose-hide, perched on the east bank. This is beautiful country for drifting, with forested banks and numerous clear streams that splash down into the river. After a while, one becomes increasingly conscious of a strange, plaintive sound in the distance, rather like the lowing of a lost steer. The moaning comes from the ungreased wooden axle of a fishwheel as its huge nets revolve in the current. Salmon scooped up by the nets drop down a chute into a box beside the wheel, from which the owner periodically gaffs them out into his boat. During a good run, some fishwheels net as many as two hundred salmon a day.

The Yukon is the largest salmon river in the world. Some seasons as many as forty million will go up it to spawn, the majority of them swimming hundreds of miles before laying their eggs in side streams. The salmon run is the basis of the economy of the Eskimo and Indian peoples living on the Yukon. The fish are caught either by means of the fishwheels, which are generally placed beside cutbanks or bluffs where there is a strong current, or in gill nets, which are strung beneath buoys at eddies in the river. The Chinook or king salmon is the largest and most highly prized. In a few places on the lower river, Chinook are dressed and sold to wholesalers who place them on ice in floatplanes and fly them to markets in Fairbanks or Anchorage. But the majority of the salmon that are dipped flopping out of the Yukon are split and dried on racks by the water's edge, not to feed man but to nourish sled dogs over the long winters.

There is frequently a fish camp at the mouth of the Chandindu River, a shallow rocky stream cutting through a meadow of knee-high grass. Here you are at an elevation of about 600 feet. This is a good place to buy fresh salmon from the Indians, although the camp should be approached with care. Sled dogs are often staked out in the grass, and it is an unnerving experience to have a pack of burly malamutes leaping at you out of the green, tugging on their chains, growling, barking, and snapping like a scene from a postman's nightmare.

During the winter, supplies of dried fish for dog food often run low, and consequently generations of hunger have made cunning and dextrous thieves of these animals. Malamutes have been known to haul themselves up the end poles of a log cabin to get at meat stored on the roof. They have climbed ladders to caches, biting their way through slab doors. A healthy and hungry dog can crunch into tin cans like so much cylindrical cardboard. Owners swear some dogs can read labels, disregarding soups, spaghetti, and the like, in favor of beef stews and other meaty combinations.

The story is told of a starving prospector, who, only a day's run from Dawson, collapsed in the snow, unable to go farther without food. The same was true of his sled dog, which had fallen in its tracks. As the gaunt prospector watched its deep and steady breathing, an idea came to him.

Unsheathing his razor-sharp hunting knife, he slashed off the animal's tail; at which the dog jerked a little in its stupor, but slumbered on. Feverishly, the prospector built a twig fire, and soon the tail was simmering in a pot. The heady aroma of cooking meat roused the sleeping dog. Man and dog devoured the tail, and thus revitalized, were able to continue across the snowfields to Dawson.

The ghost town of Forty-Mile, on the west bank of the river, about 46 miles below Dawson, was named for its distance below Fort Reliance, a trading post long since abandoned. Forty-Mile flourished briefly before the Klondike stampede. When gold in paying quantities was discovered on the Forty-Mile River, miners drifted in, throwing up tents and log cabins. Later, there would be a cigar factory, a Shakespeare club, and a saloon outfitted with Chippendale chairs. Forty-Mile had been peopled by a restless breed—the men who always kept one horizon ahead of civilization— ahead of the railroads, plowed fields, the bulge of villages into towns, of towns into cities. As might be expected, they were individualistic and sometimes eccentric. One, nicknamed Cannibal Ike, favored his moose meat raw; another, who was called the Old Maiden, packed 50 pounds of old and tattered newspapers with him, for, as he put it, "they're handy to refer to when you get into an argument." Still another early-day citizen of Forty-Mile hacked at the walls of his cabin for firewood, until there was only the thinnest partition between his living quarters and the sub-Arctic winter outside. When questioned about this peculiar activity, he replied that it let in light.

Forty-Mile was largely abandoned during the Klondike rush, but was later revitalized for a time as a steamboat stop.

About half a day's float below Forty-Mile, two monolithic rocks face each other across the river. The Indians call these the Old Man and Old Woman rocks. Their legends recount how long ago the old man returned home empty-handed from a hunt. His querulous wife nagged and ridiculed him until finally, his patience exhausted, he seized her and threw her across the river. Instantly, they both froze into stone, and there they stand today, with the Yukon flowing forever between them.

A few miles below these monoliths one comes to the border between the Yukon Territory and the state of Alaska. There is no way of knowing just where you reach the boundary, but there is a customs station at Eagle, a few miles over the border. From the water, Eagle appears to be a good-sized community. A row of large wooden buildings face the river, and behind them streets lined with frame and log cabins cut back into the forest. One walks across a quay of lank, wild grass to a rather elegant false-front. It is padlocked. All the river-front buildings are padlocked, and have been for many years.

When Fairbanks was but a clutch of rude log shelters and Anchorage not yet dreamed of, Eagle was a bustling place of three thousand population. Sometimes several steamboats would tie up at the bank in a single afternoon. The elegant, padlocked false-front was a busy customs house then. Through it, bound for the Klondike, went silks and pianos, porcelain thunder-mugs and ivory-headed walking sticks, hogsheads of whiskey and sacks of wheat. Through it, coming out of the Klondike, funneled a steady stream of gold—nuggets, dust, and bricks.

Today only a handful of families live at Eagle the year round, although there is a sizable Indian village nearby. From Eagle, a scenic road leads back to Tetlin Junction on the Alaska Highway.

Back before the gold-fever days, boundaries were somewhat casual, and no one was entirely sure where the Yukon Territory left off and Alaska began, or just what stretch of river would belong to whom day after tomorrow. The Canadians, fearing the hordes of American prospectors that poured into the Klondike might pressure annexation of the goldfields by the United States, bolstered what they considered their side of the border with the Northwest Mounted Police and the Yukon Field Force—a contingent of three hundred soldiers who, wearing red jackets and white helmets and carrying Maxim guns, had marched to their assignment up the wild interior of British Columbia, becoming less resplendent by the mile. The Americans, for their part, christened their border villages with patriotic fervor, as if the very names would solidify their position. In addition to Eagle, there were Liberty, Nation, and Star City; gold was taken from gulches such as Washington, Independence, and Fourth of July.

Perhaps 1 mile below Eagle, the river washes beneath Calico Bluff, a metamorphic hulk where bands of different colored rock have been squeezed into strange, flowing patterns. Down river some 40 miles, the ghost town of Nation lies upon the south bank of the river, half buried under shade trees, berry vines, and plants growing out of old sod roofs. This is a good place for mushroom hunting. There was once a nearby roadhouse whose woman proprietor became unladylike when winter travelers would endeavor to pass her establishment without stopping for food, grog, or at least some conversation. She reportedly would squeeze off a few rifle shots in front of the offending sleds. Few ignored such pointed hospitality.

Below Eagle, for some three leisurely days of drifting, the river continues to wind through forested canyons where clear side streams feed in from the surrounding mountains. Then the mountains begin to fall back from the river. The current slows and splits into numerous sloughs. This is the Yukon Flats, a marshy basin some 100 miles long and 50 miles wide.

For the river runner, Circle marks the beginning of the Yukon Flats; for the motorist, it marks the end of the Steese Highway, most northerly road in North America. Most float trips end at Circle, if not before. There are still several hundred miles of river between Circle and the sea, all of it wild, most of it scenic. But Steese Highway is the last connecting road. Those voyaging beyond Circle must arrange to fly their boats out, or plan to sell or give them away at whatever village is the terminus of their trip.

Strolling today around Circle, where there is a trading post and a scattering of log cabins, it is hard to visualize how in 1896 Circle boasted that it was the "greatest log-cabin city in the world." Maybe it was. There were twenty-two saloons where men gambled, sang, fought, and purchased drinks for the house with nuggets tossed casually onto gold scales. Days and nights of winter darkness were reeled away in eight dance halls where the fiddles never stopped and the rates were a dollar a dance. For the more pensive, there was a library supplied with a number of chess sets as well as the complete works of Carlyle, Darwin, Huxley, Macaulay, Ruskin, and Irving. In the two-story Grand Opera House, Shakespearean plays were produced.

Circle had style. The chief of a local tribe used solemnly to greet steamboats arriving at Circle in the early days, carefully attired in denims, cutaway coat and top hat, and brandishing a brass-headed cane. In the spring, vegetable gardens and flowerbeds sprouted on roof-tops, where the heat from wood stoves thawed the sod while the ground below was still frozen rock hard. During the winter months, a curious announcement was nailed to the door of the log-cabin jail: "Notice! All prisoners must report by nine o'clock P.M., or they will be locked out for the night. By order of the U.S. Marshal."

The most difficult navigation on the Yukon River lies between Circle and Fort Yukon. An intricate maze of sloughs and placid river mouths are traps to confound the unwary traveler. The land itself gives few clues—this is a place of endless mudbanks, myriad islets of willow growth, and swampy indentations into flat shorelines.

In the summer of 1961, a serviceman on a weekend pass hiked to a lake 2 miles off the Circle road for some fishing. He decided to return to his car by a different route, a dangerous decision in this place where lost miners in the early days were often beaten groggy by a fierce sun that hammered at them as they dragged through waist-deep mud, or were driven insane by mosquitoes that fed through the tobacco juice smeared for protection on their faces. The soldier became lost in the Yukon Flats. Sixty-seven days later he was found by moose hunters, 70 pounds lighter and nearly dead from starvation and exposure.

The United States Geological Survey puts out excellent maps of almost all of the Yukon River on a scale of 1 inch to the mile. In the Yukon Flats, however, these maps are not completely reliable, inasmuch as the topography is constantly shifting. In a few seasons, old channels become shallow and corrugated with sandbars, while new ones cut through islands shown on the charts.

Fort Yukon, just north of the Arctic Circle, has one of the greatest temperature ranges in the world. Its highest officially recorded temperature is +95 degrees; its lowest, −78. Like most towns beside the river, Fort Yukon is narrow and long, with houses scattered for some distance along the banks. Several fishwheels roll in the current, and split salmon can be seen drying on racks. This is the largest Indian settlement on the Yukon.

The Flats continue between Fort Yukon and Steven's Village as the river, which has been flowing in a generally northwestward direction throughout the trip, bends to the southwestward to sweep toward the still distant Bering Sea. Beyond Fort Yukon you meet more uncharted islands . . . wide channels that fray out into log-littered mud banks, slit through with little more than sluggish ditches . . . bars of quicksand . . . violent winds that beat shallow water into coppery waves. For all this, the Flats have a strange and lonely beauty of their own. Here, by night, the low horizons support arcs of glittering stars and sometimes dazzling displays of the Northern Lights. During the day, great flocks of ducks, geese, and sandhill cranes fan up from the water. Soft, grassy banks are crisscrossed with the tracks of bear, moose, fox, and other wildlife. The Flats are one of the world's major nesting grounds for migratory waterfowl.

What landmarks exist in the Flats have colorful names—Halfway Whirlpool, Deadman Island, Johnny Frog Cabin, Three Sleep Point, Homebrew Island, and Purgatory. Purgatory was the home of William Yanert, a retired military man whose hobbies were exploration and wood-carving. Yanert was away from his cabin much of the time, prowling and mapping the Flats, and was distressed on more than one occasion to discover that someone had pilfered food and bedding from his place. He carved a wooden devil, which at night would glower at passing steamboats from lightbulb eyes.

The thefts continued. When someone actually boosted his sheet-iron stove, Yanert had had enough. A day or so later he shot a whiskey jack (Canada jay) which he caught pecking at some bacon. He then buried the bird in a man-sized grave with rounded top near the cabin. Over it he placed a prominent headstone stating: "He robbed my camp and I shot him." Reportedly, that ended the stealing at Purgatory.

Beyond Steven's Village, the Yukon Flats come to an end as the river begins to twist through the Sawtooth and Ray mountains. Poplar-covered ridges soon steepen and become rocky at the crests. This was the site of the proposed Rampart Canyon Dam, which, had Congress authorized it, would

Here the river spreads out into the vast, marshy basin called the Yukon Flats have inundated the Yukon Flats. Estimated cost of the dam was $1.3 billion. Proponents argued that the hydroelectric power produced by the dam would induce industry to locate in Alaska. Opponents pointed out that cheaper power resources such as fossil fuel were available, and shuddered at the ecological consequences of the project. The 445-foot dam would have created a reservoir forty times larger than Lake Mead, 10 percent larger than Lake Erie; the backup would have been sufficient to put the state of Texas under 10 feet of water. Hopefully, the unrewarding project has been shelved for good.

Midway through Rampart Canyon, the charts show Rampart Rapids, a feature so gentle as to be almost nonexistent except in extremely high- or low-water. The canyon at this point is beautiful with high sweeps of forest and rock rising from the water.

The town of Rampart is typical of Yukon River settlements—a general store, some cabins strung out along a grassy cutbank above the water, and a small, mixed population of modern frontiersmen, Indians, and aged sourdoughs who remember other times. Rampart sprang up when in 1896 a Russian half-breed named Minook dug $3000 worth of gold out of a hole 8 feet square and 15 feet deep. By the following winter the Klondike rush was at fever pitch, and men paused at Rampart only long enough to pan paydirt for supplies or steamer passage to keep going upriver. Rex Beach arrived at the camp carrying a fur-lined sleeping bag, rifle, dogskin suit, and a mandolin. He lingered, finding little gold, but lots of material for the novels that would later bring him fame and fortune.

The ebbtide from the goldfields, ambitious dreamers drifting back empty-handed, also paused at Rampart during the next summer . . . and the next. One of them was a former Texan who faced the world with steady eyes set beneath thick brows. In Dawson, he had worked at a number of jobs, including promoting prizefights. He spoke of the fortunes he had gained and lost, but no one in Rampart paid much attention, since it was known that he had left Dawson penniless. Soon he drifted on to Nome, and within a year he was worth $100,000, from gambling, wheeling and dealing in mining properties. His name was Tex Rickard.

The town of Tanana lies at the junction of the Yukon and Tanana rivers, its largest tributary. It boasts the only café between Fort Yukon and the mouth of the river. A few weeks of wilderness fare and dehydrated foods can make an overcooked cheeseburger seem downright epicurean.

Tanana residents, given half the chance, are prone to bending the ears of congenial strangers with bear stories, some whimsical, others terrifying. Townspeople recall that in the summer of 1963 the bears seemed to go berserk. Bears were boldly raiding salmon wheels and sauntering into fish-smoking barns. At Manley Hot Springs a grizzly bear killed a miner in front of his cabin. Near Fort Yukon an employee of the Fish and Wildlife

Service noticed a black bear following him along the bank as he paddled a canoe downstream. When the canoe grounded on a sandbar, the bear swam out after him. The man thrashed for the other shore, where he hurriedly climbed a tree. The bear, in close pursuit, slashed at his leg as he swung up a limb, tearing off a boot-heel. The Fish and Wildlife man hurled out a knapsack containing his lunch, and while the bear ate this, slid to the ground and sprinted to a larger, sturdier tree.

Another man was camping on the Tolovana River, northwest of Fairbanks, when he was dragged out of his sleeping bag by a black bear and chewed up badly before a companion could edge in for a clear shot. He killed the bear, but not before it had inflicted wounds on the camper that required twenty-five stitches to close.

Tanana was in a state of virtual siege. Bears ambled down the dirt streets, unafraid. High school students wore sidearms when walking to school; many grammar school pupils stayed home. Armed and edgy residents blasted away at every bear that came into sight. More appeared. One bush pilot, somewhat skeptical of the villagers' tales, circled the town at a low elevation to count bears.

He spotted thirty-eight.

Rampart is the last canyon on the Yukon. Below Tanana, hills usually flank the river on one side, with flatlands on the other. The river grows larger as major tributaries flow into it—the Tanana, Nowitna, Melozitna, Koyukuk, Anvik, Innoko. There are more islands and sloughs than on the Canadian section of the river, but the current remains strong in the main channels, and the country is wooded and scenic.

Settlements are often far apart on the lower Yukon. It is 130 miles between Tanana and Ruby; 160 miles from Kaltag to Holy Cross. Villages noted on maps as lying between these points, such as Kokrines and Blackburn, are abandoned.

The towns of the lower Yukon have several things in common: they are isolated, their residents are predominantly Indian or Eskimo, and the summer salmon harvest and winter traplines are basic to the way of life. Each place, however, has uniqueness.

When gold was discovered on Long Creek shortly after the turn of the century, Ruby boomed into a town of some five thousand population. Today it is a quiet village of less than one hundred and fifty, the majority of them Indians. Although a number of fires have swept through the business district, Ruby still looks like a mining camp. Boardwalks lead up past false-fronts and log cabins. It is a pleasant place to linger in for a day, a week, or longer.

In Ruby, it is remarked that the people of the village of Galena, 50 miles farther downriver, fare badly at fishing. Galena fishermen claim that salmon sometimes bypass their wheels by flopping over Pilot Mountain, a shortcut midway between the villages. They assert that the fish have been seen leaping high up on the slopes in the moonlight, leaving a damp, slimy trail between boulders. Upriver cynics comment that the only vantage point from which this curious phenomenon has been observed is the beery depths of Galena's Yukon Inn.

Galena village, which has grown up around the fringes of Galena Air Force Base, is a ramshackle place of quonset frames and other dwellings improvised out of birch poles, sides of packing cases, and scraps of canvas and cardboard. As a group they give the impression of a kind of leaning junkyard. Most of the native inhabitants seem to harbor a feeling of predatory despair. Unless one has an irrepressible craving for a Tom Collins or a Jerry Lewis movie, the large, modern wilderness base and its attendant village are good places to avoid. Just drift on by.

Several miles below Galena a dark rock hulks on the north shore of the river. This is Bishop Rock, named for Roman Catholic Bishop Charles Sehgers, who in 1886, accompanied by two priests, scaled Chilkoot Pass. Once over the notch, the missionaries constructed boats and floated down the Yukon to Stewart River. Here the two priests lingered at a mining settlement, while the bishop pushed on with a man named Fuller. Winter overtook them at Tanana, and they paused until the river froze, continuing then by dog team over the ice. The silent miles of winter darkness pressed heavily upon the two men. The bishop, buoyed by his faith, remained cheerful. Fuller began to brood and sometimes muttered incoherently.

On the night of November 28, the bishop pitched his tent beneath the rock now named for him. Two Indian guides were on the riverbank gathering driftwood for cooking when they heard Fuller shout close to the tent. There was a shot. The natives, crouching among the darkened snowdrifts, saw Fuller stumble out of the shelter, mumbling to himself.

Fuller was taken to San Francisco and eventually brought to trial at Sitka for the murder. The two Indians went along as principal witnesses. The jury found Fuller guilty, on a reduced charge of manslaughter—his sentence was ten years. The Indians returned to their remote village, bringing strange clothing and gadgets they had bought with money earned as witness fees. They spoke of the marvels they had seen beyond distant waters—gigantic ships that must have been made from entire forests; tall, wide houses stacked on top of each other; open, stony places where it seemed that half the people of the world were gathered; the silver-and-glass oracles that men drew from their pockets and consulted to learn when it was good to sleep, eat, talk with other men, or be under blankets with a woman.

And so these Indians became renowned as story-tellers, not only in their own village but in others as well. They were envied for their experiences, and some men announced that they too were planning to go and see these things for themselves. This was only talk . . . for they had no money, no way to get there.

One young man, however, was obsessed with the idea. He noted that the killer's punishment was merely a few years' detainment in a place where he would be warm and sheltered, with food brought to his room. Around campfires, he closely questioned the story-tellers. Yes, they assured him, this was true.

One afternoon, a miner came to the village to buy fresh meat. The young man killed him, leaving the body in plain sight beside an important trail. The miner's friends soon discovered the corpse. They armed themselves and came to the village. Guardedly, they asked if anyone knew of the murder. The young man stepped forward and briefly confessed his act. While friends spoke of his fine character, and the miners watched him, he stood quietly, confident that he would soon journey to the strange places he had heard so much of.

Instead, he was bound to a spruce tree and riddled with bullets.

The Koyukuk, which enters the Yukon between Galena and Nulato, is a big river, 750 miles long and draining 26,000 square miles. There are some elusive channels where the two rivers meet, and one can almost count on brushing some mudbars before the village of Koyukuk is reached. During the 1890s gold was discovered on the chill and desolate rivers that empty into the Upper Koyukuk and a number of settlements sprang up: Rapid City, Union City, Soo City, and Jimtown. One of the camps, aptly named Coldfoot, boasted in 1902 "one gambling house, two road houses, two stores, seven saloons and ten prostitutes."

Dominic Vernetti came from Italy as a young man to seek his fortune on the Upper Koyukuk. After washing out some gold on the Hog River he left his claims to set up a trading post, little realizing that a paystreak would later be found under the site where he had pitched his tent, or that an even richer band of gold wound through the soil beneath his outhouse. Although the gold camps of the Upper Koyukuk have passed into history, the Koyukuk trading post, which Vernetti founded at the confluence of the Koyukuk and the Yukon, still flourishes. Here you can stock up on provisions, as well as buy raw furs if you have room for them.

Nulato, not far downriver, is the oldest town on the Yukon. Russian fur traders built a blockhouse there in 1838, but Indians soon burned it. Three years later Vasili Dershavin rebuilt the fort, and for the next decade managed the trading operations without serious problems. In 1851 Dershavin called a conference of Indians to discuss trade agreements. A chief named Larion, resenting the Russian's activity in his tribe's hunting grounds, killed Dershavin's messenger and sent a war party against the fort.

During a pitched battle at Nulato, the Indians were finally driven back, but not before Dershavin had been killed. Also lost in the melée was a British officer who was seeking word of the missing ships of the Franklin expedition, which had disappeared in the eastern Arctic six years earlier while looking for the fabled Northwest Passage.

At Nulato one can see an interesting Indian cemetery on a steep hill above the town. On a number of the grave markers are large mirrors, which are believed to protect the dead from evil spirits. These spirits, intent upon molesting the peaceful dead, are suddenly confronted by their own hideous reflections, which causes them to flee in horror. The mirrors have an added function; facing the town, they allow the dead to observe the activities of the living.

Between Nulato and Holy Cross lies the loneliest run on the Yukon, some 180 miles of wilderness. Holy Cross, a Catholic mission founded in 1898, marks an ethnic division on the river: above it the native population is predominantly Indian; below it, Eskimo. The town stands back from the main channel on Walker Slough, a side channel. It consists of a collection of frame houses off to one side of an imposing wooden church and other mission buildings.

The people along the Yukon River, whether they be Indian, Eskimo, or people from "outside," are extremely hospitable, and usually invite travelers in for "coffee," which generally means a hearty meal. When at Holy Cross, or below it on the river, those with squeamish stomachs should politely refuse offers of Eskimo ice cream. A local favorite, it is concocted of mashed, slightly putrified dried fish, sugar, berries, and lard.

Russian Mission, about a day's run below Holy Cross, perches upon a side hill above the west bank of the river—an attractive village of log cabins linked by warped and ancient boardwalks. Well up the slope is the Russian Orthodox church—which appears from the outside to be a humble log building. Inside, however, it is a riot of musty color, with icons, pink and red paper flowers, altar cloths, ornate silver braziers, and faded religious paintings. Yet in the entranceway one is reminded that this is frontier Alaska. On one wall are pegs where people coming from a distance can lodge their rifles before passing into the sanctuary. The stroll to church can mean danger, or, more frequently, a chance to get fresh meat.

Not far beyond Russian Mission the river hooks around Devil's Elbow, swinging to the north. For small boats, the stretch from Devil's Elbow to the ocean can be the most hazardous part of the Yukon. The river is in places 3 miles wide. Frequently, strong north winds blow in a contrary direction to the current, whipping the water into a fury of high, tossing waves. For long stretches, the main channel can be avoided by working down the sloughs which parallel it for much of the way. Here and there, however, crossings of the river trunk must be made to reach another slough. As channels shift from year to year, current U.S. Geological Survey

Emily Okitkun,
Eskimo girl, at Kwiguk
on the Yukon Delta

charts should be referred to frequently. When the winds are up this is a sporting proposition.

Some 50 miles below Russian Mission one comes to St. Mary's, another Catholic mission. A little beyond it the last hills are passed . . . ahead lies the tundra country of the Yukon Delta. On the river and in the sloughs, one has the illusion that one is passing continuously through forest country, but the trees are only a deceptive front along the banks, like the false walls of a movie set. Behind them, the spongy, open barrens of the tundra stretch away in all directions, pocked by thousands of round lakes.

Like most great rivers, the Yukon passes finally to the sea through several channels. The south channel is probably the best for ending one's voyage. It enters the Bering Sea at Sheldon's Point, a fishing camp. The only village in that part of the delta is Alakanuk. Passage to Bethel, which is served by commercial airlines, can be booked on the floatplane which periodically brings mail and supplies into Alakanuk.

The Yukon is not a whitewater river. But it is a wilderness river, running 2300 miles through undeveloped, game-filled outback. It offers voyages into America's past—somewhere along its swirling currents one begins to understand what the Columbia must have been like a century ago, the Ohio two centuries ago. We can only speculate on the future of the Yukon a century from now.

Guide Notes for the YUKON RIVER

LOCATION—The Yukon begins in British Columbia, flows to the northwest through the Yukon Territory of Canada, then describes a great arc across Alaska, opening finally into the Bering Sea.

LENGTH OF TRIP—The entire river is 2300 miles long, and one should set aside an entire summer if doing the complete voyage. The most popular float trip is from Whitehorse to Dawson, a distance of 435 miles. Most parties take from 10 to 15 days for this voyage.

FAVORABLE SEASON—From the ice break-up in late May or early June until freeze-up in the fall (plan to be off the river by mid-September) the river is navigable. One should note that mosquitoes and their unpleasant cousins are less prevalent from midsummer on into the fall.

DEGREE OF DIFFICULTY—The Yukon is not a whitewater river. There are only three rapids on the entire waterway (Five-Finger, Rink, and Rampart), and two stretches of fast water (Miles Canyon and the Thirty-Mile). Yet it is not a river to be taken lightly. It is a big river, with strong current, and the water is very chill. "Sweepers" (trees which have fallen out over the water from undercut banks) can quickly capsize a boat swept into them by the current. Should you have an accident or otherwise get into trouble, chances are you will be several days' float away from anyone who can help.

RECOMMENDED CRAFT—Raft, canoe, kayak, skiff. If voyaging as far as Circle, I would recommend that you take an outboard for a raft, skiff, and even perhaps for a canoe. In the Yukon Flats, the river spreads out into a gigantic maze of channels, mudflats, and sloughs. A little power is mighty nice to have when you find yourself deep in a dead-end slough, it is getting dark, and there is no possible campsite in view.

ACCESS POINTS—Most people voyaging the Yukon will drive up the Alaska Highway, although a delightful alternative is to take a ship up the Inland Passage. Whitehorse, capital of the Yukon Territory, is an excellent put-in place. If you wish to voyage the chain of lakes that make up the headwaters of the river, you can either drive to Carcross to shove off, or ship your vessel over the White Pass and Yukon Railroad to the ghost town of Bennett. Four places on the Dawson road afford access to the river: Lake Laberge Campground, Carmacks, Minto, and Pelly Crossing. Whereas the first three are right on the Yukon itself, from Pelly Crossing it is necessary to float about 25 miles down the Pelly River before reaching the Yukon. There are only three other places where roads approach the river and one can put-in or take-out: Dawson, Yukon Territory; Eagle, and Circle in Alaska. If traveling beyond Circle, arrangements should be made to have one's boat flown out by charter plane.

CAMPING—2300 miles of virtually untouched wilderness. Carry a water container and fill up at clear side streams; the river water is potable but muddy with glacial silt. Avoid boggy places as mosquitoes love them.

FISHING—Excellent. Record-class lake trout abound in the headwater lakes. There are pike, whitefish, and salmon in the river, grayling in the side streams.

CHAPTER EIGHT

River of Fireflies: The Buffalo

1. Buffalo River Country

The Buffalo River begins in the Boston Mountains, a crest of the Ozarks in northwestern Arkansas. It twists its way to the east, merging with the larger White River less than 150 miles from its source.

Coming into the Buffalo River country, one unpleats a roadmap against the dashboard and notices a couple of interesting things. The bold green Interstate Highway lines and red arterial highways linking places like Little Rock and Pine Bluff with Fort Smith, Texarkana, and Memphis don't cut through the Ozarks; they skirt them, and the roads of the mountains themselves are shown on the map as pale blue marks that seem to squiggle at random. They suggest, correctly, an unhurried way of life, with no need to get from one place to another rapidly.

Then you begin to notice the names of the hill-country hamlets: Blue Eye, Bug Scuffle, Evening Shade, Magic Springs, Lick Skillet, and Morning Star. When you get back into the hollows, where men in bib overalls still gather at general stores to talk about the season, the latest caper of that wild young-un of such-and-such family, or you sit on a cabin porch of a hillside farm drinking spring water poured from a battered tin pitcher by the heirs of the people who homesteaded the patch—then you begin to hear the names of the wild growing things: rattlesnake master, bastard toad flax, skull cap, mad dog, old man of the earth, pussy toes, butter and eggs, johnny-jump-up, wake robin . . .

The names—of settlements and plants—have a whimsy that seems to border on magical incantation. The country itself is no letdown.

During the warm months, the sense of greenness on the Buffalo River and its tributaries is almost overpowering. Thick stands of hardwoods and

The Buffalo River just above Richland Creek

broad-leaved shrubs seem to push against the edges of the water, squeezing it as though in a vise of fecund growth. Maidenhair ferns dangle from rock lips over which spring water trickles to drop in soft curtains; not quite waterfalls, barely more than mist. The odors of plants expanding and decaying are rich and heavy on the humid air. Fish—bluegill, suckers, and bass—glide beneath the surface of quiet mint-green pools. Turtles slip into the river from ancient, mossy logs. Numerous black butterflies mate on sandbars, wings gently pulsating.

Soon after dusk the frogs begin their strange piped chanting. Eyes closed, on the edge of sleep, the image of a primitive opera comes to mind, as bullfrogs, the principals, croak basso mysterious passions and challenges back and forth, and when they hush, tree and cricket frogs come in on cue, their chorus as relentlessly repetitive as dry notched sticks rubbed incessantly into sound.

Millions of fireflies flash overhead, festooning the forest like a Chinese carnival.

And occasionally one hears the eager yet somehow plaintive baying of hounds hard on the scent of a fox somewhere up above the river, on the ridges, in the darkness.

Unlike the canyon country of the West, this is not a region slashed open with great sweeping strokes, but rather, a region of delicate filigrees of rock carving. Clark Creek is only 3 miles long; yet in that distance it drops some 1200 feet down into the Buffalo. Early settlers who wandered up the stream, forced to wade because of thick underbrush and steep banks, discovered the spectacular alcove now known as Lost Valley. They saw waterfalls plunging off scalloped cliffs, walked through a natural bridge carved by the creek, and poked around under the immense overhang of a cave whose solid slab roof was half the size of a football field. But this was an isolated corner of the country and for more than a century Lost Valley was little known beyond the nearby farming villages of Boxley and Ponca. Sometimes local Sunday schools would convene there, followed by an all-day sing and basket dinner.

In 1931 S. C. Dellinger of the University of Arkansas conducted an archaeological survey of caves and shelters used by Indians along the Buffalo and White rivers. He listened attentively when told of miniature corncobs picked up in the large cave of Lost Valley. After hiking up Clark Creek and viewing the waterfalls and 200-foot-high cliffs, he and his assistants set to work. The cave had obviously been used as an Indian habitation in the distant past. Careful excavation brought up pieces of gourds, sunflower and other seeds the Indians had gathered, and a large cache of baskets and basket fragments. The site, now known as Cob Cave, is believed to have been used between one and two thousand years ago.

Although the report of Cob Cave was noted in scientific journals, the other delights of Lost Valley—sculpted rock and falling water—remained obscure, a local curiosity. Then, in 1945, the Arkansas publicity director, Glenn Green, heard of Lost Valley. Driving up into the Ozarks, he had to ask directions at several crossroads stores before he found someone who knew where it was. With mounting excitement, he trekked up the stream, saw sunlight gleaming against the spray of a 30-foot waterfall, passed through the natural bridge, and entered Cob Cave.

Yet there was more. Above the cave, part of the creek dropped down a 200-foot gorge in a series of four waterfalls. Another branch of the creek seemed to be spurting from the mouth of a cave. Green and his companions hauled themselves up the steep hillside, clutching at trees and brush to keep from falling back. They entered the cave, which Green describes as:

Ten or twelve feet wide and with standing room. We followed the stream a short distance inside—and began to hear another waterfall!

We tried to go farther back, but found our way blocked. After two or three tries we finally discovered a narrow passageway. We had crawled about 200 feet back from the mouth of the cave when the passage narrowed to a still lower crevice. As we squirmed through, then at last could stand erect, we were nearly overcome with the spectacle. Here we were, deep within a mountain, probing with flashlights around the walls of a circular room perhaps 40 feet high. Over a ledge near the ceiling came a splendid waterfall.

Its roar reverberated through the high-ceilinged chamber. Its sprays filled the air with icy cold mist. We stood shivering in our awe. (From *Buffalo River Country,* Kenneth L. Smith, Ozark Society, Fayetteville, Ark., 1967.)

One of the many springs that feed the Buffalo issues from a cliffside

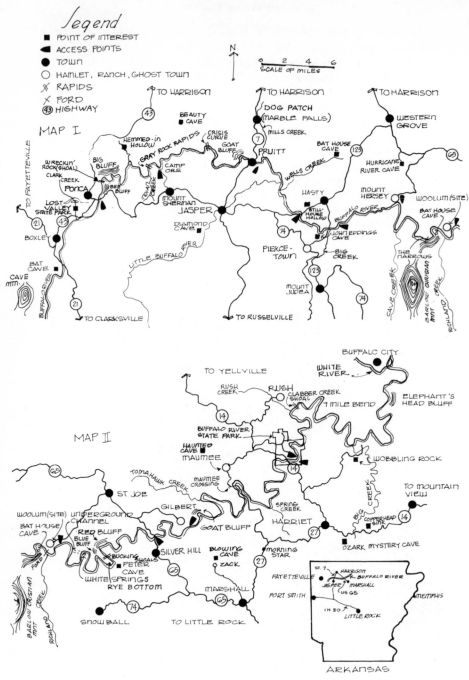

Legend

- ■ POINT OF INTEREST
- ◄ ACCESS POINTS
- ● TOWN
- ○ HAMLET, RANCH, GHOST TOWN
- ✗ RAPIDS
- ✕ FORD
- ㊸ HIGHWAY

N

SCALE OF MILES

0 2 4 6

MAP I

TO HARRISON

TO HARRISON

TO HARRISON

DOG PATCH
(MARBLE FALLS)

WESTERN GROVE

BEAUTY CAVE

MILLS CREEK

HEMMED-IN HOLLOW

CRISIS CURVE

GRAY ROCK RAPIDS

GOAT BLUFF

PRUITT

BAT HOUSE CAVE

HURRICANE RIVER CAVE

WELLS CREEK

WRECKIN' ROCK (SHOAL)

CLARK CREEK

BIG BLUFF

CAMP ORR

BEE BLUFF

PONCA

MOUNT SHERMAN

JASPER

HASTY

MOUNT HERSEY

WOOLUM (SITE)

STILL-HOUSE HOLLOW

BUFFALO RIVER

BAT HOUSE CAVE

TO FAYETTEVILLE

LOST VALLEY STATE PARK

DIAMOND CAVE

JOHN EDDINGS CAVE

THE NARROWS

BOXLE

PIERCE-TOWN

BIG CREEK

BAT CAVE

LITTLE BUFFALO RIVER

MOUNT JUDEA

CAVE MTN.

BUFFALO RIVER

TO CLARKSVILLE

TO RUSSELVILLE

CAVE CREEK

BARLOW CRISTIAN MNT. RICHLAND CREEK

MAP II

TO YELLVILLE

BUFFALO CITY

WHITE RIVER

RUSH CREEK

RUSH

CLABBER CREEK SHOAL

7 MILE BEND

ELEPHANT'S HEAD BLUFF

BUFFALO RIVER STATE PARK

HAUNTED CAVE

MAUMEE

WOBBLING ROCK

TOMAHAWK CREEK

MAUMEE CROSSING

SPRING CREEK

BIG CREEK

TO MOUNTAIN VIEW

ST. JOE

GILBERT

HARRIET

COPPERHEAD SINK

WOOLUM (SITE)

UNDERGROUND CHANNEL

BAT HOUSE CAVE

RED BLUFF

BLUE BLUFF

GOAT BLUFF

OZARK MYSTERY CAVE

BUCKING SHOALS

SILVER HILL

BLOWING CAVE

MORNING STAR

FORD

PETER CAVE

WHITE SPRINGS

RYE BOTTOM

ZACK

MARSHALL

BARLOW CRISTIAN MNT. RICHLAND CREEK

SNOWBALL

TO LITTLE ROCK

ARKANSAS

ST. 7

HARRISON

BUFFALO RIVER

FAYETTEVILLE

JASPER

MARSHALL

US 65

FORT SMITH

IH 30

LITTLE ROCK

MEMPHIS

Buffalo River

Lost Valley typifies the wilderness beauty of the Buffalo River country. Although its glades, waterfalls, caves, and bluffs have been known locally for many years, few people visit them—farm people out hunting for 'coon, possum, or running the hounds—an occasional hiker. Tourists stick to the better-traveled highways, where you can buy hickory-smoked hams and stay in AAA rated motels, or visit Dogpatch, which is a kind of Disneyland East.

Like all rivers of any size, the Buffalo cuts down through several geological formations, the deepest of which are the Boone limestones.

This is cave country. Diamond Cave, near Jasper, is held to be the third largest in the United States, after Mammoth Cave in Kentucky and Carlsbad Caverns in New Mexico. In spelunking circles, it is felt that none of these caves has been completely explored as yet, and that certain crawl-ways may lead to chambers greater than those yet found. In Diamond Cave, 2 miles of passageways have been wired to light-guided tours. Twenty-one additional miles of cave—slopes of milk-white stalagmites, thick pillars that are resonant as bells, chill pools that have existed in a windless dark since before there were men—have been explored.

In the early 1830s Sam Hudson, a millwright from Tennessee, pushed west with his brother Andy and their families. Up in the Buffalo River country they axed trees into cabins and set about taking a living from the land. Andy was as tough as a goathorn. One time he studied a flight of bees until they led him to a honey tree. Below the tree was a wallow used by a female panther that was nursing her young. The panther charged the frontiersman, who was knocked down by the rush and the slashing claws. From his back Andy ripped upward with his knife, almost disemboweling the great cat. The animal shuddered, thrashed into a sweetbriar thicket, and died.

One morning when a fresh snow was thick upon the hillsides, Sam and Andy's hunting dogs set off barking up through the oak, pawpaw, beech, and white ash trees. The brothers followed, knowing from the shrill, excited cadence that this was no 'coon or rabbit. A deer. Perhaps even a bear. Rifles hanging easy, knives in their belts, they followed the tracks to a brush-screened hole in the mountain. No sound from the dogs.

There was some dead pine around, redolent with pitch, and they ignited stubs into torches. The dark slot led down steeply into darkness; with the flickering torches the brothers eased themselves carefully down some 200 feet of a tight slanting shaft, filled with loose chockstone. At the bottom they emerged into a large chamber where the torchlight glistened on nearby cave formations. Here there were signs of a desperate battle—tufts of torn fur and blood spattered over the limestone floor. Beyond lay their dogs, dead or dying, and two dead bear. One set of bloody bear tracks lead from the carnage, and the two brothers pressed on, deeper into the cavern.

The wounded animal was on a low shelf of rock, the bear's den. As the Hudsons approached, it charged furiously, knocking the torches to the damp stone where they flickered out. In the total darkness of an unexplored cavern, the brothers fought the bear with knives, slashing and stabbing in the direction of the bear's grunts and snarls, repeatedly knocked down and then managing to roll free of its flailing claws and snapping jaws. And in the end they killed it.

The Hudsons emerged from their bizarre adventure torn up a bit, but with enough bear meat to last the season. Word of the fight and the cave spread through the hill country, and a number of people probed back into the seemingly endless passageways carrying pine torches, blazing their way with pitch drippings, charcoal marks, or twine. Locals took to guiding travelers around the known portions of the cave, charging a dime a head.

Today one can take guided tours through a number of well-lighted caves in the Buffalo River country—Diamond, Hurricane River, Shawnee, and Ozark Mystery—all of which cost somewhat more than a dime but are well worth it. The region is riddled with dark caves that invite personal exploration. Many require little more than flashlights; for others it is necessary to have a knowledge of spelunking, and equipment such as hard hats with carbide lamps, and rope ladders.

Some of the caves have been known for decades, and have been put to varied uses. A large chamber in one cave served for a number of years as a square-dance hall. As acoustics of the inner earth subtly warped the music of fiddles, guitars, and banjos, couples whirled happily in the uneven light of candles and lanterns. Bat House Cave, north of Hasty, harbored a lively whiskey still during Prohibition days. When the hamlet of Zack was a flag stop on the old Missouri and North Arkansas Railroad, Blowing Cave, across the creek, was used as a warehouse by fruit shippers.

About a mile south of Boxley, Cave Mountain slopes up from the Buffalo River. This was the site of a brief Civil War confrontation over saltpeter. In 1862 Confederates began taking nitrogen-rich earth from the floors of Bat Cave, leeching it in wooden vats, and boiling the solution in iron kettles. The finished product, saltpeter crystals, was hauled over the mountains by wagon to the Arkansas River, from whence it was shipped to Rebel arsenals for making gunpowder.

The Union Army became aware of the operation and in January of 1863 dispatched three hundred officers and men of the Iowa Cavalry to wipe it out. This was accomplished in a restrained and orderly fashion. Seventeen of the twenty Confederate soldiers on the saltpeter detail were captured, the other three, including the lieutenant in charge, having escaped.

The author's son Sean on the Buffalo River

Joseph Caldwell, the Union commander, later reported that he then "completely destroyed by fire or otherwise" the items which he cataloged as follows:

> . . . buildings, 14 in number, very extensive, entirely new and of good workmanship, together with two steam engines, three boilers, seven large iron kettles, weighing, according to the bill for the same, 800 pounds each, besides a half-ton of saltpeter, a large fire-proof iron safe (Hall's patent), three Concord wagons, two carts . . . (From *History of Newton County*, Walter Lackey.)

The destruction, however, was not as complete as the report would have it. When the troops were gone the hill people poked around the mouth of Bat Cave and found that only the rims of the iron kettles had been broken. They are all still used on farms in the Boxley area today—as watering troughs for stock, rain barrels, wash pots, and in one case as a vat for scalding hogs at slaughter time.

There are other caverns: Beauty Cave, where rare helicitites curl down from the ceiling like petrified saltwater taffy; Copperhead Sink, a 70 foot vertical shaft with snakes crawling about the perpetual gloom of the bottom, apparently living on frogs which fall into the pit from time to time; Haunted Cave, in which it is said one can sometimes hear the faint melodies of a fiddler who wandered into the cave one day and never returned. . . .

Here, under the earth as well as above it, one marvels at the delicate scrimshaw created by the action of water upon rock.

For some nine thousand years Indians lived in the Buffalo River country. Intermittently, throughout all these centuries, numerous shallow caves and rock overhangs of the region were used for shelter dwellings. Peeling away the layers of soil, scientists (and pothunters) have found their discards—scraps of woven baskets, chipped arrowheads, worn scrapers, the bones of animals they hunted. . . .

When white men came here, less than two hundred years ago, it was the hunting grounds of the Osage, and a bountiful land. There were vast herds of buffalo in upland prairies where bluestem grass grew head high; numerous deer and bear moved over trails stitching together river and ridges. The first newcomers were nomadic hunters and trappers. They were followed by settlers. Oxen pulled high-wheeled wagons up the river, trampling through cane brakes that grew thickly on alluvial bottomlands. From the wagons, women and young children, seated upon leather and wooden trunks that contained their scant possessions, gazed out with hope and curiosity mixed with some apprehension. Their men, walking beside the wagons or horseback, scanned ahead for a likely place to settle and farm.

By the time cabins had been raised and fields burned off and plowed, the Osage were gone. The Cherokee, who replaced them, were driven westward in 1828.

The Ozark settlers were an individualistic lot, with their own forms of entertainment. Every settlement had at least one story-teller of considerable prowess as well as a crackerjack fiddler. Many men came into the country with marbles of limestone and baked clay carefully wrapped in cloth and stowed in biscuit or tobacco tins as if they had been heirloom jewelry. Some of the taws, shooters, were as big as a Ping-Pong ball. On warm afternoons when there were no pressing chores men would gather to plink their taws at ringmen set in a 10-foot square, addressing the game with the concentration of billiard champions.

And they still do so today, back in Ozark towns like Blue Eye.

The hill country people solved their problems with a certain flair. Up the Little Buffalo River near Parthenon a Mrs. Hannah was getting sick and tired of hogs, deer, and other animals raiding her garden. When an agile youth informed her that there was a layer of soil on top of a large block that had eroded away from the rest of a nearby mountain, she planted her garden on the rock, reaching it by a ladder which she took down each time her work was finished, so as to keep two-footed scavengers from temptation.

Valentine Williams, who had been a Confederate soldier, farmed on the Buffalo River until his children reached school age, and then moved to St. Joe where he opened a hotel. Boarders agreed food and accommodations were excellent with one exception. Flies. Flies that in summer would swarm in through windows that had to be left open on account of the heat. A man would have to fight them off his chops and cornbread. Peach-tree-branch swatters, the usual remedy, were ineffective against the hovering horde. Williams built a fly fan, strips of paper hanging from a wooden frame, which was powered back and forth down the table (just clearing the food) by an elaborate waterwheel and linkage system. Apparently it worked.

One family, whose resources were none too ample, began to realize that someone or something was pilfering eggs. The grandfather, who had time to study the matter at length, came to the conclusion that the thief was a black snake. As bait, he laid two eggs on opposite sides of a woven wire fence. Sure enough, after a time a black snake slithered up to the first egg and swallowed it whole. Just about when it was bulging his midsection, the snake greedily lunged its head through the fence and gulped down the other egg. Unable to move forward or backward through the close wire mesh and unwilling to give up part of its feast, the snake remained inert as an hourglass until the farmer came out to terminate its digestion forever.

The first settlers and their offspring had found life bountiful in the Ozarks. The virgin soil yielded rich crops and there was game everywhere. One traveler speaks of seeing thousands of squirrels swimming across the Buffalo River, and bear hunters floated downriver with their boats wallowing under loads of meat and hides.

But with each succeeding generation there were more people on increasingly overworked land. The bottomlands were overflowing and patches began to be cultivated in remote hollows and on rocky benches. There was less game. Walter Lackey, in his *History of Newton County,* described how in 1885 the last bear in that area was killed.

> . . . with an army of hunters in pursuit, the bear was chased through Leatherwood Cove, across the river . . . down the river to Roark Bluff, from there to the top of Bee Bluff where the bear made a halt, and sat hugging a cedar tree. . . . one of the hunters shot the bear and it tumbled over a cliff.

Ten years later there were no more beaver on the Buffalo, and deer and wild turkey were going fast.

This was a logging era along the river. Vast stands of white oak were cut to make whiskey barrels and railroad crossties. Cedars, some of which measured more than 40 inches in diameter and stood more than 80 feet high, were toppled, dragged by mule or rolled to the river, then floated to a mill at Gilbert. They were chopped up to make pencils which sold for 10 cents a dozen. By 1909 the cedar was gone.

The descendants of the families who had optimistically come into the Buffalo River country in high-wheeled wagons were now leaving, the scant possessions they would take to a new life somewhere strapped to the fenders of Model-T's. Aside from those who had enough land to graze cattle, most of those who remained were too old or too poor to go. Between 1905 and 1965 half the population of the region simply went away.

Mr. and Mrs. E. R. Christian of Mount Hersey are among the few who came back. Mount Hersey is a handful of unpainted frame houses—some occupied, others not—on a dirt road that dead-ends at the river. Although the hundred-year-old, two-story dwelling they rent appears ramshackle at first glance, it must have been a handsome place at one time. It has a quality of faded elegance in spite of its loose, warped wood and overgrown yard.

Mr. Christian met his wife years ago in the Richland Valley, where she was picking cotton with her family. Mount Hersey, a few miles away, was a thriving community in those days with a water-powered grist mill, cotton gin, school, store, post office, and boarding house. The couple married and for a time lived on the mountain south of Mount Hersey that had been homesteaded and is now named for the groom's father. "Best spring water I ever had," Mrs. Christian muses wistfully.

After a time they too joined the exodus. Mr. Christian was a logger in Wyoming, California, and Montana, leading a more or less drifting life of hard work. He recalls with pride once singlehandedly building a log-cabin village for tourists out in Colorado. A large, slow-moving man in his eighties, he tends a large garden and hunts for small game, usually leaving his shoes at home in warm weather. His wife sits on the porch, watching neighbor children tumbling about in the dust and the lush foliage, remembering the pleasures and sorrows of her childhood, her family, and her travels. A pre-war Plymouth rests in front of the sagging gate, grass pushing up around its deflated tires.

"The old car played out right here," she says, pushing a loose strand of gray hair up from tired, puckish blue eyes. "Guess we're supposed to stay."

Back from the river, in the hollows and on the benches, there are numerous abandoned cabins on homesteads that have been sold to the Forest Service. The river itself snakes through a forest of second-growth trees that harbor a variety of wildlife. It is wilder today than it was seventy-five years ago. It is more like the land the Osage and the Cherokee knew. Where there are lingering hamlets on the river, Gilbert and Boxley for example, they seem throwbacks to another time. Near Boxley there is a deep hole in the Buffalo where baptisms are performed. Recently, when a mess of perch were pulled from the hole, people from up and down the valley gathered for a fish fry, and afterward sat back and softly talked while their children shouted through games under darkening trees and fireflies winked all about. There is a certain closeness in these communities that has been lost or thoroughly changed in the sprawls of houses beyond freeway off-ramps.

The bluffs, sculpted side hollows, mint-green pools, and thrashing chutes of the Buffalo have remained, although constantly threatened by merchants of highway concrete, philosophers of flatwater joy. When a powerboat becomes more important than a hummingbird, the Buffalo River will be gone, along with the Indians, the bison, the swimming squirrels, and a doomed bear clutching a tree that would soon follow its fall into the river.

2. Gliding Down the Buffalo

The Buffalo is considered to be one of the most beautiful canoe runs in America; it has aficionados who return to paddle it year after year. In terms of challenging water, spring is the most exciting time on the river—although most of the lower sections can be floated through the summer and autumn. There are a number of access points to the river, and trips can be tailored to a float party's experience and available time.

There are numerous gravel bars along the Buffalo, fine campsites. One should carry an air mattress or foam pad as well as extra-long tent stakes. In addition, a great many grassy and sandy nooks invite the traveler to rest. Veteran Buffalo boaters usually spurn such places, however scenic, in favor of gravel bars, as there is less likelihood of pests such as chiggers, ticks, sand fleas, and mosquitoes. As there are cattle along the river and communities up side branches, it is advisable to bring water containers. A number of springs beside the river trickle clear, cold water.

A driver to shuttle one's vehicle can usually be hired at Ponca, Pruitt,

Gilbert, or Buffalo River State Park. In planning a trip, 10 miles per day is a comfortable distance, allowing time for exploration ashore and swims.

The Buffalo is 148 miles long, most of it navigable by small boat. In the spring, one can put-in the river as far up as Ponca; by early summer, when the water is falling, trips usually start at Pruitt or farther downriver. Ponca and nearby Boxley are pleasant places, retaining a backcountry flavor. There is overnight camping at Lost Valley State Park.

From the concrete slab bridge over the river at Ponca one can get a good idea of water level. If the air space between the water and the bottom of the bridge is 6 inches or less, the run to Pruitt will be dangerous even for expert canoeists. Fifteen to 18 inches of air space means ideal conditions for a trip. If you drag badly in the first shoal below the bridge, the water is too low, and it is better to put-in downriver.

Between Ponca and Pruitt (a distance of 25 miles) the river winds beneath a number of towering bluffs. Big Bluff, looming well over 500 feet above the water, is the highest cliff in the Ozarks. For some decades pioneer families on the Buffalo had observed swarms of bees going in and out of a crevice high on a cliff face, and speculated on the stores of honey it might contain. In 1916 some boys built an 80-foot ladder and set it against Bee Bluff, as the face was called. That night one of them climbed the ladder and poked burning rags with sulfur into the crevice. By morning the bees were dead. Finding the crevice too tight to wriggle into, the boys bored a hole in the rock with a hand drill and inserted a dynamite stick. When it was detonated, rock went flying and streams of honey poured down the cliff. Some 400 pounds, however, remained intact and was lowered in buckets to the excited crowd below.

This is a lively stretch of water, and should be attempted only by experienced boaters. As well as noted ambushes like Wreckin' Rock, Gray Rock Rapids, Close Call Curve, and Crisis Curve, there are a number of fast shoals and chutes. During highwater, many a canoe has flipped after slamming into a willow stub.

There is much to be explored ashore. Deserted farm buildings; Goat Trail, which leads to the top of Big Bluff; and the mysterious, rugged gorge of Indian Creek, where there are waterfalls, natural bridges, and streams that disappear into dark holes in the limestone. A strenuous scramble up from the river brings one to Hemmed-in Hollow, where a 200-foot waterfall plunges off an overhang of rock and a great horseshoe of cliffs isolates the draw from all but its opening to the river. Here, in this lonely and idyllic setting, Rose O'Neil, the creator of the Kewpies, lived for a time. All traces of her cottage have long since vanished.

On any excursion away from the water keep an eye cocked for poison ivy—it flourishes along the Buffalo.

Below Pruitt, the pace of the river slackens. Pools tend to be longer, rapids shorter. From here on down to where the Buffalo joins the White, one occasionally passes johnboats from which anglers try to cast lures to within inches of the shores of emerald pools where smallmouth bass feed. Some of them get big. The traditional Ozark johnboat is constructed of unpainted wood, flat-bottomed, narrow, and square-ended. Good ones are rather graceful; bad ones look like floating packing cases.

Fed by Mills Creek, Little Buffalo River, Wells Creek, and several small branches and springs, the river grows larger. The mouth of the Little Buffalo can be readily identified as it is the only place on the Buffalo where bluffs stand close to both shores. The bluffs on this section of the river are smaller than those above Pruitt, but are multicolored and eroded into strange and subtle shapes. Some of them are almost completely maned with woodbine, which turns to a brilliant red in the autumn.

Below Wells Creek a rim of rock rises above a deep hole; from projecting slabs one can leap or dive into the water below. The pool should, of course, be sounded, as the safest place for diving fluctuates with water level. A couple of miles downriver a county road swoops out of Stillhouse Hollow and crosses the Buffalo on a low bridge of rough concrete. In moderate water the river rushes under the bridge through culverts, and in highwater often simply washes right over it. Local youngsters, in a variation of the human-cannonball act, drop themselves into intakes of the large pipes and are "shot" through them and out into the pool below. Boats, unfortunately, are not as adaptable and must be portaged over the obstacle. The large spring whose waters were once used by a neighborhood whiskey-maker is but a short walk up the hollow.

Beyond the bridge the river is tranquil and scenic. Here, as elsewhere on the Buffalo, one can spot branches and saplings whose ends have been sharpened, as if they were pencils, by the gnawing of beaver. These animals were virtually exterminated by trappers prior to the turn of the century, but are now making a comeback due to restocking by game officials. Instinctively, the energetic beavers sometimes build mud-and-pole dams, which wash out at the first rise in the river. They are not needed. Unlike their brethren in the mountain West and Far North, who construct pond lodges and store food in them against winter freeze, Ozark beavers live in shoreline burrows and are able to chew the bank hardwoods year around.

About 2 miles below the Stillhouse Hollow Road look for the entrance to John Eddings Cave on a bluff on the right-hand side of the river. It is a short, steep scramble up to the cave—perhaps 200 yards in all. The entrance is wide, and just inside are cool tapestries of hanging fern. A stream trickles out of the twilight interior where the hallway bends into darkness. There, a sunless lake, too deep to wade, extends from wall to wall. Cave explorers have paddled a rubber raft some 400 feet across this

A two-man faltboat on the Buffalo

stillwater, to small mud-floored chambers. The cave appears to go much deeper.

The backcountry road between Hasty and Mount Judea vaults the Buffalo on an ancient, one-lane iron span. Daredevil youths from nearby farms, who like as not first challenged their courage when younger by shooting the culverts of the concrete bridge upriver, have collected bets by tightwalking these rusty trusses, a good 50 feet above shallow water.

This bridge, the Highway 123 crossing, is not recommended as a put-in or a take-out point due to steep slopes, but only about a quarter of a mile downstream, at Big Creek, a rough road drops close to water level.

Mount Hersey is a bypassed place. The dirt road winding in is rutted and dusty in dry weather. When the rains come, tearing grayly at lumpy slopes, the road in places is little more than a bog. Old low-slung cars, valves wheezing, spin at gumbo. New cars rarely come. There is little left of the once-expanding community where wheat was ground and cotton ginned: five families living in snaggle-corner houses whose shingle and tarpaper roofs only serve to filter the hard storms; empty buildings where wind sweeps in through glassless windows, stirring the accumulated dust of years. At what was once the center of a bustling settlement, there are now only three rural mailboxes.

The Buffalo hustles out of Mount Hersey like a whitewater river, breaking over rocks in a long, curving shoal. You feel it is going to hammer and carve its way right down to the sea, shedding topography with wild abandon.

Delightful deception. The shoal piles into a placid stretch of water. A short, swishing run and then another pool. And another. Generations of local fishermen have named them: Akins Hole, Leafy Hole, Bat House Hole, Roughedge Hole, and Blue Hole. This is the slowest section of the Buffalo, yet an enchanting one. Fish slip around and under one's boat, without fear. In some pools, small bass and sunfish nudge against a swimmer's legs; it is like wading into an aquarium. Sometimes small fish make a series of leaps across the water, like silver skipping stones.

Over centuries, the Buffalo River and Richland Creek have carved out a neck of land whose saddle is but a few feet across. This, the Narrows, or "Nar's" in mountain terms, can be reached by a steep scramble up through

The Narrows. On the left is the Buffalo River, on the right the Richland Valley

the undergrowth on the upstream side. From the Narrows, one can look straight down to the Buffalo, some 60 to 80 feet below, or off into the Richland Valley, also a sheer drop.

It is said that two hounds owned by a man known as "Pink" Daniels once ran a fox across the knife-edge late one night. The dogs hesitated, whimpering, frightened of the height. Daniels plucked one up under each arm and carried them across in the darkness.

More recently, some high school students held a cook-out on the meadow across from the Narrows. One of the youths, who had been doing considerable damage to their beer supply, hauled himself up to the narrow rim—then jumped. The Buffalo is not deep at that point, and by all odds he should have been killed outright, but he was relaxed, lucky, and apparently suffered little harm, since he topped off the evening by seducing and impregnating a cheerleader. Or so the story goes.

Unlike the rough and wooded Buffalo River Valley, the lower end of Richland Valley is a place of broad, fertile fields. In the past, cotton has been a big crop here, and for a time there were plantations with slaves. The Civil War brought hard times. Union troops would march through, requisitioning gathered crops and trampling across unharvested fields; then Confederate units would pass by, with the same results, and in between times freebooters descended upon the unhappy landowners, taking what food remained as well as heirloom silver and an occasional comely daughter. The armies of both the North and the South seemed more interested in the crops than in their opponents, but finally in 1864 they did engage in a short, pitched battle at the mouth of the Richland. After twenty-one men had been killed, the Confederates retreated. For years afterward, local farmers plowed up rusted relics of the battle.

The lower part of the Bat House, a bluff within sight of the Narrows, resembles a human skull with eyesockets at water level. One can paddle right into the two shallow caves. The rock drops away into green depths and reputedly there is an underwater entrance to flooded chambers of an immense cave.

About a mile below, the river rolls over Woolum Ford, a rocky shallow that can be crossed only during low water. When the water is up, there is enough current to roll a wagon or stall a pickup, as some venturesome souls have ruefully discovered. The highwater detour is enough to stimulate some chance-taking; to get to the other side one must drive nearly 40 miles, back out to St. Joe and around to Snowball, much of it on rough roads. The site of the former hamlet of Woolum is up from the crossing on a grassy flat. At one time there was a cotton gin here, and stores serving the farmers of the Richland Valley. Today only a single vacant store remains.

With the addition of Richland Creek, the Buffalo River Valley becomes broader, and swings in great loops beneath high and colorful bluffs. It is here, however, midway down a river that has been growing with each tributary, that during the summer months the stream withers and shrinks. In extremely dry seasons it vanishes altogether. The missing water seeps into the gravels, collects in an underground channel, and reappears at Margaret White Springs on the other side of a large gooseneck. The springs, which are colder than the river flow, issue from cracks under the river and gently roil its surface in low water. At such a time, it is a strange experience to stand over one of these small fissures and feel the force and chill writhe up your legs and body.

Around a couple of other long bends is the place where crosstie workers used to staple logs to a cable atop the bluff, then slide them down to whack into a sandbar far below. From there, they could be floated to the mill. Peter Cave, above the river at the base of the bluff, is a snug den that has served as shelter for Indians in ages past. From below the cave, the river sweeps down Rye Bottom to be turned finally at the blue-gray bulge of Blue Bluff and the high face of Red Bluff. Rye Bottom contains the lively and well-named Bucking Shoals.

Not far from the U.S. Highway 65 bridge is the Gilbert damsite, where the Army Corps of Engineers proposed to plug up and inundate the middle Buffalo. And undoubtedly would have, were it not for the determined efforts of the Ozark Society and their friends, who regard the Buffalo as a second home.

The highway bridge affords a good access to the river, a fine put-in point, and although there is no town there, a retired river guide lays out a toothsome feast of catfish and hush-puppies on picnic tables in the screened porch of his roadside eatery. Drifting away from the bridge, toward Gilbert, take a look at the twisted iron ladder that runs up one of the concrete columns. It will give you an idea of what a high rise on the Buffalo can do. Good time to be home building an ark. According to the official gauging station at the bridge, water depth here has varied from less than 2 feet to over 30.

The 4-mile run from the bridge to Gilbert, around a large horseshoe bend, is scenic and accessible; the entire trip, with car shuttles, can be done in an afternoon. A good way to start out is with a swim in the bluff-overhung pool by the put-in place, where there is a rope swing. Downriver there are more pools, some of them with big gliding fish, and lively shoals scud below weathered bluffs.

If someone were going to do a television series set in an Ozark back-roads town (fortunately no one is) they might well use Gilbert as location. Coming down the river what one sees first is an ancient sign set back from a gravel bar, advertising the only store in town, Mrs. Noah Baker's. Then one sees an old railroad cut 2 miles downriver, and the pier of a railroad bridge rises out of the water. In spring floods, some of the worn legs quiver like loose teeth. When trains used to steam across this bridge a good many years ago, and logs were snatched out of the river by cables and dropped into gondolas, Gilbert was a boomer.

These days Gilbert is a quiet, easy kind of community of about fifty people. Mrs. Baker's store is at the center of things—for locals, canoe fanatics, and fishermen in the moderate months, mostly just for locals during dead-of-winter when weather is a topic of local pride. Gilbert is famous on Arkansas weather maps. By the time it gets chilly throughout the rest of the state, Gilbert is downright *cold*. Television meterologists usually look to Gilbert for the low end of the thermometer, and it rarely fails them.

Above Gilbert, for floating purposes, parts of the river can get mighty lean deep into a hot summer. Some jolly souls, ignoring local advice, have set off from Ponca to Pruitt during low water, and have ended up dragging their canoes for much of the way—an experience not unlike that of taking a reluctant seal on a walk down miles of rocky beach. Others have had the misfortune to have the river disappear beneath them close to Woolum; suddenly they stand, feeling grotesquely foolish, beside a boat that rests upon cracked mud or white sand, smack in the middle of the right channel.

Below Gilbert, however, there is water enough to float a canoe even during the most arid August.

The first take-out point below Gilbert is at Maumee Crossing, a good day's paddling. This is a quiet stretch of water, dropping only 3 feet to the mile, but the scenery remains superb. About 1 mile below the old railroad bridge, there is a fine launch place or camping spot at the base of Goat Bluff—venerable shade-giving elm, a deep hole for fishing or swimming, a view of sparkling water and weathered rock. The bluff is named for the goats that roam its steep flanks. The inquisitive and sure-footed animals graze all through the Buffalo River country, wherever the land is too tilted to hold crops or cattle. Halfway between Gilbert and Maumee, the clear, cold waters of Tomahawk Creek spill into the river.

Maumee Crossing is marked by a tin-roofed barn that rises out of the bottomlands beyond the riverbed, and wheel-scarred banks. The gravel road snaking off the east shore runs 8 miles out to Morning Star; the road up the west bank, which is rougher and frays into a cryptic pattern of side tracks, leads out to Highway 14. The latter is not recommended in wet weather.

Below the crossing, the pace of the river picks up somewhat. Pools are shorter. Some 4 miles beyond Maumee, Spring Creek enters the river just above the bluff of the same name. A quarter mile up stream cool, clear water pushes out of the spring itself.

Ten miles below Maumee is the Highway 14 bridge, where there is

Boaters' camp on a gravel bar near the end of the run down the Buffalo

excellent access to the river on a fee basis. Buffalo River State Park is a mile and a half beyond. The park is a lively place where yelling youngsters splash in a deep, clear pool while fathers work along the banks, casting for the big ones, and mothers chat with friends under shade trees or set out picnic lunches. Cars arrive and leave. This bustle of activity is in sharp contrast to the river that lies beyond, which is wild and lonely.

The Buffalo has a number of surprises, not the least of which is that its final 32 miles wind through wooded ridges and bluffs that crowd close to the water, as in headwaters country. Here too, as on the upper reaches of the river, there was once a farm on fertile fields inside the elbows of each wide sweep, up all the branches and in the hollows. Now the wagon tracks connecting them and leading out are faint and overgrown, the cabins and barns empty; weeds and wildflowers push up through and around rusted hay rakes. Close to vanished settlements there are graveyards, half buried in vines—wild grape, Virginia creeper, poison ivy. One tombstone reads simply:

M. D. YOCHAM
DEC. 17, 1846
SEPT. 30, 1920

*Gone, but not
forgotten*

In 100 square miles of spiny woodland, there are less than fifty people.

Eight slow-moving miles downriver from Buffalo River State Park is the abandoned zinc-mining town of Rush, which around the turn of the century had a population of over two thousand. Some half dozen buildings still stand, and there are numerous foundations and ruins. The mines were opened in the early 1880s. A decade later, a lump of pure zinc carbonate weighing 12,750 pounds was pried loose from the Morning Star Mine. Christened Jumbo, it was shipped by wagon, White River flatboat, and railroad to the 1893 World's Fair in Chicago. It won a gold medal. Speculators and miners swarmed into Rush. Pick and blasting crews bored their way into the ridges, lengthening the tunnels of mines like the Red Cloud, Lonnie Boy, Edith, and Yellow Rose. Miners called the zinc carbonate ore "turkey fat," on account of the pearly sheen it gave off in the glare of their headlamps.

Rush had begun to dwindle when World War I began. Then zinc was at a premium and the town boomed again. At the end of the war, prices fell and Rush became a ghost.

Beyond the old zinc camp the river picks up speed and throws an occasional challenge. Moving down the wide pool below Rush Creek, one hears the tumult of Clabber Creek Shoal, a long rapids with fine haystacks when the water is up. Run it right down the middle.

Here, in its final phase, the river becomes wider and deeper. Large bass glide lazily away at the approach of one's boat; schools of minnows nibble at waders' toes. The bluffs are often terraced, rising from the river in a complexity of cliffs and benches. A formation called the Elephant's Head dips a stone trunk into the water. Springs issue from secluded niches, easier to hear than to see. Most of all, it is lonesome, a place where the land has reclaimed what man once shaped. There is space and time to see, hear, and smell a thousand subtle things that have never been packaged.

Four miles below Elephant's Head the Buffalo joins the White River. Close to the White, the banks tend to be muddy, with great patches of moss. This is a result of backup due to water fluctuations controlled at Bull Shoals Dam. A massive, eroded bluff rises to the left, and there are usually a number of buzzards soaring in the thermals above it. One must stick close to this bluff, for just around a bend is the junction with the White. Floaters lingering too long in midcurrent will be swept into the White and end up at Shipp's Landing, five miles away, rather than two thirds of a mile upstream at Buffalo City. Some strenuous paddling up the left-hand bank of the White will bring one to a point where a boat can be angled across to Buffalo City, a drowsy hamlet.

The Buffalo is considered the finest wilderness river in mid-America. Since the 1950s the fate of the river has been contested by the Army Corps of Engineers, who would like to dam it, and conservation groups such as the Ozark Society, who are trying to preserve its natural beauty. In 1963 the National Park Service recommended the Buffalo be protected as a National River, updating their report in 1967. The Corps of Engineers and the Park Service are crucial protagonists in the future of America's wild rivers, a subject which is discussed at greater length in the chapter, "Our Vanishing Wild Rivers."

Guide Notes for the BUFFALO RIVER

LOCATION—Ozark Mountains of northwestern Arkansas.

LENGTH OF TRIP—The Buffalo River is 148 miles long, and about 130 miles of it—from Boxley to its junction with the White River—can be navigated by small boat. Allow 10 to 14 days for the entire trip. There are several possible shorter trips, ranging upward from a single day.

FAVORABLE SEASON—Spring and early summer are the most popular times for running the Buffalo. Mid- to late-summer trips are pleasant on the lower river, but there is usually not enough water for navigation above Pruitt. Fall and winter canoeing is also practiced to a lesser degree.

DEGREE OF DIFFICULTY—Moderate. During the spring, however, and at other times of high water, there are a number of shoals which can be challenging even to expert canoeists.

RECOMMENDED CRAFT—Canoe or kayak. A number of long stretches with little current make rafting arduous.

ACCESS POINTS—There are some twenty possible put-in or take-out places (see map, Appendix IV, for some of the most widely used). Ponca, reached by driving north on State Highway 21 from Clarksville on Interstate 40, is an excellent put-in point for an early-season trip. Later in the summer, Pruitt, reached by driving north on State Highway 7 from Russelville or south from Harrison, is a favored put-in place. The take-out point for a complete run is Buffalo City on the White River, reached by State Highway 126 south of Mountain Home.

CAMPING—Numerous attractive places. Boil water or use Halazone tablets except where water is taken from springs. Gravel bars make fine, relatively insect-free campsites.

FISHING—Good. Smallmouth bass, perch.

CHAPTER NINE

Route of the Voyageurs

1. In the Wake of the Long Canoes

By 1660, while the Pilgrims were still largely a coastal people using cod to fertilize newly cleared fields, French explorers had penetrated to the heart of the continent, paddling canoes beside the long, lonely cliffs on the north shore of Lake Superior. The Sieur des Groseilliers and his young brother-in-law, Pierre Radisson, are the first known to have come here; others would follow over the next decades. Most of these men hailed from the vicinity of Montreal and they pushed westward seeking beaver pelts. The exploration and early history of much of the North American continent, from the Arctic Ocean to the Rio Grande, was mostly due to a quirk of fashion: for better than a century no European gentleman would think of stepping outside without clapping a beaver hat atop his head.

Not far from the western shore of Lake Superior, a forested neck between two lakes marks the height of land separating the Atlantic and Hudson Bay drainages. The short Pidgeon River flows out of the chain of lakes on the Atlantic side, idles along peacefully for a bit, until, approaching Lake Superior, the momentum suddenly increases and there are several thundering rapids and three high waterfalls.

In autumn of 1731 an expedition led by the Sieur de la Verendrye, carrying a rough map sketched on birchbark by an Indian guide, toiled up an old Indian portage trail which bypassed the fast section of the Pidgeon River. The 9-mile portage was steep, hard going with the large boats, but once over it La Verendrye's party had little trouble ascending the upper Pidgeon and crossing the lakes to the divide.

Nearing Lake Superior, the Pigeon River thunders over these falls

Beyond lay a beaver trapper's paradise. For hundreds of miles to the north and west the land had been clawed to bedrock by a succession of icecaps. When the glaciers retreated for the last time, thousands upon thousands of lakes remained, connected by broad rivers and lesser waterways. On the shores of each pond, each vast and windy inland sea, each marshy creek—there were beaver lodges.

The expedition moved westward along what is now the international boundary above Minnesota, discovering that each long and wooded lake was connected to yet another by strands of river. Here and there rapids or falls had to be portaged; yet the water trail seemed to continue endlessly. Into aptly named Crooked Lake, past the tumultuous plunge of Curtain Falls, into Lac La Croix, Rainy Lake, and Lake of the Woods. The bodies of water were becoming larger. By the time La Verendrye reached the southern end of Lake Winnipeg, he was not only scouting beaver country, but was pursuing a myth as tantalizing to explorers of the northern part of the continent as the golden cities of Cibola were to Spaniards in the southern part. Surely such an intricate linking of waters must be a part of the Northwest Passage; at the end he and his weary crew would arrive at the Western Sea. Had they paddled north for a few more days, to where Lake Winnipeg opens out into a seemingly shoreless expanse of heaving blue water, as wide as Lake Erie, he might well have concluded his quest close to fulfillment. Instead, the expedition traveled up the Assiniboine River drainage, and crossed a low divide to the Missouri and a Mandan Indian village on its banks. The current of the Missouri was stronger than that of the placid rivers they had voyaged, and the Indians spoke of great mountains stretching across the horizon to the west. La Verendrye concluded that the way to the Western Sea lay elsewhere, and returned to Montreal. For the next decade he continued to seek the Northwest Passage, using the Indian portage as a steppingstone to the interior.

Although La Verendrye never came close to the Pacific, the "Western Sea," he had opened up one of the most incredible trade routes in the history of mankind. Using the Pidgeon River bypass, now called Grand Portage, Montreal fur traders fanned out into an immense complex of river systems: the Vermilion, Winnipeg, Red River of the North, Assiniboine, Saskatchewan, Churchill, Athabasca, Peace; toiling up countless feeder streams ranging from prairie sloughs to Rocky Mountain torrents, from stained waters gliding through muskeg to icy flows out of the bleak and treeless Arctic Barren Lands. The trunk route was a great arc reaching 3000 miles from Montreal to Fort Chipewyan on Lake Athabasca. Simply to paddle an empty canoe from one end or the other into the central rendezvous at Grand Portage, and then return across half a continent before the short summer faded and snow would drift across the waters, is a feat to contemplate. Yet the whole point of these epic voyages was trade; each canoe was loaded to capacity with cargo, and during the peak years hundreds of tons of pelts and supplies were freighted in a season. Birch-bark canoes 36 to 40 feet long would be paddled out of Montreal, riding low with the weight of guns, powder, balls, kettles, axes, beads, cloth, tobacco, rum, and other items. In later years one might wander into the most isolated sub-Arctic trading post and find English fabrics, Venetian glass beads, or French brandy. The route led up the Ottawa River, through Lake Nipissing, down the French River to Georgian Bay and North Channel on Lake Huron, and thence over the Sault Ste. Marie to Lake Superior. The fur-laden vessels that were propelled toward the rendezvous from out of the vast and lonely lands to the north and west were smaller, usually 25 feet long, and carried from six to ten men. At Grand Portage the cargoes were exchanged, and after a brief amount of businesslike conferences among company officials, and uninhibited whoop-up among boatmen, the return voyages would begin.

Although possessed of monumental strength and endurance, the boatmen, voyageurs, were almost never large men: weight and space were crucial factors in the big freight canoes. Bales of fur were packed so tightly that a man was sometimes unable to move his legs. On open stretches of water, a voyageur often paddled eighteen hours a day, reportedly a stroke every second, with short breaks every hour. Portages were even more demanding. Beset by mosquitoes and black flies, the short, stocky men carried loads of 180 pounds each on their bent backs, aided by a leather strap across the forehead. Some carried as much as 270 pounds. Rather than using a slow, steady gait for portaging, voyageurs preferred to dogtrot in spurts, taking frequent breaks. It took several men to carry the large Montreal canoes; two for the smaller North Country vessels.

When it came to personal effects, voyageurs traveled light. Most carried little more than a musket, bone-handled knife, kettle and cup, a pipe and a quantity of tobacco. A bright sash, worn around the waist, served as both a pocket and a symbol of his calling. Although voyageurs spent most of their waking hours on waters teeming with fish, the hectic pace of travel rarely allowed pauses for catching them. Their diet consisted mostly of pemmican—a mixture of fat, dried buffalo, and dried berries. Like the mountain men of the American West, beaver trappers of a later period, voyageurs drank deeply of strong waters whenever they had the chance. Rum, however, rather than whiskey, was the usual fare. When there was no rum in the cup, which was most of the time, voyageurs would buoy up their spirits with tobacco and song. Pipes were pulled out and fired up at every break. Songs, of which every boatman knew many, frequently accompanied the work of paddling, and took much of the tedium out of it. Indeed, strong lungs and a headful of music were considered as much a requisite for the prospective voyageur as strength and endurance.

The intrigues of rival fur-trading companies, power and boundary struggles among the nations they represented—England, France, Canada, United States—have filled volumes. Yet these things had only marginal effect upon the daily life of the voyageur—employment by a different company, a new flag flapping above the stockade of some lonely outpost. Like the mountain men, his real alliance was to the Empire of the Wilderness; his outlook was tempered with that peculiar, deep, gut-pride that comes to men whose years are spent at jobs both physically hard and hazardous. As long as there were beaver, and a demand for their pelts, his kind would endure, bright red paddles slashing into the water, one stroke a second.

During the century and a half that the fur trade flourished on waterways of the North Country, the descendants of the coastal Pilgrims and tidewater planters, and people fresh off the ships from Europe, had begun to move westward. Theirs were not the epic canoe explorations as in the North that reached hundreds of miles into the interior, but a steady migration of families in oxen-pulled wagons, plodding through gaps in the mountains, leaving wagon-ruts beside the rivers. Many shifted westward by stages, chopping and burning trees, planting, building log cabins. And after a few crops, or a decade or two, they would get restless enough to put everything back into the wagon and make scars on new grass farther west. Behind them, more and more wagons breached the gaps, the ruts became roads, and rough cabins gave way to villages of painted sawmill lumber.

As time passed, villages became towns and small cities connected by a network of roads. There had been so much chopping and burning in the river valleys that there was now more farmland than forest. As the pace of man to the south increased, that of the fur trade declined. To everyone's surprise, the supply of beaver, like almost everything else on this earth, was not inexhaustible. The beaver hats which had been all but universal among those who could afford them since the foppish proclamations of Beau Brummel in the eighteenth century, became indispensable only to repertory actors, riverboat gamblers, politicians, and other eccentrics.

Today, where there were once wagon tracks, freeways slash across the land, flanked by forests of steel, bearing wires, lights, and neon messages. Hazy cities sprawl everywhere, centers pushed skyward as if by the force of their perimeters. In the North Country, however, along much of the route of the voyageurs, beaver gnaw at trees undisturbed beside waterways less frequented than when the singers in birchbark canoes stroked their paddles in unison, once every second.

The border between eastern Minnesota and Canada is one of the least symmetrical in America. It looks like the edge of a half-finished jigsaw puzzle. For a number of years there was considerable disagreement as to where the boundary should lie, and tensions mounted to a point where logs were felled in narrow places on the route from Grand Portage to Lac La Croix, making it all but impassable. However, when the dispute was finally settled by the Webster-Ashburton Treaty of 1842, that same twisting route was selected as the international border. Much of the wilderness on either side of the voyageur trail is now protected in Quetico Provincial Park on the Canadian side and in the Boundary Waters Canoe Area on the American. As in many other designated Wilderness Areas in the United States, there are no roads, and powerboats are allowed only in a few restricted lakes. The unique clause in the Boundary Waters regulations is that cans and bottles are not permitted; no hardship in an age when a variety of dehydrated and freeze-dried foods are packaged in burnable plastic.

It seems to work. In the autumn of 1971 I took a canoe trip with friends through the Boundary Waters Canoe Area. Most of the summer visitors had come and gone, and there were few signs of their passing: charred log-ends leaning against rings of stone, lost fishing lures exposed by low water, and, at different campsites, three forgotten personal effects: a pair of socks stretched carefully upon a rock, a pouch containing highly aromatic tobacco, another pouch (this one disintegrating after perhaps several seasons) which turned out to be filled with wadded wet bills and a fistful of silver. (Only about $17 actually—but infinitely more pleasant than slicing your toe on a rusty Spam can.)

Autumn, if you luck into Indian Summer rather than days of gray, wind-blown rain, is the most lovely time on the Boundary Waters. Even on well-traveled routes, you may go for days without seeing anyone. A vast abstract pattern of interlocked lake and land stretches northward for hundreds of miles, up to where trees thin out and are waist high . . . and beyond into spongy Arctic tundra. A man could canoe a lifetime and still not know all these waters. In autumn the days can be warm enough to peel your shirt off while paddling, although the nights are chill. What few mosquitoes and black flies remain seem stupified; they alight on your arm like birds on a tree branch. There's plenty of time for a good swat before they remember their mission is blood.

Broadleaf trees are turning to orange, yellow, and crimson. Some Indians still speak of it as the time when the gods kill the Great Bear, whose blood and roasted fat drippings stain the leaves. In the clay-colored light that precedes dawn, mist rises from the smooth water, in places whirling like mock tornadoes, slow motion and in miniature. Later, when the sun is high in a clear Indian Summer sky, there seems to be motion everywhere—leaves quivering in winds that drive patterns of waves across lakes whose distant headlands shimmer like mirages. Evenings, the pulse of animal life quickens. Beaver gnaw at selected trees and push stripped branches across the darkening water. Pike and bass feed and splash in the shallows of marshy bays. Moose wade along these shores, chewing water plants with a kind of mildly baffled deliberation. Otter skim gracefully along the rims of water with strong, supple movements that make you think of both a seal and a water snake. Long after nightfall, one hears timber wolves howling back in the forest.

Here, at this time of year, storms come suddenly, theatrically. There may be stars overhead when the first lightning appears on the horizon, without sound. The first thunder is muffled, indistinct—like boulders bumping in a cave—but then wind rises with a sound of distant surf. The storm, in a solid front, advances with astonishing speed. If your tent is not up by the time you hear thunder and see the treetops whipped back and forth by the advance winds, most likely you will be pounding stakes under a sky split by lightning while being pelted by hailstones large enough to stun a chipmunk. By the time the tent is up and you are crunching around on dropped bits of the frozen sky, the concentrated fury of the storm, the violent perimeter, will have passed. Gentle rain falls as thunder and wind, lightning and hail, sweep away into distant forests as abruptly as they came.

Ely, Minnesota, is situated at the edge of the Boundary Waters Canoe Area. The main street of the town (population 4848) is lined with outfitting headquarters, where one can rent canoes, packs and other gear, or hire a guide. Some outfitters, such as Canadian Waters, offer prepacked, balanced menus for however many days you will be in the wilderness, will help you plan a route, and then give you detailed, waterproof maps. All one needs to bring to Ely is a toothbrush. For most trips, guides are an unnecessary expense, even for inexperienced canoers. The voyageur visitor center, outside of town, has a number of interesting displays. Two of the exhibits feature the taped voices of dialect narrators: a Scandinavian logger and a French-Canadian voyageur. Both turn out to have been made by the same man, who is also the voice of Smokey the Bear for the Forest Service.

The variety of voyages which can be planned out of Ely is practically limitless, and many pass along a segment of the voyageur route. An excellent week's trip begins with a drive out the Echo Trail to the Moose River. One paddles down to Lac La Croix, returning by way of Iron Lake, Crooked Lake, Basswood River, and Basswood Lake. The portages between Lac La Croix and Basswood Lake were beaten solid by the feet of voyageurs long before the advent of the modern outdoorsman.

To retrace the entire route from Grand Portage to Rainy Lake, one must drive up along the shore of Lake Superior. Watch for fish stands: smoked lake trout is one of the great flavors of the world. A reconstructed stockade and fort mark the site of Grand Portage, where as many as a thousand men used to congregate briefly each July during the heyday of the fur trade. There are several possible put-in points for a cruise over the voyageurs' highway. The most authentic, of course, would be to use the Grand Portage itself. Although the 8½-mile path to the site of Fort Charlotte is scenic, winding between lichen-covered rocks, hidden springs, and green, spongy patches of reindeer moss, one's appreciation of natural beauty is somewhat dulled if one is carrying a 17-foot canoe any distance. Few of the voyageurs remembered the trek with pleasure; they were inclined to nip from kegs of rum at their sixteen customary resting places to keep strength and spirits from failing. The trail is, however, pleasant for hiking. Two grass-overgrown rectangular mounds are all that remain of Fort Charlotte, built in the late eighteenth century. Two miles away, the river tumbles 69 feet down Partridge Falls. Although a rough road does lead to a point above the falls, the river here is shallow, rocky, and fast in places. It is rough going to Fowl Lake; canoes often have to be waded upstream.

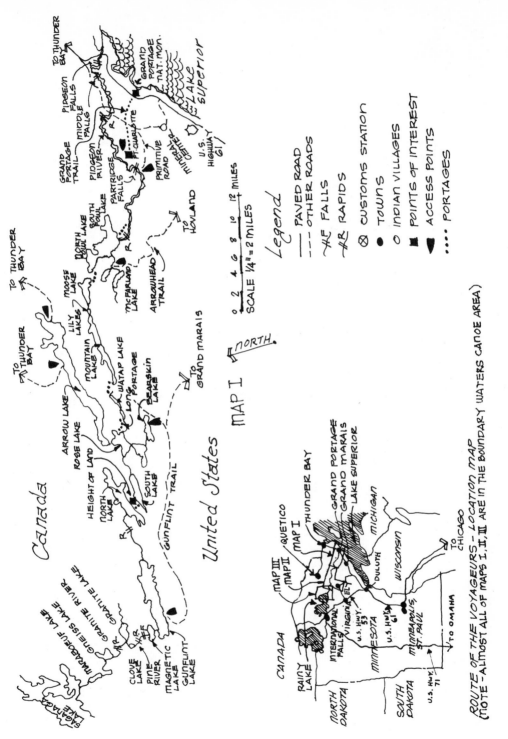

ROUTE OF THE VOYAGEURS – LOCATION MAP
(NOTE – ALMOST ALL OF MAPS I, II, III ARE IN THE BOUNDARY WATERS CANOE AREA)

MAP I

NORTH

Canada

United States

Legend

PAVED ROAD
OTHER ROADS
FALLS
RAPIDS
⊗ CUSTOMS STATION
● TOWNS
○ INDIAN VILLAGES
■ POINTS OF INTEREST
◣ ACCESS POINTS
···· PORTAGES

0 2 4 6 8 10 12 MILES
SCALE ¼" = 2 MILES

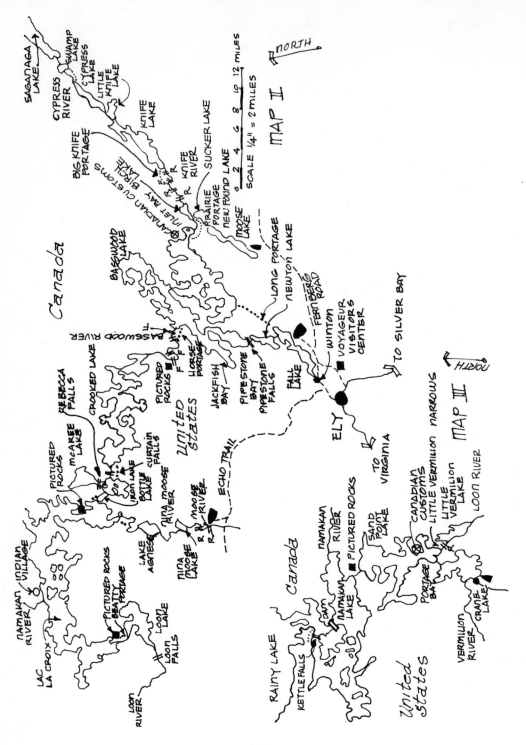

MAP II

NORTH

SCALE 1/4" = 2 MILES

0 2 4 6 8 10 12 MILES

Canada

United States

SAGANAGA LAKE
SWAMP LAKE
CYPRESS LAKE
LITTLE CYPRESS LAKE
CYPRESS RIVER
LITTLE KNIFE LAKE
KNIFE LAKE
BIG KNIFE PORTAGE
KNIFE RIVER
SUCKER LAKE
CANADIAN CUSTOMS
INLET BAY
BIRCH LAKE
KNIFE RIVER
PRAIRIE PORTAGE
NEW FOUND LAKE
MOOSE LAKE
BASSWOOD LAKE
LONG PORTAGE
NEWTON LAKE
FERNBERG ROAD
WINTON
VOYAGEUR VISITORS CENTER
BASSWOOD RIVER
REBECCA FALLS
CROOKED LAKE
PICTURED ROCKS
HORSE PORTAGE
JACKFISH BAY
PIPESTONE BAY
PIPESTONE FALLS
FALL LAKE
ELY
TO SILVER BAY

NORTH

MAP III

PICTURED ROCKS
McAREE LAKE
IRON LAKE
BOTTLE LAKE
CURTAIN FALLS
NINA MOOSE RIVER
MOOSE RIVER
ECHO TRAIL
TO VIRGINIA
NAMAKAN RIVER
PICTURED ROCKS
SAND POINT LAKE
CANADIAN CUSTOMS
LITTLE VERMILION NARROWS
LITTLE VERMILION LAKE
LOON RIVER

NAMAKAN INDIAN VILLAGE
NAMAKAN RIVER
LAC LA CROIX
PICTURED ROCKS
BEATTY PORTAGE
LAKE AGNES
NINA MOOSE LAKE
R. N. R.
LOON LAKE
LOON FALLS
LOON RIVER

Canada

RAINY LAKE
KETTLE FALLS
DAM
NAMAKAN LAKE
PORTAGE BAY
VERMILION RIVER
CRANE LAKE

United States

240

One will have a more enjoyable trip by driving out Arrowhead Trail, a dirt road, and launching at Fowl Lake. From a high precipice at the west end of the lake you can look back at the valley of the Pidgeon, a green cleft where the river shows now and again—black, green, blue, or silvery, depending upon the season and the slant of the sun. The 30-mile trip from Fowl Lake to the lower end of Gunflint Lake is largely a succession of lakes with connecting portages. The trip is not without interest. The south shore of Rose Lake is noted for lake trout fishing. Don't be logical and troll the middle of the lake—it is so shallow your lure will hit mud before you have rightly finished the cast. Try the south shore. A couple of small lakes passed through, ponds really, are skimmed with white water lilies. Beside the shore of North Lake the roadbed of the short-lived Port Arthur, Duluth and Western Railroad is still visible. The P.D. & W. inspired lofty financial optimism when it was constructed around the turn of the century: within a few years its outlook was so unrosy that people were openly referring to it as the "Poverty, Distress and Want."

Between South and North lakes a 500-year-old portage leads over the height of land, 1551 feet above sea level, 949 feet above Lake Superior. The voyageurs used to stride over this portage with relief and anticipation. After a tough, upstream haul, the currents would now favor them for hundreds of miles. In camp at North Lake, novices, or "pork-eaters," from the East would be baptized as "Nor'westers." First sprinkled with a cedar bough that had been dipped in water, the new men then repeated some initiation vows, and the ceremony would come to a boisterous and prolonged conclusion as the rum kegs were relieved of their remaining contents. The initiates were now entitled to wear colored plumes in their hats—a gaudy and proud symbol not only of having crossed over a watershed, but of having committed themselves to a hard and dangerous way of living about which few ever expressed regrets.

The Gunflint Trail, a gravel road, cuts through the woods to the western end of Gunflint Lake. There is a lodge where one can pick up last-minute provisions and fishing lures. Even if fishing has never appealed to you as a sport, you should get some cheap tackle and try it in voyageur country. Patience is not a requirement. Pike, walleye, bass, and lake trout are not coy about hitting the lures; the old reliable is a striped spoon. A man can paddle a long, long lake with a bellyful of fried pike. Putting in at Gunflint Lake, one enters the full spectrum of northern waterways—rivers, ponds, narrow serpentine lakes, vast open lakes. The rivers race through water fast enough to delight the skillful; these same stretches can be portaged on easy trails by the inexperienced. From Gunflint Lake you run down the Pine River into Clove Lake, down the Granite River into Gneiss, Maraboeuf, Saganaga and Swamp lakes, down the Cypress River into

Knife Lake, down the Knife River into Basswood Lake. The portages are generally short, rarely more than ½ mile long.

The magnificent, watery chaos of the North Country was caused by a climatic change that began more than a million years ago. At that time the country was hilly, with well-defined creeks and rivers. Lakes were rare. The country was rather like Tennessee without strip-mining. Giant tree-sloths club-footed around and mammoths and mastodons wandered the country. Gradually, the air became colder and drier. Snow came earlier and stayed later each year. Hardwood trees unable to withstand the long winters withered, died out, and were replaced by the more hardy conifers. The chill winds and changing flora pushed the wildlife southward, where many species, their adaptability stretched to breaking, became extinct. Snow fell for thousands of years without melting. The center of the cold and snow was near Hudson Bay, and after a time the bottom was compressed into clear, blue ice, and after a while longer, the weight was too much and the ice began to flow away from the pressure, slowly and massively, a system of bewitched rivers.

The glaciers moved toward the low areas ponderously; had man lived then, he could not have seen the movement, only heard it—a muffled rumbling and cracking deep within crevasses. Ice hundreds of feet thick possessed the land—covering most of what would later be Canada, with tentacles creeping as far south as the Mississippi Valley and the present site of New York City. Three times the icecap advanced and then retreated. The last contraction took place only 11,000 years ago; the glaciers pulled back to Greenland, to the high mountains of western Canada and Alaska. Some say the ice will come southward again, leveling cities despite man's knowledge of fire, electricity, and the potentials of a split atom, but no one can say for sure.

When the glaciers had melted back from the North Country, the land had been violently altered. Forests had been uprooted, the hills upon which they stood swept away. Random debris shoved before the ice now lay upon the land like soft scars; the bedrock was a scrimshaw of polished knobs, mounds, and depressions where the rock had been scraped away. Meltwater from the glaciers, sun-blasted snow, and rains satisfied the needs of gravity by creating a watershed as complex as the insides of a computer. No man today, merely looking at a map, can tell which way a waterfall plunges, what lake feeds into which river system, or where the drainage of the innumerable, small round lakes may go. Often their waters flow nowhere. Created by gigantic blocks of melting ice, these "kettle lakes," as they are called, may remain motionless for centuries, decayed vegetation building muskeg on their bottoms, until they brim over to slice a new channel, a little river, to another lake.

Beside a river or lakeshore in the North Country, you can sometimes still hear, as we did, timber wolves howling late at night. Outside of Alaska, virtually the only wolves left in the United States live in northern Minnesota. They feed upon deer and moose. Attacks upon humans have largely originated in the imaginations of writers of Far North thrillers. During winter, the large, gray animals can be called into camp by a gifted howler. Once at the flickering rim of light thrown by a campfire, far from gathering in a ferocious, salivating circle, they are shy yet curious—and perhaps somewhat disappointed at not finding a prospective mate behind the howl. Watch, too, for bald eagles and otter, moose and black bear. A loon crying over twilight waters is one of the most haunting sounds anywhere. Loons can dive more than 200 feet under the surface of a lake in pursuit of fish.

Much of the forest from Gunflint Lake to Knife Lake is virgin. Most of the timber from Knife Lake to Lac La Croix is second growth, having been logged out some years ago. Yet the jackpines and spruce come back quickly; it is hard to tell where the old cutting took place. Or the fires. A missionary, Father Jean Pierre Aulneau, wrote in 1735 that he "journeyed nearly all the way" from Lake Superior to Lake of the Woods "through fire and a thick stifling smoke" which prevented him from "even once catching a glimpse of the sun." Several times in more recent history, fires have crowned in northern forests, racing before the wind faster than a horse can run, darkening the sky hundreds of miles away with smoke. Birds were kindled in the air. An area of Wisconsin pine as large as Delaware burned in 1871, and fifteen hundred people died at Peshtigo. When flames swept out of the forest and onto the wooden roofs of Hinkley, Minnesota, in 1894, there was no place to go. People were incinerated as they ran, screaming, down the streets. Some four hundred perished. A passenger train was spared the same fate when the alert engineer, seeing the conflagration ahead, stopped the train and ran it full throttle in reverse nearly all the way back to Duluth. All that was left of Hinkley was an iron fence, the bank vault, one wall of the brick schoolhouse, and, astonishingly, a wooden privy.

In backcountry, there is always the chance of a canoe overturning and leaving your provisions at the bottom of a swift river or deep lake. In the North Country, survival is easier than in many places. Besides fish and berries—wild strawberries, gooseberries, raspberries, blackberries, blueberries, cloud berries, cowberries, and currants—a number of common plants are edible. Roots of cattails and water lilies should be roasted over an open fire. Boil the leaves of sow thistle, stinging nettle, ostrich fern, lamb's quarters, marsh marigold, chickweed, chicory, dandelion, shepherd's purse, plantain, and trillium. Three mushrooms—morels, puffballs, and shaggy manes—can be easily distinguished from poisonous varieties if one is knowledgeable about mushrooms. If unsure, don't take a chance. A book on wilderness survival should be a must for any long wilderness voyage.

Basswood Lake sprawls all over the place. Rather than a single lake, it appears to be a confederation of them somehow all joined together. Several fur companies had trading posts on Basswood Lake at one time or another. From the Indians, the traders obtained furs, fish, birchbark canoes, and an occasional wife. Although the lake is a long way from the oceans, innumerable gulls nest on its small islands during July. Much of the short Basswood River must be portaged, as there are falls and rapids.

Close to where the Basswood River flows into Crooked Lake, a rock with Indian paintings and chipped designs looms above the water. Alexander MacKenzie, discoverer of the river that bears his name, failed to notice the rock art when he passed the spot, but he commented upon another curious sight: "Within three miles of the last portage is a remarkable rock, with a smooth face, but split and cracked in different parts, which hang over the water. Into one of its horizontal chasms a great number of arrows have been shot, which is said to have been done by a war party of the Nadowasis or Sioux, who have done much mischief in this country, and left these weapons as a warning to the Chebois (Chippewa) or natives, that, notwithstanding its lakes, rivers, and rocks, it was not inaccessible to their enemies." It appears that the Chippewa, as well as the Sioux, fired arrows into the cleft, both as a defiant gesture to the Sioux and as a test of marksmanship.

Although the arrows have long since been removed from the rock, the pictures remain: crude yet strangely graceful representations of men, canoes, suns, moons, moose, loons, and what appear to be pelicans. At other sites, strange, haunting pictographs are sometimes associated with Mi-shi-pi-zhiw, Chippewa God of Water. It is believed they represent dreams he had while fasting to communicate with the Guardian Spirits.

Most of this rock art was created five hundred to one thousand years ago, although some stick figures appear to carry rifles, which would make them less than three hundred years old. At a Lac La Croix site, in among the Indian art are the initials "L.R." and the date, "1781." Most pictograph sites are next to the water, at a height from which a man could paint while standing in a canoe. Fingers were probably used as brushes, and colors came from substances readily available: soot for black, clay for white, hematite for red. The durability of the colors indicates that the binder must have been excellent. It may have been bear grease, white from gulls' eggs, beeswax, fish oil, blood, or a combination of several ingredients.

Nomadic Indians have wandered this region for some five thousand years. By the time the first French explorers arrived, the Chippewa people were the dominant tribe. Other tribes that once lived in the Boundary

Waters country had moved on: the Cree into woodlands to the north, the Assiniboine and Dakota Sioux out onto the plains. The Chippewa built birchbark canoes waterproofed with spruce or balsam pitch, and made clothing from the hides of moose and caribou, rabbit skins and beaver pelts. Like most tribes, they were skilled hunters and fishermen, and in addition harvested the wild rice that grew at the edges of many lakes and rivers. The Chippewa lived in small, interrelated family units rather than in villages of any size, yet during the time of Maple Moon in the spring many familes, many clans, would gather for feasting and celebration. Sap, collected and boiled in kettles of green birchbark, provided stores of maple sugar. They mixed it throughout the year with water to make syrup, and the syrup was often mingled with dried corn, chestnuts, berries, beans, and wild rice. At the time of the Maple Moon, members of the Midewiwin, a secret society of medicine men, gathered to talk of curative herbs and exchange shamanistic lore.

The Chippewa were highly sensitive to a world of spirits existing in wind and water, rocks, birds and bear, the sun, the moon. Virtually every aspect of their lives was conducted with ritual meaning. They traded at the voyageur stockades, apparently neither awed nor hostile around the newcomers. Most fur traders who fell victim to massacre were attacked by the Dakota-Sioux, who were unhappy about *anybody* traveling around in country they once considered their birthright. The Chippewa were always on the move to different hunting or fishing camps, to places where wild rice was ready to be harvested, or to sacred spots where tobacco might be left as an offering. When whites suggested they give up most of their lands—a treaty—most Chippewa regarded the message-bearers with cold amusement. A principal chief, Crooked Neck, was extended treaty papers to sign in 1870. Clad only in a breechcloth, his body painted vivid yellow, Crooked Neck spurned the gift of a red shirt: "Am I a pike to be caught with such bait as that? Shall I sell my land for a bit of red cloth? We will let the palefaces pass through our country, but we will sell them none of our land, nor have any of them live amongst us."

Eventually the Chippewa were forced to yield most of their lands. Yet even today whites do not live there except as the nomads the Chippewa once were—camping for a night or two and then folding up the shelter, placing it in a canoe, and paddling on to another lake, another river. There are still Chippewa villages in the Boundary Waters country, isolated hamlets reached only by canoe or floatplane. The Chippewa hunt moose and fish through holes chopped in the ice during winter, celebrate the time of the Maple Moon in the spring, and gather wild rice in late summer. The land is still wild enough to protect a certain amount of custom and dignity.

Crooked Lake, west of the Basswood River, has a lot of hustle for a lake, dropping about 12 feet from the east to the west end, and sluicing

"Curtain Falls, one of the most outrageously beautiful waterfalls in all America
. . . an avalanche of water"

currents up to 3 miles per hour through narrows. The climax of all this
movement is Curtain Falls, one of the most outrageously beautiful water-

falls in all America. It is not the highest, nor the biggest, and not even a sheer falls; but an avalanche of water whose texture and sound are different each time you look at it. There is an almost hypnotic wonder about falling water. It is the wonder, perhaps far more than a suicidal urge, that has induced men to drift over Niagara Falls inside giant rubber balls and other weird contraptions. Most have not made it, and only souvenir booklets recall their efforts.

There are no souvenir booklets about Curtain Falls. Just masses of water thundering toward a distant ocean where polar bear scramble upon ice floes. It is good to look, then close your eyes and listen. Beside rivers that run beyond the roads, sound can become vision, and vision sound.

There was once a lodge at Curtain Falls. All that remains are some foundations overgrown with grass and berry vines, broken pieces of an iron stove. Iron Lake is next, with the twin cascades of Rebecca Falls; then Bottle Lake. David Thompson, whose London pauper childhood might have been inspiration for a dozen Charles Dickens novels, was educated at a charity school, apprenticed to the Hudson's Bay Company, and wrote detailed diaries of his extensive travels in the North Country. In 1797 he and his boatmen paddled and portaged from Bottle Portage, connecting Bottle Lake with Lac La Croix, to Grand Portage stockade on Lake Superior in five days—a speed record which has not been bettered to the present time.

Lac La Croix, a beautiful, island-studded body of water that offers superb fishing, pictographs, and a Chippewa village, leads into Loon River, which in turn flows into Little Vermilion Lake, the granite walls of Little Vermilion Narrows, and on into Namakan Lake. A companion of David Thompson, Dr. John Bigsby, was neither an explorer nor a trader, but a physician who drew sketches and kept notes on his travels in the North Country. In the Namakan River he observed, with some astonishment, "a long spear erect in the water, and riding rapidly towards us. This I could not at all understand; but in a moment or two there darted down the current, from an upper bend, a canoe in full pursuit, one Indian in the bow, standing aloft on the thwarts, spear in hand; another was guiding. In striking a large fish, it had wrenched the weapon from the hand of the spearsman."

Namakan Lake crashes over Kettle Falls into Rainy Lake, named for the perpetual mist that rises from the falls on the Rainy River, on the other side of the lake. And beyond that. . . .

The voyageurs, seeking pelts, found in this northern land a complex of rivers and lakes that stretched as far as their strength could carry them before the last flocks of geese had passed overhead and ice stiffened against the banks. For modern man whose quest is for the wilderness, this is also true.

Camping overnight by island-studded Lac la Croix

2. Voyaging Through the North Woods

For some 220 miles, from Grand Portage on Lake Superior to historic St. Francis on Rainy Lake, the rivers and lakes of voyageur country wind through the north woods. The entire trip, one of the great wilderness runs of North America, can be done in three weeks to a month. Provisions should be planned with care, as they can be replenished only at Gunflint Lake, by paddling out to Ely from Basswood Lake, and at Crane Lake (see maps, pages 239, 240). The route passes through superb fishing country and your diet should be bounteously supplemented with bass, pike, walleye, and lake trout. Crayfish are also abundant and succulent, as are snails, if you happen to be an *escargot* fancier. Freshwater clams are edible, although generally tough. The voyage can be made from late spring to early fall: it should be noted that mosquitoes and black flies are most numerous and active in late May and June.

To reach Grand Portage by car, follow Interstate 35 to Duluth, then U.S. Highway 61 along the shore of Lake Superior. The first 67 miles of the voyageur route, from Grand Portage to the western end of Gunflint Lake, contains 15 miles of portages, and some tough upstream paddling on the Pidgeon River, which is described on pages 238–241. From Gunflint Lake to Fort Francis, 160 miles away, there are little more than 4 miles of portage required. This consideration, a very relevant one considering you will be carrying shelter, bedrolls, food for a couple of weeks, cooking gear, and so forth, suggests why Gunflint Lake is a popular put-in point for a trip down the voyageur route. Alternative launching places are at Bearskin Lake or Arrow Lake on the Canadian side (see maps, pages 239, 240).

To reach Gunflint Lake, one turns onto the Gunflint Trail, a scenic forest highway, at Grand Marais. At the northwest corner of the lake, a narrow strait leads into Magnetic Lake. Beyond the 1¼-mile-wide lake there are rapids followed by a falls dropping 12 feet over three steps of rock. The next 8 miles are delightfully varied—narrow lakes strung together by the Pine and Granite rivers. There are several rapids and falls necessitating portages; caution and detailed maps are essential. Lake

The author carrying an aluminum canoe over one of the many portages that connect the numerous rivers and lakes in the Boundary Waters Canoe Area

Saganaga is a beautiful body of water, with numerous rocky islands. Alexander Henry, passing through the lake during the summer of 1775, recorded that "There was formerly a large village of Chipeways here, now destroyed by the Nadowessies (Sioux). I found only three lodges filled with poor, dirty and almost naked inhabitants, of whom I bought fish and wild rice."

Swamp Lake, only ½ a mile wide, is well named. The short portage between Saganaga and Swamp ends oozily. Be careful: slipping in the mud with a canoe on your head is not fun. The somewhat longer portage from Swamp Lake to Cypress Lake consists in part of a log runway through the swamp. Cypress Lake, 5¼ miles long, was named by fur traders for the tree we now refer to as cedar. In honor of a distinguished traveler or company official, voyageurs would sometimes select a cedar on a prominent point, and create a "Mai" (or maypole) by cutting away all the branches except the uppermost, leaving a tuft of foliage at the top of the tree. The dignitary thus saluted was then obligated, by custom, to provide a round of wine or rum for all concerned. The number of "Mais" still visible in voyageur country until comparatively recent times would seem to indicate that a sizable number of important personages passed through the region, or that lesser souls were observed to be in possession of more wine than a single person might drink without grave dangers to his health.

Little Knife Portage, 66 yards long on the American side, leads to Little Knife Lake, which in turn opens into Knife Lake. Combined, the lakes are some 10½ miles long—clear, narrow bodies of water bordered by rocky, steep shorelines. They offer good walleye fishing. Big Knife Portage (about 400 yards in length) bypasses a rapids at the head of the Knife River. The ruins of a lumber company dam and log chute sprawl across the lip of the rapids. Other whitewater on the Knife River necessitates three additonal portages. At Prairie Portage, between Birch Lake and Basswood Lake, one passes a Canadian Customs house and ranger cabin. From this point a short paddle to the southwest through Sucker and Newfound lakes brings one to Moose Lake, from which the Fernberg Forest road leads into Ely. In restocking provisions, one can arrange to have someone bring them out to Moose Lake, although hitching a ride into town is less complicated. A cold beer and a little jukebox music is mighty nice for an evening after a couple of weeks in the wilds.

The route through sprawling Basswood Lake follows a Z pattern. While on the water, voyageurs customarily took a ten-minute break each hour for a smoke. Basswood was referred to as a "four-pipes lake." One of the longest portages on the western slope of the voyageur route is the 1¼-mile Horse Portage, guaranteed to lather you up a bit. The trail, which follows the American shore, skirts around Upper Basswood Falls and fast-water at the head of the Basswood River. After tumbling over two other

A blue heron takes off from the shore of Bottle Lake

falls (Wheelbarrow and Lower Basswood), the river flows into Crooked Lake. Portages around the falls are short and well marked.

Curtain Falls, at the western end of Crooked Lake, is one of the most impressive sights in the North Country. As with Upper Basswood Falls, when you hear the thunder of Curtain Falls, hug the American shore and watch closely for the portage. A ride over the lip would most likely be fatal. The trail drops steeply through forest and rock outcroppings. Midway along the portage is a fine camping spot on a grassy bench. There is excellent pike fishing in eddies below the falls.

Four-mile-wide Iron Lake comes next, and midway across it, a short side trip to the north brings you to Rebecca Falls, a magnificent twin cataract. The falls crash down from Iron Lake, so approach them cautiously. Best landing spot, and a fine campsite, is the wooded island separating the two plunging masses of water. Bottle Portage, a tough 400-yard trek, brings one into Lac La Croix. The lake, 26 miles long, has numerous beautiful island campsites and is renowned for its fishing.

The lake is believed to have been named for the Sieur de la Croix, who was crossing it with two companions in 1688 when a violent storm swept over the water. The birchbark canoe overturned. His fellow trappers managed to cling to the rolling, swamped canoe, and eventually reached shore safely. La Croix was drowned. Modern-day voyageurs should take note of this baleful event: high winds on the big lakes mean trouble and can spell disaster. Staying in camp an extra day may save your life.

The painted rocks of Irving (or Shortiss) Island were decorated by Indians and pioneer fur trappers. As Maj. Joseph Delafield commented in 1823: "The traveller has left his mark on this rock in various ways, some by name, some by date, and some by strange device."

A note on island camping on Lac La Croix: many of the most exquisite campsites are upon small domains of rock and tree, the good deadwood long since stripped out by other campers. Make wood runs to the neighboring islands or the shoreline: it is amazing how much you can carry in a canoe if it is well balanced.

There is a Chippewa village on the north shore of Lac La Croix, close to the entrance of the Namakan River.

Beatty Portage (286 yards), between Lac La Croix and Loon Lake, features a narrow-gauge track and flatcar over which one can push boats and gear with gratifying ease. Loon Lake is a narrow 5½-mile-long waterway which once was called, rather sinisterly, Un-de-go-sa or Man-eater's Lake. At Mud Portage there is another "marine railroad" (track and flatcar). The Loon River, which was fire-swept in 1917 and 1925, leads into Little Vermilion Lake. Beyond the granite walls of Little Vermilion Narrows, one can paddle south to Crane Lake, where supplies can be purchased.

Continuing on toward Rainy Lake, one passes a Canadian Customs Station just north of the entrance to Portage Bay. Sand Point Lake, 7 miles long, is connected by a narrows to 16-mile-long Namakan Lake. At Kettle Falls there is a portage around a control dam built in 1914, and from there a strong current pushes through a narrow, rocky defile and into Rainy Lake.

On the first map of this region, the large body of water (39 miles long) was called "Tecamamiouen," a Monsoni word for the mist which rises from the falls on the Rainy River. The French referred to it as Lac La Pluie. The shoreline is generally rocky, but as Major Delafield wryly observed: "In the vallies I have seen several places where I could drive a tent pin." Two miles down the Rainy River is Fort Francis, built in 1787. International Falls, close to the fort, is served by scheduled airline flights, and is at the junction of U.S. Highways 71 and 53. It is a logical terminus for this long and scenic wilderness voyage, for beyond the town, roads parallel the Rainy River all the way to Lake of the Woods.

Guide Notes for the ROUTE OF THE VOYAGEURS

LOCATION—Forms Minnesota-Canada border.

LENGTH OF TRIP—The run from Grand Portage on Lake Superior to Fort Francis on Rainy Lake is 220 miles. Since there are several access points, a number of shorter trips are possible. (See map, page 239.) Allow 3 weeks to a month from Grand Portage to Fort Francis. There are several fine sections which can be run in 1 to 2 weeks.

FAVORABLE SEASON—Late May through early October.

DEGREE OF DIFFICULTY—Lake and easy river travel. While there are heavy rapids and falls on some of these rivers, all can be by-passed on well-marked portages. Wind on the larger lakes can sweep up high waves in very little time. It is better to lay over if the weather is threatening. Extensive paddling and portaging are demanding physically—one should be in good shape for this trip.

RECOMMENDED CRAFT—Canoe. Kayaks are a possibility, but awkward to portage.

ACCESS POINTS—Most people drive into voyageur country by way of Grand Marais, Minnesota (106 miles north of Duluth on U.S. Highway 61), or Ely, Minnesota (108 miles north of Duluth on U.S. Highway 53 and State Highway 169). Out of Grand Marais, one can drive via Hovland on the Arrowhead Trail to Fowl Lake to a put-in point, or out the Gunflint Trail to launch at Bearskin Lake or Gunflint Lake. By driving up Highway 61 into Canada to the bustling city of Thunder Bay, you can approach the voyageur route from the other side of the border by driving a good many miles of forest road to shove off into Arrow Lake. There are several possible lake and river approaches to the route of the voyageurs from Ely. West of Ely, Crane Lake at the end of Echo Trail is a good take-out point unless continuing on to Fort Francis. International Falls, a long stone's throw from Fort Francis, is at the junction of U.S. Highway 71 and 53.

CAMPING—Numerous excellent campsites, many of them on islands. Most of the route of the voyageurs is in the Boundary Waters Canoe Area, where nondisposable containers such as cans and bottles are prohibited. An excellent precedent that all of our wilderness and primitive areas should enforce.

FISHING—Superb. Pike, walleye, smallmouth bass, lake trout. Here one can fill his skillet with fish as often as he cares to.

CHAPTER TEN

River of Ghosts: The Rio Grande

1. A Land of Legend

There are a lot of ghosts along the Rio Grande. Ghosts of miners who once panned placer in Colorado where the water is shallow and clear, and lichen-stained boulders from old landslides lean at the water's edge. Ghosts of the *conquistadores* who rode horses as their men trudged beside the river farther south, in what is now New Mexico, seldom stopping although the sun blazed at them and some wore armor, driving themselves to push on toward the fabled, golden Cities of Cibola, which seemed always only a little beyond where they were. The river they saw had the color of a freshly plowed field. There are ghosts too, in the hot, narrow canyons of the Big Bend country of Texas. Mexican Indians whose living comes from gathering a wax-producing plant and smuggling it across the border know of them. But they do not talk much of those things as they sit around the fading campfires until the last jerky has been quietly chewed, the last hand-rolled cigarette smoked, and men stretch out in their blankets to carry a final impression of darkly piled rock and close, mysterious stars into their dreams.

The Rio Grande, which rises in the high mountains of southern Colorado, is the second longest river in the United States. Only the Missouri-Mississippi system spans more country. For all of its 1900 miles, the Rio Grande has but a handful of tributaries, and even most of these are unstable. Their discharge varies from narrow strands that trickle together and apart, intricately braiding around dry rocks and over damp sand, to storm floods that carry uprooted trees and roll boulders in sudden, muddy torrent. People do not build riverbank houses beside these tributaries.

"There are ghosts . . . in the narrow canyons of the Big Bend country of Texas." The Rio Grande in Santa Elena Canyon

In most places across America, change is gradual, state lines a political reference; a man suddenly unblindfolded would be hard pressed to say if he were in Mississippi or Alabama, Indiana or Illinois, Oregon or Washington. The border between Colorado and New Mexico marks an abrupt change, both geographically and in numerous more subtle ways. In Colorado the landscapes are backdropped by interconnected ranges of jagged peaks, 13,000 to 14,000 feet high, where in the valleys the creeks are always filled, running or frozen. Only the Sangre de Cristo Range, which continues southward into New Mexico as far as Santa Fe, gives an impression of disregard for boundary. West of the Rio Grande the high ranges fall away below the border, becoming more gently rounded and drier with each league to the south. Still farther west are parched mesas and flatlands, cut through with spectacular arroyos that rarely carry moisture. Scattered through this piñon and bunchgrass country are Navajo hogans, from which, on a clear day, the hulk and snow of the Colorado ranges can be seen. Travelers often mistake them for clouds of a distant storm.

For most of its journey through Colorado, the Rio Grande is a valley river, where white frame houses sit back from the water and cattle and sheep graze along the banks. Once into New Mexico, the Rio Grande quickly cuts down into a broad, gently sloping plain. In places, the narrow gorge is over 800 feet deep, an almost sheer drop. Not knowing of this great trench, one might ride horseback to within a few yards of the actual rim without suspecting what is there. Below Taos Junction, the river brawls through a more conventional canyon—broken, rocksliding slopes and even enough toeholds for a highway (U.S. 64).

Now, again, after some 50 miles of wild, uninhabited canyon, there are signs of settlement. Simple crosses upon pulpits of volcanic rock; on other rocks are television aerials, often higher than the crosses, as if to gather in greater blessings. Fishermen, working their way through purple tamarisk at the water's edge, arc flies and lures toward promising eddies. When they speak, it is likely to be in Spanish, or Tiwa, language of nearby Indian pueblos. The frame farmhouses are far behind, back in Colorado. Here, villages are low huddles of adobe, surrounded by small fields of corn and chili. At Velarde, the canyon opens into the Espanola Valley, where the river winds leisurely through cottonwood groves and apple orchards, past mud houses which in autumn are festooned with strings of drying chili peppers.

From the site of San Gabriel del Yunque, where Onate founded the first non-Indian community in what is now New Mexico, you can throw pebbles into the Rio Grande. From the ancient cliff dwellings of Puye, you can see the river below, in the distance of the valley—as you can from nearby Los Alamos, birthplace of the atomic bomb.

At historic Otowi Bridge, the Espanola Valley pinches off as abruptly as it had opened at Velarde. The river then plunges through White Rock Canyon, final fastwater before the Big Bend country of Texas. From Cochiti Pueblo, end of the canyon, the Rio Grande moves placidly down the length of New Mexico. Most of the year its flow, bled by hundreds of irrigation canals, is meager. Some places, at certain times, a couple of empty beer cans and a chunk of driftwood could all but block the river.

Throughout this stretch of some 300 miles, the landscape is a paradox of desert and mountains. The dry lands—stone and sand, thorn and sapless stems—edge crumbling banks, shoved back here and there by watered

The Rio Grande (in distance) flows through a land rich in myth, legend, and history. These petroglyphs were carved hundreds of years ago by the Anasazi. This photo was taken near Otowi Bridge. Beyond here the river flows into White Rock Canyon (*Photo by Karl Kernberger, courtesy of New Mexico State Planning Office*)

fields. But beyond the final ditch, be it 50 yards or 2 miles back from the river, the desert presses against what green has been created. Yet from any place beside the river, one can see mountains: the Jemez, Sandias, Manzanos, Magdelenas, San Mateos, Black Range. None of them is a mirage. All are close, within a day's walk, octaves of blue under shifting slants of the sun, promising tall timber and chill creeks. The creeks are there, splashing down toward the unreachable river, finally slowing and then sinking into the sands of storm-clawed arroyos.

Once the river has trickled past the great smokestacks, the foundries, of El Paso, the bridges linking that city with Ciudad Juarez, it once again moves through a country with some irrigated farms close to the banks, through desert with mountains in the distance. The climate is hotter now, and only the highest mountains have trees. What little water they gather does not run off in streams, but is found in scoops of rock, called *tinajas* (watering tanks).

At the town of Ojinaga the Rio Conchos flows in from Mexico, giving the Rio Grande renewed vitality. Ahead a tangle of mountains blocks the river. For some 250 miles, from above Lajita clear down to Langtry, the waters twist and pound their way through deep, isolated gorges.

Once out of the dry, raw grandeur of the canyons, the river slows to a leisurely roll, a catfish river with trees on the banks, roads, and towns. Approaching the Gulf the heat becomes more humid, the vegetation thicker. And finally, what is left of snow and spring water from the Colorado Rockies and the Sierra Madre of Mexico, sluggishly meanders through saltmarshes and enters the sea.

The Rio Grande passes through a land of myth, legend, and mystery.

Away from the river, up side canyons at Puye and at Bandelier in northern New Mexico, are ancient, windowless cliff-houses. Beyond, in the country of mesa, arroyos, and leaning rock, are the remains of other broken cities—walls, outlines, scatters of faded pottery. Some of them were immense. More than fifty million pieces of rock were quarried and mortared into the construction of one typical community house. In another place a kiva, a religious vault, was covered with a layer of thin, carved planking that reverberated like a gigantic drum—the pulse of the earth itself—when shamans danced upon it. Over centuries, the cities of sun and rock grew and flourished. The people were becoming more skillful in fashioning objects important to them—dwellings, hunting and farming tools, pottery . . . the carved animal bones and feathers that were used in dance and song to dramatize the eternal mysteries: life, death; rain, drought; darkness, light.

Late in the thirteenth century and early in the fourteenth century, when these cities had reached their highest point of development, they were abandoned. There is no evidence of attack from outside or civil strife, no signs of burning or destruction. Most belongings were taken by departing residents. No burial sites or religious places were vandalized.

Scientists have proposed that increasing dryness triggered the migrations. Yet comparisons of annual tree-ring growth indicate people left the great community houses of Chaco Canyon a century before there was a drought. And in Frijoles Canyon, cliff-houses and bottomland structures were deserted beside a stream that always flowed. Epidemic? If so, burial sites give no sign of it. Did erosion destroy the croplands? This not only runs contrary to the drought theory, but that within a mere century it could have forced abandonment over such a scattered area seems hardly credible.

After leaving the cliff-cities, many groups made their way to the valley of the Rio Grande, where they built pueblos close to the river. Their descendants still live there today. In these villages, stories are told of how, in the distant past, people had left places it had taken generations to build.

One story tells how a people lost favor with the great plumed snake that was both protector and provider for the place in which they lived. The snake, reacting to some ceremonial offense, mounted into the sky higher and higher until he became the band of stars we call the Milky Way. Abandoned by their principal deity, the people's life could no longer be good. So they moved down to the river, to learn new ways of life, ways of communicating with new gods.

While Indians living along the Rio Grande told and retold myths that interwove with their daily lives—myths of the sun, the stars, certain animals, and the river itself—Spanish galleons were swaying westward over the seemingly endless reach of the Atlantic Ocean. On them, noblemen, adventurers, and soldiers talked and dreamed of distant legends—places where the sands were made of gold and precious stones lay strewn about like common pebbles. There were Catholic priests aboard whose belief that Indians, once taught of Christ's Passion, would come to regard their pagan fetishes as mere playthings was also myth. Among most tribes even today, a corn dance evokes as deep, if not deeper, feelings than a Mass, an eagle feather as much emotion as the Cross.

For Hernando Cortés and the men who followed him, the legend became reality. Hearing of the strange beings that had landed upon the beaches, the rim, of his known world, Aztec emperor Montezuma sent gifts—an image of the sun, in pure gold, larger than a carriage wheel; an even larger silver moon; gold figurines; parrot-feather headdresses—in hopes the intruders would go away.

Cortés sent the messengers back with three cloth shirts and a Venetian glass cup. And then proceeded to conquer Mexico.

Mexico, or New Spain, as it was now called, yielded more riches than had been dreamed of. Restless *conquistadores* looked for new legends to vindicate.

North of the ancient Aztec empire, greenness gradually receded, spaces became more infinite, hollow, with brilliant sunlight and arcs of stars, mountains hulking stark and eroded. Surely, it was thought, this landscape must be drab camouflage to rich empires beyond. After a time, stories, shaped as much by the listeners as the tellers, began to be defined and seem real. To the north were the Seven Cities of Cibola, where rooftops were tiled with gold and entire streets were lined with the shops of sliversmiths. And there was Quivira, where strings of golden bells tinkled in the wind.

The first Spaniards to enter the fabled lands north of New Spain had little interest in treasure; rather than wanting to explore the unknown, they wished only to escape from it. Three Spaniards and a Negro slave, Esteban, were survivors of the ill-fated Narvaez expedition, which landed in Florida in 1528. For seven years they lived among Indians along the Gulf Coast and in the Southwest, at times enslaved to dig roots or other menial tasks. (Esteban's thoughts at working beside a former master reduced to the same status have not been recorded.) Later they became known as men who could heal the sick and raise the dead. They began a long trek, guided by the setting sun, seeking outposts of New Spain which they knew to lie somewhere to the west. They were starving and ragged when they reached Indian villages on the Rio Grande, close to the present site of El Paso. Their fame as medicine men had gone before them and the villagers shared what meager food and clothing they possessed. They trudged on and eventually reached a Spanish settlement.

When Esteban returned to the north country of legend, he wore bright clothes and carried a gourd rattle. Bells jingled at his wrists and ankles. Two greyhounds beckoned to his call. The former slave was now guide to an advance party seeking the Seven Cities of Cibola. At Hawikúh, a Zuñi pueblo, the chief was angered rather than pleased when Esteban had a runner deliver the gourd rattle to him. The talisman was similar to those used by an enemy tribe. There was a fight, in which Esteban and several Indians with him were killed. Friar Marcos, leader of the scouting party, arrived after the battle was over. But seeing the great terraced city, he was sure it was the first of the seven cities they were seeking. He returned south with an optimistic report for the governor of New Galicia, Francisco Vásquez de Coronado.

Commissioned by Crown and Viceroy, a massive expedition led by Coronado started north the following winter from Culiacan—two hundred and thirty caballeros, numerous foot soldiers, five friars, almost a thousand Indian porters and servants, herds of horses, sheep, and cattle.

Coronado, a handsome young man with blue eyes and blond hair, moustache and beard, who rode a horse as though it became a part of him, was eager and confident . . . only time and distance separated the expedition from kingdoms as rich, if not richer, than those of the Aztecs and the Incas.

Distance stretched agonizingly into time. The expedition was strung out for miles, moving slowly northward across the maze of canyons which slash the western flank of the Sierra Madre Mountains of Mexico. Impatient, Coronado pushed ahead with a hundred men, passing through desert country in what is now southern Arizona, arriving at Hawikúh in midsummer. The Indians made a line of sacred cornmeal before their city, warning the Spaniards not to cross it. When they did, a war horn was sounded, and arrows were loosened from taut bows. But arrows and leather shields were no match for mounted men protected by armor and chain mail, who had harquebuses, swords, and lances. The horses, especially, were frightening, and after the Zuñi defense was quickly broken, word spread among the pueblo peoples that these tall, strange beasts ate men.

At Hawikúh, there were no gilded rooftops nor streets of silversmiths. The Spaniards helped themselves to Indian food stores, which they badly needed, and thought of the six months of grueling effort that had brought them to a rock village containing nothing of worth. Still, the dream persisted. Perhaps they had not gone far enough.

As Coronado waited for the rest of his legions to reach Hawikúh, he sent out exploration parties. Melchior Díaz went west with twenty-five men, crossing the barren *Camino del Diablo,* an Indian trail, to the banks of the Colorado River. Hernando de Alvarado went east with twenty soldiers and a priest, and after a week's travel, gazed down upon a wide, brown river, lined with cottonwoods and willow. P'osoge, or Big River, the Indians called it. Alvarado had reached the Rio Grande near the present site of Isleta. Marching northward along the river, he exchanged presents with head men of the river pueblos, and had crosses erected before each village. The Pueblo Indians, never habitually warlike, received the Spaniards well.

Coronado decided to winter his army on the Rio Grande, and it was at this bivouac, near the present-day town of Bernalillo, that he heard Alvarado's report. Alvarado had much to tell, not only of places seen, but of stories heard. It seemed that to the east was a place with great cities near a river wider than most lakes. People traveled on the river in long canoes with sails and golden eagles on the prows, and sometimes fish larger than horses were caught. Table service was made from silver; other vessels from gold, and the emperor took his rest under a tree from which golden bells dangled, tinkling in the breeze.

It was called Quivira.

Years before, in Spain, a friend of Coronado's had prophesied he would go to distant lands, rising to a position of high power, and then suffer calamitous downfall. Coronado had gone to New Spain, become a provincial governor, and now seemed on the verge of finding the shimmering empire he sought.

Troubles began. An Indian claimed a soldier had raped his wife, but identification of the culprit was inconclusive, since the Spaniards looked very much alike to the Indians, just as the Indians looked very much alike to the Spaniards. As ice began forming along banks of the river, Coronado sent officers to collect clothing from the pueblos, as his men had come from hot climates, and were unprepared for the biting cold. From some pueblos, food was foraged as well as cloth and hides. Regarding them as guests, the Indians had shared food with the Spaniards, although they had little surplus. Tribute was another matter.

Young men of the tribe had sportively wrestled with the newcomers. They were mortal. Only their horses gave them power.

One afternoon, Indians from the pueblo of Arenal attacked two herdsmen guarding the garrison's horses, and drove the animals across the river. Some were killed; others scattered. Inside the open square of the pueblo, horses screamed with pain and fright as arrows were shot at them from rooftops. The Spaniards made overtures for peaceful surrender. The Indians angrily refused. Shouting their battle cry—*Santiago!*—the soldiers attacked with crossbow and harquebus. A log was used as a battering ram to open a breach at the base of the pueblo, into which burning brush and wood was stuffed. Soon the interior of the many-celled structure was afire, and men leaped from the walls to escape choking smoke. Some were held as captives, others lanced, and yet others, as an example, were tied to stakes and burned as if they had been witches.

The Indians made another defiant stand, at the pueblo of Moho on the west bank of the river. After a fifty-day siege, the Indians, almost out of provisions and water, attempted to steal away from the pueblo in darkness. Only a few managed to cross the river to safety, the rest were killed or wounded by cavalry. For miles downstream, brown bodies floated on the brown slow water, catching on snags and slowly revolving in eddies.

Resistance was broken. But for the men of the pueblos, normally a peaceful yet a proud people, certain things would not be forgotten. At least not until after other centuries of bloodshed.

Coronado could now turn his attention to Quivira. Traveling eastward across the plains as far as what is now Kansas, he saw herds of buffalo stretching as far as the eye could see. In all this vast sea of lank grass, there were no cities, only Indians who lived in grass huts and hunted the buffalo; no emperor listening to golden bells, only a naked, white-haired chieftain whose sole wealth was a copper band around his neck.

Returning to the Rio Grande, Coronado prepared for another winter's bivouac. His belief in Quivira, although ebbing, was not gone. He would search for it the following spring.

Coronado loved horses, and during a spirited race with one of his officers his saddle girth broke, throwing him into the path of the other horse. Struck by a flashing hoof, for a time he was close to death. When he had recovered, Quivira seemed more distant than ever. And so, in the spring of 1542, the army of Coronado, a man of shattered vision, struggled back toward Mexico.

Writing of Coronado after his return, Lorenzo de Tejeda stated: "Francisco Vásquez came to his home, and he is more fit to be governed in it than to govern outside of it. . . ."

In the country of the Rio Grande, men would continue to search for gold and silver. And would eventually find them, not as bells hanging from a tree or on shelves of mud houses, but rather, in the rock of mountains rising back from the river. That time, however—an era of jack-hammers and dynamite, player-pianos and stagecoaches—would come much later.

Priests and settlers followed in the wake of the *conquistadores,* and a number of missions and farming hamlets were established in the Rio Grande Valley. Over 500 miles of harsh, uninhabited country separated the colony from Chihuahua, closest Spanish outpost of any consequence. It appeared there was no mineral wealth whatsoever, and farming was possible only in parts of the river valley and up some tributary canyons. Yet there were Indians to be converted, and officials set to the task with zeal. Kivas were demolished. *Caciques,* Pueblo priests, were tried for heresy— some were flogged, others executed. Such abuses triggered frequent Indian revolts, and for one twelve-year period the Spaniards were completely driven from the upper Rio Grande.

The settlers, living in isolation and constant fear of Indian attack, began to evolve a culture which was as distinct from that of Mexico as Mexico's was from that of Spain. Language took on special nuances, as did music, folklore, architecture, and religion.

The Penitente Order observed Easter week with intense rituals that dramatized the Passion story. Hooded figures marched to symbolic Stations of the Cross, lashing each other's bare, bleeding backs with yucca whips. On Good Friday evening, Penitentes gathered in an adobe *morada,* where the only light was from one white candle, representing Christ, and twelve yellow candles, signifying the disciples. A hymn would be sung, then a psalm recited, and one of the yellow candles would be extinguished. This was repeated until only the white candle continued to burn, which in turn would then be hidden. In utter blackness shrieks, wails, banging of wooden devices, and clanking of heavy chains would shatter the silence—a pandemonium vividly commemorating that day of horror when darkness descended, the disciples fled, the earth shook, boulders split, and the dead were cast out of their graves. After perhaps half an hour the white candle would again be brought forth, the tumult cease, and a hymn would close the ceremony.

Old stories of witchcraft and werewolves, easy to shrug off in the bustle of European cities, were not taken lightly when a colonist's family gathered around their fireplace of an evening, the door barred against Indians, bear, or whatever might be in the dark, humped hills that stretched off into unknown lands. In lonely bottomlands and on rocky sidehills, people reported seeing *brazas,* mysterious balls of fire, or hearing the ghost wails of *llorana,* the crying woman. Certain old women of the villages were said to be able to make potions for love or death, to be able to change themselves into wolves and other animals at will.

The *conquistadores* had come into the country of the upper Rio Grande, resplendent in armor and plumes, seeking the stuff of legends. After the turn of the last century, the mountain men began appearing along streams that fed into the Rio Grande, wearing filthy, worn buckskins. Cantankerous, self-sufficient, restless and unbelievably tough, they themselves were the stuff of myth and legend. The price of beaver pelts drew them into the largely unexplored lands of western America, and of those who survived long enough to tilt a jug of corn whiskey and recount, each had his own odyssey: of being chased naked by a score of armed Indians, outrunning all but one, killing him with his own lance, and then plodding on for days to safety, feet full of cactus spines and numbed from high pass snowfields; of being lashed to a cottonwood raft that got flung through the most godawful stretch of river rapids on the American continent; of killing an enraged grizzly bear with a clasp knife; of days wandering amid sun-sucked desert ranges and almost dying of thirst; of exploring canyons so deep that clouds seemed to rise out of them, and chasms so narrow that the sunlight never leaked in.

At Taos, as much as anyplace, the mountain men holed up for the winter and relaxed from their wanderings. There was lots of "Taos Lightning," a local *aguardiente* that was a powerful relaxant, except when a man needed a head of steam for a good-natured brawl. Taos Lightning could do that too. Gambling and outlandish lying were acceptable pastimes, and *fandangos* were real events. Most of the town would turn out. To the throb of guitars and the sawing of violins, Spanish dandies and lanky, bearded trappers vied for the attentions of shapely senoritas. When interests conflicted, as they frequently did, monumental fights would ensue, often knives against the flying fists of howling, buckskinned madmen who seemed harder to hurt than shadows.

Kit Carson was a short, wiry youth who drifted into Taos after running away from a saddler to whom he had been apprenticed in Franklin,

Missouri. His former employer offered a one-cent reward for his return. The penny went begging, since Carson seldom returned anywhere for long; he was always on the move, pacing back and forth through the western states as though they were a cage scarcely big enough to contain him. His exploits became legendary. While guiding John Frémont to California, an expedition that was to result in the annexation of that area, Carson and his companions were besieged by Modoc Indians near Klamath Lake. The Modocs had an overwhelming advantage in numbers and things looked rather grim for the travelers. Carson somehow managed to slip out through the enemy perimeter and, killing an Indian every few minutes from different vantage points, soon had them wondering if it were not they, rather than the Frémont party, that was surrounded. The Modocs withdrew.

In later years, Carson spent a good deal of time in Taos. During a serious illness, he one day raised up from his buffalo robe and requested a solid meal and his pipe. Warned they might prove fatal, he retorted: "No matter. Bring me some fust-rate doin's, a buffler steak, my pipe and a big bowl of coffee." He ate two pounds of meat, took some long pulls at his pipe, and died.

Taos was winter headquarters for Bill Williams, who originally came west sober and upright as a white picket fence, obsessed with the notion of converting every Indian he laid eyes on to Christianity. Somewhere along the way, a spell of the backcountry laid hands upon him, all that sky and distance, and he dropped his ministry for outright roaming, and later took up with so much cussing and drinking that even the mountain men around Taos respected him. Old Bill Williams ended up with a considerable town named after him, a good-sized river (when it runs), and a mountain range. An honor which, for the record, was never bestowed on any frontier evangelists.

One of Bill Williams' drinking cronies at Taos was a husky young trapper named Tom Smith, who would soon be known throughout the mountain West simply as "Pegleg," a nickname he acquired in about the roughest possible way. In the late fall of 1827 Smith was trapping on the North Platte. Smith, aided by Ceran St. Vrain, was setting traps when an Indian fired from cover, hitting him in the right leg. St. Vrain dropped to his stomach, cradling his rifle to fend off the anticipated charge. There was no other gunfire as the Indian, hearing the approach of other trappers, slipped away.

Smith's companions carried him back to camp on a crude litter, and uncorked some Taos Lightning for him to pull on. The injured man's leggings were cut away, revealing a hopelessly shattered limb. Smith lifted up and looked himself. "Cut her off," he ordered. When no one moved, not knowing how to go about it, Smith requested a knife from the camp cook. After a couple of long shots from the jug, he began the amputation himself.

Midway through, he passed out, and Milton Sublette finished the job, taking the leg off below the knee. The operation had been primitive, to say the least, and it was expected the patient would be dead by morning. Instead, he was very much alive, cursing with vigor. After a day or so, during which time Smith seemed to grow stronger, camp was broken and the party headed west. Their journey, up over deep soft snow in the Park Range, down through the dense scrub oak of the Little Snake River country, was rugged going even for healthy men. Smith was carried on a litter suspended between two horses, which at one point lost their footing, tumbling him into a ravine. He reacted, as was his wont, by stringing together some of the most imaginative cuss words ever bellowed at a winter sky.

The trappers made winter camp in the valley of the Green River, where some friendly Ute had also dug in. Up to this point, Smith had survived on sheer will power; what remained of the leg was still in bad shape. An old Ute medicine man said he knew of a remedy. Next day, after gathering up a quantity of a certain root, he and several of his people carefully chewed the tubers, then came up in turn to spit the juice upon the stump. It healed rapidly.

While snow piled up in drifts outside, Smith lay upon buffalo skins in his warm lodge, meticulously whittling out the wooden leg he would be known by from St. Louis to the Golden Gate.

Pegleg continued to trap as long as the market for beaver pelts held up, but when prices began to drop he turned to other vocations, such as horse stealing. For several years he raided Mexican ranches in Chihuahua and California, always elusive, usually successful in plundering a number of animals, which he sold at Bent's Fort on the Arkansas.

According to contemporary accounts, he was still a formidable man in a fight. Isaac Wister was heading west when he encountered Pegleg in Independence, Missouri, in April of 1849. The irascible old mountain man was none too happy at being locked out of all the saloons in town. As related in Wister's autobiography, Pegleg

> therefore blew off the lock of one of them with his rifle and entered upon four border-desperadoes, deep in the fascination of poker, who instantly opened fire. Pegleg's gun being empty, he promptly jerked off his hickory leg and at one blow extinguished all the candles on the table and began feeling for the enemy. The general net result of the engagement was—two men killed by the wooden leg, another *hors de combat,* and the fourth shot with a captured weapon as he was making his way out. Having been variously wounded in the encounter, Pegleg's blood was up, and he was for remaining to fight the town, but his friends applied the *similia similibus curantur* and with the aid of more whiskey, managed to get him away among the Kaw Indians

across the boundary, and no one in Independence hankered for the job of capturing this famous character on the open prairie. (From *Auto-biography of Isaac Jones Wister,* Isaac Wister, 1914.)

Sometime in either 1865 or 1866 Pegleg and a companion set out to walk from Yuma, Arizona, to San Diego. Three days of trudging across the sun-scaped Colorado Desert was enough for the companion, who returned to Yuma. The sixty-nine-year-old man continued, leaving the prints of a boot and a peg on the salt of dry lakes; plodding over endless sand dunes, across miles of desert pan where the wind had stripped away everything but billions of smooth pebbles. Losing his way in the mountains, he climbed a peak to get his bearings. On the way down, he pocketed some soft rock that looked like gold ore although it was black. Eventually, he stumbled into San Diego, delirious from starvation and exhaustion. He was taken to a hospital. A nurse placed the black rocks in the window of his room, and later they were sent to the San Francisco mint for assaying. Records reveal that the rocks were analyzed at the mint, and found to be extremely rich gold ore blackened by volcanic activity. A check in the amount of $1452 was sent to the San Diego hospital, where there was no one to receive it.

Pegleg Smith had left. Somehow he made his way to San Francisco, where he died in October of 1866 at the city hospital, unaware of the magnitude of his discovery. The search for the source of the black rocks, referred to as the Lost Pegleg Mine, has been going on ever since.

The mountain West that Pegleg knew as a young man was an immense domain of solitude, where a trapper might walk hundreds of miles without seeing another white man. North of Taos there was only a handful of forts, maintained by fur barons, scattered over an area the size of Europe. Entire river systems and mountain ranges were unknown.

By the time of his death, in all that area there were virtually no rivers or creeks that had not been attempted in log rafts (with frequent fatalities), almost no gulches or passes that had not been tramped over. Maps showed towns clustered against mountain ranges like berries (although many had been built and abandoned within a month, and others were mere phantoms in the minds of men who sold mining stock). From 1848, when a nugget was picked up from the sluiceway of Sutter's Mill in northern California, until well after the turn of the century, every state from the Rockies on West was the site of scores of bonanzas—gold and silver stampedes.

Mining camps sprang up in the mountains on either side of the upper Rio Grande: Bland, Albermarle, Twining, Hopewell, Midnight, Summitville. Creede, Colorado, which boomed after two prospectors located the Holy Moses Mine close to the headwaters of the Rio Grande, soon became one of the most flamboyant mining towns anywhere. Its population was estimated to be around ten thousand during the 1890s, and conditions were so crowded that for a time Pullman cars of the Denver & Rio Grande Western served as a makeshift hotel on a siding near the station between runs. Creede was hit frequently by fires and floods. It seemed that no sooner would a burned section of town be rebuilt over barely cold ashes than flood waters would come sweeping down Willow Creek, ripping apart buildings—running all that half-charred lumber down the Rio Grande toward Mexico. A journalist, observing the enthusiasms of Creede's early inhabitants, commented that "at night there are no policemen to interfere with the vested rights of each citizen to raise as much Cain as he sees fit."

The mining booms were accompanied by a frenzy of railroad building: everywhere branch lines probed away from continental trunks.

The Denver and Rio Grande Western line from Antonito, Colorado, to Santa Fe, dubbed the "Chili line," was an informal road. For much of its distance the tracks ran beside the Rio Grande—up White Rock Canyon, through the Espanola Valley and the lower Taos Box—and many a time the steam engines throttled down to either drop off or pick up a solitary fisherman or wildflower buff. Mail, newspapers, and sometimes babies were delivered by the train crew. One accommodating engineer used to funnel scalding water from his boiler into the wooden washtubs of women who had come by wagon from the dry-farming community of Carson, greatly facilitating their weekly wash.

Trains ran on the Chili line until the advent of World War II, when the tracks were taken up for scrap metal. Some of the engines were shipped to Skagway, Alaska, and were used on the White Pass and Yukon Railroad.

There are old people living along the Rio Grande who say that from time to time they still hear train whistles, distant and mournful in the night. There is a windowless adobe near the rutted weed-rank right-of-way in which, it is related, one cannot spend a comfortable night. Those who go there with bedrolls and wait awake all night will be disappointed. Nothing will happen. But if one falls asleep, uneasy dreams follow. At some point in a dream something will shriek, high and piercing. You will wake and hear the sound again, far up the canyon, repeating itself. A steamwhistle. Unmistakably. And then the rhythmic huff of the engine, coming closer. The din increases, is amplified, until it seems the train is hurtling right at the house, into it. One cannot bear it, must rush outside into a sudden hush of glittering stars and empty fields. Only the nearby river moves, dark and gently swirling.

Even now, in the age of space voyage, there are some curious things in the villages back away from the river and the highway, places settled by Spanish colonists more than three centuries ago.

At Santuario Chapel, north of Santa Fe, built in 1816, there is a pit of red-clay earth in an anteroom to one side of the altar. The afflicted rub this clay, a healing earth, against the parts of their bodies that are failing them.

In the anteroom hang dozens of crutches and braces to which are attached scrawled testimonials in Spanish. Many people take jars and pouches of clay home with them, for family or relations too ill to travel. Yet the level of red clay seems to remain the same.

In the chapel there is a statue of the infant Christ, fully dressed, with soft shoes upon wooden feet. It is said the infant, troubled by things of our modern world, paces in the chapel, and under the trees before it. No one has seen this. But every few months the shoes are found to be worn through, and must be replaced.

Not far from Santuario is a deep cave. Smoke from large fires built inside it, they say, will emerge hours later from fissures in Black Mesa, more than 15 miles away. Black Mesa itself—high, isolated, slabbed with dark rock—seems a good setting for mystery. Indians speak of a cannibal giant who once lived in a cave on the north side. Inside, the mesa was riddled with passageways and chambers. To these places the giant would carry his victims.

Near some villages darkened *moradas* still resound to shrieks and the clanking of chains on Good Friday Eve, and heavy crosses are dragged to secret crucifixion sites.

In the villages today, if one asks about *brujas* the response will be a shrug and an indulgent smile. Yet as late as 1887 a woman was stoned to death in a mountain hamlet for being a witch. If one persists long enough, it is discovered there are certain *viejas* who mix herbs into broths said to have unusual powers, and who are able to pass from one place to another without motion.

In lonely ranch houses amid the dark, humped hills, people whose supper cooks upon wood stoves and whose rooms are lighted with kerosene lamps, talk softly of strange things seen or heard: a ball of rolling fire, perhaps, or the sobbing wails of *llorana*.

The Rio Grande passes through a land whose rocks are stained with ancient blood; where myth, dreams, and reality have often touched in curious ways.

It is a river of ghosts.

2. Cruising the Upper Rio Grande

The upper Rio Grande is a variety of rivers: its setting ranges from mountain meadows to narrow, rocky gorges, and it offers gentle runs for beginning boaters, exciting water for skilled whitewater enthusiasts, and in places is virtually impassable. A popular Colorado run is from the old mining camp of Creede to South Fork, a swift, exciting section where large trout await the resourceful angler. This is the site of an annual boisterous raft race, sponsored by the Alamosa Chamber of Commerce.

The Rio Grande Gorge—more than 50 miles of fast river cut through basalt layers spewed from ancient volcanoes—begins undramatically a few miles north of the Colorado-New Mexico border. At Lobatos bridge, popular launching place for boat trips, the river slips quietly through an immensity of sky and parched flatlands. To the north, highpiled in the distance, is 14,317-foot Blanca Peak—sacred to the Navajo tribe. Southward lies a sweep of prairie where antelope browse amid sage and chamisa, and volcanoes swell softly against the horizon. Passing through this prairie, the river slices gradually into the land. Shallow cliffs give way to deep walls of lichen-stained rock. At the New Mexico border the gorge is 200 feet deep. Where the Red River enters the Rio Grande, it is 800 feet deep.

Only two bridges cross the gorge. For a single brief stretch, on the east rim, a dirt road parallels it. With a few exceptions, trails into the canyon and beside the river are rough or nonexistent. The variety of wildlife and plants is extraordinary.

It is fitting, then, that the Rio Grande Gorge was one of eight rivers selected to comprise the initial National Wild and Scenic Rivers System, that on May 13, 1970, it was the first American river to be formally thus dedicated.

The 24-mile run from Lobatos bridge to Lee Trail is rated Class II on a difficulty scale of I to VI—"mild rapids, intermediate run." Lobatos bridge can be reached by driving east from Antonito on State Highway 248, or west through Mesita. The Rio Grande is usually run May through September. There may be one or more barbed-wire fences in the water before the mouth of the canyon is reached. When you spot one, paddle for shore and portage. They can do nasty things to rafts.

Once into the canyon, the water quickens, fed by cold springs. Willows and tall grass line the banks, camouflage for mule deer, bobcat, and coyote. Swallows and songbirds swoop and flutter against rock and willows. Sometimes, high overhead, a golden eagle can be seen, drifting in the air currents, watchful for prey. Beaver and muskrat slip from bank to water. The snowy egret nests here, as does the great blue heron.

The Colorado-New Mexico border is noted by a concrete marker set in a low mound of boulders on the east rim. From here to Taos Junction bridge, the gorge is protected by the U.S. Wild River Act. Some 9 miles from Lobato bridge, Costilla Creek comes in from the east; usually dry, it is known to rip and tear when thunderheads are piled up over the mountains. It is a favorite camping nook for boaters.

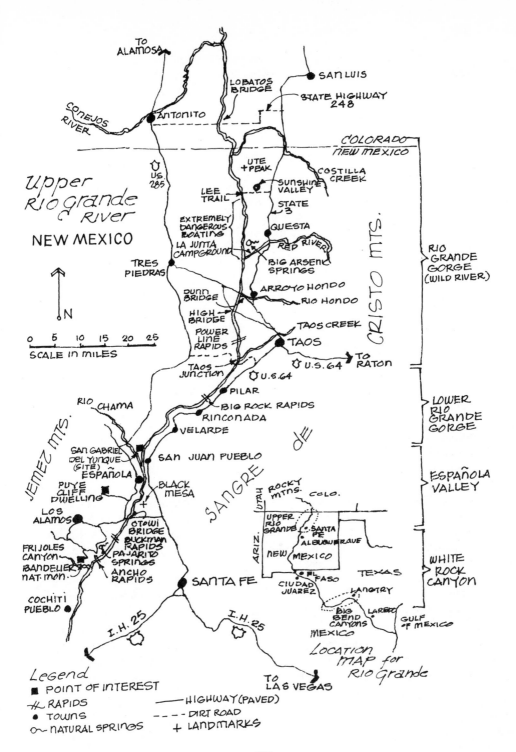

Upper
Rio Grande River
NEW MEXICO

TO ALAMOSA
SAN LUIS
LOBATOS BRIDGE
STATE HIGHWAY 248
CONEJOS RIVER
Antonito
COLORADO
NEW MEXICO
US 285
UTE PEAK
LEE TRAIL
SUNSHINE VALLEY
COSTILLA CREEK
STATE 3
EXTREMELY DANGEROUS BOATING
QUESTA
LA JUNTA CAMPGROUND
RED RIVER
TRES PIEDRAS
BIG ARSENIC SPRINGS
RIO GRANDE GORGE (WILD RIVER)
DUNN BRIDGE
ARROYO HONDO
RIO HONDO
HIGH BRIDGE
SANGRE DE CRISTO MTS.
POWER LINE RAPIDS
TAOS CREEK
TAOS
TAOS JUNCTION
U.S. 64
TO RATON
U.S. 64
RIO CHAMA
PILAR
BIG ROCK RAPIDS
RINCONADA
LOWER RIO GRANDE GORGE
VELARDE
JEMEZ MTS.
SAN GABRIEL DEL YUNQUE (SITE)
ESPAÑOLA
SAN JUAN PUEBLO
SANGRE DE
ESPAÑOLA VALLEY
PUYE CLIFF DWELLING
BLACK MESA
LOS ALAMOS
OTOWI BRIDGE
BUCKMAN RAPIDS
PAJARITO SPRINGS
FRIJOLES CANYON
BANDELIER NAT. MON.
ANCHO RAPIDS
SANTA FE
WHITE ROCK CANYON
COCHITI PUEBLO
I.H. 25
I.H. 25
TO LAS VEGAS

Location Map for Rio Grande
ROCKY MTNS.
UTAH
COLO.
UPPER RIO GRANDE
SANTA FE
ALBUQUERQUE
ARIZ.
NEW MEXICO
EL PASO
TEXAS
CIUDAD JUAREZ
LANGTRY
BIG BEND CANYONS
LAREDO
GULF OF MEXICO
MEXICO

0 5 10 15 20 25
SCALE IN MILES

N

Legend
■ POINT OF INTEREST
╫ RAPIDS
• TOWNS
∽ NATURAL SPRINGS
——— HIGHWAY (PAVED)
- - - DIRT ROAD
+ LANDMARKS

Close to Lee Trail, the canyon becomes deeper, the water swifter. The trail is reached by driving west from New Mexico Highway 3 through Sunshine Valley to the canyon rim and then south along the rim for 2½ miles. Roads in this area turn to gumbo in wet weather. The trail starts from the Achilles tendon of a boot-shaped promontory between the Rio Grande Gorge and Sunshine Canyon. There are other rough trails in the area, but in carrying boats up from the river, one's spine is in less danger of total disintegration by following Lee Trail, 220 steep feet from water to rim. Other trails in the area, unless one has rich Sherpa blood, should be ascended with no more than a fishing rod.

Those unfamiliar with the river would do well to have a friend waiting at the base of the trail, with fire burning if it is late, steaks and *refrescos* at the ready. For if Lee Trail is missed, the next 12 miles will be pure nightmare. Between the trail and the confluence of Red River, the Rio Grande drops 650 feet. Immense, spray-slick boulders often choke the channel. The water thunders down in cataracts, gushing through narrow slots of glistening rock.

Boating experts rate this one of the most difficult stretches of water in America—Class VI in rating.

In the spring of 1970, a California housewife who works for a river-guide organization probed the upper Rio Grande to see if it offered tour possibilities. She was enchanted with the canyon until Lee Trail was behind her, and deep-roar rapids came up around every bend. She and her party— two boatmen, two New Mexico Fish and Game Department employees— found themselves plummeted through wild chutes, and lining boats through rapids impossible to run. Lining is not only hard work; it is dangerous work.

You are often waist deep in icy water, with the boat jerking at ropes like a wild horse. If, in bracing yourself against the current, you happen to thrust your foot against a mossy rock—you will be lucky to get to shore with only bruises, lucky not to lose the boat. If unlucky, the river will draw you into it like a helpless marionette . . . hurl you into the bursting of water against rock.

On the fourth day, having negotiated only 4½ miles, the lady decided, "This is it, we can't make it. We were exhausted. I remember pushing some spider webs out of the way so I could crawl under a rock to rest."

They struggled out toward the canyon lip, toward the normal world without the incessant, threatening rush of a river gone berserk. Near the sharp, sliced rim of the gorge, they encountered two semihysterical fishermen who had come upon the body of a rafter who drowned in the stretch they had been attempting.

Once the Red River is reached, the Rio Grande slows somewhat, as if exhausted from the crescendo of its furious descent. The run from here to

John Dunn bridge is rated Class III, a "challenging intermediate run." An excellent trail switchbacks up from the junction of the two rivers to La Junta Campground: 800 vertical feet. A trail winds upcanyon from where the rivers meet, leading to Big Arsenic Springs, where 5400 gallons of water per minute issue from great rockslides. In spite of the forbidding name, water from Big Arsenic is refreshing and cold. Large brown and rainbow trout glide through pools and eddies in this section of river. Crayfish are their favorite natural food: using them as bait, anglers have reeled in fish weighing as much as 10 pounds, and 2-pounders are frequently hooked.

Several miles below the Red River, the Rio Hondo rushes in from the east. The only road to enter the canyon swings down the trench carved by the Rio Hondo, spans the Rio Grande over John Dunn bridge, and switchbacks up the other side, headed towards Tres Piedras. Most boaters who enter the water at the Red River take-out here. The next 17 miles pose a challenge to the most skillful whitewatermen and is rated Class V, "exceptionally difficult."

A couple of miles below the bridge, eroded remains of an old wagon road cut steeply down to the river from both canyon rims. Viewing the abrupt, narrow pitches today, it is hard to envy bygone teamsters on the descent, or their horses pulling up the other side. At the crossing, a man named Manby once had a way station and bathhouse. Only the walls remain of the building, although the hot springs still flow. On warm summer days, there are usually a few young people at the spring, hair loose over their shoulders—bathing, laughing, or simply stetched quietly in the sun.

The Rio Grande Gorge high bridge, which spans the canyon from rim to rim, is another 2 miles downriver. From the water, the bridge is quite a sight; just as the river is from the bridge. The Washington Monument could be placed under the span with 100 feet to spare. There are usually a number of tourists peering into the abyss from the bridge; they wave when they spot boats far beneath them. A couple of seasons ago, however, some youths playfully dropped pebbles as boats passed below. Pebbles falling 650 feet do unplayful things to a person's head. Fortunately, no one was hit.

There is no trail from bridge to water level. The stretch from here to Taos Junction bridge is the wildest on the river, a trail-less solitude of soaring rock and plunging rapids, where the animals rarely hear the sounds of man. About midway through the run, a power line crosses the gorge at rim level. Beneath it is one of the toughest navigable rapids on this or any other river. On the west bank, where boaters beach to look over the cataract, is a registration book in a mailbox. Landslides have dammed the river at this point, and the water rushes over the obstruction. The sensation

Rough going in "The Slot." Running "The Slot" is a favorite of New Mexico whitewater enthusiasts. The narrow passage is just below Glen Woody Bridge between Pilar and Embudo, where the river is easily accessible by road

of running Powerline Rapids is perhaps most aptly stated by "Stretch" Fretwell of Los Alamos, New Mexico, who has gone through it numerous times: "You aim your boat for the right place and get spat out like a watermelon seed. Hopefully right side up."

The next 5 miles are difficult boating—a continuous succession of rapids, violent back eddies, whirlpools, looming boulders.

Where Taos Creek comes into the river from the east, the wild river gorge is ended. Here, at Taos Junction bridge, boats can be taken-out or put-in. Below, the canyon continues to be scenic, but the walls are broken and eroded down into benches beside the water. From the bridge to the farming village of Pilar, a dirt road borders the river. Currents swing in easy drifts. It's an excellent stretch to boat with a nonaquatic girl friend, or with children.

From Pilar to Rinconada the velocity of the river picks up as it twists down through a tamarisk-lined canyon. The run is rated as Class IV, or "expert." U.S. Highway 64 parallels the east side of the river along here, with numerous overlook pullouts. Each May these pullouts resemble city parking lots as hundreds of spectators perch on rocky slopes above the river to watch the Rio Grande boat race. Rafts and kayaks leave at one-minute intervals from the starting point near Pilar. Places are awarded on how long it takes them to cover the rocky 4.4-mile course. Not everyone completes it. Just below Glen Woody bridge a rockslide pinches the entire river into "The Slot," only 5 feet wide at its narrowest point. At the end of the rapids, a giant boulder splits the river. To the right is a short drop: to the left, a foaming, narrow chute. From wet personal experience, I recommend the right-hand drop. During the race, Big Rock Rapids usually weeds out several competitors. The race ends at Rinconada, another farming village, and here, too, is an end to fastwater. For the next 10 miles, to Velarde, at the mouth of the canyon, the river is rated Class I, an easy, scenic trip. Throughout the canyon, on the west side, one can see segments of the roadbed of the historic "Chili line." Near Embudo, there is an old yellow, wooden water tower.

For the next 28 miles the river slips lazily through the Espanola Valley—a good place for beginning boaters to get the feel of the water and their craft. The river is some distance from the highway, passing through farm and ranch lands, often bordered by stately cottonwood groves.

If there is a dance at San Juan Pueblo, one can hear from a drifting boat the deep throb of drums, the chanting of singers. The Indians say that there were once two villages not far from there, facing each other across the river. So that they might have commerce, medicine men began building a bridge, of parrot feathers from one side, magpie feathers from the other. When the spans met in mid-river, there was much rejoicing, and people

The Rio Grande near Embudo, New Mexico

passed freely from one village to the other. But one day evil witches caused the bridge to break. All that were upon it fell into the river and were changed into fish.

Below San Juan Pueblo the Rio Chama washes into the Rio Grande from the west. During late March, April, and early May there is excellent whitewater boating in the canyon of the Rio Chama. The put-in point is at the El Vado Ranch, a private fishing lodge west of Tierra Amarilla. For 20 miles, to Christ in the Desert Monastery, a good take-out place, the river drops rapidly through a canyon reached only by water or rough trail. Fishing is excellent. The run is rated Class III, a "challenging, intermediate trip." There are a number of good campsites, and most boaters prefer to make the trip an overnight one. From Christ in the Desert Monastery, a Benedictine retreat founded in 1964, a 13-mile dirt road leads back to U.S. Highway 84. It is possible to continue on down the canyon for several miles, past the buildings of the Gallina Bench Ranch, and then take-out where a road to an operating ranch parallels the river for about 3 miles.

Just below the confluence of the Rio Grande and the Rio Chama there is a diversion dam of old car bodies, a snaggle of rusty metal that is best shied away from. The river continues to roll on placidly, under the highway bridge at Espanola, past the isolated bulk of Black Mesa east of the river.

Otowi bridge, on the Santa Fe-Los Alamos highway, marks the beginning of White Rock Canyon, most popular whitewater run in New Mexico. For 24 miles the Rio Grande twists its way through spectacular cliffs of basalt and pumice before emerging into flatlands near Cochiti Pueblo. The run is rated Class III, although Ancho Rapids can be Class IV during highwater. The average drop is 10 feet to the mile. The canyon can be run in a single strenuous day, but an overnight trip is more enjoyable. Near the river, in side canyons or against rimrock, there are subtle, lovely things—the clear seep over moss of an unexpected spring, wildcat tracks, strange flutings in ancient rock, Indian petroglyphs, the liquid stare of a mule deer poised for flight. It is best to have time to beach and scramble about at whim.

Three and one half miles from Otowi bridge is Buckman Rapids, and the deserted settlement of Buckman, where there are artesian springs. This is good water, but canteens should be carried, as the river water is not safe to drink.

A wide, sandy arroyo breaks through the canyon walls on the east side of the river. When the Chili line was running, the narrow-gauge tracks followed this wash down from Santa Fe, and then swung northward through the canyon to Otowi bridge, a lunch stop. A rough dirt road, the only one to enter the canyon, winds up the arroyo to Santa Fe.

Three miles beyond Buckman, on the west side of the river, the cool, crystal flow from Pajarito Springs drops over a small waterfall—an excellent campsite. Close by, a weathered wooden cross marks the grave of a sheepherder. Pajarito Rapids, which lie upstream from the springs, is exciting but not difficult. There are other rapids downriver, occurring where storms have brought rock and debris out of side canyons: Water Canyon, where a large island splits the river; Ancho; Frijoles; Capulin; and Sanchez, which being shallow and rocky is toughest in low-water. Ancho Rapids is the most impressive stretch of whitewater on the run, and should be carefully scouted. In 1961 an Albuquerque youth started through the rapids in a rubber raft, neglecting to put on his life-jacket. He drowned.

An attempted power run through White Rock Canyon came to an abrupt watery halt when both boat and outboard were pulverized on the rocks of Ancho.

At Frijoles Canyon, 2½ miles beyond Ancho Rapids, there is a good trail leading up to Bandelier National Monument Headquarters. A few hundred yards downstream from Frijoles Canyon, a spring bubbles from rock. Wild burros and other animals can sometimes be seen in the surrounding tangle of brush and scrub trees. Approaching Cochiti, the canyon walls drop and the river slows. Ahead, swarms of heavy-equipment vehicles rumble at their task: construction of the 5½-mile-long Cochiti Dam. When it is done, water will back up as far as Buckman, burying rapids, springs, and petroglyphs. Land developers are already moving in with blueprints for housing tracts for the canyon rims and "lakeside sites."

Another section of wild river will no longer exist.

Guide Notes for the UPPER RIO GRANDE RIVER

LOCATION—Begins in the Rocky Mountains of southern Colorado, and flows southward through New Mexico.

LENGTH OF TRIP—The Rio Grande Gorge is some 50 miles long, and there are some fine runs to the north of it in Colorado, as well as to the south as far as Cochiti Pueblo, not far from Santa Fe. Trips are usually made in segments of 1 to 3 days, due to a wide variance in difficulty.

FAVORABLE SEASON—The spring run-off, from May through mid-June, is the best time to run the upper Rio Grande. The river is extremely rocky and the water level drops rapidly as the summer progresses. This is mountainous country, quite cold in the winter.

DEGREE OF DIFFICULTY—There's something for everyone. There are gentle stretches, suitable for novices; intermediate runs; whitewater that should be attempted only by experts; and one segment, choked with immense boulders, where even the most skilled boater will spend most of his time lining or portaging his craft (the drop is close to 100 feet per mile). It is especially important that the guide material be carefully read on this river, because a drowsy current can quite quickly become a boiling nightmare. Take-out points must be scouted in advance, unless known from previous experience.

RECOMMENDED CRAFT—Again, it depends upon which section. For most of it, rafts and kayaks are more suitable, but there are also some delightful canoe runs.

ACCESS POINTS—There are several possible put-in and take-out points, all of which are relevant to the skills of a particular boater. Study guide material and map carefully.

CAMPING—There are a few developed campsites and several beautiful undeveloped sites along the upper Rio Grande. Most are mentioned in the text or shown on the map (see Appendix IV).

FISHING—Good trout water, best on the upper reaches in Colorado and in the Rio Grande Gorge.

3. Through the Canyons of the Big Bend

The canyons of the Big Bend country, where the Rio Grande marks the boundary between Texas and Mexico, offer spectacular boating. In the vast solitude of deep chasms, stony flatlands, and desert mountains there are few signs of civilization: some abandoned ranches, an occasional goat ranch or farming village on the Mexican side, a few fishing camps, and two picnic areas within Big Bend National Park. In the National Park, one- and two-day float trips can be made. Beyond the park, it is possible to float for a week without encountering another human being.

Although there are a number of springs coming into the Rio Grande, fresh water should be carried. Some of the spring water, which is mostly hot or warm, is potable. River water should be boiled before using.

In terms of both climate and a high water level, the best season for boating extends from October through February. Hotter weather and shallow water make the months from March through May less desirable. From June through September the canyons are extremely hot and water levels fluctuate wildly. Because the Rio Grande is prone to flood, especially during the summer months, campsites that are well above the water should be selected.

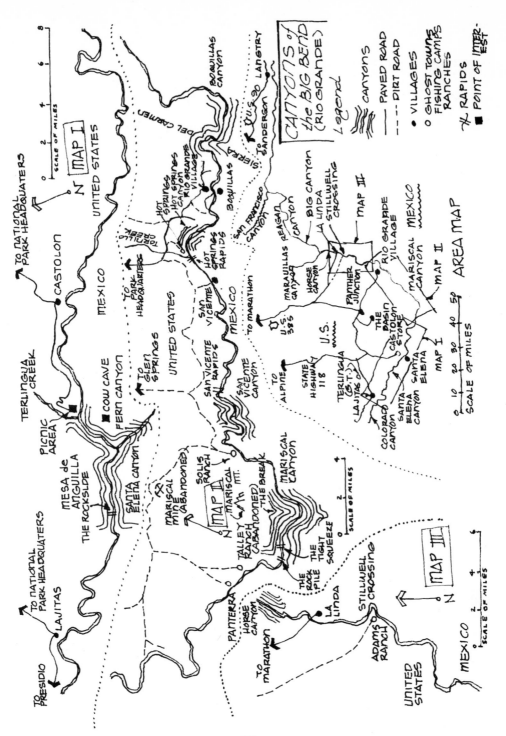

CANYONS of the BIG BEND (RIO GRANDE)

Legend
~~~~ CANYONS
——— PAVED ROAD
----- DIRT ROAD
• VILLAGES
○ GHOST TOWNS FISHING CAMPS RANCHES
≈ RAPIDS
■ POINT OF INTEREST

AREA MAP

MAP I

MAP II

MAP III

279

The point of departure at Lajitas, Texas, on the lower Rio Grande

About 24 miles west of Lajitas on Highway 170, Anvil Rocks, a formation next to the river, marks the put-in point for Colorado Canyon. The canyon, which is usually done in two days, features a number of rocky rapids and passes through rugged terrain. The best take-out place is at Lajitas, which is on a side slough rather than the main river.

Lajitas itself consists of a general store situated at a shallow ford which crosses the river into Mexico, where there are scattered ranches in the backcountry. Giant catfish heads on strings dangle from the branches of a shade tree beside the store like grotesque yuletide ornaments. One of the broad eyeless heads is 9 inches across. The ford behind the store is the put-in point for Santa Elena Canyon. If rocks are showing across most of the ford, the water level is ideal for the run. If, however, the rocks are covered with rising muddy water, an alternate canyon run should be considered. The Rockslide, just inside the canyon, is extremely dangerous in high water.

A short distance below Lajitas the slough enters the main channel, and a little more than a mile beyond that is an interesting, but not difficult,

On the Rio Grande below Lajitas, before entering Santa Elena Canyon

rapids beneath a dark, igneous cliff capped with limestone on the Texas side. For 11 miles, from Lajitas to the canyon entrance, the river winds its way into increasingly rugged country, banks lined with willow, seepwillow, mesquite, and tamarisk. Approaching Santa Elena Canyon, the river twists sharply through mild rapids. The entrance is awesome. The river points straight at the 3884-foot-high limestone bulk of Mesa de Anguilla, and rushes into it through a narrow vertical crack. There are good campsites just outside the opening, and most boaters either unroll their sleeping bags here or below the Rockslide on the Mexican side.

Inside the canyon the river drops swiftly between sheer walls, and the current is strong—crossrips, hidden rocks, and undercut cliffs can present problems. The Rockslide is a little less than 1 mile into the canyon, around the first major bend to the left. It is first seen as a fan of rubble suspended from the vertical cliff on the Mexican side. Soon the river is blocked by several huge rocks, with narrow gaps between them. This is the first barrier. Beyond it is a small bay, or clear area, where boats can always be beached safely on the Mexican side, and can be landed on the Texas side during normal water. About 100 yards ahead, the river is choked with house-high boulders, a dangerous maze of abrupt drops, suckholes, and blind alleys. This is the Rockslide, in which a number of parties have lost boats and equipment, and which quite possibly has been the site of drown-

A fast ride entering Santa Elena Canyon

ings in the past. A few seasons back a man and his dog were thrown into the water when their raft capsized in a suckhole of the Rockslide. The man managed to get to shore below the rapids, bruised and shaken. The dog was never seen again.

Those who elect to run the Rockslide must carefully memorize a route from above, on the shore. Once careering through the slide in a canoe, raft, or kayak, there is no way to see over or around the massive boulders. The first 75 yards of the slide are the most difficult, although none of it is easy. Except in highwater, boats can be lined and portaged down the Texas side. The safer portage over the rockslide on the Mexican side, hard against the cliff, is steep and rough. There are no difficult stretches from below the Rockslide to the end of the canyon. Sheer walls continue to squeeze the river into a narrow bed. The current is swift, with occasional crossrips and boils.

Eons ago, ocean tides surged across this area, and deep beds of limestone were deposited. Long after the sea had dried, and the river had established its drainage, molten material from deep in the earth heaved at the limestone from beneath. Over centuries, the river held its course by cutting through the great block of limestone as it rose.

In the last one-fourth of the canyon, the river makes a big bend to the left. A slotted opening on the Mexican side, Fern Canyon, is well worth exploring. It contains narrow spring-fed pools, tinkling falls, tapestries of fern and other plants, dapples of sun and shade upon sculpted, polished rock. Beyond Fern Canyon there is a huge cave high on the Mexican side. Variously called Cow or Sheep Cave, it may be reached by ledge from the upstream side.

A mile or so farther on, the great cleft of Santa Elena ends as abruptly as it began. One can take-out here, as it is only about 100 yards from the river to a picnic area maintained by the Park Service. The Chisos Mountains, in which Big Bend National Park Headquarters is located, dominate the skyline to the east. Terlingua Creek, which enters the Rio Grande at the mouth of Santa Elena Canyon, usually carries only a feeble trickle of water. But during summer and autumn storms, when tributary creeks like Rough Run, Goat, Calamity, Crystal, and Javelina are running bank to bank, Terlingua becomes a muddy torrent. The Terlingua watershed is parched, eroded country, sparsely covered with creosote bushes, clusters of prickly pear, cactus, ocotillo, and other desert plants. This was not always so. The area was once heartland of the G-4 Ranch and site of a farming community, Terlingua Abaja. James Gillett, who had been foreman of the G-4, later reminisced that in 1885 Terlingua Creek was a "bold running stream, studded with cottonwood, and was alive with beaver. At the mouth of Rough Run there was a fine grove of trees, under the shade of which I have seen at least one thousand head of cattle." Today what cottonwood

Camping in Santa Elena Canyon

remain are mostly sun-bleached snags, victims of drought and erosion. The fields around Terlingua Abaja, where vegetables, wheat, and corn once grew, have long since been washed away. The houses slowly crumbled under storm and wind.

A paved road follows the river from the picnic area at Santa Elena to the historic trading post at Castolon, a distance of 8 miles, then swings northeast toward Park Headquarters in a high basin of the Chisos Mountains. Close to Castolon, a ford leads across the river to Santa Elena, Mexico, a small farming village. For the next 40 to 50 miles the river rolls quietly through open country, and few boaters run it save for anglers on the prowl for big catfish. There are a few fishing camps on the American side of the river.

At the southernmost tip of the Big Bend, Mariscal Mountain blocks the course of the river, and again, the waters plunge through a spectacular canyon. Boats can be shoved off at either Panterra or the abandoned Talley Ranch, reached by rough backcountry roads. Road conditions should be checked when fire permits are picked up from rangers at Panther Junction, and, as when doing any desert travel, several gallons of extra water, a shovel, and towrope should be tossed onto the load.

Mariscal and Santa Elena canyons have a number of similarities. Both were formed by the river cutting through limestone as it was gradually uplifted; both begin abruptly without preamble—the river simply slips into narrow cracks wedged by towering rock. Like Santa Elena, Mariscal Canyon has a rockslide not far from the entrance.

The Rockpile in Mariscal is just a hundred yards inside the opening. It is much less formidable than the Santa Elena version; nevertheless, river runners should beach on the gravel bar a little upstream from the rocks on the Texas side and look it over. A number of boaters, ignoring this ritual, have been unceremoniously dumped into the water.

About ½ mile below the Rockpile, a massive block of stone has fallen into the river, forcing the water to churn through a 5-foot gap on the left, and a 10-foot gap on the right. Like the Rockpile, this, the Tight Squeeze, has caused a number of unplanned swims. The left-hand gap is not recommended. Current in the right-hand slot piles up on another rock, forcing a tight turn to the left. It is best to enter the right-hand slot from close to the Mexican side, which gives one the best angle for avoiding debacle or outright disaster. Inexperienced boaters can line or portage boats along the rocky Mexican shore, a practice followed by even the most seasoned boaters in highwater. When the river is running 5 feet high or more, it surges over the midstream rock, creating a dangerous waterfall.

Below the Tight Squeeze, the river is mild, and although dunkings do occur, they are occasioned by boaters rubbernecking the soaring delights of this canyon to such an extent as to forget the equilibrium of their craft. In places the walls are from 1500 to 1800 feet high. White boulders rise from the shores, polished by centuries of silt-laden floods.

Midway through the canyon the sheer walls drop away for about ¼ mile at The Break, a great rift caused by folding and faulting. It is as though a giant finger had been drawn down the length of the mountain while the rock was soft and doughy. There is a shallow rapids here, and on the Mexican shore, some sod dugouts that have been occupied from time to time in the past. This is a lonely place. When the night wind swoops down the dry creekbed on the Mexican side, shaking spiny yucca and whistling against the cliffs, it seems a thousand miles from the nearest streetlight or well-trimmed lawn.

Yet the crossing here is an old one, and the trails that wander up the rift on either side of the river, splitting into numerous smaller paths back on the mountain, have been used often, usually at night. No one knows for how many centuries Indians have walked the trails, but on a boulder of the west wall of the dry creek petroglyphs representing turtles, centipedes, a cross, and other, more obscure, designs have been pecked into the rock. Comanche war parties used the trail when raiding Mexican ranchitos for horses and other livestock; they were followed by former buffalo hunters, renegade sheriffs, and ne'er-do-wells from shanty towns of the southern plains, who also took to running off Mexican ponies. In turn, gangs of Mexican cutthroats stormed up the rift, seeking Texas longhorns and Indian babies which could be sold into slavery.

In more recent times the trails have been used by a variety of smugglers who, moving their pack trains by night, carried illegal firearms, gold, liquor, and wax from the candelilla plant. Originally, the pale green plant was considered useful only as a rustic cure for venereal disease, but the wax now commands good prices as a component for candles, phonograph records, floor wax, and shoe polish. The trail heads at the north end of Mariscal Mountain are largely concealed with brush; from lookouts the smugglers can scan the surrounding desert for members of the Border Patrol or others who might be inhospitable to their ventures, before proceeding northward or making contact with buyers.

Rangers at Big Bend National Park estimate that three to four pack trains bearing illicit candelilla wax cross the border and pass through portions of the park each month. In remote camps, mostly on the Mexican side, the gathered candelilla plants are dumped into 55-gallon oil drums cut lengthwise. The vats contain boiling water laced with a small amount of sulfuric acid which causes the wax to separate and float to the top. It is then ladled out, allowed to harden, and packed upon burro trains. The Rangers, of course, have no mandate over customs matters, but they are concerned over the gathering of the plant within the park boundaries, principally on Mariscal Mountain and Mesa de Anguilla, and must apprehend pack trains for not possessing a commercial license to operate within the park. Recently, six horsemen escorting forty-three loaded burros were arrested in the park. Such men are usually armed. They are poor; the animals represent most of their material wealth, and the wax can be the result of weeks or months of hard work. Confiscations are not lightly regarded by either side.

Below The Break the river glides smoothly between high walls, which through one stretch have been eroded into a fantasy of pinnacles and towers, like a setting for goblins and trolls. There is a good campsite about 1 mile below The Break on the Mexican side, a high sandbank with a view of the pinnacles. The river breaks abruptly out of the depths of Mariscal Mountain to wind sluggishly through rolling desert country. It is about 2 miles to the site of Solis Ranch, usual take-out point for Mariscal Canyon float trips.

Most float parties leave a shuttle vehicle at Solis and then drive around the north end of Mariscal Mountain to either Talley Ranch or

Panterra. En route they pass the ruined processing plant, offices, and residences of the Mariscal Mine, a cinnebar (mercury ore) mine that has largely been inactive since the 1920s. Hardier souls can leave their vehicle at Talley Ranch, drift through, cache their boats, and then hike back over Mariscal Mountain. The trails are unmarked, faint and waterless; but experienced and prepared backpackers will find the trek enjoyable—there are spectacular views of the canyon, at least one former smuggler's house, and a number of large bat caves. The Mariscal Canyon float trip is 7 miles long, and can be done in four or five hours (with, of course, additional hours needed for shuttle driving).

Between Solis Ranch and Boquillas the Rio Grande cuts through two other canyons: San Vicente and Hot Springs, with a stretch of fairly open country between them. Although they are not sheer-sided gorges like Santa Elena or Mariscal, their eroded cliffs do display interesting formations. There are only two rapids in the entire run, neither of which should present problems. After passing through San Vicente Canyon, one quickly reaches the rapids of the same name, created by boulders washed down by flash floods in Glenn Draw. The other fastwater is at Hot Springs Rapids, located at the mouth of Tornillo Creek. Here an island splits the river. The Mexican channel is recommended.

In these canyons, one occasionally sees the brush huts of a candelilla camp or flocks of goats scrambling along cliff-sides, and where the banks are gentle there are scattered farms on the Mexican side. The small Mexican hamlet of San Vicente was originally established as a fort in 1774. On the other side of the river, San Vicente, Texas, is today marked by ruined adobe and stone houses as well as a graveyard on a gravel hill to the north. A short way downriver, there are other reminders of the past—the abandoned store and somewhat primitive tourist courts of Hot Springs, which operated from 1909 to 1942. There are a number of warm springs trickling into both sides of the river, and on the Mexican side, some people have created their own spas—small bathing pits dug in the riverbank silt.

San Vicente and Hot Springs canyons are usually run as an extension of a Mariscal Canyon float trip—two or three days would be ample time. A good take-out place is Boquillas Ford. The trip can be shortened by taking-out at Glenn Draw, reached by rough road (four-wheel drive recommended), or at Hot Springs, from which an improved road leads back to blacktop.

Boquillas Ford may well be the most informal border crossing in the country. American tourists camping at nearby Rio Grande Village are ferried back and forth across the river on burros provided by barefooted Mexican boys.

At one time this was country where most people carried a gun and expected to use it. Max Ernst, who in 1908 was justice of the peace for the area, stopped a bullet while returning home from business in Boquillas. He managed to reach a neighbor's house before dying. In his pocket, his wife found a note he had managed to scrawl: "Am shot, I expect by one of Solis at gate. First shot hit, two more missed." Although Martin Solis and his four sons were sharply questioned by a grand jury, the case was eventually dropped.

Eight years later the community of Glenn Spring was besieged by sixty or seventy bandits from south of the border. Glenn Spring, a village of about sixty people, was situated a few miles up the wash from the mouth of San Vicente Canyon. There were nine U.S. soldiers camped at Glenn Spring the night of the raid, and during some lively gunfire, four of the soldiers, the son of the storekeeper, and several raiders were killed. After looting the store and putting the torch to three other buildings, the bandits headed back toward the dry mountains of Mexico.

Below Boquillas, the river winds through the middle of the Sierra del Carmen. Schott Tower, highest peak in the range, rears up from the Mexican side of the water; it is visible from a number of places in the canyon. The Boquillas Canyon run is excellent for novice boaters or family outings as there are no rapids of any consequence. The canyon itself is 17 miles long, and it is 25 to the customary, and best, take-out place at Stillwell Crossing. This should be an overnight trip at the minimum, and most backcountry aficionados will want to take three days, allowing time for exploration of side canyons. Some of the canyons contain exquisite glens and wildly eroded rock formations.

At Stillwell Crossing there is an old cable footbridge. Permission to leave shuttle cars at Stillwell Crossing can be obtained from the U. J. Adams Ranch (P.O. Box 426, Marathon, Texas; Heath Canyon exchange number 376-2212).

Stillwell Crossing is gateway to one of the loneliest stretches of river anywhere. From here a man could drift for a week—all the way to Langtry, over 130 miles downriver—without seeing another human being. Canyon after canyon slashes through gaunt, dry ranges; sunsets flame over tortured rocks where no one has ever walked; coyote yip at dusk and dawn; and the press of immense solitude is either exhilarating or vaguely ominous to the infrequent traveler. Senses sharpen. A distant tumbling pebble, kicked loose by a lizard or a roadrunner, can be heard distinctly. The muggy smell of the river and damp-rooted plants beside it rises strongly through the warm air. In caves and alcoves of the mountains, panther sprawl during the afternoon heat, waiting for the cool and darkness of night to hunt. Bands of peccaries, far more dangerous to man, root up side draws. Close to the river, the bird the Mexicans call *brasita de fuego* (little coal of fire), darts between willows at water's edge, black wings fanning against red body.

Such a setting would seem almost flawed without a lost mine, and, of course, there is one. Back in the 1880s four brothers by the name of Reagan had a ranch that was roughly defined as running upstream from the canyon now bearing their name to the mouth of Maravillas Canyon, an amorphous spread where cattle simply drifted to wherever they could find any sort of thornless plant to chew on, like as not across the river on the Mexican side. One morning a valuable horse was found to be missing from the *remuda*. Lee Reagan and Bill Kelly, a cowhand who was half Negro, half Indian, set out to find the horse—Reagan covering the American side of the river, Kelly the Mexican. At dusk they met, as arranged, near the mouth of Maravillas Canyon. When the rancher asked Kelly if he had spotted the pony, he shook his head and then grinned in the failing light.

"I've found something better." He reached into his *morral*—saddle-horn pouch for small objects—and pulled out a lump of ore. "I've found a gold mine. Right over there! In a canyon just wide enough to ride a horse through."

Reagan, for whom at that time all rocks were just a diabolic device to keep feed from coming up, could not have distinguished between gold ore and petrified wood, and was damn sure his employee knew even less. A good sight less. And so, far from sharing Kelly's excitement over the rock, he was merely irritated that they had not found the horse.

Kelly hung onto the ore, and after a time hoboed a freight train to take it to his friend Lock Campbell of San Antonio, a conductor for the Southern Pacific. Campbell, as it turned out, was out on a run, but Kelly left the ore sample with a mutual friend and returned to the Reagan ranch.

Campbell had the ore assayed. Results were $80,000 to the ton, enough to induce gold fever in the most stolid man. As soon as he could get leave from the railroad, he hurried down into the remote **Rio Grande** canyon country, seeking Kelly. He never found him. About the time word of the assay results reached the Reagans, Bill Kelly disappeared. Foul play was strongly suspected.

As might be expected of men with a bonanza somewhere in their sprawling back yard, the Reagans began to take a lively interest in minerals, but for all their ceaseless prowling were never able to locate the strike made by their departed cowpuncher. Lock Campbell probed for the mine, as did a number of other hopefuls, finding nothing but spectacular country and intriguing clues.

Will Stillwell, who with his brother Roy ranched upriver from the old Reagan spread, may have actually found the Lost Kelly Mine. Around 1914 or 1915, he encountered an old sick Indian woman while on a cattle-buying trip into Mexico. The woman seemed close to death, but Stillwell and his companion, a Mrs. Murphy, managed to nurse her back to health. In gratitude, she gave them directions to a gold mine. Up a certain **canyon,** she related, they would find a large boulder with a tomahawk buried on one side. The mine was farther up the canyon, covered with poles and dirt.

The finale to the episode was later related to Virginia Madison. She describes it in her book, *The Big Bend Country*.

> . . . they found the boulder and they found the tomahawk. They knew they were almost to the mine then, but they were without water. The nearby *tinaja* was dry and a water seep a little farther up the canyon was not enough for their horses. They had no tools to dig with and bandits were hot on their trail, so they were forced to abandon their hunt and retreat across the Rio Grande to Texas. They decided to stay out of Mexico until the revolution had died down.
>
> Will Stillwell was certain that he had, at last, located the rich gold mine. (From *Big Bend Country of Texas,* Albuquerque: University of New Mexico Press, 1955.)

Stillwell apparently gave the author no particulars as to where the mine was located, although he did tell his brother Roy. Soon after, Will joined the Texas Rangers and was killed in a fight, and Roy died as the result of an accident while hauling feed to his ranch.

In more recent times an American gold-seeker, Xanthus "Kit" Carson and a Mexican, Guerra Menchaca, plodded over a faint trail that once connected the Stillwell Ranch with the Mexican village of Musquiz. Menchaca had spun an interesting yarn. He had been a soldier with the Mexican army, which in 1910 was skirmishing with revolutionaries in the Big Bend country. He became friendly with a prospector named Virgil Ellis, who lived in Musquiz, where, some three decades before, Bill Kelly had also made his home. Ellis made a tidy living packing gold out of a remote mine he had discovered, the location of which he described to Menchaca.

Fearing pillage by revolutionaries, the prospector suspended operations for a time, concealing the entrance with rubble from dynamite blasts. He was killed in an accident not long after. Menchaca, for rather obscure reasons, had sat upon the secret for forty years.

For Carson the treasure hunt was apparently as perilous as Stillwell's had been years before: there was some doubt whether Menchaca, suffering from heart trouble, would endure the strenuous hike; the heat was withering; and they had to "fight the hordes of rattlesnakes in the cactus patches every step of the way." In a narrow, sheer-sided canyon, they found boulders inscribed as Menchaca had said they would be. The mine itself was covered with rubble from flash floods and Ellis' dynamite blasts, rendering development prohibitively expensive. There seems little doubt they had found the Ellis diggings, and there are strong arguments that the site was the one approached by Will Stillwell and is the Lost Kelly Mine to boot. Kelly would have used this route in passing from the Reagan Ranch to Musquiz.

Yet lost-mine stories are rarely wrapped up that neatly, especially when the gold remains hidden. A member of a float party may yet, while hiking up a side canyon, stub his toe upon a fortune, and it just may be the one that Billy Kelly never collected.

Bob Burleson, president of the Texas Explorers Club, says of the lower Big Bend canyons: "[There are] many tough rapids, some of which require a portage, and almost a continuous canyon for three fourths of the trip. This trip is for properly prepared and experienced river runners, and could be a very arduous and miserable trip for the careless or ignorant adventurer."

Bill Kugle, another member of the Texas Explorers Club, elaborates: "I have often thought of the bad situation which could result if someone broke a leg. There would be no other way to get an injured person out other than to float out over a period of several days. It would be extremely difficult to float an injured person out in a canoe without capsizing several times. The discomfort attendant upon being thrown into the rapids with a crudely splinted broken leg can hardly be described. For this reason I gave strict instructions to the members of our expedition before leaving: 'Don't break no legs.' "

A run through these canyons, in terms of both rugged scenery and whitewater challenge, offers one of the great adventures in American wilderness boating. Persons contemplating the trip should write the Texas Explorers Club (Bob Burleson, President, Box 844, Temple, Texas) for a copy of their detailed notes on the run. This material also includes names and addresses of ranches on the bottom end of the run. Although most float trips start at the Adams Ranch at Stillwell Crossing, there are a number of possible take-out points, including one at Bone Watering and another at the Bootleggers Highway. Prior permission must be obtained from ranchowners to use any of them.

Not far below the Adams Ranch one can see the Dow fluorspar plant at La Linda, Coahuila, and pass under the bridge over which fluorspar is trucked to the Marathon railroad depot. As soon as the bridge fades from sight you are in wild country, immediately running Horse Canyon, short but deep, and then drifting into a more open stretch with mountains looming back from the river. This is lost-mine country. The narrow canyon which Xanthus Kit Carson and Guerra Menchaca explored slices through rimrock on the Mexican side. A few miles beyond is Maravillas Canyon, where Bill Kelly is said to have displayed his ore sample to Lee Reagan. Maravillas Canyon is usually dry and wide, filled with white boulders. There is a burned ranch house at the mouth of Maravillas, and a rough road leads up the creek to Black Gap Headquarters—a 20-mile hike and the last thread back to civilization for at least four days.

One shoves off. Across the expanse of Outlaw Flats, famous for mirages, the flat-topped bulk of El Capitan lifts a sheer 1000 feet above the desert floor, shimmering like a mirage itself. Downstream the water quickens, funneling into Big Canyon, where the river breaks loose into several fine rapids. And then comes Reagan Canyon, which twists through the rock for some 40 miles, and thunders through the most dangerous rapids on the lower river: Hot Springs, Burro Bluff, Horseshoe Falls, and Panther Canyon. Here and there warm springs rise at riverbank, and occasionally one spots a ruined cabin or a cave. Dr. R. T. Hill, in his account of explorations in these canyons, aptly described the country below Panther Canyon: "The sculpture is marked by queer, eccentric pinnacles projecting above the ragged skyline—spires, fingers, needles, natural bridges, and every conceivable form of peaked and curved rocks."

Below Reagan Canyon there are other deep gorges, strange rock formations, hot springs, and whitewater. Then, gradually, the country becomes more open and cattle can be seen grazing; now and again a ranch road will come right down to the river. And finally one reaches Langtry, a quieter place now than when the principal building carried an imposing sign:

> THE JERSEY LILLY
> SALOON
> JUDGE ROY BEAN
> JUSTICE OF THE PEACE
>
> COURT HOUSE
> THE LAW WEST OF THE PECOS
> WHISKEY WINE AND BEER

But at Langtry, beyond the huddles of abandoned adobe huts, there are a gas station and a blacktop highway leading away from the wild and solitary canyons of the Rio Grande.

Guide Notes for the CANYONS OF THE BIG BEND

LOCATION—That section of the Rio Grande which makes up the border of Texas and Mexico, running between Lajitas and Langtry, Texas. The long section of the river between Cochiti Pueblo, New Mexico, and Lajitas, Texas, is not particularly wild or interesting.

LENGTH OF TRIP—As with the upper Rio Grande, one can choose from a variety of trips, depending upon time and skill on the water. You can spend a weekend or close to a month drifting these canyons (allowing time for prowling up side canyons, a temptation few seem able to resist). Take a gander at the guide material and map and see what fits your schedule and temperament.

FAVORABLE SEASON—October through February. Blazingly hot weather and lower water levels make other seasons less attractive.

DEGREE OF DIFFICULTY—The canyons on the edge of Big Bend National Park—Santa Elena, Mariscal, Hot Springs, San Vicente, Boquillas—are not rough even for inexperienced boaters if they know where to look for a couple of big rapids. The Rockslide, less than a mile inside Santa Elena, is formidable. Even experts look it over and often decide to portage in highwater. The Rockpile, in Mariscal Canyon, can also be a challenging piece of water. Boquillas Canyon is an excellent place for a novice to get the feel of his paddles. From Stillwell Crossing, end of Boquillas Canyon, to Langtry, the river is isolated, probably more than any waterway outside of Alaska in the United States. There are challenging rapids. This stretch is for expert boaters only. In highwater some rapids may be unrunnable and should be portaged.

RECOMMENDED CRAFT—Canoe, kayak or raft. In several stretches the current is slow and makes one work in a raft.

ACCESS POINTS—There are several good put-in and take-out places, depending on how long a trip you care to make. Most of them can be reached by driving into Big Bend National Park, south of Marathon, Texas, on U.S. Highway 385, or south of Alpine on State Highway 118. Langtry, ultimate take-out point for a canyon trip, is on U.S. Highway 90 west of Del Rio.

CAMPING—Semidesert country with many good campsites. River water is potable but muddy and will need some settling. Watch for springs and fill up there.

FISHING—Excellent fishing for big catfish.

CHAPTER ELEVEN

Our Vanishing Wild Rivers

Wild rivers are a vanishing species. People have settled beside most waterways in the United States; roads and railroads parallel them. Many are badly polluted. The surface of the Cuyahoga in Ohio is so thickly skimmed with oil and chemical wastes that in 1969 it actually caught fire. There is a certain amount of black humor in the spectacle of firemen attempting to put out a river. A once beautiful and famed trout stream in Massachusetts carries effluvium away from a chemical plant. Now, not only have the fish and other waterlife gone, long since poisoned, but no vegetation grows within several feet of the banks.

It is not pollution, however, which threatens most of our remaining wild rivers—but dams. Since the time when man crouched in caves, gnawing raw meat from bones, he has constantly struggled to control his environment. Gradually, over centuries, he has got better at it. During the past one hundred years our technology has expanded to the extent that our control is now awesome and rather frightening.

In the past, dams have contributed much to the standard of living in America through irrigation, flood control, and cheap hydro-electric power. The Bureau of Reclamation and the Army Corps of Engineers, the principal agencies concerned with dam building, have done much that is commendable. Like all institutions or individuals, they would like to continue to do what they do well—even if there is no longer a need for it. How does bureaucracy phase itself out? It doesn't. It hires public-relations men who are experts at constructing justifications. Most of the pitch is slanted toward the Chamber-of-Commerce sort of sentiment that *any* growth is Progress, in and of itself.

These days, dams of any size are usually built to provide water, power, or both. Much of the scramble to get dams authorized for water gains is paradoxical. The flow of the Colorado, for example, has already been overapportioned. An additional dam would further decrease the amount of available water, due to evaporation and seepage. At a time when we pass out vast amounts of money in the form of crop subsidies to keep land out of production, proposals that we spend millions on irrigation projects to cultivate yet more land appear to be conceived by a most peculiar form of economic algebra.

Power needs are something else again. The demand for energy in the United States is growing at an incredible rate—doubling every fifteen years. Yet to assume that it should continue to do so, as most experts believe, may be a fallacy. Whether the present younger generations are going to consider electric carving knives and three cars in the garage as necessities in the future is highly debatable—especially when such a rate of increase will mean the systematic destruction of much of what remains of our natural environment.

Even if power demands fall far short of what the graph-plotters predict, a vast amount of energy will still be needed. How much of this future energy can be generated from "clean" sources (nuclear fission, geothermal heat, solar energy, wind, and the like) will depend on how much money and time we are willing to spend on making them practical. How much is the environment worth?

As the search for power sources continues, many of our most beautiful wild rivers will inevitably be coveted by power companies. Yet the damming, the destruction, of virtually every wild stretch of water in the United States would add only a drop in the bucket as far as power needs go. By damming our remaining wild rivers, we would have sacrificed one of our most magnificent recreational resources—for nothing.

In 1968 Congress passed the Wild and Scenic Rivers Act to protect natural waterways. Sections of eight rivers were initially included in the system: Rogue, Clearwater, Middle Fork Salmon, Rio Grande, St. Croix, Wolf, Eleven Point, and Feather. A number of other rivers are being considered for inclusion. Yet many outdoorsmen feel the bill is being implemented too slowly; there are only so many wild rivers, and they are rapidly being bulldozed out of existence. River running is one of the fastest growing sports in America.

The clerk radiated a healthy, tanned cordiality.
"Now, which river did you wish to take?"
"Grand Canyon. We understand it has the most exciting rapids, spectacular scenery."

"Certainly does." The clerk thumbed through a number of bound pages while the young couple waited anxiously.

"Here we go. We can get you on an August trip in 1980."

"But that's six years away!"

"Sorry. Best we can do."

If this projected dialogue sounds far-fetched, consider a couple of statistics. In 1869 the expedition of John Wesley Powell made the first recognized voyage through Grand Canyon. Between the time of Powell's epic journey and the mid-1950s, less than one hundred and fifty adventurers had ever floated through the canyon. By the summer of 1969, some 5192 people had made the trip; by September 1, 1970, the count was

"Every wild river in America will be gone before our children can come to know them, unless the dam builders are blocked." The Snake River choked behind the $230 million dam of the Idaho Power Company at Hell's Canyon on the Idaho-Oregon border (*R. J. Brown Photo from Freelance Photographers Guild*)

7863, with more boats yet to come. Other wild rivers are likewise feeling
the press of population.

California, the golden state, needs lots of power and water. Virtually
all of the once wild and beautiful streams tumbling out of the western slope
of the Sierra Nevadas have been dammed, or followed as access through the
mountains by roads and railroads. One of the few segments of wild river
that remain in the state, the Stanislaus River from Camp 9 to below Parrot's Ferry, is scheduled to be inundated by the New Melones Dam, despite
vigorous opposition by conservation groups. New Melones Dam was originally conceived as a flood-control project, a low barrier which would have
backed little water into the wilderness canyon. But the dam-builders,
perhaps growing a bit hysterical at the threat of their own obsolescence,
have proposed a high dam that will turn the canyon into a reservoir,
justifying this as creating a recreation resource. People will be able to water-
ski. It will allow more people to fish. Nobody will have to scramble down a

Meanwhile, in Oregon the Rogue River still tumbles wild and free—but America's wild rivers face an uncertain future unless a sounder sense of values prevails
over wholesale pollution and damming

mountainside to get to the water; blacktop roads will loop in and "sports-men" can throw out bobbers for perch. The warmer water will have killed the trout.

Wild river Stanislaus brings in close to half a million dollars' worth of business to local merchants through guided tours, trout fishermen, back-packers. Reservoir recreation is a common commodity in northern Cali-fornia (there are 200,000 acres of flatwater, created by dams, within 75 miles of the Stanislaus). Visitor use of many of these bodies of water has declined over recent years, despite the population boom. Over a short period of years, the merchants of the region around wild river Stanislaus stand to lose if the dam-builders are given their way. In the long run, a great deal more will be lost.

A field of flowers can be destroyed, and return the following spring. A forest can be logged out or burned, and within a few decades the scars will have completely healed to all but a highly trained eye. A river, cutting into rock, becomes itself through hundreds of centuries.

Every wild river in America will be gone before our children can come to know them, unless the dam-builders are blocked, forced to learn another trade. Perhaps constructing make-believe wild rivers for Disney-lands. Because soon, unless more people care more, the only "wilderness river adventures" left in America will be in Disneylands . . . voyages of make-believe.

CHAPTER TWELVE

106 Wild Rivers to Run

Most river runners have their favorite waters, to which they return time and again, developing an almost paternalistic feeling. Inevitably, there will be some devoted outdoorsmen who will rise up in wrath upon reading this section of *Wild Rivers of North America* to discover that some lovely sections of river have been omitted. It is almost like sending out invitations to a large party (if we invite them, then we have to invite *them*—why does he mention *that* muddy refugee from a drainpipe when he could have included the . . .).

This section, presenting 106 wilderness rivers to run, is a sampler. It would require a volume (albeit a thin one) to discuss every stretch of wild river in the continental United States, and additional volumes to consider those in Canada, Alaska, Mexico, and Central America. A great many fine runs have been omitted because of lack of space; others because their wilderness credentials are tarnished by dams, pollution, parallel highways, towns, farmlands, and other encroachments of civilization. Some runs that you will find here, such as Cross Mountain Canyon of the Yampa, and the Neversink, are whitewater of utmost difficulty. On the other hand, there are a number of gentle waterways suitable for novices and family groups. I have included backcountry rivers which pass through jungle, desert, mountains, swamp, woodlands, and tundra; stretches that can be run in a day and voyages requiring a month or more.

Rivers are grouped in the following sections: Central America and Mexico, Western United States, Central United States, Southern United States, Eastern United States, Eastern Canada, and Western Canada and the Far North.

In most cases I have selected rivers for which more detailed supplemental descriptions are available. Before setting out to do any of these rivers you should send away for pertinent material (see Appendix II). *Always* check locally as to water level before casting off. Each river has brackets of flow, measured by cubic feet per second (cfs), within which it can be enjoyably or safely run.

Readers for whom a river is still only something to be crossed on a bridge—or which, through a complexity of pipes, fills their bathtubs—should beware. You will be entertained by running one of these waterways, probably intrigued after finishing the second, and most likely hooked midway through the third. You may miss a lot of weekend television. That's something to be considered.

Central America and Mexico

Rio Coco (*Central America*)

The governments of Honduras and Nicaragua have for many years locked horns over border disputes. Occasionally, illtrained and disinterested militia from one side or the other are sent out to jungle outposts on the frontier, where, out of boredom, they shoot at anything that seems to run, swim, crawl, fly, or even grow. These differences notwithstanding, Rand McNally, never one to trifle with geographical vagaries, places the border smack down the Rio Cocos.

It is an admirable jungle river. One drives from Managua to Wiwili (good road as far as Ocotal, fairly rough on in). Shove off from Wiwili into a river which has an average depth of 24 inches during March. The waters are gentle on down to Wamblan, and beyond, but it is good to hire a guide at Wamblan. One of the best is Rosa Palacios (male, in spite of the name) from the nearby village of Piedras.

Downriver, at Walakitan, the water begins to get rough. There one can hire men to portage boats and equipment around Walakitan Rapids. In the stretch between Walakitan and Carrizal there are several rapids and a waterfall. Kiuras Falls is spectacular—especially if one drifts into it amidstream, finding the banks just a mite too far away. Kairasa Rapids, not far below, are also soul food for the compulsive kamikaze. As with all whitewater rivers, when you hear bigwater ahead, put ashore and scout it out. At the village of Raiti, men can be hired to lug boats at about $3 per man per portage.

Below Carrizal the river broadens and becomes calm. There are villages where one can obtain bananas, rice, beans, possibly even a suckling pig. The river reaches the ocean at Cabo Gracias a Dios. A charter flight out should be arranged before leaving Managua.

February and March, the dry season, are the best months to tackle the Rio Coco (or any other Central American rivers). The river is low enough then to expose midstream sand and gravel bars, excellent camping places. Shoreline camping is mostly in the jungle, which can be itchy or worse. One should allow a week to ten days for the voyage.

Periodically, the border situation gets a little testy, but this can easily be checked out beforehand from officials in Managua. Boats, life preservers, and other camping equipment are expensive and hard to come by in Central America. Bring your own.

Rio Patuca (Honduras)

Like the Rio Coco, the Patuca is a big river in Central American terms. It is a river to be run in January or February when the sandbars are showing and the insects are relatively inactive. The entire waterway drains volcanic highlands and winds some 500 miles to the sea. This is mostly a jungle river—lots of parrots, monkeys, and an occasional tapir. The Indians are friendly. Best voyage is the 300-mile stretch from Catacamas (a fly-in) down to Awas near the Caribbean.

Usumacinta (Mexico)

The ancient Maya called the Usumacinta the River of the Sacred Monkey. Rising as swift mountain streams in the mountains of Chiapas and Guatamala, it is a large, broad flow where it cuts through the jungle of what was once the heart of the Mayan empire. Two of the finest Mayan ruins, Yaxchilan and Piedras Negras, lie close to the main river; Bonampak and Petex-Batum are on tributaries. Although tourists can now charter flights in to the major ruins, this is remote country. Bonampak's twenty-eight temples and superb wall paintings were not discovered until 1947; there may well be other lost cities buried under jungle growth. Some two hundred Lacandone Indians, descendants of the Maya, still live in the Usumacinta region. Unfortunately, most of their small villages have been visited by so many ethnic pilgrims—anthropology professors and Vassar graduates in pith helmets—that they initially strike one more as camp-followers than natural primitives. Why not? They have been enthusiastically viewed as specimens for so long, that to demand your jacket or wristwatch for the pleasure of witnessing their lifestyle is credible. The beautiful, long-haired Lacandone suffer from overexposure.

The country does not. Most of the rain-forest trees crown out at about 150 feet high, and little sunlight leaks through. In places one has to chop a tunnel with a machete, elsewhere you walk freely through a dimness roofed by a rampant growth—a strange sort of temple to Fecundity, with mysterious aisles running off in all directions between the mahogany, rubber and chicle gum trees, the hanging vines. Tributary rivers, winding out of the

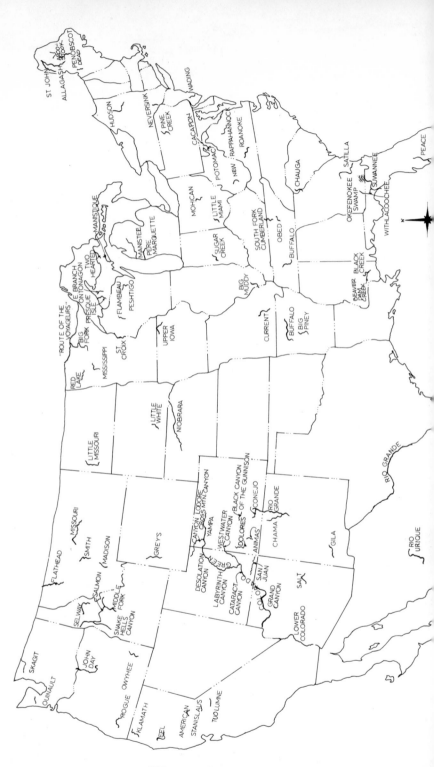

ST JOHN
ALLAGASH
PENOBSCOT
KOOK
DEAD

WADING

NEVERSINK

HUDSON

PINE
CREEK

CACAPON

POTOMAC

NEW

RAPPAHANNOCK
ROANOKE

PEACE

MANISTIQUE

MOHICAN

LITTLE
MIAMI

CHAUGA

SATILLA

OKEFENOKEE
SWAMP

SUWANNEE

WITHLACOOCHEE

MANISTEE
PERE
MARQUETTE

SUGAR
CREEK

SOUTH FORK
CUMBERLAND

OBED

BUFFALO

BLACK
CREEK

"ROUTE OF THE
VOYAGEURS"

E BRANCH
ONTONAGON

TWO
HEARTED

PRESQUE
ISLE

FLAMBEAU

PESHTIGO

BIG
MUDDY

BEAVER
CREEK
CREEK

BIG
FORK

ST
CROIX

UPPER
IOWA

CURRENT

BUFFALO

BIG
PINEY

RED
LAKE

MISSISSIPPI

LITTLE
WHITE

NIOBRARA

LITTLE
MISSOURI

RIO GRANDE

MISSOURI

SMITH

MADISON

GREY'S

CANYON LODORE
CROSS MTN CANYON
YAMPA

WESTWATER
CANYON

BLACK CANYON
OF THE GUNNISON

CONEJO

RIO
GRANDE

CHAMA

GILA

RIO
URIQUE

FLATHEAD

SALMON

MIDDLE
FORK

DESOLATION
CANYON

LABYRINTH
CANYON

CATARACT
CANYON

DOLORES

ANIMAS

SAN
JUAN

COLO

SALT

SELWAY

SNAKE
HELLS
CANYON

GRAND
CANYON

LOWER
COLORADO

SKAGIT

JOHN
DAY

OWYHEE

QUINAULT

ROGUE

KLAMATH

EEL

AMERICAN
STANISLAUS

TUOLUMNE

302

RIO PATUCA

RIO COCO

RIO USUMACINTA

RIO GRANDE de SANTIAGO

highlands, are fast. Sections of the Lacantun, Jatate, and Lacanja rivers have been run by alligator hunters, and an occasional kayaker with a yearn to get into one of the few lost pockets that remain on planet Earth. Many other magnificent streams have not even been walked beside for decades—let alone voyaged.

The most interesting Usumacinta voyage is from Tres Naciones to Tenosique, a distance of about 160 miles. The river flows past the ruins of Yaxchilan and Piedras Negras, and bucks through several stretches of heavy whitewater. Tenosique is reached by road, but one must hire a bush pilot to get to Tres Naciones. This is no run for a novice. Grand Canyon of San Jose, above Tenosique, squeezes the Usumacinta into a narrow, roiling gorge. Big water. Skilled boatmen in a ten-man raft should have no trouble navigating it at most water levels, but there are rapids a man in a kayak or decked canoe should scout carefully. Portages, when necessary, are neither marked nor tramped. Few people come this way. The country is beautiful—dense green foliage from which there are the chatter of monkeys and squawks of tropical birds. The walls of San Jose Canyon are several hundred feet high.

Although there are four varieties of poisonous snakes in the region, here, as elsewhere, the Jungle Snake Menace is greatly exaggerated. One runs more of a risk in the southeastern United States. Falling tree limbs are a greater hazard than snakes in the jungle. Be careful where you pitch your tent. Also, if you run onto a pack of peccaries, don't argue—head for the nearest tree. The little pigs can be very nasty. On the other hand, if you bring along a gun for camp meat (permit from the Mexican government required), peccaries are fine when roasted over campfire coals, as are monkeys and wild turkey. If angling, one should bait up for catfish, gar, and a harmless relative of the South American piranha. Papayas, plantains, avocados and other fruit sometimes can be found growing wild or can be purchased from Indians.

The best season to voyage the Usumacinta is from January through March, the dry season. Bring insect repellent and a tightly meshed tent. Allow plenty of time for exploring Mayan ruins: one could easily spend a summer on the Usumacinta. Allow at least ten days. Below Tenosique, the Usumacinta is sluggish and the country somewhat more settled. For someone looking for a short, easy, and accessible run, however, the trip downriver to Balancan or Zapata makes an enjoyable jungle excursion.

Rio Grande de Santiago (Mexico)

The Rio Grande de Santiago, which flows out of the Mexican highlands near Guadalajara and winds its way down to the Pacific, offers both whitewater adventure and views of interesting backcountry. There are several spectacular rapids, especially on the upper portion of the trip, but since a good mule trail parallels most of the trip, portages can be taken when needed.

The voyage from Santa Rosa Dam, 35 miles out of Guadalajara, to Santiago Ixcuintla, a good take-out point near the coast, should take from a week to ten days. Because of its turbulence, the river is more suitable for rafts and kayaks than canoes. Except in very low water, which is no fun for anyone, this is no place for novices to learn about rivers.

At Guadalajara, one should ease by the Hydroelectric Power Department to glean whatever river information may be dispensed. No matter what the directions are, be alert while on the river itself. A recent rafting party almost floated over a 30-foot dam, built in 1907, that the Power Department officials had forgotten to mention. (Note: This potential wipe-out will probably be encountered on the second day out from Santa Rosa Dam.)

The trip is splendid, a slice of off-the-highway Mexico: thatched hut villages, a canyon of slashed red cliffs, *vaqueros* driving lean cattle to water at sundown, warm Coca-Colas in mud *tiendas,* Indians poling dugout canoes. In places it appears there are rocks floating in the water—chunks of pumice. Although alligators have been hunted as food for centuries, they still doze on mudbanks of the lower river, banana plantation country, where there are also iguanas and roseate spoonbills.

The main street of the red-light district in Santiago Ixcuintla drops right down to the water. Without doubt the best place to take-out.

Western United States

Tuolumne (California)

The rivers which tumble out of the Sierra Nevadas are fast, clear, and immensely scenic. Unfortunately most of them have been dammed, their canyons inundated with reservoirs, water bled off by diversion tunnels, or are bracketed by highways and railroads. Of the few remaining wilderness stretches, a run of the Tuolumne from Lumsden to Wards Ferry Bridge offers some of the most challenging whitewater in the state. This is a river for experts. The drop from Lumsden Bridge to Clavey River is 50 feet to the mile; from Clavey River to Wards Ferry Bridge 35 feet to the mile. Clavey Falls is usually portaged. In addition to life jackets, extra paddles, crash helmets, and wetsuits are recommended for kayakers. Only one professional outfitter, American River Touring Association, of Oakland, California, has taken raft parties down the run at the time this is written.

The Tuolumne rises from the Mount Lyell glacier, flows through the meadows of the Yosemite high country, enters Hetch Hetchy Reservoir, and joins the San Joaquin River 158 miles from its source. Although fishermen for years have scrambled down what wild section yet remains of the Tuolumne, it was not until the last few years that boaters began making runs down it. Most voyaged the 18 miles from Lumsden Bridge to Wards Ferry Bridge, but at least one party tried the river from the confluence of Cherry Creek to Lumsden Bridge. They found the gradient steep, some 100 feet to the mile, with numerous rapids, but felt the run was possible for experts in low water. In 1970 it was announced that the Tuolumne was one of forty-seven rivers being studied for possible inclusion under the National Wild Rivers Act. A growing number of people hope it will be indeed so designated, as there are very few stretches of wild river left in the entire state of California.

American (California)

Branches of the American River wind through the hills of the Mother Lode country, offering several possible boat runs. The North Fork of the American is rated a Class II voyage between Highway 49 and Folsom Lake. One must paddle 2 to 4 miles across flatwater to take-out at Rattlesnake Bar.

The Middle Fork from the washed-out Greenwood Bridge to Murderer's Bar may be Class II or Class III, depending upon water level. It's best to scout the take-out carefully. The 15 miles above Greenwood Bridge, beginning at the confluence of the Rubicon and Middle Fork, can be run by experts when the water is up sufficiently. This stretch features a number of rapids and fine wilderness scenery. At one point the river oxbows back to within 50 feet of its starting place. Early-day miners blasted a tunnel through the neck. One can paddle through the opening, but the tumultuous chute leading to it is all but impossible (although it has been negotiated by kayaks). Rucky Chunky Rapids, where the river booms down through huge boulders in three steep plunges, will require portaging. The bottom of Rucky Chunky is only about 1 mile from Greenwood Bridge.

There is superb boating on the South Fork. Above Coloma, where James Marshall discovered the flecks of gold that triggered the California stampede, the river is rated Class IV. From Coloma to Lotus the current is gentler, rated Class II and III, with gold-rush relics providing color, and rapids named "Old Scary" the principal excitement. Beyond Lotus the run is rated Class IV once more, with a number of rapids in a beautiful canyon above Folsom Lake, the take-out place. The trip from Chile Bar to the lake makes for a leisurely two-day journey.

Klamath (California)

The Klamath, pushing its way through the coast range of northern California, offers boaters remote mountain scenery and whitewater adventure. The two-day run between Happy Camp and Ti-Bar is popular with skilled rafters and kayakers. The stretch includes a number of large rapids, including Hamburg Falls and Rattlesnake. Since the Klamath is a controlled river, it can be run throughout the summer and into the autumn. There is an abundance of wildlife in the area, including great blue heron, osprey, bald eagle, mink, beaver, and bear.

Eel (California)

In northwestern California, there is a good stretch of wilderness on the main fork of the Eel River. A two-day run from Hearst Ranch to Dos Rios is rated Class III (on a scale of I to VI) for most of the way. The trip from Dos Rios to Alder Point should take two or three days and is rated Class II and III. For much of this distance the river forms a boundary to the Round Valley Indian Reservation. June and early July are considered the best times for boating.

Lower Colorado (California-Arizona)

In spite of the London Bridge being relocated to Lake Havasu City, there is a lot of fine wilderness country on the lower Colorado. To the author's way of thinking there can be no more pleasant a way to see this, America's greatest desert, than to drift through it on a river. If you get hot, just plunge in. Bare, contorted mountain ranges with needles and other spectacular formations rise back from either side of the water. Fishing is excellent.

If one puts-in at Bullhead City, below Davis Dam, Needles, or Topock, it is probably advisable to have some kind of motor for getting across the flatwater of Lake Havasu. Below Parker Dam, however, there is current almost all the way to Picacho Campground, north of Yuma. This run is great for novice boaters or just anyone who wants to get far away from the thundering herd.

Salt (Arizona)

The Salt River has cut its way down through an impressive canyon in east-central Arizona. A 52-mile run from Highway 60 to Highway 288 passes through a beautiful wilderness region—and features a number of tough rapids. The trip, which should be attempted only by skilled rafters or kayakers (an undecked canoe would have serious trouble here), must be made during spring or early summer to ensure sufficient water. Four hundred to 1000 cubic feet per second is good water: over 1000 cfs is hazardous. Flow information can be obtained by calling 273–5900 in Phoenix. The average gradient in the canyon is 23 feet per mile, although in one place it is 45 feet per mile. Several rapids should be scouted; some portaging may be necessary. Plan about four days for the trip.

San Juan (Utah)

The San Juan River, principal tributary of the Colorado River, opens up some fine wilderness country to float parties. Rising mostly in the high country of southwestern Colorado, the river winds through ranching country and past oil derricks in New Mexico, its flow usually twice that of the fabled Rio Grande. Out beyond Shiprock and over the border into Utah, the San Juan moves into wilder country—vast undeveloped spaces of mesa and sky, canyons and towers of rock.

Now that Lake Powell has backed up into much of the lower river, the most interesting run is the 81-mile stretch between Bluff and Clay Hills Crossing. The trip can be broken into two segments: from Bluff to Mexican Hat (24 miles), and from Mexican Hat to Clay Hill Crossing (57 miles).

The first segment has the advantage of accessibility; Clay Hills Crossing is a long way from anywhere over back roads. The put-in point is at Sand Island Campground, 4 miles out of Bluff. The river is muddy and one should bring an ample supply of drinking water. San Juan Canyon is deep and scenic, with cliffs rising to some 1500 feet above the river. Before entering the canyon proper, one is likely to see Indian herders with flocks of sheep: the San Juan forms the northern boundary of the Navajo reservation. There are two impressive cut-off goosenecks in the canyon. Eight-Foot Rapids are close to the second of these formations, about midway along the run. The rapids, which have been rated 3 on a scale of 1–10, should present no problems to boaters of moderate experience. Around a sharp bend to the left from the rapids are the Narrows, where gray-and-black cliffs rise up from both sides of the water.

Vegetation is sparse along the river, with tamarisk predominant close to the water, but there is no lack of wildlife on the wing. One sees chukars, yellow warblers, cliff swallows, and numerous canyon wrens. Highwater may offer delightful roller-coaster boating over large waves—a specialty of the San Juan. One can take-out at Hat Rock Campground or Mexican Hat itself, about 2 miles beyond.

On the other side of Mexican Hat the river kinks its way through the famed San Juan Goosenecks. On the saddle of Mendenhall Loop, which the river has almost cut entirely through, there is an abandoned stone cabin. Vivid canyon walls rise some 1400 feet in the Goosenecks; further on they reach a height of 2500 feet. Each bend of the river reveals strange and beautiful rock formations. There are several side canyons that invite hiking. Far up some of the larger ones, such as Slickhorn and Grand Gulch, there are isolated, rarely visited cliff dwellings. The only whitewater of any consequence on the run, Government Rapids, is about 20 miles up from Clay Hills Crossing.

John Day (Oregon)

Most of Oregon's famed whitewater runs, such as the MacKenzie, are bordered by highways and villages. On the east side of the Cascades, however, where the landscape is drier and less populated, there are some interesting wilderness runs. The John Day River, which winds through ranching country in central Oregon, is best run in November and again in March, April, or May. During summer months the water level is too low for an enjoyable voyage.

Once the John Day leaves Highway 19 at Service Creek it wanders for 157 miles through backcountry before emptying into the Columbia. Bring plenty of provisions, as there are only a handful of access points and scattered ranches along the route. Keep an eye out for barbed wire across the channel, and portage where necessary. Watch for rattlesnakes on shore. Overall this is not a difficult river. There is however, a steep, dangerous pitch below Clarno, and there are falls 8 miles above the mouth which require a portage.

Owyhee (Oregon)

The Owyhee, in the southwestern corner of the state, is even more remote and unfrequented. The 53 miles from Rome to Owyhee Reservoir are not difficult if the water level is sufficient, but this should be determined locally before setting out. Best time of year is May or June. The landscape is high desert, with lava flows and old craters. As the route which leads to the take-out comprises more than 30 miles of rough dirt road, it may be easier to have someone pick you up than to attempt a car shuttle.

The voyage, which should take from four to five days with plenty of time for side hikes and swimming, is down canyons and through sagebrush country so wild and remote that much of it has been explored only by boat. The only outposts of civilization are a few scattered ranches. In places along the Owyhee one can see wooden waterwheels that were once used to supply power for irrigating lonely ranches. Although there are several stretches of sportive whitewater, the only heavy rapids occur close to Marcom Ranch, where a crude rock diversion dam has been bulldozed into the river.

Not far beyond an old stone cabin which once served as a hideout for rustlers, the river enters a 10-mile gorge whose walls rise 1000 feet high— sheer cliffs thrusting directly out of the water. At many places along the run there are strange rock formations, and patches of wildflowers in season. Deer are often seen along the banks, and sometimes bobcat. Hawks, eagles, and vultures ride thermals high above the river. There are a few miles of slackwater paddling across the headwaters of Owyhee Reservoir (which takes one over the drowned hamlet of Watsonville), to the take-out point at Leslie Gulch.

Quinault (Washington)

You can run every river in this book without benefit of a guide if skilled enough—with one exception: the Quinault of Washington. Tumbling out of the high country of Olympic National Park, the river shoves its way through the almost unbelievable lushness of the Northwest coastal rain

"On the Quinault." Taken by the famous photographer of the American Indians, Edward S. Curtis (from his classic work, *The North American Indians,* Vol. IX, 1912)

forest before opening into the Pacific. The best run is from Lake Quinault on Highway 101 to Taholah on the coast—a 35-mile trip through thick growths of salal, spruce, and hemlock, the water mostly gentle but sometimes churning down staircases of rock. Not a particularly difficult stretch for an experienced river runner.

The only way you can make this voyage is in a dugout canoe with an Indian guide, for the river rambles through the beautiful, wild heartland of the Quinault Reservation, where no private boats are allowed. Why not? This is the forest home of the Quinault Indians, and to voyage with them is to step back briefly toward a time when Lewis and Clark were still trudging over the Bitterroot Range, or when Edward Curtis first photographed them. The Quinault canoes are traditional—hollowed-out cedar logs about 30 feet long, with a 30-inch beam. The logs are carved out with hand adzes, a task that sometimes takes as much as a year to complete. The

Indian's control of the dugouts in fastwater is masterful. A trip down the Quinault usually takes about 8 hours, allowing a bit of time for looking or fishing (native cutthroat can be taken all year long and there is a surge of steelhead in the autumn). Rates are far more reasonable than is the case with other wilderness outfitters who publicize the merits of their wilderness chefs. Your Quinault guide will expect *you* to bring a sack lunch for him. Put something special in it: this is a river for good feelings.

Skagit (Washington)

The Skagit River of Washington is not exactly a wilderness waterway, but comes close to it. A road that parallels the river, used mostly by logging trucks, it well screened by stands of fir and cedar, as well as thick underbrush. There are numerous fine places to camp. Most towns up the Skagit have a flavor of the past. Some were early-day logging camps; others mining centers. Marblemount, founded in the 1880s, has hotels and log cabins dating from gold rush days.

The Skagit rises in British Columbia, and drains some of the most beautiful and rugged country of the Cascade Mountains. Some authorities consider it the finest steelhead stream in the world. Up to thirty-five thousand of the sea-going trout, weighing up to 20 pounds each, are caught each winter. Salmon taken from the Skagit in August may run up to 50 pounds. Summer floaters can dine well on the Skagit. In addition to an abundance of fish and waterfowl, one can usually pick a quart of raspberries or blackberries within minutes. Bear and deer are often seen. The stretch from Newhalem to Marblemount is fast and rocky. There are a number of rapids, some of which are rated Class IV, in highwater. Below Marblemount the river becomes larger and slower yet is still exciting water. The best take-out place is probably Hamilton, as beyond it the river becomes increasingly murky and splits into myriad channels.

Selway (Idaho)

A river guide once told me "Years ago you'd never see anyone on the Middle Fork of the Salmon except maybe a smoke jumper once in a while—workin' his way downriver after fightin' a fire. Nowadays to get that kind of solitude you have to go up to the Selway."

Tumbling out of the Bitterroot Mountains, the Selway is indeed one of America's most beautiful and unfrequented rivers. Swift and rocky, it can be boated only during spring run-off, usually in June. Rapids are frequent and have hair on them. It is a river of whitewater excitement, a challenge for skilled boatmen. Thick forests of pine and cedar occasionally fall back, opening to grassy meadows where elk and moose graze. In places, rock walls squeeze the river into deep, narrow gorges. Mountain goat and bighorn sheep gluefoot their way along high, almost nonexistent ledges. The trout are not big by trophy standards—but they are numerous and feisty.

The most practical wilderness run in terms of access is the 49-mile trip from Whitecap Creek to Selway Falls, which should take from four to five days. Whitecap Creek is at the end of a Forest Service road that heads into backcountry from Magruder Ranger Station. There are a number of fine campsites along the river.

Rapids mentioned in the following log have been rated on a scale of 1 to 10 as to difficulty when water conditions are optimum.

SELWAY RIVER LOG
(*Mileage from Whitecap Creek*)

Mile 4: Slalom Slide Rapids (3–4). Followed by a good campsite with a deep, 75-yard-long fishing pool. Down a straight stretch and around a bend to the left one encounters three heavy rapids within the space of a mile—Galloping Gertie (6), Washerwoman (6), and Cougar Bluff (6). Around a sharp bend from the last rapids is a fine, large campsite at Driftwood Bar.

Mile 7: Running Creek. Ranch and airstrip. There is a shallows (3) below the mouth of the creek.

Mile 12: Goat Creek Rapids (5). Rocky.

Mile 13: Fine campsites on left side of river.

Mile 14: Shearer Fire Guard Station and Airstrip. Around a large horseshoe bend is Selway Lodge, a hunting retreat accessible only by airplane, boat, or trails.

Mile 16: Bear Creek, a large tributary.

Mile 18: Rodeo Rapids (3), which features a large standing wave, is followed by Indian Creek Rapids (3).

Mile 24: Ham Rapids (6). Lots of rocks. Beyond is a deep, narrow canyon —a beautiful place.

Mile 27: Moose Creek, a major tributary. Here one drops into a canyon where for 6 miles there are virtually no campsites and the water is turbulent. Named rapids include Double Drop (two falls, 75 yards apart, the first rated 6 and the second 5); Ladle (7), wide and rocky without any easy channels, can be sneaked on the far right; Little Niagara (5), which should be run to the right as there are falls against the other bank; No Slouch (6); and Osprey (7), which should also be run to the right, with efforts taken to avoid the bluff and sharp rocks at the last drop.

Mile 33: Good campsite with swimming holes.

Mile 38: A little beyond the mouth of Pinchot Creek is Jim Creek Rapids (7–8), probably the toughest on the upper river. Lots of boulders to the left; a big hole near the bottom of the rapids cannot be avoided. These rapids should always be scouted. Two miles below is a fine, large campsite.

Miles 38 to 49: Gentle section of the river. Lots of time for water fights or lazy looking. Take-out at Selway Falls, which is, for all practical purposes, unrunnable. There is a road to the falls.

Flathead (Montana)

The Bob Marshall Wilderness Area, south of Glacier National Park, is one of the most beautiful and unfrequented regions of America. The South Fork of the Flathead River, which runs through the middle of it, has seldom been run. As might be expected, access is difficult, involving a trail of 20-some miles from Seeley Lake over a pass to the upper reaches of the river. Anyone who has ever lugged a boat up a steep slope will appreciate the advisability of hiring a packer with some stout horses. The South Fork is floatable, if shallow and multichanneled, down to Big Prairie Ranger Station. Beyond, the river passes into a clay-walled canyon in which there are several easy yet interesting rapids. There is excellent fishing on the river as well as in Big Salmon Lake, a short side hike.

It is not until one passes Black Bear Creek that the going gets not only rough, but impossible. At one place the river is squeezed by an immense boulder into a jet less than 5 feet wide; beyond, it enters a boiling cleft where a boat would almost certainly be capsized and sucked under. It is essential to take-out above this danger zone. One man is known to have entered it in a rubber raft: he drowned. The portage necessitates reaching the main trail, several hundred feet above the river, by a rough spur path. From there it is a long trek down to Meadow Creek Fire Guard Station. Once again, pack horses are well worth the money. It is an easy float from Meadow Creek down to the KLN Ranch (where one can rent pack animals and leave shuttle cars). Anyone planning this trip should read Oz Hawksley's detailed account of his exploratory run down it in 1964 (see Appendix II), as well as consulting with forest rangers and packers who are familiar with the area.

Running the North Fork of the Flathead is a much less complicated affair that does, however, include encounters with some very large rapids. A gravel road parallels the river as far as the Canadian border, affording easy put-ins, but it is rarely visible from the water and lightly traveled. Those who camp on the opposite side of the river from the road will have the illusion of pure wilderness for most of the trip. There are supurb vistas of the peaks in Glacier Park (of which North Fork is the western border), as well as whitewater excitement all the way. The trip from the Canadian border to confluence with the Middle Fork takes an average of five days.

Madison (Montana)

Like most rivers of western Montana, the Madison is clear and lively—good trout water with mountains to rest your eyes on in just about every direction. The run from Varney Bridge, about 13 miles above Ennis, to Ennis Lake, is easy floating, popular with fishermen. Like their counterparts throughout the mountain West, most of them prefer rubber rafts to canoes. Approaching the lake, the river splits into a number of channels, which should cause no problems except in very low water.

Below Ennis Dam the Madison twists through Beartrap Canyon, a difficult stretch of whitewater. Abrupt drops and lots of boulders make this one of the more challenging runs in southwestern Montana. The canyon is scenic and relatively inaccessible, although short. It opens into a broad valley through which the river meanders. One can take-out at the Highway 289 bridge or continue on into Three Forks. Rattlesnakes are prevalent, especially in the area of Beartrap Canyon.

Smith (*Montana*)

The Smith River, which begins near the ghost town of Castle in central Montana, is an interesting and little-traveled waterway. Much of it flows through a semiwilderness that contains caves and limestone cliffs with Indian paintings. Tributaries, such as Rock and Tenderfoot creeks, are acclaimed for their rainbow and brown trout. Browns up to 9 pounds have been taken. There are numerous fine camping spots. The best float trip is probably from the Fish and Game access near Fort Logan to the county road running between Cascade and Eden. Be careful of fences stretched across the river.

Missouri (*Montana*)

For 160 miles, from Fort Benton to Robinson Bridge, the Missouri is little changed from when Lewis and Clark passed beside it. Five to seven days is ample time for a voyage down this historic wilderness waterway. The broad, muddy river winds through a region of lonely bluffs and buttes. Some of the more spectacular formations include Steamboat Rock, Dark Butte, Cathedral Rock, White Cliffs, and Hole-in-the-Wall. The state is developing a campsite at Hole-in-the-Wall and fresh water may be obtained there. There are good camping places all along the river. Willow, cottonwood, and rose bushes grow close to the water, pine higher up. Beaver are frequently seen. This is a fine catfish river—10-pounders are often caught; also sturgeon weighing 30 pounds and better.

Black Bluff Rapids is 5 miles up from the mouth of Marias River. There are rocks and rough water in midstream which can be bypassed on either side. One's voyage can be shortened by putting-in at either Loma Ferry, by the mouth of Marias River, or Virgelle Ferry 16 miles farther on. Deadman Rapids are a little up from the mouth of the Judith River and should be run to the left. The remains of Fort Claggett lie close to the Judith River. It was occupied about one hundred years ago, and people still dig up old inkwells, buttons, cartridge shells, and the like. There is a ferry below the mouth of the Judith and 3 miles beyond this is Birch Rapids. Run it to the right of the island—but keep away from the right bank. Most other named rapids on this stretch of the Missouri are glorified riffles. This is not a difficult run.

At Chimney Bend there is a deserted ranch and a cliff inscription reading "General Meade. 1880." Who put it there is something of a puzzle, as the general died in 1872. At Cow Island one passes the spot where Chief Joseph and his Nez Percé band forded the river on their flight toward Canada. This is a fine section of wilderness water, well worthy of inclusion under the National Wild and Scenic Rivers System. Detailed maps made of this section of the Missouri can be obtained by writing the National Parks Service (see Appendix II).

Greys (*Wyoming*)

Greys River is a fast mountain stream running through a deep valley between the Salt River and Wyoming Ranges. Some 50 miles of navigable water range from moderately difficult to rapids that should be attempted only by experts. A Forest Service road parallels the river, which permits scouting of difficult portions. As with most high-country rivers in the Rockies, trout fishing is good, and one can expect excellent campsites.

From a put-in point at Corral Creek Fire Guard Station to Lynx Creek Campground the river clips right along but there are no serious rapids. If experienced, one can run it in an open canoe. Be on the alert for obstructing logs. Below Lynx Creek the river rumbles through the remains of an old landslide. This rapids is between 1 and 2 miles long—a continuous drop with little or no opportunity for pausing in eddies. The canyon opens out at a point a little above the Forks of the Greys River Campground, and is comparatively easy on down to the bridge at Squaw Flat. Only experts should attempt the rapids below Lynx Creek. Gradient for the 43 miles from Corral Creek Campground to a point just below Squaw Flat is 39.5 feet to the mile. Beyond Squaw Flat the river foams through a canyon which appears to be Class V or better. It may be completely unrunnable in most water levels.

Cross Mountain Canyon of the Yampa (*Colorado*)

It is a magnificent moment when man conquers that which has been considered impossible in terms of rock, water, a stopwatch. . . . Unlike Dr. Roger Bannister's breaking of the four-minute mile, or the first ascent of El Capitan, in Yosemite, the successful kayak run of Cross Mountain Canyon of northwestern Colorado in 1965 received little publicity. Yet anyone who has viewed the gorge from the air—a boulder-choked cascade that drops 80 feet in its first mile, 60 feet in the succeeding two miles—will appreciate the achievement of Calvin Giddings, Bruce Christensen, and Paul Schettler.

Bus Hatch, an almost legendary western river guide, attempted the gorge in the late '30s with several companions in wooden Galloway-type boats. Dan Tobin, superintendent of Dinosaur National Monument, recalls the venture: "They successfully navigated the first two falls, the first of which was described as having a terrible backlash, but lost their craft in the third one. After much difficulty they were able to work their way back upstream to safety."

In 1951 or 1952 some airmen from Lowry Air Force Base had a go at the canyon; their 20-foot metal pontoon structure got no farther than the second drop. In the following years others attempted Cross Mountain in a raft of lashed oil drums, and in a Japanese rubber raft. The violent cataract soon separated the adventurers from their boats and, although no one was drowned during the capers, there were some wet, sorry hikes up to the canyon rim. In 1964 two men passed through the canyon in a kayak, but since their craft was lodged more frequently upon their shoulders, portaging, than upon the raging water, they justifiably considered the attempt a failure.

Giddings and company made their successful run in early August, when the river was flowing in the vicinity of 1000 cubic feet per second. Only expert kayakers could hope to navigate its boulder-choked whitewater. Even so, the conquering party covered their bets; following the action from the shore were three friends, one of whom could whip an innertube on a rope to a capsized kayaker with the accuracy of an Annie Oakley. He was needed, perhaps preventing a fatality, certainly saving a boat, on more than one occasion. Nevertheless, one expedition kayak still remains irretrievably wrapped around rocks of the canyon—fortunately it was being lined, rather than paddled, at the time of the misfortune.

The immense boulders of the Cross Mountain Canyon make the passage of a large raft impossible; the rapids are too tough for a small raft or a decked canoe. Kayak is the only way. Giddings estimated there are nine lengthy rapids of Class IV or higher, but allowed it is tough to tell where one chute ends and another begins. It is mainly a continuous 3-mile rapids. Most kayakers, however talented, will decide to portage or line a rapid or two. The gorge offers no easy walkabout turf; this is slippery boulder-and-cliff country, and one drowns just as surely from falling into a rapid from a rock as from a boat.

To get to this challenging gorge, take the dirt road north near the hamlet of Cross Mountain in northwestern Colorado, on U.S. Highway 40. The road crosses the river at the portals of the canyon. Giddings' detailed account of his passage through the gorge should be obtained if possible. It was published in *American White Water,* Spring, 1966 (see Appendix II).

Yampa (Colorado)

Below Cross Mountain Canyon the Yampa is joined by the Little Snake River and the combined flows meander through Deerlodge Park, a broad valley. Deerlodge Park, reached by dirt road that branches off U.S. Highway 40, is the put-in spot for a spectacular 45-mile run through Dinosaur National Monument to confluence with the Green at Echo Park. Although not nearly as hazardous as Cross Mountain Canyon, there are big rapids on this voyage that demand the skills of experienced boatmen. The trip is popular with guided raft parties.

Within sight of Deerlodge Park the river enters a deep, precipitous gorge. The canyon walls are almost continuous all the way to Echo Park, and have been eroded into beautiful formations, such as Haystack Rock, Cleopatra's Couch, and the Crow's Nest. In places there are small openings in the narrow canyon: Harding Hole and Castle Park, site of the Mantle Ranch. The Yampa cuts back into the mountains in a series of horseshoe bends. Air distance to Echo Park is nearly half that of the river mileage. The rapids below Tepee Gulch, Big Joe, and Warm Springs Draw can be rough in high water, especially the last one. There are fine campsites along the river, caves to explore at Harding Hole. One can take-out at Echo Park or continue on through Whirlpool and Split Mountain canyons on the Green.

Conejos (*Colorado*)

The Conejos River flows into the Rio Grande several miles south of Alamosa. West of Antonito, the Conejos meanders through a beautiful mountain valley, where stands of spruce, cottonwood, and aspen alternate with grassy meadows, and here and there one drifts by abandoned log cabins of early settlers. The trout fishing is excellent.

The Conejos River Canyon is reached by driving west from Antonito on State Highway 17. One of the most pleasant floats begins at the highway bridge close to Elk Creek Campground. From this bridge to the next bridge downriver at the Ponderosa Fishing Camp, the current is fast, but there are no obstacles other than two barbed wire fences which cross the river and necessitate portages. The run, which takes about forty-five minutes, is excellent for novice boaters. The Ponderosa Camp bridge has large beams which V down almost to the water, but boats can sneak along the right-hand side without difficulty.

For a couple of miles below Ponderosa Camp the river continues to move briskly without rapids. Then the pace begins to quicken. There are numerous fallen trees and boulders in the water. After a series of good-sized riffles, the current slams into a log jam on the right-hand side, makes a tight S-turn, and rushes through a narrow, rock-squeezed chute, a tricky combination in high water. Just beyond the chute is Aspen Glade Campground, usual take-out point. The entire run from the highway bridge takes from two to three hours, depending upon water level.

One can also put-in at Spectacle Lake Campground, several miles above Elk Creek, or continue beyond Aspen Glade. The trip beyond Aspen Glade, however, is through more open, settled country, and one encounters a number of barbed-wire barriers.

Gila (*New Mexico*)

The Gila Wilderness, in southwestern New Mexico, is little changed from the days when Geronimo and his braves would camp there after raiding ranches to the south, on the flatlands. Bears shamble through conifer forests of the Mimbres and Pinos Altos ranges. Over 250 species of birds live here; it's an extraordinary natural aviary. Older than the scattered campfire ashes of the Apache or than the ghost mining camps that decay on the fringes of the wilderness are cliff dwellings inhabited some six hundred years ago. On rocks above the Gila River their inhabitants painted stick people, animals, zigzag vertical lines, curious whorling circles. They used the red and orange pigments of one rock, hematite, to decorate the blander faces of granite and sandstone.

For some 40 miles the Gila River runs through this beautiful, wild region, a superb canoe run. Like may rare and lovely things, it is hard to catch. At most, there are only three weeks a year when the water level is sufficient to float a canoe, usually the last week in March and the first two weeks of April. Check with New Mexico whitewater clubs (see Appendix VI) for conditions.

Drive out State Highway 527 to the river crossing and put-in. One will likely see wild turkeys, bald eagles, blue herons, and all manner of ducks during the voyage, which will take from two to three days. Elk often graze in the meadowlands that flank much of the river. Above Sapello Creek, the cliffs drop directly into the water for a stretch. Near Skeleton Canyon a small waterfall drops through a chute until sprayed upward by a lip of rock, creating an altogether satisfying effect against a background of stained rock.

Boats can be taken out of the river at Turkey Creek, or, more practically, at Sapello Creek farther on, where a dirt spur road leads to pavement only ¼ mile away.

Central United States

Little Missouri (*North Dakota*)

There is a stretch of the Little Missouri, which runs down from a country road a few miles northwest of Amidon to Medora on Interstate Highway 94, where for some 60 miles the river is about the color of second-day coffee with cream and rapids are all but nonexistent. There are fish in the river—but they are impossible to see in the murk of suspended clay particles. One canoeist reported accidentally whacking a fish with the stroke of his paddle.

Yet for all this, the Little Missouri offers a wildly beautiful float trip, winding through the heart of the western Dakota badlands. Strangely eroded bluffs rise on all sides; some are solid in color, more frequently they are banded in hues of white, red, blue, green, gray, yellow, tan, and black.

The bluffs are some hundreds of feet high; but with scant vegetation to give perspective they often seem to lift thousands of feet above the water.

Throughout the badlands there are burning coalbeds, which have baked the overlying claybeds into a natural red brick, scoria. One coal seam, observed to be burning by settlers in the 1880s, still smolders today. Nearby, a stand of junipers are straight and columnar, as if imitating spruce trees. This peculiar growth pattern is believed to exist only in the badlands at this one location; when the trees are taken elsewhere and replanted, they soon bend into the gnarled and sprawling posture of conventional junipers. Botanists suspect the persistently burning coal, possibly by the emission of sulfur dioxide, may have caused the mutation.

The run from Amidon to Medora takes about three days. When the water levels are high, however, the trip could probably be extended to as much as 280 miles, from Marmarth to some 40 miles downstream from the north unit of Theodore Roosevelt National Memorial Park. Information may be obtained from Park Headquarters at Medora or the National Forest headquarters in the same town. Be sure to check water level, since the river is sometimes too shallow to float. The pertinent U.S.G.S. contour maps are those for Watford City and Dickinson; scale 1:250,000.

For much of its length the Little Missouri passes through scenic wilderness. As such, it is definitely a candidate for our Wild and Scenic Rivers System (before someone decides to push a road up along it, with the inevitable baggage that follows: junk curio shops, greasy spoon eateries, pastures of rusting automobiles, and trail bikes ripping up into the soft slopes of the badlands).

Little White (*South Dakota*)

The Little White River, a clear, swift stream, meanders through the Rosebud Sioux Reservation of South Dakota—a fine place for canoeing. Much of the country seems little changed from the days when Indians hunted buffalo here. Close to the river there are groves of cottonwood, green ash, American elm, box elder, and juniper, while bur oak and stands of Ponderosa rise on the canyon sides. Above are treeless grasslands now browsed by herds of beef cattle.

From Ghost Hawk Campground, a good put-in place, the river runs for some 10 miles through Crazy Horse Canyon, which is from 3 to 10 miles wide and about 300 feet deep. Watch for beaver. On some of the numerous gravelbars one can find quartz crystals and pieces of petrified wood. In places there are small standing waves, but there are no rapids of any consequence. Below Highway 18 the pines thin out and the valley opens up. Trees and scrub growth crowd the river; in places fallen trunks block the passage, making for slow progress. Some canoeists prefer to bypass this 15-mile stretch, putting in again where the Ring Thunder Community Road crosses the river. From here to the take-out point where the river passes close to Highway 83 (about 17 miles) the banks are mostly open and grassy. In this stretch the current, cutting its way through shale, drops through some exciting rapids of moderate difficulty.

Niobrara (Nebraska)

The Niobrara River traverses virtually all of northern Nebraska while rarely even coming close to a parallel highway. For much of this distance it slides through shallow, wooded valleys where there are frequent meadows. As with the Little White River to the north, the surrounding countryside features gently rolling grasslands and occasional farms. The Niobrara is considered all but unnavigable for a few miles below Box Butte Dam; it is gentle all the rest of the way to Lewis and Clark Lake on the Missouri.

St. Croix (Minnesota)

Some 5 percent of Minnesota is water, equaling the area of Rhode Island and Connecticut combined. About 25,000 miles of rivers and streams flow through a region that is predominantly farmlands in the south, forest in the north. A variety of wilderness waterways offer a wide range of scenery and degrees of difficulty.

One of the finest runs is down the St. Croix River on the Minnesota-Wisconsin border, which is being considered for inclusion in the National Wild and Scenic Rivers System. Although the St. Croix can be navigated for more than 120 miles, all the way from the woods of Burnett County, Wisconsin, down to confluence with the Mississippi, the wilderness portion extends 68 miles from Danbury, Wisconsin, to Taylor Falls, Minnesota. Below Taylor Falls there are roads beside the river and numerous towns.

The St. Croix is a wide, clear river with excellent forest campsites and numerous sandy islands. The rapids are not generally dangerous for moderately experienced canoeists. Some 22 miles below Danbury the river splits into two channels at the Kettle River Rapids. These rapids are followed by Paint Pot Rapids—some 5 miles of whitewater in all.

Big Fork (Minnesota)

The Big Fork winds through a magnificent valley to join the Rainy River close to International Falls. From source to mouth the banks are shaded by stands of pine, spruce, hardwoods, and fragrant balsam. On the upper reaches one paddles past fields of wild rice. There are beaver dams up almost every tributary and moose graze in marshy areas. The current is fairly strong—be on the lookout for submerged logs and rocks. There are a number of rapids whose difficulty varies with water depth and season. Information may be obtained by contacting the Pine Island State Forest Office in Big Falls. Little American Falls and Big Fork Falls must be portaged at any water level.

The Big Fork was a major water route for Indians, and later was used by fur traders. There was once a Hudson's Bay post at Keuffner's Landing,

30 miles up from Rainy River. A good put-in point is at Dora Lake, 173 miles from the confluence with the Rainy, although there are a number of other access points. Some of the principal rapids, with mileage given from Rainy River, are as follows: Ostby Creek (45), Big Fork Falls (52), Powell's (97), Little American Falls (106), Muldoon (116), Rice (134), Huck's (152), and Robb's (157). This is a trip for experienced canoeists. There are good campsites.

Red Lake (*Minnesota*)

When considering Minnesota, one usually thinks of lakes or thick forests. The upper reaches of the Red Lake River, however, offer a different and intriguing landscape: open, marshy country beyond the river's corridor of stately trees. The first 12 miles of Red Lake River pass through a true wilderness, a part of the Red Lake Indian Reservation. Wildlife is abundant: this is a good place to bring a camera with a telephoto lens. The flow is clear and gentle; it should provide no problems for novice boaters.

The put-in point is where the river leaves Lower Red Lake, reached by Highway 1. Twelve miles downstream there is dam which should be portaged on the right. There are no good camping places above the dam. Beyond the dam the country changes; there are no swamps and few trees. Toward the end of the run there are scattered farms. The take-out point is at Thief River Falls, 54 miles from Red Lake. The 40-mile run between Thief River Falls and Huot features rapids and high cliffs, but also passes through a more developed and populous area.

Mississippi (*Minnesota*)

There is great fascination in the source of a mighty river, be it the Nile or our own "Father of Waters." The first European to reach the banks of the Mississippi was Hernando de Soto in 1541, yet it was not until 291 years later that Henry Schoolcraft accurately determined the source as Lake Itasca in north-central Minnesota. For 80 miles from its source to Lake Bemidji, the river winds through pine forests and marshlands where one has ample opportunity to spot wildlife, including moose.

This section provides a fine run for canoeists seeking wilderness, for its winding course is virtually untouched by industry or concentrated settlement. Three overnight landings have been completed: Bear Den Landing, 5 miles south and 3 miles southeast of Selway, is readily accessible; Pine Point Landing may be reached by car over the forest road which leaves the blacktop road 2 miles north of Becida; the Iron Bridge Landing, west of the Iron Bridge on the Bemidji-Becida road, is accessible only by canoe or other boat. Water levels and other information may be obtained by writing the Forest Station at Itasca State Park.

Eight miles beyond Lake Bemidji the Ottertail Power Dam must be portaged on the right, and a few miles downstream the river flows into Cass

Lake, one of two large bodies of water on this stretch of the river. Lake Winnibigoshish, 10 miles below, covers an area of 114,800 acres and is 15 miles across. One should venture across this lake only if the weather is calm. Two other dams must be portaged before Grand Rapids is reached. The 100 miles of river between Lake Bemidji and Grand Rapids are scenic, passing through Chippewa National Forest and Leech Lake Indian Reservation. There are a number of fine campsites and fishing is excellent.

Between Grand Rapids and Brainerd the river enters a huge swamp basin and later winds past the Cuyuna Iron Range. At the mouth of the Crow Wing River, a few miles beyond Brainerd, the Mississippi has all but described a gigantic circle, having traveled 376 miles to a point only 70 air miles from its source. Crow Wing State Park, where there is a ghost town dating from the 1860s, is a good take-out place. One can, of course, continue on downriver all the way to New Orleans; yet from this point on, the Mississippi enters more settled country, and its wild-river characteristics diminish as it flows southward.

Peshtigo (Wisconsin)

The Peshtigo River, which flows through Nicolet National Forest in northeastern Wisconsin, features the most challenging stretch of long continuous whitewater in Wisconsin. Roaring Rapids, as this section is aptly known, actually consists of six separate drops, with a gradient of 47 feet to the mile. Roaring Rapids is rated Class IV in difficulty, while the rest of the run is considered Class II or III depending upon water level.

The put-in point for a 20-mile run to a point close to Cauldron Falls Reservoir is at the first bridge below Cavour. There are camping spots en route but drinking water should be carried. The Peshtigo is a stream where sections of quiet water alternate with rapids that tumble between granite boulders. For some 9 miles there are no rapids of such difficulty as to make scouting necessary (unless in an undecked canoe during high-water). Then one reaches Michigan Rapids and Ralton's Rips, both of which are steep and should be looked over.

Roaring Rapids begins about 2½ miles from the take-out point (bridge of Marinette County Highway C). First Drop, where the river rushes down a sloping granite ledge, is within sight of Second Drop. Kussokavitch Rapids, about ½ mile below Second Drop, is not particularly difficult in itself—but runs directly into Five-Foot Falls, which are precisely what the name suggests. A narrow chute near the left bank is the best route. A gentle curve to the right, visible from Five-Foot Falls, marks the beginning of Horse Race, a Class IV rapids some 300 feet in length. Beyond is S Curve, final whitewater of the run. All of Roaring Rapids should be scouted.

Flambeau (Wisconsin)

In contrast to the wild Peshtigo, the gentle flow of the Flambeau River is suitable for novice boaters. Only two rapids will be encountered on a 23-mile run through Flambeau River State Forest, and neither of these is considered hazardous. The put-in point is where County Highway W crosses the North Fork of the Flambeau. Cedar Rapids, not far beyond the junction of the North and South forks, flows around a large island. Float parties often run this several times, portaging back up the east bank. The island makes an excellent campsite. The other rapids of note, Beaver Dam, features a drop of some 3 feet in a fairly short distance. The customary take-out point is at one of the private lodges along Big Falls flowage, reached by roads running north from Tony or Glen Flora. Inquire locally.

Upper Iowa (Iowa)

The Upper Iowa, which is being considered for inclusion in the National Wild and Scenic Rivers System, is one of the most beautiful streams in the American midlands. Between Kendallville and Decorah the spring-fed river flows between high limestone cliffs, which in places tower 400 feet above the water. Stands of native cedar grow from cliff ledges as well as on top of the bluffs. There are numerous good camping spots. The current moves along at a good pace, and although there are a number of shoals, no rapids are considered dangerous. Among the visual delights of this trip are Coldwater Creek, a trout stream which winds through a park-like meadow; the massive stone monuments known as Chimney Rocks; and Malanphy Springs, a waterfall.

The 30-mile stretch between Kendallville and Decorah makes a fine weekend float. Upriver, a 24-mile trip from Lime Springs to Kendallville is also popular. While the scenery is not as spectacular as that of the lower run (the upper part flows mostly through flatlands), the smallmouth fishing is excellent. Boaters should keep a sharp eye out for fences across the river.

Big Muddy (Illinois)

The Big Muddy of southern Illinois is neither appreciably larger nor more turbid than many midland streams. It flows through Shawnee National Forest, an engaging corner of wilderness in this distressingly developed state. A good put-in point is located ¼ mile east of Sand Ridge at a county bridge. Here the river winds through a forest of bottomland hardwood species. The pileated woodpecker is often heard, if not seen, and deer are common. Tread carefully: there are rattlesnakes, copperheads, and cottonmouth moccasins in the area. Abenyville Rock and Swallow Bluff are interesting formations, as is Little Grand Canyon, where there is a campsite. One can take-out at Rattlesnake Ferry east of Grand Tower, or paddle on to the mouth and then down the Mississippi to Cape Girardeau, Missouri. The voyage from Sand Ridge to Rattlesnake Ferry is a pleasant overnight trip, with smooth water all the way.

Sugar Creek (Indiana)

Whenever Hoosier river runners get together the conversation usually touches on Sugar Creek, a historic waterway that is still relatively unspoiled. Although the calm waters (mostly Class I) are now for the most part the province of canoeists, in 1843 a flatboat 50 feet in length, with a 16-foot beam, passed down Sugar Creek into the Wabash, the Ohio, and on to New Orleans, fully loaded with a cargo of flour, bacon, and lard. Paddling around some of the tight kinks of Sugar Creek today, one has to marvel at the feat. The best section of the river is a 40-mile run from Crawfordsville to the Wabash. It is then but a few miles down the Wabash to the take-out point at Montezuma. The annual Sugar Creek canoe race begins at Crawfordsville and ends at Shades State Park. The most scenic portion of the river, featuring cliffs, bluffs, and stands of virgin timber, is the 11-mile stretch between Shades and Turkey Run State parks. If you are continuing on to the Wabash, there is a dam to be portaged below Turkey Run State Park.

Mohican and Little Miami (Ohio)

Although it is impossible to boat for any distance in Ohio without running smack into civilization, there are a few interesting short runs. The Mohican and Little Miami rivers both have good stretches. Near Loudonville, one can put-in to Clear Fork of the Mohican at Hemlock Grove Camp, located in a beautiful wooded ravine where there are campsites. Some 4 miles downstream Clear Fork joins Black Fork to form the main river, which can then be floated to Mohawk Dam. This trip is generally considered safe for novices. Good fishing.

Below Clifton the Little Miami River plunges into a deep and spectacular gorge. As there are rapids and falls in the canyon, this is strictly for skilled boaters. Inquire locally. A number of miles downriver, one reaches the Spring Valley Wildlife Area, a wooded region where there are campsites.

Presque Isle (Michigan)

Upper Michigan thrusts out like a knobby arm between Lake Michigan and Lake Superior. Sparsely populated, it boasts a number of wilderness rivers. In the course of a 96-mile run from U.S. Highway 2 near Marenisco, the Presque Isle River drops swiftly to its mouth on the shore of Lake Superior. Falls and heavy rapids make this a run for experts. The banks are usually high and wooded, with cliffs in some places and occasional swamp country. Except in the marshes, the bottom is largely solid rock. Fishing is good for bass, trout, and pike. The stretch from U.S. Highway 2 down to State Highway 28 begins dramatically. There are four falls close to the put-in point at the bridge. There are several other drops on this section which will require portages. The river is somewhat calmer between Highway 28 and the lake, yet there are still hazards, most notably a falls encountered soon after entering Porcupine Mountains State Park. From a campground at the mouth of the river a forest road leads back to Wakefield.

Ontonagon—East Branch (Michigan)

This fast stream, largely within the Ottawa National Forest, offers a fine 60-mile, two-day cruise through backcountry. There are several rocky rapids and one should be on the alert for logjams and deadheads. This is a good trout stream. The put-in point is at Sparrow Rapids Campground near Kenton. On the lower part of the run, steep clay bluffs rise sharply from the riverbed. Where the river bisects Forest Road 208, which runs between Mass and Trout creeks, one passes the remains of a bridge that washed out in 1963. The 8 miles from here to the take-out place at the U.S. Highway 45 bridge are almost continuous whitewater—Class II to III. When the water is up there are high standing waves, but no falls or ledges that require portaging.

Manistique (Michigan)

This is an excellent wilderness river for the long weekend. The 90-mile run from State Highway 44 north of Blaney Park to the town of Manistique on Lake Michigan should take from three to four days. Except for an occasional intrepid fisherman, you will be out of contact for the entire voyage, so bring enough provisions. With any luck your diet will be bountifully supplemented with perch and walleye. Good campsites. The run begins in Seney National Wildlife Refuge and then passes through Manistique River State Forest. A shorter, 50-mile, two-day trip can be made down the West Branch of the Manistique. The put-in point is at the West Branch Forest Campground on Highwater Truck Trail. Directions can be obtained at the Manistique Field Office of the Conservation Department. Much of this trip will be on the main river after the two flows converge.

Two Hearted River (Michigan)

Over on the other side of the peninsula, the Two Hearted River cuts through equally wild country. This is a more demanding river in terms of boating skills. The 2- to 6-foot-deep water is fast and some portaging is necessary over logjams. Experts only. The countryside is rolling and forested: there are a number of excellent campsites. There are feisty rainbow and brown trout in every section of the river. The put-in point is at the High Bridge Campground on a forest road north of Newberry. Take-out at the hamlet of Two Heart on Lake Superior. Michigan name-givers, at least when it comes to rivers, were not lacking in imagination. Predictably, there are your Indian, Pine, and Fox. But also, in addition to the Two Hearted, there are the Paint, Misery, Jordan, Thunder Bay, Bad, Paw Paw, and Firesteel—just to mention a few.

Manistee (Michigan)

The Manistee River rolls across a considerable chunk of western Michigan, much of it through backcountry. All told, one can boat for 215 miles, a trip requiring at least ten days, with minimal interference from villages, roads, and dams considering that you are in an industrial state— our unceasing fountain of automobiles—rather than in the wilds of northern Canada or Honduras. Putting-in at the Manistee River Hunt Club off the State Highway 72 west of Grayling, one pushes off into a shallow river that twists for 28 miles through cedar swamps. This is trout country. It is 60 miles to the hamlet of Sharon. Beyond the State Highway 66 bridge, the pace of the river picks up and it writhes all over the landscape. There are good campsites. If low on grub, park your canoe at the Highway 37 bridge and walk into Sherman. Not far beyond is 8 miles of slackwater behind Hodenpyl Dam, dull for boating but a good place to fish for pike, bass, and panfish. Take-out for portage on the north side of the dam. The run down to Tippy Dam is scenic, but frequented. The best stretch of the Manistee is from below Tippy Dam to Manistee Lake—90 miles of wilderness. This river offers coho fishing in season.

Père Marquette (Michigan)

The Père Marquette River of western Michigan is being considered for inclusion in the National Wild and Scenic Rivers System. It would be a fine choice. From the put-in point on Highway 37 south of Baldwin, the river winds through Manistee National Forest, a run for experienced boaters. There are numerous rapids, as well as logjams, overhangs, and quick turns. Rainbow Rapids, which will be encountered about an hour after passing beneath Bowman Bridge, is especially tricky. If in doubt, portage on the south side. The river offers lots of places to camp, and trout fishing. There are several access points to the Père Marquette, and one can plan to boat for a weekend or a full week on the river. Good take-out points are located at the edge of the National Forest (road south of Custer), or at Père Marquette Lake next to Lake Michigan.

Southern United States

Current (Missouri)

The Current River of south-central Missouri, a spring-fed flow that winds through a sparsely populated region of the Ozarks, was the first American river to be given permanent protection from dam builders and developers. In 1964 about 100 miles of the Current and some 40 miles of its tributary, Jacks Fork, became the Ozark National Scenic Riverways.

French trappers named the river *La Rivière Courante* (the running river), but later inhabitants of the region, lanky Anglo-Saxons who farmed the hollows and hill patches, shortened the name to Current. As with the Buffalo River country in Arkansas, sparse economic resources are responsible for much of the Current's present wilderness condition. What hardwoods were accessible were logged off decades ago; thick second-growth forest has now replaced them. As thin, overworked soils failed to produce, settlers moved away. Bypassed by freeways and major railroads, the Current River country has never attracted any industry to speak of. What few towns have grown up near the river—Eminence, Owl's Bend, and Van Buren—are pleasant country-crossroad hamlets.

Some 60 percent of the Current's flow pushes out of natural springs. The most impressive is Big Spring, largest single-orifice spring on the continent, which produces 250 million gallons of clear, chill water every twenty-four hours. Many of the springs issue from limestone formations in which there are numerous caves and sinkholes. Round Spring Cavern, privately owned and open to the public, has more than 6000 feet of passageways.

There is an abundance of wildlife in the region: kingfishers, green heron, pileated woodpecker, wood thrush, raccoon, bobcat, rabbit, squirrel, opossum, gray and red fox, muskrat, mink, and beaver. Fishermen can select their lures for rock and smallmouth bass, red horse, channel cat, and walleyed pike. Three fourths of the park is forested with sycamore, cottonwood, maple, and birch close to the water, and with oak, pine, hickory, gum, dogwood, and redbud on the hills, which rise up to 400 feet above the water.

The river is swift enough to be of interest to experienced canoeists, but is not dangerous for those of moderate skill if reasonable precautions are taken. Canoes can be rented at several places along the river. For information write one of the whitewater clubs in the area (see Appendix VI).

Big Piney Creek (Arkansas)

Big Piney Creek flows south out of the Boston Mountains, a crest of the Ozarks that also gives rise to the Buffalo River. The Big Piney passes through a lovely, isolated canyon where there are large, water-carved boulders at water's edge. In the spring, the vivid hues of dogwood, azalea, redbud, service berry, and other flowering plants stand out against the green forest; in autumn it is the hardwoods' time for riotous color. The Big Piney alternates between long, quiet pools, where there is good smallmouth fishing, and fast rocky chutes. After a rain, when the water is up, the Big Piney provides a wild whitewater ride. The run from Indian Creek to Long Pool is rated Class II to III; the stretch from Long Pool to Double Bridges is somewhat easier. There are good campsites and lots of wildlife—deer, turkey, coyote, squirrel, duck.

Black and Beaver Dam Creeks (*Mississippi*)

Perhaps no section of Faulkner country has retained as much backwoods dignity as parts of De Soto National Forest north of Gulfport. Two creeks—Black and Beaver Dam—slip away from towns and cultivated soils to wind through the kind of forest Major de Spain or Sam Fathers might have hunted. The 42-mile run down Black Creek from Big Creek Landing to Old Alexander Bridge is on open, meandering waters. Numerous broad sandbars offer excellent campsites. The current eases along at about 1 mile per hour, a nice pace for dropping a hook down to the bass, bream, and catfish that glide under the surface.

Beaver Dam Creek, an 8-mile run from Spring Branch into Black Creek below Janice Campground, is as narrow and twisting as worms just shoved onto the hook. Its flow, although stained by the tannic acid that leaches from decaying vegetation, is both safe and refreshing to drink. Massive trees join their leaves overhead, creating what amounts to a tunnel into the wilderness.

Satilla (*Georgia*)

Canoe enthusiasts of Waycross, Georgia, are twice blessed. Not only do they have the swamp trails of the Okefenokee close at hand, but the Satilla River flows just out of town. The 149-mile stretch from Waycross to Woodbine is one of the few remaining wild and scenic rivers in the state. It is a peaceful river with no rapids of consequence. Early-day trappers used to bring bales of fur out of the Satilla country, and it is still renowned for wildlife. Animals frequently seen include duck, squirrel, raccoon, wild turkey, and deer. Fishing is good, with largemouth bass (called "trout" in these parts) being the most sought-after species. There are numerous excellent sandbar campsites. So strong is the pull of the Satilla wilds on local youths that one boy, unable to afford a canoe, used his dad's welding torch to make one out of old car fenders. The ungainly, tippy craft made it all the way to Woodbine without mishap.

Buffalo (*Tennessee*)

In 1968 Tennessee became the first state to protect her rivers with the Tennessee Scenic Rivers Act, legislation which antedated the National Wild and Scenic Rivers Act by six months. The Buffalo, a pastoral stream in the western part of the state, was made a part of the state scenic rivers system, and later became part of the National Wild and Scenic Rivers System. Beginning in Lawrence County, it flows north on a course parallel to the Tennessee River for some distance before merging with the Duck River. The river can be floated for 110 miles, most of it through lovely woodland country. Numerous gravel bars make excellent campsites. Although not considered primarily a whitewater river, there are shoals and rapids. A float map can be obtained from the Game and Fish Commission (see Appendix II). Fishing is good for bass and catfish.

Cumberland—South Fork (Tennessee-Kentucky)

The South Fork of the Cumberland has carved out a wild, spectacular canyon on the Tennessee-Kentucky border. Float trips can be divided into two sections: from New River to Leatherwood Bridge, and from Leatherwood Bridge to Kentucky Highway 92. The entire run can be made in three days, or longer if one lingers to fish and explore. Overall, the upper section is more demanding, with a good deal of Class III water and some Class IV whitewater (Jake's Hole Rapids). The longer, lower section is rated Class II if two falls are portaged.

The put-in point for the upper run is at the town of New River on Highway 27. For 9 miles one follows the rather leisurely New River, which flows through a wild, steep-sided canyon. Approaching confluence with South Fork of the Cumberland there are some fair-sized rapids, and then the canyon opens into a gorge with sandstone cliffs rising from 300 to 400 feet high. Dogwood and a profusion of other plants grow where there is purchase. Hardwoods and pine rise at water's edge. In Jake's Hole there is a series of steep drops where the 100-foot-wide river rushes through boulder gardens, creating a grand confusion of combing waves, deep holes, and fast chutes. It is no place for the novice or anyone in an undecked canoe.

Just below Leatherwood Bridge (at Scott State Forest west of Oneida) is Angel Falls, a boulder jam that can be run by experts on the extreme left side in certain water levels. Most people portage. When it has not rained for a few days, there is excellent smallmouth bass fishing in the gorge. Fine camping spots are available. There are Indian cliff dwellings underneath the canyon rims, but to get at most of them requires mountain-climbing gear. Devil's Jump Falls, across the Kentucky line, has been run at certain water levels, but must be portaged if the river is up.

Obed (Tennessee)

Like the South Fork of the Cumberland, a section of the Obed owes its wilderness character to the deep and relatively inaccessible gorge it has carved. This scenic whitewater canyon is located in the Catoosa Wildlife Management Area, north of Rockwood. The superb 12½-mile trip could be made in a single day, but one would have to be crazy to do it. It would mean taking blind chances on rapids that should be scouted, refraining from throwing lures into clear pools where big muskies lurk, paddling doggedly past beautiful sand beaches, natural swimming holes, and odd crannies that beg to be explored afoot. Take two days. Or three, if you really want a breather from civilization.

From put-in at the bridge over Big Daddy Creek (16 miles out of Crossville), it is a 2-mile run down into the Obed. The biggest rapids in the gorge, rated Class IV, is about 3 miles below where Big Daddy Creek enters the Obed, doubling its flow. There are a number of Class III rapids in this section. Below Clear Creek the river is quieter. Rapids are less violent; pools are longer. As well as muskie, there are bass, bluegill, and catfish in these waters. From confluence with the Emory River it is a short run to take-out at Nemo Bridge.

Withlacoochee (Georgia-Florida)

The Withlacoochee winds through the lowlands of south Georgia and then joins the Suwannee over the Florida line. This is a wilderness waterway for the most part, bordered by sandy banks and dense foliage. In places it skirts swamp country; elsewhere there are limestone outcroppings. Along the 56-mile run from Highway 94 west of Valdosta to the Suwannee River there are plenty of good campsites. Shorter trips may be made between any of the four highway bridges that span the waterway. Unlike the Alapaha, a placid (although pleasant) river to the east, the Withlacoochee has several sportive rapids. High waves are generated during the rainy season (March through May). The river is rated Class III in difficulty. A variety of wild-life inhabits the banks of the Withlacoochee. Fish bite almost any time of the year, but insects bite less in the winter months.

Peace (Florida)

If you don't have a chance to get to the Usumacinta of Mexico or the Rio Coco of Central America this year, try the Peace as a surrogate. From Bartow in Polk County to Charlotte Harbor across the bay from Punta Gorda, the Peace offers 105 miles of navigable water—long stretches of it through subtropical wilderness. In places you can look at the dense, green foliage, close your eyes and listen to a frenzy of birdsounds, and swear you are in the unmapped jungle. There are a number of access points. Inquire locally as to water conditions. A take-out at the Highway 761 bridge will avoid the long ocean-bay paddle to Charlotte Harbor.

Chauga (South Carolina)

Sometimes westerners (like myself) have grown up with an image of Carolina rivers as stately tidewater flows whose brackish elbows nudge the lawns of historic mansions on their ordered marches to the sea. The Chauga, however, comes brawling out of the mountains like the beautiful running rabble of the Rockies, plunging over and under rocks, ripping against cutbanks as if to create canyons overnight. Generally, the Chauga has only enough water for a float trip during the spring: by late summer it is only a jumble of mossy boulders through which rivulets trickle. The run from South Carolina (secondary) Highway 290 to Hartwell Reservoir is only 20 miles—yet it encompasses dynamic whitewater and the natural beauty of Sumter National Forest. There are trout in the upper reaches, and fair to good bass fishing in the lower stretches. This is a voyage for experienced boateis who should be prepared to portage around several falls and rapids.

Rappahannock (Virginia)

One of the finest wilderness runs in the East lies only 50 miles from Washington, D.C. as the crow flies. The woods are much the same as they were when Grant marched his Army of the Potomac through them more than a century ago. Although there are no historical markers on the river, one feels the nearness of old battlefields: Manassas, Brandy Station, and Chancellorsville.

Put-in close to Remington. If at all interested in fishing, don't forget your tackle box. This section is seldom fished, and smallmouth bass have thrived. The first real whitewater is about 5 miles downstream from Remington, Kelly's Ford Rapids. The rapids are perhaps 1¼ miles long in a wide section of the river. After the first ¼ mile one should keep well to the left bank to avoid a ledge with a heavy flow. Beyond Kelly's Ford, just below the rapids, there are no places to take-out or even walk out easily for some 26 miles, until close to Fredericksburg. There are no farms or roads near the river. A ½-mile stretch of rapids at the confluence of the Rapidan can be dangerous in highwater. Keep to the left bank here also. Other fast shoals will be a delight to skilled whitewater enthusiasts, or make life miserable for the novice. The take-out place is within 3 miles of Fredericksburg, where a road touches the river on the right bank above a sharp left bend.

Roanoke (Virginia)

Ironically, the Roanoke, a name freighted with historical connotations, has some of the most primitive riverbanks in the East. A 60-mile stretch, from Leesville Dam downstream to the head of Kerr Reservoir, seems to elude civilization with gratifying ease. The scenery and whitewater are especially glorious between Long Island and Brookneal.

The river rises in Montgomery and Floyd counties, bursts through the Blue Ridge Mountains, and tames out in tobacco country, close to the North Carolina border. Virginia is criss-crossed with roads, yet only in a few places can cars get close to the Roanoke. Otter still play there, sliding down slick banks. What better reason could there be for canoeing it if, indeed, one needs a stated reason?

Cacapon (West Virginia)

Caudy's Castle is a high spur of rock up the Cacapon River of West Virginia, a fast mountain stream that has remained delightfully wild in spite of its close proximity to Washington, D.C., Baltimore, and other urban centers. Local folk claim that Caudy was an ancestor of Buffalo Bill—a self-reliant frontiersman who wriggled his way up the rock while trying to escape from eighteen hostile Indians. Caudy made his stand around the hook of a ledge only about half a moccasin wide. One by one, as his attackers arrived, he violently clubbed them with a pine limb and then shoved them off into space. Only the eighteenth Indian perceived the futility of the assault, and scrambled back down to the river. As a youth, George Washington surveyed up the Cacapon: the landscape—where hawks sweep over remote meadows, and stands of hardwoods press right up against high cliffs of limestone and sandstone—is little changed from when he saw it.

Far above Caudy's Castle, the Cacapon begins as the Lost River; it wanders through some thickets before going underground. Miles away it pulses out of the ground, a clear flow—the Cacapon. A good put-in point is at Capon Bridge, the beginning of an exciting two-day, 21-mile trip to a take-out at Largent. Watch for deer and wild turkey. Many bankside trees are slashed at their bases, not by overanxious outdoorsmen with hatchets, but by beaver. On some high ledges you may see goats that have gone wild. This is a whitewater river, with some pitches rated up to Class III.

New (West Virginia)

River running in rubber rafts has never gained the popularity with easterners that it has in the West. Although certain whitewater east of the Mississippi is as challenging as that to be found anywhere, the rapids are not as likely to feature the high-standing waves and haystacks that are the delight of the rafter. The New River comes hustling out of the Appalachian foothills, entering the "Grand Canyon of the East" southeast of Charleston. In the turbulent 30 miles between Prince and Fayette Station the river is wide and powerful, with heavy rapids and huge waves. The biggest of these rapids are rated up to Class V—a run for experts unless one is in a guided raft party (see Appendix V). The pleasures of the New River are by no means confined to whitewater thrills. There are also quiet stretches where one has time to lean back and enjoy the beauty of the canyon: towering wooded hills, rock formations, and wildlife.

Potomac (West Virginia)

Most wilderness runs in the East tend to be in rugged country and feature whitewater: the bottomlands, where canoeing is easy, are often agricultural or otherwise developed. The Paw Paw Bends of the Potomac, however, which parallel the Cacapon, offer a comparatively easy cruise through wild country. There are some ledges, but the rapids are not difficult. The put-in point is at Paw Paw, and the take-out place at Little Orleans, 20 miles downriver.

Eastern United States

Pine Creek (Pennsylvania)

Spread out a map of Pennsylvania and look for where there is least showing. Few towns or roads. Up north from the center. Pine Creek, which has carved the "Grand Canyon of Pennsylvania" and is being considered for inclusion in the National Wild and Scenic Rivers System, works its way through the backcountry up there. One can put-in for a lusty run at Galeton, on U.S. Highway 6, but the creek can't shake the blacktop for 13 miles until it reaches the hamlet of Ansonia and swings south. Here the waters drop into the gorge and push through comparatively wild country. There is a good fast current with some rapids rated Class II. Spur roads reach into campsites beside the stream, yet by and large the landscape is as pretty and unmanicured as can be found in this part of the nation. Take-out at Blackwell, where the pace of the water gets slow and that of civilization picks up.

Wading (New Jersey)

Even in a highly industrial state like New Jersey it is possible to boat "far from the madding crowd." The Delaware River, which forms the border between New Jersey and Pennsylvania, is a very popular cruising river with fine scenery and campsites. Less well known and more remote, the Wading River in the southern part of the state winds through the sandy, wild, Pine Barrens before emptying into tidewater near Great Bay. Much of the trip is through the Wharton State Forest. Two other good canoeing rivers, the Mullica and Batsto, also flow through the Wharton tract. A 25-mile run can be made on the Wading River if the put-in is at Chatsworth, but unless the water is up the stream will be too small for canoeing until it passes under the Highway 563 bridge near Speedwell. At this writing canoes can be rented inexpensively at the village of Jenkins on this road.

Neversink (New York)

New York has an abundance of wilderness waters, most of them lying within Adirondack Park. As with the Boundary Waters Canoe Area of Minnesota, most longer trips involve short segments of different rivers, lots of lake travel, and some portaging. Among the individual rivers of the state, however, none is discussed with more awe by whitewater buffs than the Neversink, a tributary of the Delaware running through Sullivan and Orange counties. The name Neversink carries a ring of irony when one considers the magnificently rugged 10-mile gorge between Bridgeville and Oakland Valley. There are no roads in the gorge, for the simple reason it would have been necessary to blast them out of vertical cliffs. For two decades prior to 1960 a number of intrepid boaters attempted the chasm in kayaks, decked canoes, and foldboats. A succession of boulder-strewn rapids, rated as high as Class V even under the best of water levels, demolished some boats and forced the parties to portage most of the way. Rubber rafts, whose *forte* is bouncing off the boulders of big rapids, are considered useless here—the rocks are too sharp.

In the spring of 1960, nine boats assaulted the gorge, manned by members of the Kayak and Canoe Club of New York. Listen as Walter Burmeister describes part of their whitewater adventure:

> By far the most difficult rapid was the hair-raising drop of Upper Denton Falls. Hidden behind a sudden turn, it begins with a display of complex, rocky standing waves. Suddenly, beyond the bend the steep incline of the roughest portion lies ahead. Constricted between converging walls, the compressed flow sluices madly over huge rocks and vertical ledges. There is no easy way through this turmoil. Deep sink-holes, powerful chutes, cascading side water, towering standing waves, and vicious breakers are everywhere. There is no time to admire the grandiose setting. It is little wonder that most of the foldboats capsized and the decked canoe was swamped. (*American White Water,* February 1961.)

After 10 miles of this watery mayhem, the group emerged from the gorge triumphant, wet and battered, having portaged around only two high falls. Like the conquest of Cross Mountain Canyon of the Yampa, mentioned earlier, it was an epic feat of courage and skill. Once a mountain such as the Matterhorn or the North Face of the Eiger has been ascended, subsequent adventurers find the going easier: routes have been discovered, expansion bolts and pitons left in the rock. In a gorge such as that of the Neversink, routes that worked in one water level might be suicide in another. Nothing is left behind except a boat or two wrapped around rocks. The challenge remains intact.

Hudson (New York)

Between Manhattan and the Jersey shore, the Hudson River carries hearty gobs of just about every waste product expelled by modern man and his industries past the greatest concentration of people on the American continent. Yet near its headwaters, a stretch of the Hudson flows clear and fast through one of the wildest areas of the eastern United States.

Between Newcomb, which is at the geographical center of Adirondack Park, and the village of North River on State Highway 28, the Hudson is a backcountry stream far from highways or resorts—a long hike out should one's boat be smashed in rapids. The run, which takes from two to three days, should be attempted only by experienced boaters. Long, placid ponds alternate with fast chutes and rocky shoals. There is a variety of wildlife in the area, including black bear as well as fine fishing. Campsites are numerous.

For about 1 mile below the put-in point at the State Highway 28–N

The wooded upper Hudson River between Newcomb and Glens Falls, New York

bridge the river is broad and slow. Then the canyon becomes narrow and the river plunges over Ord Falls. Below the confluence of the Goodnow River there is a long placid stretch known as Blackwell Stillwater. Between the Stillwater and the mouth of the Cedar River there are rapids that should be scouted. At the mouth of the Indian River the Hudson swings to the east and its canyon deepens. There are several rapids in this spectacular gorge.

The annual Hudson River Whitewater Derby is contested over a 7-mile course near North Creek, usually in May.

Penobscot—East Branch (Maine)

Many New England rivers are sportive, but there are Dixie cups floating in Walden Pond and the shoals of the Merrimack now entrap bald tires and discarded girdles. Let us move on to Maine. A fine voyage, one of many, is to paddle the East Branch of the Penobscot as it winds through forest and meadowlands, much of it within sight of the 5258-foot-high hulk of Mount Katahdin.

Even the name Penobscot has a good ring to it. Back before World War I, when 60 million feet of logs might be jockied down the Connecticut River during the spring drive, Penobscot Indians were often hired to scout the water. Oldtime loggers, who with their caulk-boots and peaveys rode the shifting, grinding masses of logs all the way to the mills, still talk of how the Penobscot could guide their bateaux casually through the wildest rapids. Lumberjacks called them the greatest natural rivermen in the world, which they may well have been.

The best put-in point is below the dam at Grand Lake Matagamon, reached by gravel road out of Patten. Here one begins a 40-mile wilderness voyage to the village of Grindstone. The East Branch is not essentially a whitewater trip, but good maps and caution are necessary, for there are impassable falls and a few heavy rapids. The river is dangerous only in that the outdoorsman—fishing, birdwatching, or just plain looking—might drift into fastwater above a falls or cataract without having a chance to put ashore. Stair Falls, Haskell Rock Pitch, Pond Pitch, Grand Falls, Hulling Machine Pitch, Bowlin, Whetstone, and Grindstone Falls are all heavyweights. Some of these can be run by experts if the water levels are right; others are forthright manglers. This is a magnificent wilderness river to cruise if one is willing to portage a bit. A marvelous float if you know where to anticipate the danger points (consult *Appalachian Mountain Club New England Canoeing Guide;* see Appendix II).

Allagash (Maine)

The Allagash River flows through the largest semiwilderness in all of the eastern United States. Its fame and popularity among river runners is entirely justified. For 98 miles the river pushes through forest that is a habitat for moose, bear, and other wildlife. There are lazy stretches of water, rapids, and large lakes.

Thoreau cruised the headwaters in 1847, and wrote that the scenic waterway should be preserved. More than a century later, in 1966, the Maine legislature established the Allagash Wilderness Waterway. The Allagash does not flow through undisturbed wilderness as do many rivers discussed in this book; the virgin pine forest has been logged out and is now replaced by spruce, and one may camp only at designated sites. Yet the region is unpopulated, the river beautiful.

The most popular put-in point for running the entire river is at Telos Landing, reached by back roads out of Greenville, Millinocket, or Patten, although some canoeists prefer to be flown in to one of the lakes along the system. The 43 miles from Telos Landing to Churchill Dam is mostly lake paddling. Lock Dam, between Chamberlain and Eagle lakes, was originally constructed so that Allagash water could be diverted to float logs into the Penobscot River system. Allagash lumbermen, who had little enough water for their own log drives, dynamited the structure. For a time it appeared the North Woods were about to erupt with violence, but the "Telos War" was finally settled with a bloodless compromise. The remains of a tramway that seems to start nowhere and go nowhere lie close to Lock Dam. Built in 1902–1903, it was used to transport logs from Chamberlain Lake ¾ of a mile to Eagle Lake. The 16-mile Eagle Lake and Umbazooksus Railroad was later built on the site. Rails and two giant oil-burning steam locomotives today rust in the forest.

Below Churchill Dam the 8 miles of Chase Rips provide whitewater excitement for experienced canoeists. Poling skill is often helpful here, especially in low-water. The 11-mile paddle through Umsaskis and Long Lake can be hard if there is a strong north wind. The 27 miles from Long Lake Dam to Michaud Farm are mostly fastwater, although there are no serious rapids. This is one of the most scenic sections of the river, especially above Round Pond. At the entrance of Musquacook Stream one can clearly see where a tornado once ripped through the timber for a considerable distance. Overall the run from Michaud Farm to Allagash village is less attractive than the upper river, as there are several camps and a logging road on the left. Allagash Falls, however, 3 miles below Michaud Farm, is a spectacular sight, plunging over a drop of close to 40 feet. The portage is on the right. The most challenging rapids on the river, rated Class II-III, are in the last 14 miles below the falls.

A private logging road between Ashland and Daaquam allows access at a point between Umsaskis and Long lakes. Permits, however, must be obtained from the joint owners of the road, the Great Northern and International Paper companies. Canoeists must register with rangers when entering the Allagash Wilderness Waterway, or at checkpoints en route.

St. John (Maine)

The St. John River follows a parallel course to the west of the Allagash before the two rivers converge at the village of Allagash. If anything, it is more remote and less frequented than the Allagash. The final 83 miles from Northwest Branch to Allagash village must be run in its entirety, as there are no places to return to civilization. This section demands experienced boaters, as there are heavy rapids. There are fewer lakes and ponds on the St. John than on her sister river; consequently the water tends to drain out more rapidly after the spring thaw. The ice generally goes out in April, and the river can be best floated from mid-April to late June, when the water is usually quite low. Early trips are recommended, since high-water tends to smooth out rapids and the slapping misery of the black fly season can be avoided.

Best access is from the Canadian side of the border. The International Paper Company has private roads which cross the St. John by Baker Lake and at Northwest Branch, 29 miles downriver. A permit must be obtained from the company office at Chisholm, Maine. Unlike the Allagash, where there are generally rangers around to help out should you get into difficulty, you are very much on your own canoeing the St. John. This is wild country. There are fine campsites. Seventeen miles below the site of Seven Islands, once a thriving community, Big Black Rapids rips and tears, one of two major rapids on the river. The other, Big Rapids, is 36 miles downriver. Both stretches of whitewater have drowned the incautious and are rated Class III. Scout them carefully.

Aroostook (Maine)

The branching headwater streams of the Aroostook River wind through wild country in northern Maine. They offer fine canoe runs when there is sufficient water. By mid-July of a dry summer some of them can get a bit rocky. The Aroostook proper begins at the confluence of Munsungan and Millinocket streams. Access to both streams is most practical by air. The 16-mile paddle down Munsungan is through wooded, scenic country. The current is swift for the most part, with a number of rapids rated up to Class II. Munsungan Falls has been run by experts in high-water, but is usually portaged. The 6-mile float down Millinocket is through alternately fast and calm waters. From the junction, it is an easy one-day trip down the Aroostook to Masardis (when the water is high). Masardis makes a good take-out point, since there you reach the highway. Beyond, the country becomes somewhat more settled.

St. Croix Stream, which enters the Aroostook at Masardis, is another fine canoeing stretch. The hamlet of Howe Brook, which is on the Aroostook and Bangor Railroad, is a good starting point. There are no access roads into the area, but canoes can be shipped in by rail. The pleasant two-day trip to Masardis is principally down smooth water, although there are minor rapids.

Machias River, another tributary of the Aroostook, flows through mountainous, heavily wooded country. From a put-in point at Big Machias Lake, it is a 32-mile, one- to two-day, fastwater trip down to the Aroostook. The lake is reached by spur road off a private forest road running west from Ashland (permit and fee required). As there are several long stretches of intermediate whitewater, only experienced canoeists should try this one. A portage is necessary around a logging dam.

Dead (Maine)

Contrary to its name, the Dead River boasts some extremely lively water. As well as magnificent falls, the river contains the longest stretch of continuous heavy rapids in New England. By putting-in at Long Falls Dam and running to the Forks, expert canoeists can enjoy 22 miles of rugged scenery spiced with whitewater thrills. A 6-mile paddle through marshlands brings one to Dead River Dam, a broken log dam. Take-out here and portage (left) around Grand Falls, a sheer 30-foot drop not far beyond the old dam. A spring offers clear, cold refreshment after the work of the carry. From the mouth of Spencer Stream, only ¼ mile beyond, the wide, boulder-strewn current drops swiftly between cliffs, ledges, and steep forested slopes. The gradient is 30 feet to the mile, and the river tosses through almost continuous rapids (Class IV). The toughest stretches of whitewater, Spencer Rips and Poplar Hill Falls, often have to be lined.

Eastern Canada

Miramichi (New Brunswick)

Most New Brunswick rivers which have road access are pastoral, flowing through mixed woodlands and farming country where villages are a feature of the landscape. The Southwest Branch of the Miramichi from Half Moon to Boiestown is a delightful exception—a wilderness run renowned for its Atlantic salmon and sea trout fishing. This voyage of some 50 miles involves lots of whitewater. If you are inexperienced, a guide is recommended. From Boiestown to tidewater, a distance of 67 miles, the river is wide, swift, and frequently floated. The country is more settled, however, and Highway 8 parallels the river. Historically, the Miramichi has been used as a route to the interior since the days of the birchbark canoe.

Metabetchouan (Quebec)

In the seventeenth century a fur-trading post and Jesuit mission were established on Lac Saint-Jean at the mouth of the Metabetchouan River.

Trappers and missionaries paddled the entire length of the Metabet-chouan, an important segment of what was called the "Jesuit Trail."

Today one can follow a section of the Metabetchouan on a well-marked canoe trail through Laurentides Provincial Park, a short, scenic drive north of Quebec City. A series of lakes leading into the river affords a 60-mile trip that can be run with ease in four days. Although a forest road parallels part of the trip and there are established campsites, the region retains a wilderness flavor. Canoes may be rented from the Parks Service.

The put-in point is at Lac Montagnais, 17 miles west of Lac Kiskisink on a gravel road. The route involves some fourteen short portages, mostly around rapids, although the longest (taking about twenty minutes) is between lakes. One need not encounter rapids of more than Class II difficulty. There are Class III and Class IV rapids on the run, all of which can be bypassed by portage trails. The route describes a rough V-shape: the take-out point is back at the Kiskisink Road.

Swampy Bay—Kaniapiskau—Koksoak (Quebec)

The mining town of Schefferville, close to the Quebec-Labrador border, is a long way from anywhere. It is as far north of New York City as Manhattan is north of Miami. Beyond Schefferville there are no roads or railroads, only a few settlements, mostly Eskimo trading centers. This is the jump-off for one of the more challenging canoe voyages of the Far North, down the Swampy Bay River past the ruins of the old Hudson's Bay Post of Fort McKenzie, into the Kaniapiskau River and down it to the Koksoak River. Logical terminus for the trip is Fort Chimo on the Koksoak, not far from Ungava Bay. This is a 450-mile wilderness voyage. There are no permanent habitations en route and during the three weeks required for the journey, canoeists will probably not encounter another human being. Prepare accordingly. Because of strenuous portages, canoes are preferable to rafts or kayaks. Mosquitoes can be very bad. The trout fishing is superb.

From Sept-Iles on the St. Lawrence River one can board a mixed freight-and-passenger train of the Quebec, North Shore and Labrador Railroad for Schefferville, a 200-mile, eleven-hour journey to the north. It is generally possible to hire an Indian guide at the mining town, although he will more likely speak French than English. Gunshot Lake, above Schefferville, is the starting point for the run down the Swampy Bay, a watercourse of long, narrow lakes joined by segments of whitewater river—gorges, chutes, falls, and rapids. Much of the country stretching back from the river is marshy, and dry campsites are sometimes hard to find, although in places there are high rises covered with white caribou moss—a superlative bed.

One does not frequently see game on the Swampy Bay, although there are a number of caribou in the area. Fishing is another matter. Virtually no anglers have fished the river and its lakes since the decline of the fur trade

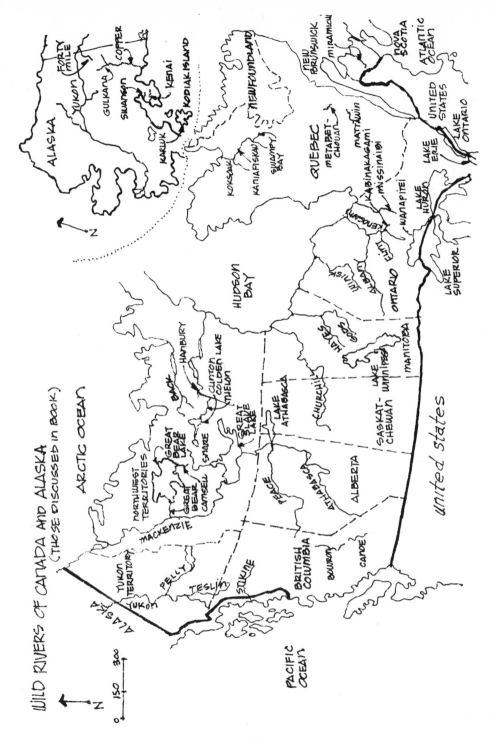

WILD RIVERS OF CANADA AND ALASKA
(THOSE DISCUSSED IN BOOK)

341

years ago. One need only cast a few times to reel in speckled trout up to 2½ pounds, lake trout up to 6 pounds.

Some rapids can be run, others lined. The toughest portage is at High Falls below Otelnuk Lake, where the river thunders over a 65-foot drop, with extensive rapids above and below. The 4-mile carry is pretty much a trail-less scramble. Old Fort McKenzie is situated close to the confluence with the Kaniapiskau. Near its roofless buildings lie rotted freight canoes— 24-footers that took eight sturdy men to portage. The Swampy Bay is 100 to 200 yards wide; the Kaniapiskau is twice that size, and pushes with a strong current. Here the country is more hilly, and there are numerous sand and gravel bars. This is the edge of the barrens, and the trees—spruce and tamarack—are stunted and tend to cluster together as if for defense. There is an old portage trail, long unused, around Limestone Falls, a 60-foot drop 15 to 20 miles above where the Kaniapiskau joins the Larch River to form the Koksoak. There is also a somewhat overgrown 2½-mile portage trail around Manitou Gorge below the falls. At Fort Chimo, which is on tidewater and populated largely by Eskimos, one can fly out to Montreal on scheduled aircraft or obtain charter service.

Mattawin (Quebec)

The Mattawin River of eastern Quebec is not a river for the Sunday-afternoon paddler. It is 60 miles of rapids, chutes, and waterfalls where placid stretches of any length are few and far between. An official of the Consolidated Paper Company, which logs in the region, concluded a letter of response to a query about the Mattawin by commenting: "The canoeists should note the rather numerous crosses along the river and govern themselves accordingly." The water flow is contolled by the outlet of Taureau Dam, and there is always the possibility midway through the trip of the water's dropping so low as to make the river unnavigable. The Mattawin passes through wilderness, where the only sign of loggers one is likely to encounter are the pulp logs that occasionally come careening down the current. South of the river there are no settlements for some 50 miles. To the north there is only one distant road between the Mattawin and the North Pole.

In short, the Mattawin is a scenic challenge for whitewater experts. The run begins at Taureau Dam, east of Mount Tremblant Provincial Park. Knowledge of French or at least a French dictionary is a must for this trip. In all likelihood this will be the sole language of the dam-keeper, and discussion as to how much water will be released over the following week (average length of the trip) is obviously crucial. The shuttle car should be left at the town of Mattawin on Highway 19.

The run begins with a roar—Empty Barrel Rapids. One is never far from the cadence of whitewater; there are eleven named rapids, some of them extremely rough, and numerous unnamed rapids. Even for skilled boatmen, some of the rock gardens and drops will appear foolhardy (there are rapids rated Class V or better). Line or portage if in doubt. This wild flow, a long way from help, has been a killer, and will probably be so again. At two fierce rapids—Red Pine and Rapide du Crapeaud—there are no shelves close to water level for lining or portage. Tough, high portages are delineated by heavy wire stretched up through brush and rock.

George Sears, who ran the Mattawin in 1967, describes the lower half of Les Rapides de L'Arrachis as follows:

> Most of the river ran through a narrow chasm on the right, dropping 10–20 feet in some really awesome waves. We were able to skirt this cataract in a small side channel with only two or three short carries. As we worked our way down, we could look over the central island at the main channel, seeing the waves and spray repeatedly thrown high in the air. Although we saw no evidence, this was certainly the number one candidate for a cross on the river bank!

On down the river, close to its end, a plume of mist and thunderous roar announces Chute de la Grandmère—Grandmother's Falls. The river rolls off a ledge to burst upon boulders 35 feet below. Boats and supplies can be roped straight down, or a circuitous portage can be made.

The entire Mattawin drops at a brisk 15 feet per mile, but for 11 miles the descent averages 30–55 feet per mile. It is a challenging river that winds through wild forest. Good water. Dangerous water.

Missinaibi (Ontario)

The Missinaibi River, which was a principal route for Hudson's Bay Company traders between Lake Superior and James Bay, offers scenic wilderness cruising and ample opportunities for wildlife photography. The 200-mile run from Mattice to Moosonee should take seven to ten days, and should be attempted only by experienced river runners. There is fastwater in places and the average party will make use of some eight portages. Mattice, a village 42 miles west of Kapuskasing, is on Highway 11 (Trans-Canada Highway) as well as the Canadian Pacific Railroad. The historical settlement of Moose Factory, close to the end of the run, is well worth a visit. From Moosonee one can return to Cochrane and Highway 11 on the Polar Bear Express of the Ontario Northland Railway.

Albany (Ontario)

The Albany River, northwest of the Missinaibi, was once a major artery of Hudson's Bay Company trade. Fort Albany, close to James Bay, is the oldest post in continual use to the present day. It was established in 1683. The company quickly extended its influence up the river and its tributaries, across to other watersheds, so that within a decade voyageurs were carrying supplies out of Fort Albany to a network of subsidiary posts as far west as the Rainy and English rivers, returning laden with furs.

The old voyageur route from Sioux Lookout to Fort Albany (650 miles) is as much a wilderness today as it was 2½ centuries ago. What few Indian communities still exist on the river (a trading post and cluster of cabins, perhaps a school or a mission) receive most outside supplies by airplane. This run is a wilderness adventure of major proportions—one should plan for a full month on the water. The river is large, swift, and passes over a number of rapids and falls, demanding a high degree of whitewater skills. En route, there are few sources of supplies or assistance. Some thirty portages will be necessary.

From the start at Sioux Lookout, pass through Lac La Seul and then portage over the height of land to Lake St. Joseph. Highway 599 crosses the route between Lake St. Joseph and Osnaburgh Lake, and one can cut off a great many miles and several days of lake travel by putting-in here. The upper portion of the journey is rolling country forested with black and white spruce, jackpine, poplar, and white birch. The lower portions of the river are more typical of a northern muskeg environment. Fishing for pike, pickerel, and brook trout is good. At Martin Falls, 200 miles upstream from Fort Albany, the wide portage over which the voyageurs once moved the large York boats on rollers can still be used. From Fort Albany one can fly out to Moosonee, railhead of the Ontario Northern.

Kabinakagami—Kenogami (Ontario)

A shorter, easier voyage to Fort Albany can be made down the Kabinakagami and Kenogami rivers, which flow into the Albany. This is a 250-mile trip, requiring about a week—two-thirds of it on the Albany. It is usually not necessary to portage on this trip, although some rapids may have to be lined. To reach the starting point travel 22 miles west of Hearst on Highway 11, then drive 27 miles north on Rogers Road. The put-in point is at Limestone Rapids of the Kabinakagami. Guides may be hired at the nearby Calstock Indian Reserve.

Winisk (Ontario)

With considerable justification the Winisk River has been called the most exciting run in northern Ontario. The lower river winds through expanses of Arctic tundra, denning grounds of the polar bear, and habitat of moose, caribou, Arctic fox, snow geese, and other wildlife. Seal, walrus, and beluga whale thrive in the chilled waters beyond the mouth of the river. The wilderness is absolute between the Hudson's Bay Post at Winisk Lake (the beginning of the voyage), and the village of Winisk on Hudson Bay. Supplies must be carried for the entire 250-mile trip. Winisk Lake is well over 100 miles from the nearest road (a gravel affair connecting places like Pickle Crow and Central Patricia), and hence air transport must be arranged to the starting point. There is scheduled air service out of Winisk. Experienced guides of the Webiqui tribe can be hired for the downriver voyage; canoes are also available (see Appendix II). The trip generally takes about two weeks. There is fine brook-trout fishing in parts of the river and in side streams. The Winisk begins in one of the most remote preserves in the world, Wild River Provincial Park, and meets the sea in an equally unfrequented enclave, Polar Bear Provincial Park.

Flint (*Ontario*)

Wilderness boating in Ontario is, of course, by no means confined to ventures of expedition proportions. There are numerous two- and three-day excursions, ideal for the cross-country traveler who happens to have a canoe or kayak lashed to the roof of his car. The Flint River is such a run. One puts-in at Klotz Lake Provincial Park on Highway 11 out of Longlac. From Klotz Lake one passes into Flint Lake, a fair-sized body of water, and then into the river. The 30-mile trip to the Canadian National Railroad near Flintdale requires only six portages and should take no more than three days.

If hooked on the country, one has the option of passing on down into the Kenogami and the Albany. In such a case, prepare well before leaving the railroad, for that run is *not* a brief outing.

Wanapitei (*Ontario*)

Huron Indians called the forested country on the north shore of Georgian Bay *Ouendake,* or "One Land Apart." It is indeed a special place—hill country with thousands of lakes and waterways, much of it set aside by the Canadian government as a Recreational Reserve. The put-in point for a scenic 85-mile cruise is at the bridge of Highway 637, a gravel road that branches off the Trans-Canada Highway, 23 miles south of Sudbury. The Wanapitei flows mostly through backcountry, tumbling through challenging rapids in places. Portages are not always clearly marked.

WANAPITEI RIVER LOG

Mileage

0   Wanapitei River at Highway 637. Portage 150 yards around rapids.

2¾   Rapids; portage.

4   Rapids; portage.

6   A series of rapids; portage 50 yards. Good campsite here, portage rapids and old bridge 75 yards. Portage stretch of fastwater.

7½   Bear chutes; rapids for 300 yards with 6-foot drop. The northernmost 150 yards can be pulled through; the bottom 150 yards must be portaged.

8½   Rapids; 3-foot drop; portage 40 yards.

8¾   Sturgeon chutes; 11-foot drop; portage 100 yards.

10¼ Take the east fork to Wanapitei Bay.

13   North end of Wanapitei Bay. The Canadian National Railroad (CNR) can be reached from here by traveling 3 miles east through Hartley Bay. The mouth of the Pickerel River can be reached by progressing southward along the east shore of Wanapitei Bay for approximately 1 mile. Then

take the channel southeasterly into Ox Bay; follow the eastern side of the big islands at the west end of Ox Bay. Cut southeast and follow the south shore of Ox Bay eastward to the mouth of the Pickerel River.

16 Mouth of the Pickerel River.

19 CNR Settlement of Pickerel River.

28 Highway 69.

36 Falls; 3-foot drop; portage 65 yards.

36½ Rapids; 2-foot drop; portage 240 yards.

40 Squaw Lake. For the next 6 miles, the river is uneventful and winds considerably.

46 Horserace Rapids. The next 2 miles of river get rougher; the shoreline is higher and frequent rapids are encountered, necessitating portaging and lining.

49 Sand Rapids. The next mile of river gets even rougher; there are shallow rapids for nearly the whole distance; the canoe must be pulled or floated the whole way.

50¼ Portage to Portage Lake. To avoid bad chutes and rapids upriver, portage from the Pickerel River to Dollars Lake (Kawigamog Lake) via the east end of Portage Lake. The north end of the portage is hard to find but it is in fair condition. There are two clearings on the north side of the Pickerel opposite the portage. Portage 880 yards to Portage Lake, and from the southeast bay 440 yards to Dollars (Kawigamog) Lake. This latter portage is marked and in good condition.

51 Dollars (Kawigamog) Lake. This lake has fairly low shorelines and a number of cottages. Travel southwest through Ess Narrows to the long east-west arm. Travel east to Smoky Creek.

61 Portage 200 yards from Kawigamog Lake to Smoky Creek via the west side of the creek; ¾ mile south, there is a high beaver dam; portage 40 yards on the east side.

62 Portage 365 yards from Smoky Creek to Smoky Lake; this portage is marked and in good condition. Travel southwest on Smoky Lake to Naganosh Lake.

65 Smoky Lake and Naganosh Lake have rugged and rocky shores, and there are few cottages.

68 South end of Naganosh Lake. Portage 1760 yards southeasterly to Sunny Lake.

69 Sunny Lake. Portage 190 yards from the south bay of Sunny Lake to a narrow bay of Portage Lake. This is a very beautiful lake with a rugged shoreline. After leaving the bay, swing southwest to the end of the lake and portage 200 yards to Island Lake.

70 Island Lake. This lake has a generally high (20-30 feet) rocky shoreline. There are some cottages. Traverse southwesterly on Island Lake to the end of the long southwest arm that narrows to Three Snye Falls and Rapids.

73   Three Snye Falls and Rapids. Drop of 13 feet; good 120-yard portage. From here to Byng Inlet, the shore is low, rocky and somewhat abrupt.

73¾ Two sets of rapids begin; portage 70 yards; go across a pool and portage 60 yards.

74½ A long series of falls and rapids begins (Thirty Dollar Rapids). Portaging is necessary. The trail is poor to fair. Portage on the south side, 1¾ miles, crossing the CNR.

79¼ Farm Rapids and Falls. A series of falls and rapids for the next mile. Portage 145 yards around a 14-foot falls; pull through rapids and portage 125 yards around 5-foot drop.

80¾ Falls; 4½-foot drop; portage 150 yards either by trail or river bed.

81½ Red Pine Rapids. Drop of 2 feet; portage 65 yards.

82   Two sets of rapids; the first involves a pull-through; the second is a 25-yard portage. During highwater periods, a 600-yard portage over Highway 69 is necessary.

82½ Highway No. 69.

85   Byng Inlet.

Hayes and Gods Rivers (Manitoba)

During the fur-trading era, the Hayes River was a major route between Hudson Bay and Lake Winnipeg. If anything, this long waterway flows through more of a wilderness today than it did a century ago. Even historic York Factory, at the mouth of the river, is now deserted. The full voyage from Norway House to Hudson Bay is 350 miles. At only one place en route, Oxford House, is it possible to obtain supplies. If rendezvous with a charter plane is not arranged at the mouth of the river, one must travel a considerable distance back up the Nelson River to reach a take-out point on the Canadian National Railway. Obviously, this is a trip requiring careful advance planning. The voyage can be greatly shortened by flying in to Oxford House and leaving from there.

From Norway House, the route crosses Little Playgreen Lake and enters the Nelson River, which is a mile wide and studdied with islands in this section. Sea River Falls, 17 miles downriver, is a chute with a 4-foot drop. Most rapids on the trip can be run by experienced canoeists. Five miles beyond, at the High Rock, one paddles eastward on the small and marshy Echimamish River. A short portage is required to get into the Hayes River, where the longest portage of the trip, 1300 feet, must be made to avoid a 45-foot drop in the river. There are two rapids where the river slices through a narrow ravine 7 miles beyond Robinson Lake, and Waipinaipinis (the Angling Place), is a 6-foot chute where the river drops into a marsh that opens into Oxford Lake. The lake is about 30 miles long and 9 miles wide, with numerous islands and long peninsulas to enhance the scenery and break the wave fetch. Oxford House is situated on a rise of land in the northeast extremity.

After leaving Oxford Lake, the river runs southeast for 11 miles before entering Knee Lake. Trout Falls, encountered just before Knee Lake, must be portaged. This narrow body of water is 40 miles long. Not far downriver is Swampy Lake, a rather misleading name as there is only a peat bog on a short section of one shore. After Swampy Lake it is a river run all the way to Hudson Bay. For some 30 miles the current is split by many islands, and runs swiftly, often breaking into whitewater. Beyond a rapid known as The Rock, for the gray, coarse gneiss it exposes, the character of the Hayes changes. The river is bordered by clay banks, there are no more rapids or islands until tidewater.

If one opts to return via the Nelson rather than being picked up by charter plane, Marsh Point, separating the two great rivers, must be paddled around. If tides and weather are right, this can be an exciting trip; one can see the remains of old Port Nelson, wrecked ships in the harbor, seal, whale, and possibly even polar bear. However, if there has been a storm in Hudson Bay, it may take days for the water to calm enough for a canoe, and even in the best of weather one needs to stand 11 miles out to sea in order to catch the incoming tide around vast mudflats. Those impatient enough to attempt a land portage between the river mouths will find themselves wallowing through 8 miles of waist-deep muskeg. If returning by way of the Nelson, write for all the information you can get. You'll need it.

A variation of this voyage would be to fly in to one of the four fishing lodges on Gods Lake (reached only by air) and then run the Gods River down to Shamattawa, where one could be picked up by floatplane. Although a much shorter run than the Hayes, this trip wanders its way through the same lonely wilderness, and is noted for the excellence of the brook-trout fishing along the way. For a longer run on the Gods River, one could continue beyond Shamattawa on down into the Hayes and on out to the site of York Factory.

Western Canada and the Far North

Bowron (British Columbia)

The Bowron River winds through the forests of central British Columbia—a true wilderness waterway. To reach the put-in point one drives east on a secondary road from Quesnel, and passes through the old gold-rush town of Barkerville. During its gusty peak a century ago, Barkerville was rated the largest town west of Chicago and north of San Francisco. The voyage begins at Bowron Lake Provincial Park, a few miles beyond Barkerville. The trip down to where the river enters the Frazier should take five to six days. Most of the distance is on leisurely water, but there are a few small canyons where the pace picks up.

The upper Bowron is fairly small, even at highwater stages. One will probably encounter logjams necessitating portage, and possibly beaver dams as well. The frequent ponds and marshes make an ideal moose habitat: float parties will likely see several. The first canyon is wide, with gently sloped sides. In highwater the passage is swift and contains enough boulders to make things interesting, yet there are no dangerous rapids. In other water stages, however, people have reported 10-foot falls, obviously something to keep an eye peeled for. The canyon is short, and soon one is on quiet water, once again.

As on so many North Country wilderness rivers, one finds windowless cabins, their roofs collapsed under seasons of snowfall, onetime homes to trappers or gold seekers. About midway down to the Frazier one passes through five short but scenic canyons. The third canyon, Portage, offers the most challenging whitewater on the entire run. The tricky boils of fastwater in upper Portage Canyon Falls are climaxed by 8- to 10-foot waves at the base. A reasonably easy portage is possible. The final canyon is a box canyon, steep with colorful rock formations. Surprisingly, the water is mostly smooth.

Below the canyons one may encounter gargantuan logjams. Scouting afoot will reveal channels and portages if necessary. One can take-out at Highway 16, or paddle around a long horseshoe bend into the Frazier, leaving the water 2 miles down the big river at a car ferry.

Canoe River (British Columbia)

The Canoe River offers 80 to 90 miles of fine wilderness boating from Valemount, on the Canadian National Railroad west of Jasper, to Boat Encampment, where the stream flows into the Columbia and there is a mountain road leading back to civilization (Highway 23). It is usually a four- to five-day trip. There are no dangerous rapids, and, in case of trouble, a dirt road used by loggers parallels the river for part of the trip. One may encounter logjams, which can be hazardous.

Boats can be shipped by railroad to Valemount on the Canadian National Railroad, or hauled up by car. The trip begins in a V-shaped valley with thickly wooded slopes. Plant life is luxurient—raspberries and giant fern crowd at the water's edge. Where there is a profusion of berries, bear follow. More than one expedition down the Canoe has had its provisions scattered by a prowling bear.

About the third day the country becomes more open and somewhat marshy. This is a good place to see moose. Boat Encampment, the take-out point, is at the confluence of the Canoe and the Columbia.

Stikine (British Columbia)

Picture it: a wide, green river flowing through virgin forests of spruce, past lofty, jagged peaks so remote and numerous that many have not even been named. One hundred and fifty-three miles of wilderness water, where place names indicate abandoned homesteads or trappers' cabins rather than towns. Beside the river one sees crystalline waterfalls plunging over palisades; bear and moose at the rim of the woods and mountain goats on high ledges; glaciers that sweep out of the mountains to within yards of the water. Unlike so many beautiful rivers in the Far North, the Stikine does not require air travel. Getting there is much of the fun. From Wrangell, Alaska, historic port on the Inland Passage, a 64-foot riverboat, the *Margaret Rose,* makes frequent upriver runs to the former gold-rush tent city of Glenora. The 153-mile trip takes four days. Season is from mid-May through September. Stow your canoe, raft, or whatever on the *Margaret Rose,* and then leisurely float back down the river from Glenora. If you are driving up the Alaska Highway, and 236 miles (one way) of rough roads through wild country are your cup of tea, Glenora can be reached by a branch road leaving the Alaska Highway at Watson Lake. Drift down and take the *Margaret Rose* back to your car.

From Glenora, on the western side of the Cassiar Mountains, the river winds through a country of meadows, with fine stands of aspen and vine maple. In high-walled Little Canyon the Stikine breaches the Coast Range. From here to the Pacific, 80 miles away, spruce forests become increasingly dense, the individual trees larger. Large cottonwoods rise at water's edge. It is often midmorning before the ocean mists burn away. Watch for beaver and otter. The Stikine is not all that far from the land of the Midnight Sun; by midsummer it is not solidly dark until after 11 P.M. It is a hefty paddle from the mouth of the Stikine to Wrangell and it would be prudent to arrange with someone in Wrangell for a pickup by powerboat.

Churchill (Saskatchewan)

The Churchill, a long, large river which strings together numerous beautiful lakes, was one of the most important northern waterways during the fur-trading era. As early as 1776 a fort and trading post was constructed at Ile à la Crosse. A year later Peter Pond discovered the nearby Methye Portage, which leads to waters that run into both the Pacific and the Arctic oceans. This opened the entire western part of Canada and much of the United States to the fur trade. Many of the illustrious figures in beaver trapping and exploration voyaged the Churchill, including Alexander Mackenzie, whose epic east-west crossing of upper North America preceded that of Lewis and Clark by ten years.

A superb 240-mile wilderness trip begins at historic Ile à la Crosse. There is only one community en route, Snake Lake, and there are only scant signs of the numerous people who have traveled the Churchill over the past two centuries: portage trails, an occasional cabin, rocks rolled around old campfire ashes. The journey involves a good deal of travel on lakes, some of them quite large. Detailed maps are essential. You can cut down on your grub weight by carrying fishing tackle; northern pike and walleye abound in this waterway, and large lake trout can be taken in some waters.

Most of the trip is through low, rocky country forested with willow and poplar, with a scattering of birches and conifers. One section of the route (between Knee and Drager lakes) is marshy, and it is here that one will see great flocks of geese and ducks in the fall. Moose and other wildlife are frequently seen. Cree Indians still hunt, trap, and fish the Churchill, although most have forsaken the rigors of paddling for outboard motors. There are from 15 to 20 whitewater stretches which have to be portaged, depending on the skill of the boatman. Some drops, such as Needle Falls, must be portaged. In several cases, there are no portage trails around rapids that can be dangerous. If in doubt, line your boats through. Whitewater chances that one might take on a short run in the Ozarks without a second thought would be insane here in the vastness of the North Country. The take-out point is at the Highway 2 bridge near Otter Rapids. There is no way to miss it. There is no other bridge on the entire voyage. This is an adventure for expert canoeists, and should take from fourteen to eighteen days. Beyond Otter Rapids the Churchill continues for several hundred miles, opening into Hudson Bay at the town of Churchill, which is at the end of a spur of the Canadian National Railroad.

Mackenzie
(Athabasca, Peace, Snare, Camsell, Great Bear)

The 2525-mile-long Mackenzie River, "Mississippi of the North," is immensely appealing to those whose fingers often hover over the great unpopulated areas of the globe. The Mackenzie and its tributaries offer a staggering mileage of wilderness flat country. The broad Mackenzie is eminently navigable, which makes for more than 1000 miles of easy canoeing, yet also provides passage for a quarter-million tons of freight hauled each summer. The barge traffic and its residue—rusted bankside oil drums and the like—detract from the quality of the wilderness experience. Scenically, much of the great river is rather monotonous flatlands and seemingly endless scrub forest.

Tributaries of the Mackenzie are generally more interesting. The Athabasca River forms the eastern border of Wood Buffalo National Park in Alberta; the Peace River runs right through it. Wood Buffalo is a gigantic wilderness park, with roads, developed campsites, lodges, and self-guided nature trails conspicuously absent. The jump-off on the Peace is Fort Vermilion; on the Athabasca it is Fort McMurray. Close to the western tip of Lake Athabasca, waters of the Athabasca and Peace rivers merge to form the Slave River, which empties into Great Slave Lake, official headwaters of the Mackenzie. One can fly out from Fort Smith on the Slave or drive out from the town of Hay River on the lake.

North of Yellowknife, on Great Slave Lake, it is 130 miles by air to

Jolly Lake, height of land: eastward, the waters run to Hudson Bay; westward to the Mackenzie basin. From here, one can move eastward through MacKay, Alymer, and Clinton and Colden lakes into the Hanbury and Thelon rivers and hence to Hudson Bay. To the west, 1½ miles from Jolly Lake, one can scratch down a series of small lakes connected by necks of water generally too small to be floated; the beginnings of the Snare River. One portages perhaps 4 of the first 13 miles, then the water gets deeper, the banks wider. Below Snare Lake the river drops into canyons where the water rips into unrunnable cataracts. This can be circumvented by puddle-hopping nine small lakes to the south, not all of them connected. Figure about ten portages totaling 3 miles, and you are back on the Snare, once again runnable. From either Indian Lake or Kwejinne Lake, work north through whatever pattern of lakes seems most feasible (here lake and land are interlocked like the fingers of a dozen people playing a crazy game) to the head of the Camsell River, which was an important part of the old Indian trade route between Great Slave Lake and Great Bear Lake. The Camsell runs mostly through bedrock, with forested banks, often lingering in ponds and lakes.

The Camsell opens into the vast, lonely reaches of Great Bear Lake, where abrupt faces of granite rise hundreds of feet above the water. On your own, it is at least twelve days' paddling to the outlet of the Great Bear River, but a tow can usually be arranged with a nearby fishing camp. The clear Great Bear River mostly zips over a rocky bed only 3 or 4 feet deep, so swift that the 80-mile trip can be made in a single day's run. It enters the Mackenzie near Fort Norman.

A Northwest Passage by freshwater? Quite possible, but it would probably take three summers. Up the Thelon and Hansbury; 400-yard portage to the Lockhard; westward through Clinton-Colden, Aylmer, Mackay and Jolly lakes; down the Snare and Camsell rivers to Great Bear Lake; across Great Bear Lake and down the Great Bear River into the Mackenzie; then the backbreaker, up 50 miles and 1000 feet on the Rat River to McDougall Pass; down the Bell, the Porcupine, into the Yukon, and on to the Bering Sea. No place for full-rigged sailing vessels. The Northwest Passage really does not exist—unless you have whitewater skill, endurance, time, and a yen for traversing the demanding sub-Arctic rim of North America. If you have all of these, the dangers and toil are still there—yet so is the exaltation that has come to all strong men who have passed through lonely places.

Hanbury—Thelon (Northwest Territories)

There are perhaps a dozen vast areas of virgin wilderness left upon the earth; certainly the largest upon our continent, and one of the most interesting anywhere, are the Barren Lands. Contrary to popular myth, the lonely landscape between the final stunted trees of Canada's great north forest and the Arctic Ocean are not perpetually sheeted with snow, completely flat, or even barren. Barren Land rivers thunder through rapids and over falls; escarpments are in places over 1000 feet high. Although at least one strange, isolated forest does exist deep within the Barrens, the country is generally treeless, yet there is a ground cover of coarse heath, low willow, and dwarf birch. During the summer, carpets of wildflowers and red and yellow lichens turn much of the land into a dazzle of color.

The Barrens are an ornithologist's delight. As well as great flocks of Canada geese, canoeists will see pintail ducks, herring gulls, Arctic terns, ptarmigan, peregrine falcons, and, if fortunate, whistling swans. The large mammals of the Barrens are numerous, but wary. The Arctic wolf and the Barren Grounds grizzly generally flee at the scent, sight, or sound of man. The shaggy musk-ox is tamer, and will generally watch an approaching boater with curiosity, or, if in a herd, form their distinctive defense ring, the bulls facing outward with cows and calves inside. Small herds of from one hundred to three hundred caribou are seen frequently, and herds estimated at better than 150,000 animals have been observed.

Roughly speaking, the Arctic summer extends from mid-June to mid-August. Because of the vast distances between settlements in the Barrens, trips must be carefully planned with regard to schedule and provisions. Out there you are a long way from any kind of help. More time should be allowed for scouting, lining, and portaging rapids than is the case in less demanding environments. An upset in icy water, in a region where there is little fuel, can be and has been fatal. Although a good roaring fire for warmth is hard to come by in the Barrens, one can usually gather enough twigs from willow and buckbrush for frugal cooking. A stove can thus be regarded as optional equipment, and a compass might just as well be left at home, as the proximity to the magnetic pole plays havoc with readings.

An experienced Barren Lands canoeist has written: "On a warm, cloudy, windless day, the insect life on the Barrens defies description. The fact is that such days are rare. Bugs and wind cannot go together; and most of the time it is windy." Nevertheless, a canoeist who neglects to bring head nets, a tight tent, and insect repellent is guaranteed some extremely unpleasant moments. An informative booklet on preparing for a Barren Lands voyage can be obtained by writing TravelArctic (see Appendix II).

One of the finest Barren Lands canoe adventures is a 500-mile voyage down the Hanbury and Thelon rivers. The most practical way of beginning such a journey is to have your canoes flown to Sifton Lake, close to the source of the Hanbury. (Canoes can be lashed very snugly to the pontoons of a chartered Otter.) If the canoe is rented from the Hudson's Bay Company, one can leave it at the post at Baker Lake, end of the run.

The Hanbury is a swift, boisterous river, cutting across rolling plateau country. The river requires some 7 miles of portage, mostly short treks, although there is a tough 2½-mile hike around Dickson Canyon, where the water drops 200 feet within about 1 mile. Sixty-foot Helen Falls is another thunderous spectacular on the Hanbury. Portaging in the Barrens is facilitated by the numerous caribou trails that run beside the rivers.

The Thelon is a quieter river than the Hanbury: on the principal stretch of 350 miles no portaging should be necessary. Here, as the trees become ever more stunted and sparsely scattered, one begins to see big game, especially musk-ox and caribou. The Thelon Game Preserve was created in 1927. Aberdeen Lake, where waves can travel 40 miles, may put a limp in one's schedule. Since wind directions change with some frequency, it's better to lay over rather than to fight a severe headwind.

A Barren Lands canoe voyage is one of the supreme outdoor adventures of our continent. Few have done it: those who have, have felt bounteously rewarded for the planning and effort necessary.

Back (Northwest Territories)

Possibly the ultimate challenge in Barren Lands river running is the Back, which rises as a small stream near Alymer Lake and rambles for 615 miles before emptying into the Arctic Ocean. Unless someone has voyaged the remote waterway since 1963, it appears likely that only three parties *have ever* traversed the entire river. George Back, for whom it was named, prepared to run it in 1834 to search for Captain John Ross, who in turn had been seeking the fabled Northwest Passage. Ross turned up before Back could get underway, but the intrepid Englishman made the hazardous trip anyway in only three weeks. Twenty-one years later, James Anderson, Chief Factor of the Hudson's Bay Company, led a party down the Back in search of the Franklin expedition, lost while they also probed for the Northwest Passage. Austin Hoyt, a Buffalo newspaper reporter, rounds out the roll-call. He and three companions voyaged the Back in 1963.

This is fine country for viewing the big-game animals of the Barrens— caribou and musk-ox. It is also an extremely arduous trip, with some 80 falls, cascades, and rapids. Back wrote that stretches on the river "foamed and boiled, and rushed with impetuous and deadly fury." Anyone contemplating a jaunt down the Back, probably the least traveled of all American rivers of any size, should consult Hoyt's account for particulars (see Appendix II).

Teslin (Yukon Territory)

In an age when wilderness rivers are a vanishing breed, the Yukon Territory, whimsically speaking, has wild rivers to burn. They come plunging out of the high glacial peaks of the St. Elias Range, the Mackenzie Mountains, spinning leaves through moose pastures, slipping through rotten pilings supporting boardwalks thrusting out from empty-windowed towns gone back to forest. All rivers in the Yukon are wild. And unlike eastern Canada, where good rivers wind through an infinity of timbered flatlands, here mountains rise up to catch the winds at 19,000 feet; the streams have to gouge, rip, and fight their way down gravity. There is a river for every aesthetic taste, for every skill, in the Yukon. An easy one for boaters is the Teslin, which has an average gradient of only 2.5 feet per mile, with no portages involved. Although it runs parallel to and joins the Yukon, one does not have to portage Whitehorse Dam or paddle the length of Lake Laberge—it is a smooth 200-mile cruise from Johnsons Crossing on the Alaska Highway down into the Yukon, with a take-out at Carmacks. Or one can run on down the Yukon to Dawson, Eagle, or wherever. The Teslin was floated by a number of the Klondike stampeders who had come up the Ashcroft and Stikine trails rather than crossing Chilkoot Pass.

Pelly (Yukon Territory)

Want to see moose? Try the Pelly, which is the major river draining the west side of the Mackenzie Mountains. Unlike the Yukon, into which it flows, the Pelly has never known a gold boom, or resultant steamboats, and consequently the wildlife is a good deal more relaxed and at home. Best place to put in is at Ross River, on the recently completed Robert Campbell Highway. Buy supplies before heading up from the cut-off at Watson Lake on the Alaska Highway.

Some 34 miles beyond Ross River the Pelly cuts north into wilderness. There are a couple of rough places (ask locally, since they vary depending upon season and water level). Above Ross River, at Hoole Canyon, the Pelly is not only nasty, but probably unrunnable.

It is a fine run down to Pelly Crossing, on the Dawson Highway, and beyond, into the Yukon. Where to take-out depends on how much time you have.

As for moose, I can almost guarantee you one, to lodge in the sights of your camera or gun. But beware. Some years back, when I was drifting the Pelly, a companion saw massive rustling in the alder, threw his 30-0-6 against his shoulder, and almost squeezed on an Angus bull. *Angus bull? Black-haired hulk from the plains of Texas, the feedlots of K.C.? Hallucination.* We were a hundred miles down a wilderness river; hadn't seen *Homo sapiens* in days. A camouflaged moose? No way. We paddled ashore and met two siblings from Saskatchewan, dignified and black-bearded. They reckoned they had the most northern cattle ranch in America. We reckoned so too.

The Pelly is a wonderful floating river but aside from the Saskatchewan Brothers' ranch (close to the junction with the Yukon), this is emphatically a wilderness river. There are no friendly farmers or townships to hike to if you get into trouble. Plan your trip accordingly.

Copper (Alaska)

The Copper is a broad river, laden with glacial silt, that has cut its way through the rugged Chugach Mountains to the Pacific. The upper river is bordered by the Glenn Highway, but below Chitina, an old, picturesque mining settlement, the current swings out into the wilderness of Copper River Canyon. Although the peaks in this part of the Chugach are no more than 7000 to 8000 feet high, a low timberline, jagged profiles, and snow-plastered slopes tend to give many of them the grandeur of Himalayan giants. The range spawns a number of massive glaciers. This is salmon water. Brown, black, and grizzly bear stalk the spawning fish up side streams, while seal pursue them downriver. Other wildlife, including moose, trumpeter swan, and bald eagle are abundant.

The 85-mile voyage from Chitina to Alaganik on the marshy Copper River Delta takes about five days. The Copper is a big river, with a strong current, although not noted for heavy whitewater. Highlight of the trip is Miles Lake, a slow section created by sediment deposited by Miles Glacier. The 300-foot face of the glacier rises directly out of the water, and massive ice cliffs split off and plummet down with regularity. Icebergs drift slowly in the current. There is a rapids where nearby Childs Glacier meets the river. If cars are shuttled to Valdez over the Richardson Highway, transportation can be arranged over the road segment between the Copper River Delta and Cordova. There is both air and boat service from Cordova to Valdez.

Forty-Mile (Alaska)

The Forty-Mile River, a tributary of the Yukon, is an excellent waterway to float for hunting, fishing, or just plain looking. The 117-mile run from the Taylor Highway bridge at Milepost 49 to the Clinton Creek Road, close to the Yukon, is not difficult navigation for the most part, although there are a few rapids of Class III and IV. The overall gradient is 9 feet to the mile.

The first 32 miles of the voyage, from Milepost 49 to where the Taylor Highway again recrosses the river (Milepost 75), is fastwater, dropping 25 feet to the mile. Rapids, although numerous, are either small or of the haystack variety, and should pose no problems. Below the Milepost 75 bridge, the river becomes gradually broader and the current slackens. There are, however, six dangerous rapids on the middle and lower sections of the river. They are located: (*a*) 5 miles below the Milepost 75 bridge, (*b*) immediately below the confluence with North Fork, (*c*) 2 miles upstream from the highway bridge at Milepost 112, (*d*) close to the Alaska-Yukon Border: Deadman Riffle and Eldon Landing Rapids, (*e*) 5 miles upstream from the take-out point at the Clinton Creek Road. This final unnamed rapids is the roughest. It is in two sections and should be lined from the north bank during highwater.

In spite of the fact that the Taylor Highway crosses it at three places, this is very much a wilderness river. Most of its course is distant from roads or settlements. Gold-seekers panned the Forty-Mile before the turn of the century, and here and there old cabins decay on the riverbanks. Moose, bear, and other wildlife abound; fishing is good for grayling, burbot, and sheepfish.

One can take-out at the Clinton Creek Road bridge, or paddle down to the ghost town of Forty-Mile on the Yukon River. The scenic Yukon run from Forty-Mile down to Eagle contains no rapids, although the current is swift.

Gulkana (Alaska)

The village of Paxson, on the Richardson Highway, is the turn-off for Mount McKinley National Park. Paxson Lake, a few miles south of town, is a source of the Gulkana River. For some 45 river miles the Gulkana meanders off to the west of the highway, and finally returns to parallel it at Sourdough.

The put-in point is at the Paxson Lake Campground. There are several miles of lake travel before one reaches the river itself. The first 3 miles after leaving the lake are fast and of moderate difficulty—rated Class III. Below the junction with the Middle Fork the river calms and is smooth-floating until Canyon Rapids are reached about midpoint in the trip (18 miles below the lake). For 8 miles in the canyon, the river has a 50-foot gradient and is rated Class IV. There is a marked trail for portage or lining along the left bank. The remainder of the run on into Sourdough is Class II water.

One can continue 35 miles down to Gulkana, all of it moderate water, but the close proximity of the highway tarnishes the river's wilderness credentials on this section.

Swanson and Kenai (Alaska)

There is some fine wilderness canoeing on the Kenai Peninsula, much of it within the Kenai National Moose Preserve. Well-maintained forest roads provide easy put-ins and take-outs.

The Swanson River offers a leisurely voyage through game-filled woods and open lands of rock and moss. Turning north at Sterling, one drives to almost the end of the Swan Lake Road, entering the water at Paddle Lake. From Paddle Lake to Jean Lake at the head of the Swanson, the canoe trail leads through a chain of narrow lakes. Portages are generally short (the longest is ½ mile), and the run should take no more than a day unless one lingers for extensive fishing.

The Swanson itself is a gentle stream, rated Class I. It is 19 miles to the Swanson River Campground, which is on a roadhead, 24 miles from there to Cook Inlet on the Pacific. Shuttle cars can be driven to that point over the North Kenai Road. Fishing is good for both rainbow and Dolly Varden in the lakes and river. There is a run of silver salmon on the Swanson during the summer months.

The Kenai River is less remote than the Swanson (in places roads parallel it), yet it throws out some challenging rapids. The put-in point is the bridge at Milepost 49 of the Sterling Highway. For some distance the river wobbles fairly close to the road. Schooner Bend, a Class III rapids, lies just beyond the next (and final) highway bridge. Below the confluence of Jean Creek, the Kenai swings away from the road, entering a 2-mile-long canyon. Here there are tough rapids, Class IV in most any kind of runoff. The stretch should be walked along and pondered, even by skilled whitewatermen.

Once the river enters Skilak Lake, there is a 6-mile journey to Upper Skilak Lake Campground. The lake is large, and dangerous when windy. One can take-out at the upper campground, driving several miles to the lower campground, or stroke on down the lake. It is 51 miles from Lower Skilak Lake Campground to the town of Kenai, with a number of possible take-outs en route. Most of it is easy going, although there is a Class III rapids 12 miles below the lower campground. Pink, silver, and red salmon all ascend the Kenai to spawn.

Karluk (Alaska)

Interested in big bear? Try the Karluk on Kodiak Island, which runs right through the turf of the Kodiak brown bear, largest carnivore in the world. During the summer months, when salmon swarm up the river to spawn in such quantities as sometimes to give the illusion one could walk across their thrashing backs, the big brownies hang around the river. Salmon is good eating, for man or beast. Younger bear often chase fish through shallow water, eventually coming up with one grabbed in their jaws. Mature bears, who have had a few years to contemplate the matter, usually select a good spot to sit in the water, and swat fish out to the bank as they swim past.

Salmon intent on reproducing are not interested in feeding, but will snap peevishly at a large, flashy lure such as a spoon. This is a good place to take a barbless hook, as you will probably catch many more 8- to 12-pound sockeye salmon than your party can eat. Kings run to 30 pounds and more. There are also rainbow, steelhead, Arctic char, and Dolly Varden in the river.

The Karluk is a short river—some 25 miles long. A Widgeon owned by Kodiak Airlines can be chartered to drop river runners at Karluk Lake, headwaters of the river. Midway to the sea there is an overnight accommodation, the "portage cabin." The trip ends at Karluk lagoon, a long way from anywhere. The plane will pick you up there.

For some time the Karluk has been considered a sort of ultimate by hunters and fishermen. Now some floaters are just shooting film. Or just looking. Ever see a wild swan? You should.

Selected Bibliography

General

American Red Cross, *Canoeing.* 1956.

Buck Ridge Ski Club, *Basic River Canoeing.* Swarthmore, Pennsylvania, nd.

Makens, James C., *Makens' Guide to U.S. Canoe Trails.* Irving, Texas: Le Voyageur Publishing Company, 1971.

Nesbitt, Paul; Pond, Alonzo; and Allen, William, *The Survival Book.* New York: Van Nostrand & Co., 1959. (Also Funk & Wagnall paperbook edition.)

Porter, Eliot, *In Wildness is the Preservation of the World.* San Francisco: Sierra Club, 1962.

Riviere, Bill, *Pole, Paddle and Portage.* New York: Van Nostrand Reinhold Co., 1969.

Russell, Jerry and Renny, *On the Loose.* San Francisco: Sierra Club, 1968.

Rutstrum, Calvin, *New Way of the Wilderness.* New York: The Macmillan Co., 1966.

Urban, John T., *White Water Handbook for Canoe and Kayak.* Boston: Appalachian Mountain Club, nd.

Journals

American Canoe Association, *American Canoeist,* Philadelphia.

American White Water Affiliation, *American White Water* (issued to members). San Bruno, California.

CHAPTER TWO. The Irascible Rogue

Magazine Articles

Chapman, Art, "Old Reelfoot—Scourge of the Siskiyous," *Frontier Times.* August–September, 1966, pp. 32–60.

Goldrath, Bert, "Conquering the Wild, White Rogue," *Popular Mechanics.* May, 1962, pp. 104–106.

Sunset, "The Rogue," June, 1966, pp. 77–85.

Booklets

Bureau of Land Management, *The Rogue Wild River.* Medford, Oregon, nd.

"Rogue River and Tributaries" (may be obtained from Glen Wooldridge, river guide, 913 SW "H" St., Grants Pass, Oregon).

CHAPTER THREE. River of No Return: The Salmon

Brown, Mark Herbert, *The Flight of the Nez Perce*. New York: Putnam, 1967.
DeVoto, Bernard, ed., *Journals of Lewis and Clark*. Boston: Houghton, Mifflin, 1953.
Idaho Federal Writers Project. New York: Oxford University Press, 1950.
Wolle, Muriel Sibell, *The Bonanza Trail*. Bloomington: Indiana University Press, 1958.

Magazine Articles
Brokaw, Tom, "That River Swallows People. Some It Gives Up; Some It Don't," *West* (Los Angeles Times Sunday Magazine), November 1, 1970, pp. 12–19.
Craighead, John and Frank, "White-water Adventure on Wild Rivers of Idaho," *National Geographic,* February, 1970, pp. 213–239.
Kelly, Charles, "Hermit of the Middle Fork," *True West,* February, 1970, pp. 26–27, 40.
Kimball, Ethel, "River Rat Pioneer," *True West,* December, 1963, pp. 30–31, 50–53.
Randal, J., "Sylvan Hart is Alive and Well in the Wilderness," *Avant Garde,* January, 1969, pp. 46–49.

Booklets
Detailed maps with descriptive material may be obtained from the U.S. Department of Agriculture, Forest Service, Intermountain Region, Ogden, Utah.
Sheepeater Indian Campaign. Boise: Idaho County Free Press, 1968.

CHAPTER FOUR. Treasure of the Sierra Madre: The Rio Urique

Bennett, W. C., and Zingg, R. M., *The Tarahumara*. Chicago: University of Chicago Press, 1935.
Cassel, Jonathan, *Tarahumara Indians*. San Antonio: Naylor Press, 1969.
Lister, Florence, *Chihuahua: Storehouse of Storms*. Albuquerque: University of New Mexico Press, 1966.
Pennington, C. W., *Tarahumara of Mexico*. Salt Lake City: University of Utah Press, 1963.
Wampler, Joseph, *New Rails to Old Towns*. Berkeley, California: Private printing, 1969.

Magazine Articles
Jenkinson, Michael, "The Glory of the Long Distance Runner," *Natural History,* January, 1972, pp. 53–65.
O'Reilly, Mary Ellen, "Lady on a River of Rock," *Sports Illustrated,* October 21, 1963, pp. 26–33.

CHAPTER FIVE. River of the Shining Mountains: The Colorado

Abbey, Ed, *Desert Solitaire: A Season in the Wilderness*. New York: McGraw-Hill, 1968.
Crampton, C. Gregory, *Standing-up Country: The Canyon Lands of Utah and Arizona*. New York: Knopf, 1938.
Dellenbaugh, Frederick S., *A Canyon Voyage*. New Haven: Yale University Press, 1962.

Hughes, J. Donald, *The Story of Man at Grand Canyon.* Grand Canyon Natural History Association, np, 1967.

Kolb, Ellsworth L., *Through the Grand Canyon from Wyoming to Mexico.* New York: Macmillan Company, 1915.

Krutch, Joseph Wood, *Grand Canyon: Today and Its Yesterdays.* New York: William Sloane and Associates, 1958.

Porter, Eliot, *The Place No One Knew.* San Francisco: Sierra Club, 1963.

Powell, John Wesley, *Canyons of the Colorado.* Flood & Vincent, 1895, Dover paperback edition, 1961.

Stanton, Robert Brewster, *Down the Colorado.* Norman: University of Oklahoma Press, 1965.

Stegner, Wallace, *Beyond the Hundredth Meridian.* Boston: Houghton Mifflin Co., 1954.

Waters, Frank, *The Colorado.* New York: Rinehard & Co., 1946.

Watkins, T. H. and contributors, *The Grand Colorado.* Palo Alto, California: American West Publishing Co., 1969.

Booklets

Belknap, Buzz, *Grand Canyon River Guide.* Salt Lake City: Canyonlands Press, 1969. (May be obtained for $3.95 from Canyonlands Press, P.O. Box 21021, Salt Lake City, Utah; waterproof edition, $5.95.)

Powell Society Ltd., *River Runners Guide to the Canyons of the Green and Colorado Rivers: Volume I: From Flaming Gorge Dam through Dinosaur Canyon to Ouray; Volume II: Labyrinth, Stillwater & Cataract Canyons.* Denver. nd.

CHAPTER SIX. River of the Trembling Earth:
The Suwannee and Okefenokee Swamp

Kennedy, Stetson, *Palmetto Country.* New York: Duell, Sloan & Pierce, 1945.

Matschat, Cecile Hulse, *Suwanee River: Strange Green Land.* New York: Literary Guild of America, 1938.

Magazine Articles

Sands, Tom, "Suwanee River," *Southern Telephone News* (Southern Bell Telephone Co.), September, 1960.

Booklets

Elkins, Leston, *Story of the Okefenokee,* private printing, np, 1946.

Okefenokee National Refuge, Box 117, Waycross, Georgia, maps and other booklets.

Suwanee River Authority (P.O. Box 13-D, Trenton, Florida), river map of the Suwannee.

CHAPTER SEVEN. River of Gold: The Yukon

Becker, Ethel Anderson, *Klondike '98.* Portland: Binfords and Mort, 1959.

Burton, Pierre, *Klondike.* Toronto: McClelland and Stewart, 1962.

Schwatka, Frederick, *A Summer in Alaska.* Philadelphia: John Y. Huber Co., 1891.

Winslow, Kathryn, *Big Pan-Out.* New York: W. W. Norton & Company, 1951.

Magazine Articles
Alaska Sportsman. Assorted issues.
Jenkinson, Michael, "Ghosts Along the Yukon" ("Bennett: Yukon Ghost," "Fort Selkirk: Where the Steamboats Pass No More," "Dawson: Paris of the North," "Forty-Mile: A Restless Breed," "Eagle," "Circle: Where the Road Dead-ends," "Rampart," "Ruby"), *True West*, eight-part series from June, 1965, through August, 1966.

CHAPTER EIGHT. River of Fireflies: The Buffalo

Smith, Kenneth L., *Buffalo River Country*. Fayetteville, Arkansas: Ozark Society, 1967.

Magazine Articles
Hedges, Margaret, "The Buffalo River at Its Source," Ozark Society Bulletin, Spring, 1960.
Jones, Robert F., "The Old Man and the River," *Sports Illustrated*, August, 1970, pp. 28–34.
Ozarks Mountaineer, assorted issues.

Booklets
Ozark Society, *Buffalo River Canoeing Guide*, Fayetteville, Arkansas, nd.
U.S. Government Printing Office, *Proposed Buffalo National River*, 1968.

CHAPTER NINE. Route of the Voyageurs

Burpee, Lawrence, ed., *Journals and Letters of Pierre Gaultier de Varennes de la Verendrye and His Sons*. Toronto: The Champlain Society, 1927.
Denis, Keith, *Canoe Trails through Quetico*. Toronto: The Quetico Foundation, 1959.
Gates, Charles, ed., *Five Fur Traders of the Northwest*. Minneapolis: University of Minnesota Press, 1933.
Mackenzie, Alexander, *Voyages from Montreal through the Continent of North America to the Frozen and Pacific Oceans in 1789 and 1793, with an Account of the Rise and State of the Fur Trade*. New York: A. S. Barnes and Company, 1903.
Nute, Grace Lee, *Rainy River Country*. St. Paul: Minnesota Historical Society, 1950.
Nute, Grace Lee, *The Voyageur's Highway*. St. Paul: Minnesota Historical Society, 1941.

CHAPTER TEN. River of Ghosts: The Rio Grande

Horgan, Paul, *Great River*. New York: Rinehart, 1954.
Madison, Virginia, *The Big Bend Country of Texas*. Albuquerque: University of New Mexico Press, 1955.
New Mexico Federal Writers Project. New York: Hastings House, 1940.
Tate, Bill, *The Penitentes of the Sangre de Cristos: an American Tragedy*. Truchas, New Mexico: Tate Gallery Publications, 1966.

Magazine Articles
Carson, Xanthus Kit, "Dig Here for Bill Kelly's Millions," *Argosy*, August, 1966, pp. 34–36, 80–82.

Hurt, Wesley R., Jr., "Witchcraft in New Mexico," *El Palacio* (magazine of the Museum of New Mexico, Santa Fe), April, 1940.

Kline, Doyle, "The Rio Grande: First to Go Wild," *New Mexico Magazine,* Spring, 1971.

Smith, Alson J., "Pegleg Smith," *Frontier Times,* October–November, 1964.

Booklets

Big Bend Natural History Association, *Guide to Backcountry Roads and the River,* Big Bend National Park, Texas, 1970.

Burleson, Bob, *Notes on the Canyons of the Big Bend,* Temple, Texas: Texas Explorers Club, nd.

Carnes, Cecil, *Running the Rio: A Guide to River Canoeing and Rafting in Northern New Mexico,* Los Alamos, New Mexico, nd.

Sources of River-Running Information
by States and Provinces

A great deal of free or inexpensive information on river running can be obtained by sending away for it. In many cases the best information on a given river can be found in magazine articles. Travel and outdoor magazines have run numerous accounts of river voyages over the last twenty years. I have narrowed the magazine material in this section down to those waterways discussed in "106 Wild Rivers to Run." I refer often to *American White Water,* because of its attention to specific rapids in challenging rivers, and its invaluable guide material not usually found in general travel or fishing publications. Back issues of *American White Water* can be ordered from George Larsen, Box 1584, San Bruno, California 94066.

With the exception of the back issues of magazines (whose prices vary with their rareness), all of the material listed in Appendix II is free unless otherwise stated.

	Information and Materials Available
Alabama	
John V. Orr, Forest Supervisor, U.S. Forest Service, U.S.D.A., P. O. Box 40, Montgomery, Alabama 36101.	General information.
Alaska	
Bureau of Land Management, P.O. Box 2511, Juneau, Alaska 99801.	*Alaska Canoe Trails,* detailed pamphlet, with maps, describing eleven float trips.
Bureau of Sport Fisheries and Wildlife, U.S. Fish and Wildlife Service, P.O. Box 500, Kenai, Alaska 99611.	

Arizona

Bert Coleman, Travel Information Section, Suite 1704, 3303 N. Central Ave., Phoenix, Arizona 85012.

General information.

Arkansas

Harold Bly, Box 343, Upper Eleven Point River Association, Pocahontas, Arkansas 72455.

Information on Eleven Point River.

The Ozark Society, P.O. Box 38, Fayetteville, Arkansas 72701.

Information on Arkansas rivers.

Ozark Society Book Service, Box 725, Hot Springs, Arkansas 71901.

Buffalo River Country, an excellent illustrated guidebook ($4.95).

Ozark Wilderness Waterways Club, P.O. Box 8165, Kansas City, Missouri 64012.

Bulletins on Ozark float streams.

U.S. Department of Interior, Superintendent of Documents, U.S. Government Printing Office, Washington, D.C. 20402.

Buffalo National River, an illustrated booklet with map (50 cents).

Jack Wellborn Jr., 1625 Slattery Bldg., Shreveport, Louisiana 71101.

A Guide to Canoeing the Cossatot.

California

American River Touring Association, 1016 Jackson St., Oakland, California 94607.

Information on California rivers.

American White Water, Vol. XV, No. 3 (Autumn 1970): "The Upper Stanislaus Gorge," by Mary Ellen Whitmore.

American White Water, Vol. XV, No. 4 (Winter 1970): "The Tuolumne River," by Robert H. Hackamack; "The Wild Middle American," by Charles Martin.

Field and Stream, November 1964: "Desert Boating" (Lower Colorado).

Colorado

American White Water (Spring 1966): "Cross Mountain Conquered," by J. Calvin Giddings.

American White Water (Spring 1968): "The Animas of Colorado," by Bill Winn.

Colorado Department of Game, Fish and Parks, 6060 Broadway, Denver, Colorado 80216.

General information.

Connecticut

Appalachian Mountain Club, 5 Joy St., Boston, Massachusetts 02108.

A.M.C. New England Canoeing Guide ($5). Detailed river routes, maps, of New England.

Connecticut Development Commission, State Office Building, Hartford, Connecticut.

Information on Connecticut and Housatonic rivers.

Farmington River Watershed Association, Inc., 24 East Main St., Avon, Connecticut 06001.

The Farmington River and Watershed Guide (book, $2.50; map, 50 cents).

Delaware

State Development Dept., 45 The Green, Dover, Delaware 19901.

Boating, Camping and Fishing, a folder.

Florida

Department of Natural Resources, Larson Bldg., Tallahassee, Florida 32304.

Proposed system of canoe trails.

Division of Commercial Development, 107 W. Gaines St., Tallahassee, Florida 32304.

Canoe Trips in Florida, a booklet outlining twelve river cruises, mostly in northern Florida. There is also a pamphlet, *Withlacoochee River Trail.*

Game and Fresh Water Fish Commission, 620 South Meridian St., Tallahassee, Florida 32304.

Specific river information upon request.

U.S. Department of the Interior, National Park Service, Everglades National Park, Box 279, Homestead, Florida 33030.

Boating information and maps.

Georgia

Coastal Plain Area Tourism Council, P.O. Box 1223, Valdosta, Georgia 31601.

Pamphlets on Withlacoochee and Alapaha River trails.

Folkston County Chamber of Commerce, P.O. Box 276, Folkton, Georgia 31537.

Same.

Slash Pine Area Planning and Development Commission, Box 1276, Waycross, Georgia 31501.

Pamphlets on Satilla River and Okefenokee Swamp.

Idaho

Department of Commerce and Development, State House, Boise, Idaho 83707.

Idaho Water Fun (booklet).

Hells Canyon Preservation Council, Box 691, Idaho Falls, Idaho 83401.

Information on the last remaining segment of the wilderness Snake River, and how it is threatened.

Forest Service, U.S.D.A., Intermountain Region, Ogden, Utah.

Pamphlet with description and map of the Middle Fork of the Salmon.

Forest Supervisor, Salmon National Forest, Salmon, Idaho 83467.

Pamphlet with description and map of the Salmon River.

Forest Supervisor, Tagghee National Forest, St. Anthony, Idaho 83445.

Map showing Henry's Fork and the Upper Snake.

Illinois

The Chicagoland Canoe Base, 4019 North Narragansett Ave., Chicago, Illinois 60634.

Canoe Trails.

Department of Conservation, Boat Section, 106 State Office Bldg., Springfield, Illinois 61106.

Illinois Canoeing Guide, which describes twenty-three river trips (with maps).

Indiana

Department of Conservation, 612 State Office Bldg., Indianapolis, Indiana 46209.

Canoeing Trails in Indiana, a booklet describing sixteen trips.

Iowa

Conservation Department, East 7th and Court Sts., Des Moines, Iowa.

Iowa Canoe Trips, detailed booklet describing thirteen river trips.

Kansas

Department of Economic Development, State Office Bldg., Topeka, Kansas 66612.

General information.

U.S. Forest Service, U.S.D.A., P.O. Box 727, Winchester, Kansas 40391.

Daniel Boone National Forest float trip (summary and map).

Louisiana

Louisiana Wildlife and Fisheries Commission, P.O. Box 44095, Capitol Station, Baton Rouge, Louisiana 70804.

General information.

State Parks and Recreation Commission, Old State Capitol, P.O. Drawer 1111, Baton Rouge, Louisiana 70821.

Booklet on State Parks—some boating information.

Maine

American White Water (Spring 1963): "By Kayak Through Darkest Maine" (Penobscot), by J. Raymond Hudkinson.

Appalachian Mountain Club, 5 Joy St., Boston, Massachusetts 02108.

A.M.C. New England Canoeing Guide ($5). Best source of information on Maine waterways.

Department of Economic Development, Tourism Division, State House, Augusta, Maine 04330.

Escape to Maine, and Wild Maine (booklets describing canoe routes).

Field and Stream, July 1963: "Why We Must Save the Allagash," by Justice William O. Douglas.

Great Northern Paper Co., 6 State St., Bangor, Maine 04401.

Sportsman's map of Allagash, Chesuncook, and Chamberlain canoe country.

Maine Forest Service, Augusta, Maine 04330.

Maine Forest Service Campsites (booklet describing locations of three hundred free campsites, many along waterways).

Rangeley Lakes Region Chamber of Commerce, Rangeley, Maine 04970.

Detailed map of canoe routes in Rangeley Lakes—Azicoos area.

Scott Paper Company, Northwest Division, Winslow, Maine 04901.

Map and description of the Moosehead, Upper Kennebec waterways.

St. Croix Paper Co., Woodland, Maine 04694.

Map of Grand Lake canoe area.

State Parks and Recreation Commission, Augusta, Maine 04330.

Allagash Wilderness Waterway (booklet with map).

Maryland

Blue Ridge Voyageurs, P.O. Box 32, Oakton, Virginia 22124.

Blue Ridge Voyages, Vols. I and II, by Roger Corbett and Louis Mantacia ($2.50 each).

Thomas L. Gray, 11121 Dewey Rd., Kensington, Maryland 20795.

Canoeing Streams of the Potomac and Rappahannock Basins ($1.00).

Maryland Department of Forests and Parks, State Office Bldg., Annapolis, Maryland 21404.

General information.

Massachusetts

Appalachian Mountain Club, 5 Joy St., Boston, Massachusetts 02108.

A.M.C. New England Canoeing Guide, best source of information on Massachusetts rivers.

New England Electric System, Turnpike Rd., Westboro, Massachusetts 01581.

Canoeing on the Connecticut River (booklet with map).

Westfield River Watershed Association, P.O. Box 114, Middlefield, Massachusetts 01243.

Map and information on the Westfield River.

Michigan

Forest Supervisor, Huron National Forest, Cadillac, Michigan 49601.

Michigan Canoe Trails and *Michigan Water Access Sites* (booklets).

Huron-Clinton Metropolitan Authority, 1750 Guardian Bldg., Detroit, Michigan 48226.

Detailed maps showing campsites, portages, access points, on the Huron River.

West Michigan Tourist Association, 136 Fulton East, Grand Rapids, Michigan 49502.

General information.

Minnesota

Aitkin County Park Commission, Court House, Aitkin, Minnesota 56431.

Mississippi River Guide (50 cents).

Bigfork River Canoe Trail, Box 356, Bigfork, Minnesota 56628.

Bigfork River Canoe Trail (folder).

City Administrator, 218 S. Main St., Le Sueur, Minnesota 56058.

Booklet (with map) on the Minnesota River.

Cook County Civic Council, Grand Marais, Minnesota 55604.

Canoeing information for Arrowhead country.

Crow Wing Trails Association, Box 210, Sebeka, Minnesota 56477.

Crow Wing River information.

Department of Conservation, Division of Parks and Recreation, 320 Centennial Bldg., St. Paul, Minnesota 55101.

Minnesota Voyageur Trails, large, detailed booklet describing sixteen rivers and Boundary Waters Canoe Area. Contains good maps ($2).

Department of Economic Development, 51 E. 8th St., St. Paul, Minnesota 55101.

Information on canoe routes and outfitters.

Earl's Tree Service, Rushford, Minnesota 55971.

Root River Canoe Trail (folder).

Ely Chamber of Commerce, Room 117, Community Bldg., 30 S. 1st Ave. E., Ely, Minnesota 55731.

Information on Boundary Waters Canoe Area—pamphlets from outfitters.

Muller Boat Company, Taylor Falls Canoe Company, Taylor Falls, Minnesota 55084.

St. Croix River (folder).

Pine County Soil and Water Conservation District, Hinckley, Minnesota 55037.

Kettle River Canoe Route (folder).

State Documents Section, 140 Centennial Bldg., St. Paul, Minnesota 55101.

Snake River information.

Forest Supervisor, Superior National Forest, Duluth, Minnesota 55801.

Canoeing information on Boundary Waters Canoe Area (with map).

U.S. Department of Agriculture, Forest Service, Cass Lake, Minnesota 56633.

Folders and map of Chippewa National Forest (Turtle and Rice rivers).

Missouri

S. G. Adams Printing Co., 10th and Olive Sts., St. Louis, Missouri 63101.

Maps of Current and Jacks Fork rivers.

Argosy, August, 1969: "Our First National River" (Current and Jacks Fork), by Larry Nicholson.

Conservation Commission, North Ten Mile Dr., Jefferson City, Missouri 65101.

Missouri Ozark Waterways, by Oz Hawksley ($1). Detailed guide to thirty-seven canoe trips.

Ozark National Scenic Riverways, Box 448, Van Buren, Missouri 63965.

Maps and information on Current and Jacks Fork rivers.

Mississippi

Supervisor, De Soto National Forest, Box 1291, Jackson, Mississippi 39505.

Pamphlet (with map) on *Black Creek Float Trip.*

Montana

American Canoeist (October 1967): "Historic Missouri," by Byron Grosfield.

American White Water (Spring 1965): "Pioneering the Flathead," by Oz Hawksley.

American White Water, Vol. XV, No. 4 (Winter 1970): "Down the Wide Missouri," by Ann Schafer.

American White Water, Vol. XIV, No. 4: "Lewis & Clark's Real Route" (Missouri River), by Dean Norman.

Department of Fish and Game, Helena, Montana 59601.

Montana's Popular Float Streams (booklet); "Floating through the Yellowstone Waterway" (reprint from *Montana Wildlife,* maps of Blackfoot, Clark Fork, and Bitterroot rivers).

U.S. Department of the Interior, National Parks Service, 1709 Jackson St., Omaha, Nebraska 68101.

1893 maps of the Missouri River between Fort Benton and Fort Peck Lake. As there have been few changes on the river since then, these handsome maps are still valid.

Yellowstone River Guide, 2047 Custer Ave., Billings, Montana 59102.

Floating, Fishing and Historical Guide to Yellowstone Waterway, Gardiner to the Big Horn River, by Burdge & Ross ($2).

New Hampshire

Appalachian Mountain Club, 5 Joy St., Boston, Massachusetts 02108.

A.M.C. New England Canoeing Guide ($5), the best source of information for New Hampshire rivers.

Department of Resources and Economic Development, Concord, New Hampshire 03301.

Canoeing on the Connecticut River (booklet).

New Jersey

Delaware River Basin Commission, 25 Scotch Rd., P.O. Box 360, Trenton, New Jersey 08603.

Maps of the Delaware River ($1 per set).

Division of Economic Development, P.O. Box 400, Trenton, New Jersey 08625.

Brief descriptions of several New Jersey canoe routes.

Rutgers University Press, 30 College Ave., New Brunswick, New Jersey 08903.

Exploring the Little Rivers of New Jersey, by James and Margaret Cawley ($1.95).

Upper Raritan Watershed Association, Inc., P.O. Box 44, Far Hills, New Jersey 07931.

Information on the Raritan River.

New Mexico

Base Camp, 121 San Francisco, Santa Fe, New Mexico 87501

Information on Rio Grande and Chama Rivers (25 cents).

Ms. Helen Redman, Route 1, Box 177, Santa Fe, New Mexico 87501

Publisher of *Rio Grande Gurgle,* a news-sheet about New Mexico river running.

New York

American White Water (February 1961):
"We Vanquish the Neversink," by Walter F.
Burmeister.

Department of Environmental Conservation,
Albany, New York 12226.

Adirondack Canoe Routes (pamphlet).

North Dakota

Fish and Game Department, Bismark, North
Dakota 58501.

Opportunities for Outdoor Recreation at Wakopa, a folder describing a canoe trail developed
by the state.

Ohio

Department of Natural Resources, Division
of Watercraft, 1350 Holly Ave., Columbus,
Ohio 43212.

Ohio Canoe Livery, Loudenville, Ohio
44842.

Ohio Canoe Adventures, a booklet with descriptions and maps of
numerous river trips.

Folder on the Mohican River.

Oklahoma

Department of Wildlife Conservation, 1801
North Lincoln, Oklahoma City, Oklahoma
73105.

Scenic Rivers (pamphlet).

Oregon

Grants Pass Chamber of Commerce, Grants
Pass, Oregon 97526.

Information on the Rogue River.

State Marine Board, Agriculture Bldg.,
Room 109, Salem, Oregon 97310.

Oregon Boating Guide (has little
information on wilderness rivers,
but does show access points for
more traveled waterways).

Pennsylvania

American Youth Hostels, 6300 Fifth Ave.,
Pittsburgh, Pennsylvania 15232.

Canoeing Guide to Western Pennsylvania and Northern Virginia
($1).

Delaware River Basin Commission, 25
Scotch Rd., P.O. Box 360, Trenton, New
Jersey 08603.

Maps ($1 per set).

Pennsylvania Fish Commission, Harrisburg,
Pennsylvania 17120.

*Boating Guide to Pennsylvania
Waters* (rather sketchy).
Canoeing in Delaware and Susquehanna Watersheds.

Pennsylvania State University, College of
Agriculture, Agricultural Experiment Station, University Park, Pennsylvania 16802.

Stream map of Pennsylvania
($1). This shows virtually all
waterways.

Rhode Island

State Department of Natural Resources, Division of Conservation, Veterans Memorial
Bldg., Providence, Rhode Island 02903.

Pawcatuck River and Wood River
(booklet).

South Carolina

State Travel Division, P.O. Box 1358, Columbia, South Carolina 29202.

General information.

U.S. Department of Agriculture, Forest Service, Southern Region, Box 1437, Gainesville, Georgia 30501.

Canoeing the Chattooga.

South Dakota

American White Water, Vol. XIII, No. 3 (Winter 1967–68): "Canoeing Crazy Horse Canyon," by Dean Norman.

Tennessee

American White Water (Summer 1962): "Pioneering a Tennessee River" (South Fork of the Cumberland), by John Bombay.

American White Water (Spring 1963): "River Reports: Cumberland So. Fk.," by John Bombay.

American White Water (Autumn 1964): "River Reports: Tennessee's Obed," by John Bombay.

Game and Fish Commission, P.O. Box 9400, Nashville, Tennessee 37220.

Tennessee Recreational Waters (float maps of Buffalo, Duck, and Harpeth rivers).

Scott County Chamber of Commerce, Oneida, Tennessee 37841.

Co-sponsors of Angel Falls-Devil's Jump Canoe Race (South Fork of the Cumberland).

Sierra Club Bulletin, January 1969: "Volunteer State Shows the Way" (Tennessee Scenic Rivers Act of 1968), by William L. Russell.

Wild Rivers, Inc., P.O. Box 18, Oneida, Tennessee 37841.

The Oneida Trail.

Texas

Superintendent, Big Bend National Park, Texas 79834.

Big Bend National Park (folder with some information on the river).

Bob Burleson, President, Texas Explorers Club, P.O. Box 844, Temple, Texas 76501.

Information on the Rio Grande River.

Vermont

Agency of Development and Community Affairs, Montpelier, Vermont 05602.

Canoeing the Connecticut River (booklet with maps).

Appalachian Mountain Club, 5 Joy St., Boston, Massachusetts 02108.

A.M.C. New England Canoeing Guide (the best source of information on Vermont rivers).

Vermont Development Commission, Montpelier, Vermont 05602.

Vermont Canoeing (booklet).

Virginia

Appalachian Outfitters, Box 11, 2930 Chain Bridge Rd., Oakton, Virginia 22124.

Canoeing White Water (a detailed book describing rivers of Virginia, West Virginia, and the Great Smokies of North Carolina $4.75).

Commission of Game and Inland Fisheries, Box 1642, Richmond, Virginia 23213.

Canoe Trails of Eastern Virginia (booklet).

Louis Matacia, 7414 Leesburg Pike, Falls Church, Virginia 22043.

Blue Ridge Voyages, Vol. I ($1.75); Vol. II ($2). Gives detailed information.

State Travel Service, 911 E. Broad St., Richmond, Virginia 23219.

Virginia's Scenic Rivers (booklet).

Washington

American Canoeist (Spring 1970): "Raingear, Will Paddle" (Skagit), by Ann Schafer.

Angle Lake Cyclery, 20840 Pacific Highway So., Seattle, Washington 98188.

Washington River map ($1.15).

Signpost Publications, 16812 36th Ave. W., Lynwood, Washington 98036

Kayak and Canoe Trips in Washington ($2.25).

Sunset (October 1963): "Down the Quniault in a Cedar Canoe."

Washington Kayak Club, 5622 Seaview Ave., Seattle, Washington 98107.

General information and river map ($1).

Wisconsin

Northwestern Wisconsin Canoe Trails, Inc., Gordon, Wisconsin 54838.

Canoeing the Wild Rivers of Northwestern Wisconsin ($3).

Wisconsin Conservation Department, Box 450, Madison, Wisconsin 53701.

Wisconsin Water Trails, a detailed booklet.

Outing Director, Wisconsin Union, University of Wisconsin, 800 Langdon St., Madison, Wisconsin 53706.

Guide to White Water in the Wisconsin Area, by Andres Peekna ($1.25).

West Virginia

American White Water (Spring 1964): "The Great Cacapon," by Lamarr Knapp.

American White Water (Spring 1967): "Blue Ridge Voyageurs on the Cacapon," by Louis J. Matacia.

Blue Ridge Voyageurs, P.O. Box 32, Oakton, Virginia 22124.

Blue Ridge Voyages, Vols. I and II ($2.50 each).

West Virginia Wildwater Association, Route 1, Box 95, Ravenswood, West Virginia 26164.

A Canoeists Guide to the Whitewater Rivers of West Virginia ($2.50).

Wyoming

American White Water (September 1966): "Hoback, Grey's and Wind Rivers of Western Wyoming," by Oz and Dorothy Hawksley.

U.S. Department of the Interior, National Park Service, Grand Teton National Park, Moose, Wyoming 83012.

Floating the Snake River.

Canada

Canadian Camping Association, Suite 203, 102 Eglinton Ave. East, Toronto, Ontario.

Centenary Journey Canoe Trip Log, details of a coast-to-coast canoe voyage ($2).

Canadian Government Travel Bureau, Ottawa, Ontario.

General information.

Alberta

Alberta Government Travel Bureau, Edmonton, Alberta.

General information.

N.W. Voyageurs—Youth Hostels, Box 444, Edmonton, Alberta.

General information.

British Columbia

British Columbia Travel Bureau, Department of Recreation and Conservation, Victoria, British Columbia.

Bowron Lake Provincial Park canoe routes.

Manitoba

Manitoba Government Travel, 408 Norquay Bldg., Winnipeg 1, Manitoba.

Large package of booklets, pamphlets, and maps includes descriptions of river trips and canoe trails.

New Brunswick

Griff-Inns, Boiestown, New Brunswick.

Information on guides and boat rentals for the Miramichi River.

New Brunswick Travel Bureau, Box 1030, Fredericton, New Brunswick.

Booklet on canoe trips in New Brunswick, list of guides and outfitters.

Northwest Territories

TravelArctic, Yellowknife, Northwest Territories.

General information. Also: "Across the Barrens by Canoe," reprinted from *North* magazine (Hanbury and Thelon rivers); "Summer Travel in the Canadian Barrens," and "Fresh Water Northwest Passage," both reprinted from *Canadian Geographical Journal.*

Ontario

Department of Tourism and Information, Province of Ontario, Parliament Bldgs., Toronto, Ontario.

Northern Ontario Canoe Routes (an excellent guidebook with map). Also, a list of canoe outfitters in Ontario, and booklets on canoe routes of North Georgian Bay Recreational Reserve and Quetico Provincial Park.

Quebec

American White Water (Summer 1967): "The Roaring Mattawin," by George W. Sears, Jr.

Department of Tourism, Fish and Game, Parliament Bldgs., Quebec City, Quebec.

Booklet and map on Metabetchouan River in Laurentides Park; booklet and map of canoe routes in Verendyre Park; list of outfitters; beautifully illustrated material on fishing.

Outdoor Life (March 1970): "Water All White" (Swampy Bay, Kaniapiskau, Koksoak), by David Jarden.

Saskatchewan

Department of Natural Resources, Province of Saskatchewan, Regina, Saskatchewan.

Detailed material on twenty-six canoe routes.

Chief Ranger, Prince Albert National Park, Waskesiu, Saskatchewan.

Information on canoe routes within Prince Albert Park.

Yukon Territory

Alaska Magazine Book Department, Box 4-EEE, Anchorage, Alaska 99509.

A Guide of the Yukon River, by Don and Vangie DeHart ($1.75).

Department of Travel and Publicity, Box 2703, Whitehorse, Yukon Territory.

General information, and some boating information.

Mexico and Central America

American White Water (Winter 1958–59): "Mexican Hay (Stack) Ride," by Lillian Lasch.

A voyage down the Rio Santiago of Mexico.

Summit, Vol. XI, No. 9 (December 1965): "Jungle Camping in Mexico," by Robert F. Moseley, Jr.

Valuable material for anyone contemplating a jungle voyage.

Wilderness Holidays Publications, Box 7097, Charleston, South Carolina 29405.

River of the Sacred Monkey, a book on the Usumacinta River ($2), by Dimitar Krustev.

Conservation Societies

American Forestry Association
919 17th St. N.W.
Washington D.C. 20016
Friends of the Earth
72 Jane Street
New York, New York 10014
Sierra Club
1050 Mills Tower
San Francisco, California
Wilderness Society
5850 Jewell Ave.
Denver, Colorado 80222
Wildlife Society
Suite S 176, 3900 Wisconsin Ave. N.W.
Washington, D.C. 20016
NOTE: Most of these societies sponsor river tours for their members. Other important conservation groups, such as the American River Touring Association of Oakland, California, and the Ozark Society of Arkansas, are listed in Appendix II.

Where to Obtain Maps

A number of map sources have been listed by region in Appendix II. Within the United States, the most important map source for the backcountry traveler is the U.S. Geological Survey. For free indexes, write to either of the two following locations: U.S. Geological Survey, Washington, D.C. 20242; or U.S. Geological Survey, Federal Center, Denver, Colorado 80225. To obtain indexes for Canadian maps, write to Map Distribution Office, Department of Mines and Technical Surveys, Ottawa, Ontario, Canada. For certain rivers, magnificently detailed scroll-like maps have been lovingly prepared by Leslie Jones of Heber, Utah, a legendary river runner. Rivers and their preservation are less of a hobby than a lifelong passion with him, and he combines this zeal with his skills as a professional draftsman. The results are works of art in their own fashion, and are generally quite accurate. The maps have been printed and are sold as a non-profit public service, in hopes that people will go down the rivers, become enriched by them, and help to preserve them. Currently available are maps of Green River Lake to Daniels ($2.50); Green River—Red Canyon, Canyon of Lodore, Split Mountain Canyon, Desolation Canyon ($3.00); Colorado River—Gore Canyon to Grand Junction ($2.80); Westwater Canyon ($1.80); Cataract Canyon ($1.10); Grand Canyon ($3.20); Yampa River ($1.80); Dolores River ($2.75); Black Canyon of the Gunnison ($2.50); San Juan River ($1.80); Hell's Canyon of the Snake ($2.50); Middle Fork Salmon ($2.00); Salmon River ($2.30); Clearwater of Idaho, and Selway ($3.00); Rogue River ($2.00); Mackenzie of Oregon ($1.80); Columbia in British Columbia ($2.50); Canoe of British Columbia ($1.50); Frazier—Tête Jeune—Yale of British Columbia ($3.00); North and South Fork of the Flathead of Montana ($3.00); and the Grijalva of Mexico ($1.50). Altogether a monumental work.

The maps may be ordered from Leslie Jones, Star Route, Box 13A, Heber City, Utah 04032.

Outfitters

A complete list of outfitters and guides who serve the outdoorsman in North America would require a volume in its own right. Most of these guides cater to hunters and fishermen, and can be contacted by writing local chambers of commerce. Many of the big, rapids-strewn western rivers can be run with guided parties, usually in large neoprene rubber rafts. Reservations ordinarily must be made well in advance of the voyage. In the Boundary Waters Canoe Area, which straddles the Minnesota-Canada border, outfitters will rent canoes, packs, and virtually everything else needed for a jaunt through the backcountry.

Western River Guides Association

Most of these outfitters run Grand Canyon. Other popular rivers are the Green (Canyon of Lodore), Yampa, Rogue, and Middle Fork of the Salmon. Western River Expeditions has taken tours down Mexican rivers such as the Rio Grijalva. The American River Touring Association has the most varied schedule, running rivers from Alaska to Peru, and even cruising Australia's Great Barrier Reef. As tours vary from year to year, a person wishing to join one of these exciting voyages would be well advised to send postcards to each outfitter, requesting information on its upcoming tours.

Allen, Sylvester—RFD, Springville, Utah 84663.
American River Touring Association—1016 Jackson St., Oakland, California 94607.
Amoss, Dudley—1949 Laird Ave., Salt Lake City, Utah 84108.
Canyonland Tours—295 Blue Mountain Dr., Monticello, Utah 84535.
Cross Tours and Exploration—272 W. 1400 So., Orem, Utah 84057.

Frontier Expeditions—1779 Michigan Ave., Salt Lake City, Utah 84108.
Grand Canyon Expeditions—P.O. Box 21021, Salt Lake City, Utah 84121.
Harris-Brennan Expeditions—250 N. 500 E., Centerville, Utah.
Hatch River Expeditions—411 E. 2nd No., Vernal, Utah 84078.
Holiday River Expeditions—519 Malibu Dr., Salt Lake City, Utah 84107.
Mexican Hat Expeditions—Box 157, Mexican Hat, Utah 84531.
Missouri River Cruises—Box 688, Jordan, Montana 59337.
Moki Mac Expeditions—5340 Highland Dr., Salt Lake City, Utah 84117.
Sanderson Brothers Expeditions—Box 1574, Page, Arizona 86040.
Western River Expeditions—1699 E. 3350 So., Salt Lake City, Utah 84106.
Whitewater River Expeditions—Box 1249, Turlock, California 95380.
Wonderland Expeditions—3862 So., 825 W., Bountiful, Utah 84010.

Boundary Waters Canoe Area

In recent years the town of Ely, Minnesota, has derived much of its income from the numerous outfitting firms which supply summer canoeists. Even for inexperienced paddlers, guides are a luxury rather than a necessity. In the author's opinion, the best outfitter is Canadian Waters (113 E. Sheridan St., Ely, Minnesota 55731), who provide their customers with detailed waterproof maps, among other niceties. There are, however, a number of other fine outfitters who will send you pamphlets on their services if you write the Ely Chamber of Commerce.

Other Outfitters

United States
Arizona River Runners, Inc., c/o Fred Burke, Box 2021, Marble Canyon, Arizona.
Canyoneers Inc., P.O. Box 957, Flagstaff, Arizona 86001.
Colorado River and Trail Expedition Corporation, 1449 East 30th Street, Salt Lake City, Utah 84106.
Fort Lee Co., P.O. Box 2130, Marble Canyon, Arizona 86036.
Georgia Clark, Royal River Rats, P.O. Box 12489, Las Vegas, Nevada 89109. (Trips through Grand Canyon.)
Grand Canyon Dories, Inc., P.O. Box 5585, Stanford, California 94305.
Grand Canyon Use Expeditions, Rt. 2, Box 755, Flagstaff, Arizona 86001.
Idaho Outfitters and Guides Association, P.O. Box 95, Boise, Idaho 83701. (Information on Idaho wilderness resorts, guides, and whitewater trips.)
Oars, Inc., 1313 20th Street, Santa Monica, California 90406.
Outdoors Unlimited, 2500 5th Avenue, Sacramento, California 95813.
Prince Helfrich, Vida, Oregon. (Information on whitewater trips in the Pacific Northwest.)
St. Croix Voyageurs, c/o Mr. George Dwelly, Belgrade, Maine 14917. (Allagash River tour.)

Tour West, Inc., P.O. Box 333, Orem, Utah 84057.

Wilderness Voyageurs, P.O. Box 97, Ohiopyle, Pennsylvania 15470. (Raft tours down the Youghiogheny River near Pittsburgh.)

Wilderness World, 1342 Jewel Avenue, Pacific Grove, California 93950.

Wildwater Expeditions Unlimited, c/o Jon A. Dragan, P.O. Box 799, Large, Pennsylvania 15025. (Raft tours on the New River Canyon of West Virginia.)

Wildwater, Ltd., Long Creek, South Carolina 29658. (Canoe and raft trips down the Chattooga River, where the film *Deliverance* was filmed.)

Canada

Canadian Quetico Outfitters, P.O. Box 910, Atikokan, Ontario. (Quetico Provincial Park. Canoe rentals and guides.)

Hudson's Bay Company, Northern Stores Dept., 79 Main St., Winnipeg 1, Manitoba. (U-Paddle Canoe Service. Canoes may be rented at one Hudson's Bay post and dropped off at another at the end of the voyage.)

Wilderness Expeditions Ltd., 11445-143 St., Edmonton, Alberta. (Rivers of the Far North.)

NOTE: A complete list of Ontario outfitters may be obtained by writing to the Ontario Department of Tourism and Information, Parliament Buildings, Toronto, Ontario.

Upon request, nearly all of the outfitters listed in this section will send out booklets or pamphlets describing their activities.

Whitewater Organizations

The American Whitewater Affiliation, P.O. Box 1584, San Bruno, California 94066, is America's leading wilderness river-running organization. Its chapters are listed by states below, with Canadian chapters at the end.

California

John Wesley Powell Boat Club
  Charles Martin, Representative
  1329 Henry
  Berkeley, California 94709

Sierra Club
River Conservation Committee
  Scott Fleming, Rep.
  2750 Shasta Rd.
  Berkeley, California 94708

Haystackers Whitewater Club
  Tom Johnson, Rep.
  Box 675
  Kernville, California 93238

Sierra Club
Lomo Prieta Paddlers
  Joe Kilner
  185 Loucks Ave.
  Los Altos, California 95901

Ballona Creek Paddling Club of Los Angeles
  John Evans, Rep.
  933 N. Orlando Dr.
  Los Angeles, California 90069

Feather River Kayak Club
  Mel Schneller, Rep.
  1773 Broadway St.
  Marysville, California 95901

Sierra Club
Mother Lode Chapter
  Sam Gardali
  914 Stanford Ave.
  Modesto, California 95350

Idlewild Yacht Club
  Robert N. Symon, Rep.
  3900 Harrison St., No. 23
  Oakland, California 94611

Sierra Club
San Francisco Chapter
River Touring Section
  Francis Cutter, Rep.
  94 El Toyonal
  Orinda, California 94563

YMCA Whitewater Club
  Gary Gray
  640 N. Center St.
  Stockton, California 95202

American Guides Association
  Box B
  Woodland, California 95695

Colorado
Colorado White Water Association
  Ira Lee
  Route 1, Box 76
  Beverly Hills Estates
  Castle Rock, Colorado 81201

Connecticut
Appalachian Mountain Club
Connecticut Chapter
  Bill and Janet Blaha
  83 North St.
  Guilford, Connecticut 06437

Georgia
Georgia Canoeing Association
  Clyde Woolsey
  4725 Silverdale Rd.
  College Park, Georgia 30337

Illinois
Belleville Whitewater Club
  Linda Seaman, Rep.
  No. 3 Oakwood
  Belleville, Illinois 66223

Prairie Club Canoeists
  Sneakin Deacon Kiehm, Rep.
  2019 Addison St.
  Chicago, Illinois 60618

Indiana
Kekionga Voyageurs
  E. Heinz Wahl, Rep.
  1818 Kensington Blvd.
  Fort Wayne, Indiana 46805

American Camping Association
  Ernest F. Schmidt, Rep.
  Bradford Woods
  Martinsville, Indiana 46151

Kansas
Ozark Wilderness Waterways Club
  Milton Noltensmyer, Rep.
  3305 W. 50th Terrace
  Shawnee Mission, Kansas 66205

Maryland
Explorer Post 757
  Nancy Rayburn, Rep.
  203 Longwood Rd.
  Baltimore, Maryland 21210

Canoe Cruisers Association
  John Thomson
  23 Grafton St.
  Chevy Chase, Maryland 20015

Monocacy Canoe Club
  David Meadows, Rep.
  Route 7, Box 371
  Frederick, Maryland 21701

Massachusetts
Phillips Academy Outing Club
  George H. Edmonds, Rep.
  Phillips Academy
  Andover, Massachusetts 01810

Kayak and Canoe Club of Boston
  John Urban, Rep.
  55 Jason St.
  Arlington, Massachusetts 02174

Cochituate Canoe Club, Inc.
  Guy F. Newhall, Rep.
  99 Dudley Rd.
  Cochituate, Massachusetts 01778

Appalachian Mountain Club, Boston
  Biff Manhard, Rep.
  45 Wesley St.
  Newton, Massachusetts 02158

Appalachian Mountain Club
Worcester Chapter
  Bob Osthues
  2 Merrimount Rd.
  West Boylston, Massachusetts 01583

Michigan
Kalamazoo Downstreamers
  Carl D. Bennett, Rep.
  1529 Hamelink Dr.
  Kalamazoo, Michigan 49002

Minnesota
Minnesota Canoe Association
  Joseph R. Conrad, Rep.
  Box 14177
  Minneapolis, Minnesota 55414

American Youth Hostels, Inc.
Minnesota Council
   R. Charles Stevens, Rep.
   6506 Knox Ave., So.
   Richfield, Minnesota 55423

Missouri
Meramec River Canoe Club
   Al Beletz, Rep.
   3636 Oxford Blvd.
   Maplewood, Missouri 63143

American Youth Hostels, Inc.
Ozark Area Council
   P.O. Box 13099
   St. Louis, Missouri 63119

Central Missouri State College Outing
Club
   Dr. O. Hawksley, Rep.
   Warrensburg, Missouri 64093

New Hampshire
Ledyard Canoe Club
   Jay Evans, Rep.
   201 McNutt Hall
   Hanover, New Hampshire 03755

New Jersey
Adventure Unlimited
   Homer Hicks, Rep.
   Box 186
   Belvidere, New Jersey 07823

Kayak and Canoe Club of New York
   Ed Alexander, Rep.
   6 Winslow Ave.
   East Brunswick, New Jersey 08816

Murray Hill Canoe Club
   Al Hahn
   R.D. 1, Dutch Lane Rd.
   Freehold, New Jersey 07728

Mohawk Canoe Club
   Gerald B. Pidcock, Rep.
   Jobstown-Wrightstown Rd.
   Jobstown, New Jersey 08041

Boy Scouts of America
National Council
   Mart Bushnell, Rep.
   New Brunswick, New Jersey 08903

Appalachian Mountain Club
New York Chapter
   George N. Thomas, Rep.
   24 Barnard Ave.
   Oakland, New Jersey 07436

New Mexico
Albuquerque Whitewater Club
   Glenn A. Fowler, Rep.
   804 Warm Sands Dr., S.E.
   Albuquerque, New Mexico 87123

Explorer Post 20
   J. H. Fretwell, Rep.
   4091 Trinity Dr.
   Los Alamos, New Mexico 87544

New York
Niagara Gorge Kayak Club
   Michael J. McGee, Rep.
   147 Lancaster Ave.
   Buffalo, New York 14222

Cornell Outing Club
   John R. Lyons, Rep.
   937½ E. State St.
   Ithaca, New York 14850

Ka Na Wa Ke Canoe Club
   Chuck Berg, Rep.
   2877 Amber Rd., R. No. 1
   Marietta, New York 13110

Adirondack Mountain Club
Genesee Valley Chapter
   Douglas Smith, Rep.
   769 John Glenn Blvd.
   Webster, New York 14580

Genesee Downriver Paddlers
   LeRoy Dodson, Rep.
   Proctor Rd.
   Wellsville, New York 14895

Ohio
American Youth Hostels, Inc.
Columbus, Ohio, Council
   Charles H. Pace
   650 Noe-Bixby Rd.
   Columbus, Ohio 43213

Warner and Swasey Canoe Club
   Wayne McRobie, Rep.
   406 Mill Ave., S.W.
   New Philadelphia, Ohio 44663

Keel-Haulers Canoe Club
  John A. Kobak, Rep.
  1648 Allen Dr.
  Westlake, Ohio 44145

Pennsylvania
Endless Mountain Voyageurs
  Louis Hopf, Rep.
  285 Short Hill Dr.
  Clarks Green, Pennsylvania 18411

American Youth Hostels, Inc.
Pittsburgh Council
  Bruce E. Sindquist
  210 College Park Dr.
  Monroeville, Pennsylvania 15146

Central Ski Club of Philadelphia
  Paul A. Liebman, Rep.
  345 S. 18th St.
  Philadelphia, Pennsylvania 19103

Pennsylvania Canoe Club
  4900 Ridge Ave.
  Philadelphia, Pennsylvania 19128

Wildwater Boating Club
  Richard S. Brown, Rep.
  P.O. Box 77
  Pine Grove Mills, Pennsylvania
  16868

Sylvan Canoe Club
  Terry D. Sanders, Rep.
  1935 Hampstead Dr.
  Pittsburgh, Pennsylvania 15235

Penn State Outing Club
  John R. Sweet
  118 S. Buckhout St.
  State College, Pennsylvania 16801

Buck Ridge Ski Club
  H. Buehler, Rep.
  1155 Schoolhouse Lane
  West Chester, Pennsylvania 19380

Tennessee
Tennessee Valley Canoe Club
  Robert P. Shepard
  4403 Montview Dr.
  Chattanooga, Tennessee 37411

Bluff City Canoe Club
  L. Migliara
  Box 4523
  Memphis, Tennessee 38104

East Tennessee White Water Club
  Don Jared, Rep.
  P.O. Box 3074
  Oak Ridge, Tennessee 37830

Texas
Texas Explorers Club
  Bob Burleson, Rep.
  Box 844
  Temple, Texas 76501

Utah
Wasatch Mountain Club, Inc.
  J. Calvin Giddings, Rep.
  904 Military Dr.
  Salt Lake City, Utah 84108

Vermont
Norwich University Outing Club
  L. J. Hurley, Rep.
  Northfield, Vermont 05663

Canoe Cruisers of Northern Vermont
  Mrs. Nan Smith
  Shelburne Farms
  Shelburne, Vermont 05482

Virginia
Explorer Post 999
  Thomas J. Ackerman, Rep.
  Mansion Circle
  Hopewell, Virginia 23860

Blue Ridge Voyageurs
  Ralph T. Smith, Rep.
  129 Hill Crest Dr.
  Manassas, Virgina 22110

Coastal Canoeists
  R. L. Sterling, Rep.
  309 Mimosa Dr.
  Newport News, Virginia 23606

Washington
Washington Kayak Club
  Al Winters, Rep.
  8519 California Ave. S.W.
  Seattle, Washington 98116

West Virginia
West Virginia Wildwater Association
  Idair Smookler, Rep.
  2737 Daniels Ave.
  South Charleston, West Virginia
  25303

Wisconsin

Wisconsin Hoofers Outing Club
   Steve Ransburg, Rep.
   3009 Hermina St.
   Madison, Wisconsin 53714

Sierra Club
John Muir Chapter
   Tom O'Rourke, Rep.
   708 South Oneida St.
   Rhinelander, Wisconsin 54501

Canada

B. C. Kayak and Canoe Club
   Erich Kozak, Rep.
   P.O. Box 2237
   Vancouver 3, British Columbia
Canadian Youth Hostels Association
Maritime Region
   Ruth Mackenzie, Rep.

   6405 Quinpool Rd.
   Halifax, Nova Scotia
Montreal Voyageurs
   Rene Bureaud, Rep.
   360 Barberry Place
   Dollard des Ormeaux
   Montreal 960, Quebec

Boat Builders and Distributors

Most Army surplus stores and larger sporting-goods stores carry river-running craft, or can order them for you. A number of leading manufacturers and distributors, listed below, will send information upon request.

Inflatables

Inflatable Boats Unlimited, P.O. Box 21021, Salt Lake City, Utah 84121. (Manufacturer of rafts ranging from the 7-foot Sportyak to the 37-foot Colorado model.)

Leisure Imports, Inc., 104 Arlington Ave., St. James, New York 11780. (Importer of the Pyrawa inflatable canoe.)

Rubber Fabricators, Inc., Grantsville, West Virginia 26147. (Manufacturer of 8-, 10-, and 12-foot neoprene and nylon rafts.)

Seagull Marine Sales, 3107 Washington Blvd., Venice, California 90291 (Distributor of the British Avon Raft, which comes in a number of sizes and models.)

Kayaks

Hans Klepper Corp., 35 Union Square West, New York, New York 10003. (Manufacturer of kayaks and foldboats.)

Hauthaway Kayaks, 640 Boston Post Road, Weston, Massachusetts 02193.

High Performance Plastics, Inc., Hingham Industrial Center, Bldg. 56, 349 Lincoln St., Hingham, Massachusetts 02043.

Old Town Canoe Company, Old Town, Maine 04468. (Manufacturer of canoes and kayaks.)

Surf/Kayak Company, Box 218, Encinitas, California 92024.

Canoes

Cadorette Canoes, Inc., P.O. Box 518, Grand Mère, Quebec, Canada.

Feather Craft, Inc., 450 Bishop Street N.W., Atlanta, Georgia 30318.

Fleet Products Co., Inc., 1930 Placentia, Costa Mesa, California 92627.

Grumman Boats, Grumman Allied Industries, Inc., Marathon, New York 13803.

Lincoln Fiberglas Division, Lazott Co., Inc., Milk Street, Westboro, Massachusetts 01581.

Lund Boat Co., P.O. Box 10, New York Mills, Minnesota 56567.

Northway Canoes, 10015 Green St., Hebron, Illinois 60034.

Sawyer Canoe Co., 4496 North U.S. 23, Oscoda, Michigan 48750.

Stowe Canoe Co., Stowe, Vermont 05672.

White Canoe Co., Old Town, Maine 04468.

Whitewater Equipment (General)

The Dartmouth Co-op, Main St., Hanover, New Hampshire 03755.

Water Meister Sports, P.O. Box 5026, Fort Wayne, Indiana 46805.

Base Camp, 121 West San Francisco, Santa Fe, New Mexico 82501

INDEX